Public Places, Private Journeys

Public Places, Private Journeys

ETHNOGRAPHY, ENTERTAINMENT, AND THE TOURIST GAZE

ELLEN STRAIN

RUTGERS UNIVERSITY PRESS
New Brunswick, New Jersey, and London

LIBRARY OF CONGRESS CATALOGING-IN-PUBLICATION DATA

Strain, Ellen, 1968–
  Public places, private journeys : ethnography, entertainment, and the tourist gaze /
  Ellen Strain.
    p. cm.
  Includes bibliographical references and index.
  ISBN 0-8135-3186-1 (cloth : alk. paper) — ISBN 0-8135-3187-X (pbk. : alk. paper)
  1. Tourism—Social aspects.   2. Exoticism in motion pictures.   3. Tourism and the arts.
  I. Title.

  G155.A2 S669   2003
  306.4'8—dc21

                                                                      2002068043

British Cataloging-in-Publication information is available from the British Library.

Manufactured in the United States of America

CONTENTS

Preface and Acknowledgments   vii

Introduction: The Filtering Eye of the Tourist   1

——— PART ONE   FOUNDATIONS

ONE   Defining the Tourist Gaze   15
TWO   Touristic Births: Placing the Tourist   37
THREE   Technological Identification: Stereography and the Panama Canal   74

——— PART TWO   THE CINEMATIC TOURIST GAZE

FOUR   Moving Postcards: The Politics of Mobility and Stasis
         in Early Cinema   105
FIVE   Jules Verne: Travel and Adaptation   124
SIX   Snapshots of Greece: *Never on Sunday* and the Politics
         of Touristic Narrative   154
SEVEN   Corporeal Geographies: E. M. Forster on Film   175
EIGHT   Global Mappings: Michael Crichton's Postmodern Travels   191

——— PART THREE   BEYOND FILM

NINE   *Millennium:* Tourist Stand-ins and Hyphenated Anthropologists   213
TEN   Narrativizing Cybertravel: CD-ROM Travel Games   230
ELEVEN   Virtual Reality and the Challenges of Reembodied Tourism   248

         Conclusion   274

         Notes   279
         Bibliography   293
         Index   303

PREFACE AND
ACKNOWLEDGMENTS

IN THE FALL of 1994, I attended an orchestral concert entitled "Around the World in Eighty Minutes" at the Hollywood Bowl in Los Angeles. I was enjoying the voyage, so to speak, letting images of Spain swirl through my head as I listened to the familiar music of Georges Bizet's *Carmen*. Aided by a glance at the program, I soon realized that the music was not Bizet's but rather Franz Waxman's pastiche of Bizet composed for the Jean Negulesco film *Humoresque*. This triggered a belated acknowledgment of another misrecognition: these images of Spain were not my own (at that time having never been to Spain), but an amalgam of scenic moments that, like the music that accompanied them, were stolen from the silver screen.

At any other concert venue, such a program, boasting of a tour around the world, might have referred to a sampling of musical pieces written by notable composers of various nationalities, each parading the musical styles and traditions associated with his homeland. At the Hollywood Bowl, however, any world tour would be filtered through the lens of Hollywood cinema, a fact that seemed to have temporarily slipped my mind. What surprised me was not this brief mental lapse nor my mistaken recognition of Bizet but rather the aura of authenticity attached to both the music and my borrowed images of Spain. The authenticity surely did not stem from the composers, which included a German-born composer imitating a Frenchman's attempt to capture the spirit of Spain (Waxman's version of *Carmen*), a transplanted Hungarian creating a musical backdrop for India (Miklós Rózsa's score for Zoltan Korda's film *The Jungle Book*), or an American composing the score for a Middle Eastern adventure (Maurice Jarre's music for David Lean's film *Lawrence of Arabia*). Nor did it find roots in any pretense to realism on the part of the concert organizers; after all, our grand tour was rounded out with a fantastic flight back to London via the "Flying Theme" from Steven Spielberg's *E.T. The Extra-Terrestrial.* Perhaps in the absence of any firsthand experiences of the Ukraine, India, or Japan, for instance, these films—Korda's *The Jungle Book,* Joshua Logan's *Sayonara,* and J. Lee Thompson's *Taras Bulba*—filled some empty slot in a mental map of the world. With their visual and aural plenitude, the films seemed to insist upon their indexical links to actual geographies and to paint a world with greater vibrancy than even some memories of my own rained-in, fogged-out overseas adventures. And now these films' scores re-created at the Hollywood Bowl evoked memories of childhood cinematic experiences imbued with a kind of nostalgia that one might associate with a past journey.

This musical global tour, punctuated by a British homecoming in the form of George Frideric Handel's *Music for the Royal Fireworks,* was truly a celebration of our worldliness, and if my own lack of cosmopolitanism was any measure, it was a worldliness gained not from years of wanderlust but from a lifetime of cinephilia on the part of an audience living in the heartland of moviemaking. Even after the concert, I continued to reflect on the extent to which we access the world and its distant locales through filmic images and popular culture in general. These images not only fill in the gaps of firsthand experience but also provide points of reference during actual travel and may even predispose us to viewing foreign cultures in predetermined ways. Perhaps a tutored gaze, a touristic way of viewing and understanding, could be discerned and theorized. In other words, not merely a set of postcard images may mediate our vision of distant geographies but a culturally constructed set of strategies for perceiving the "exotic"—and for turning cultural difference into postcard visions in the first place—may inflect and possibly even shape to a good extent the nature of our cross-cultural perception.

My thoughts regarding a tourist gaze lay fallow until I embarked on a project on the history of entertainment technologies touted as immersive due to their ability to deliver the sensation of "being there." I positioned film as the centerpiece of this study, bookended by precinematic entertainments such as world fairs and stereographs and, on the other side of the historical spectrum, by computer games and virtual reality. Following in the tradition of scholars like Lynn Spigel and Carolyn Marvin, I focused this cross-media study on the discourses surrounding a new technology's introduction. I soon arrived at a new structure and a more defined set of concerns with a single observation that harked back to my observations at the Hollywood Bowl. My analysis of the texts used to introduce new entertainment media to the public revealed that the exoticized environment consistently has been used as the ideal testing ground for immersive technologies' reality effects. From Auguste and Louis Lumière's early cinematic world tours to touristic romps courtesy of CinemaScope to early digital flight simulators' missions through sublime desert landscapes, the foreign landscape and its inhabitants have been deemed the most impressive route for displaying a medium's immersive powers.

SINCE THIS MANUSCRIPT has been years in the writing, albeit with generous breaks for other academic projects as well as for life's typical exigencies, assistance has come in many forms and from many fronts. Various portions of the manuscript have been published in other forms, and I thank the editors of those publications who helped me to further refine the expression of my thoughts: Cristina Degli-Esposti, Jane Gaines, Henry Jenkins, Nancy Lutkehaus, Scott Mac-Donald, Tara McPherson, Mark Nowak, and Frank Tomasulo. I am particularly grateful to the numerous helpful archivists who have assisted me at the University of Southern California's Special Collections, the Human Studies Film Archives at the National Museum of Natural History of the Smithsonian Institution, the Film Study Center at the Museum of Modern Art, the Film Archives at the University of California at Los Angeles, the California Museum of Photography at the University of California at Riverside, and various divisions of the Library of Congress. I am grateful to Robert Kolker and Janet Murray, who provided valuable comments on an early version of the book's introduction. My thanks also go to Leslie Mitchner at Rutgers University Press, who has given me ample assistance and far more patience than I have deserved. Particular recognition goes to my friends and colleagues who have formed my intellectual community in Los Angeles and Atlanta: Jay Bolter, Arianne Gaetano, Diane Gromala, Richard Grusin, Tara McPherson, Rebecca Merrens, Alan Rauch, Jeff Reznick, Greg VanHoosier-Carey, Karen Orr Vered, and Paul Young. Especially deserving of recognition are Greg and Paul, my two generous colleagues and collaborators, whom I hope I can soon assist in the way they have helped me through the final phases of book writing. Other supporters whose contribution to my sanity cannot be underestimated include Amy Bruckman, Diane Gromala, Dana Randall, and a group I affectionately refer to as the Weehawken roommates, who did their best to steady my nerves as I completed revisions under a sea of smoke floating across the Hudson River. My mentors at the University of Southern California include Nancy Lutkehaus, Michael Renov, Amy Richlin, and Lynn Spigel. Marsha Kinder, as director of my dissertation committee, was essential in bringing the issues of this book into focus. My gratitude goes out to her for her continued support of my work. Without the compassion, generosity, and intellectual camaraderie of Ian Seymour I would have never seen my way through the final pages of the manuscript. His assistance has ranged from the mundane details of word processing to the many intangibles of his companionship, which I will always cherish. And finally, I acknowledge the support of my family; for my parents' supreme talent in challenging me to greater heights while always making clear their indefatigable faith in me, this book is dedicated to them.

Versions of the second, third, sixth, seventh, ninth, and tenth chapters previously appeared in the following sources and are used with the permission of the editors and publishers. Chapter 2: *Wide Angle* 18, no. 2 (special issue *Movies Before Cinema,* part 1; Scott MacDonald, guest ed.), pp. 70–100 (April 1996); chapter 3: *Visual Anthropology Review* 12, no. 2 (special issue *Consumerism: Bodies, Images, Commodities*), pp. 44–58 (fall/winter 1996/1997); chapter 6: *Journal of Film and Video* 49, nos. 1–2, pp. 80–93 (spring/summer 1997); chapter 7: *Cinema and the Postmodern,* ed. Cristina Degli-Espoti (New York: Berghahn Press, 1998); chapter 9: *Cross Cultural Poetics* 4 (special issue *Voyage/Voyageur/Voyeur*), pp. 60–77 (April 1999); and chapter 10: *Hop on Pop: The Politics and Pleasures of Popular Culture,* ed. Henry Jenkins, Jane Gaines, and Tara McPherson (Durham, N.C.: Duke University Press, 2003).

Public Places, Private Journeys

INTRODUCTION

The Filtering Eye of the Tourist

AS MORE CRITICALLY INFORMED postcolonial perspectives gradually seep into Americans' sense of history, and as religious and ethnic discord continues to plague the international arena (hitting closest to home with the attacks of September 11, 2001), Americans seem to be increasingly aware of what euphemistically could be called globalization's sticking points. Conversations across national borders are weighted down by and filtered through the baggage of past political machinations, continued imbalances in economic power, and shifting hierarchies and alliances crystallized in terms like "superpower" or "third world." Yet despite this growing awareness of political entanglements that exist on a global scale but play out on the local level, American culture remains indelibly marked by a more naive tradition of cross-cultural contact, a belief in the potential for fulfillment in more private or personal border crossings. Americans continue to be captivated by the idea that somewhere on the highest mountain or in the densest jungle the triumphant traveler, through her perseverance, can stumble upon a political blank slate where it is possible to step outside the burdens of national identity to forge contact across cultural divides. This belief, or touristic predisposition, shaped by romanticized travel tropes of the past, is not entirely untouched by more contemporary understandings of international tension and histories of colonialist exploitation. However, as read through popular culture, this romantic touristic imagination is extremely resilient, only recently laboring under the strain of reinvention.

These areas of strain reveal what lies beneath, like shafts of light illuminating the mechanics of Western travel mythologies and touristic pleasures undergirded by technologies of representation, an intermixing of anthropology and fantasy, and a faith in authentic human experience. The wear and tear of these myths, the belabored nature of the attempt to reinvent travel tales in forms appropriate to the contemporary age, holds significance beyond the slight fading of a stubbornly persistent fantasy. At the heart of this phenomenon is a shifting faith in knowledge, experience, and representation, played out in what is believed to be the last bastion of authenticity. The tensions of globalization, an awareness of omnipresent mediation and simulation, and a dimming belief in untouched hidden worlds have in some ways made the maintenance of such myths more essential. The resurrection of tales of discovery, first contact, and individual adventure in virgin landscapes are more frenzied and desperate, pulling out all the stops in the technological simulation of exotic worlds. Ultimately, however, the contradiction between the desire to grasp through mediation this depleting supply of authenticity, and representational technologies' ability to exceed, supplant, or invent the real produces the very textual cracks that provide such a unique perspective on contemporary experience in a postmodern age.

—— Immersion and the Tourist Gaze

Through historical analysis of entertainment technologies' travel representations in Western culture, with a particular emphasis on the traditions that have shaped contemporary American culture, *Public Places, Private Journeys* explores the operations of representation, authenticity, knowledge, and experience within what I term the *tourist gaze.* As an ambivalent pursuit of the exotic and as an experiential structure, the tourist gaze is mobile, portable, and even culturally promiscuous. It can further be defined as historically and epistemologically linked to the development of vision-supplementing technologies and to a set of precepts and biases that are widely held but formalized within classical anthropology. With the adjective *mobile* I reference the virtual or actual mobility of the tourist-spectator, the vicarious movement of the armchair tourist or the traveling eye of the tourist moving through geographical space.[1] My reference to portability recognizes the surfacing of the tourist gaze within diverse cultural practices ranging from ethnographic fieldwork to more mundane activities such as perusing issues of *National Geographic.* In describing the movement of touristic perception across such practices as promiscuous, I draw attention to its flouting of conventional borders between popular or entertainment-based practices and so-called scientific or intellectual endeavors, as well as between actual travel and simulated immersion within an exoticized environment.[2] In short, the tourist gaze is far from confined to tourism alone.

The tourist gaze's ability to resurface in diverse cultural practices, from tourism to movie watching to anthropological investigation, can be explained in part by modernism. The tourist gaze shares with other cultural formations a series of social, historical, and economic determinants. As part of the cultural logic of modernism, it is linked to other social phenomena that are similarly expressive of modernism, its epistemologies, and its worldview. Its portability, then, is really the conductivity of modernist culture, which facilitates the free passage of the tourist gaze between similar materials or all that is part of the fabric of modernism. Thus, the observation put forth in the preface—that is, the historical consistency of the use of foreign landscapes to foreground entertainment technologies' immersive effects—makes sense in light of both tourism's and many visual technologies' roots in modernism. Even without resorting to such an explanation, the reliance on exotic environments for displaying a new technology's immersive realism seems logical. The world's wonders, from Norwegian fjords to the Khajuraho temples, seem particularly appropriate for demonstrating the power used to create a sense of spatial immersion. The proven appeal and entertainment value of such sights help to balance out the risk of presenting a brand new entertainment technology to an audience, whether it be those viewing film for the first time in 1898 or virtual-reality inductees of the following century.

Further explaining the use of travel stories and exoticized imagery in immersive entertainment forms, modernist visual technologies (with cinema as a paradigm, here) and the travel mystique both partake in what I call *the illusion of demediating mediation.* This myth of demediation produces the illusion that certain types of experience can strip away the typical mediations that intervene in the experience of reality, or that certain technologies, through their radiant powers of representation, can somehow reverse the postmodern eclipse of authenticity.[3] In the same way that film has been credited with presenting raw reality that breaks through the fog of everyday experience, travel to foreign lands has been mythologized as a cleansing process that renews perception.

This conundrum of demediation continues to occupy a nodal position within both tourism studies and film studies. The tale of tourism studies' birth necessarily begins with Dean MacCannell's 1976 book *The Tourist* and its analysis of the motivations that impel the tourist to make the trek to exotic lands.[4] MacCannell's lasting contribution—and the spark that would ignite several years of debate—was his description of the holy grail of tourism: authenticity. MacCannell suggests that this quest for authenticity is a reaction to the alienation that grew out of industrialization and the subsequent fragmentation of modern society. In other words, a fading of a sense of reality and oneness with the world impels the tourist out into the world. Within this search, more so-called primitive societies hold out the greatest promise for recommuning with that elusive entity known as the real and for reinvigorating perception of one's surroundings. In the words of MacCannell, "Modern man has been condemned to look elsewhere, everywhere, for his authenticity, to see if he can catch a glimpse of it reflected in the simplicity, poverty, chastity or purity of others."[5]

The debate between MacCannell and subsequent tourism scholars such as Daniel Boorstin and Paul Fussell, who view the tourist as a debased figure all too willing to accept commercialism's fakery and fatuousness, has been the fuel propelling tourism studies into realms beyond the field's industry-driven interests in sociology, economics, and business management. In their portraits of the tourst, Boorstin and Fussell reveal elitism in their differentiation of the traveler who seeks and knows how to recognize authenticity from the tourist who either gladly or unknowingly accepts Disneyland's versions of the world's wonders. The traveler designation in these tourist/traveler distinctions is reserved for the explorer of past eras or for intellectuals of the contemporary era. In both cases, a tacit class— and often gender—distinction separates the traveler from the tourist, who is at home within the supposedly degraded, fatuous, and overcommercialized state of the contemporary travel industry.

Specious tourist/traveler distinctions and the unresolved debate over the tourist's relationship to authenticity are best replaced with a more complex view of the tourist derived from a semiotic analysis of tourism. Such a semiotics of tourism reveals travel practices to be culturally determined and the resultant experiences to be mediated by expectation, societally shaped viewing practices, and a dense process of culturally situated interpretation. Yet, within the practice of tourism, the myth of demediating mediation obscures this semiotic filtering process. As a core component of the tourist gaze, the illusion of demediation offers the false promise of communion with authenticity and an escape from the very mediation that the semiotics of tourism unveils.

Not only is the promise of demediation standard to the marketing discourse of tourism, but it is constitutive of the travel mythos as propagated by the very travelers that Fussell and other self-declared "antitourists" celebrate. The more contemporary travel writer and novelist Michael Crichton sums up this discourse of travel's demediating power, writing, "Stripped of your ordinary surroundings, your friends, your daily routines . . . you are forced into direct experience."[6] Other noted travel writers who preceded Crichton in the construction of this mythos have similarly suggested some type of recovered ability to fully experience reality by way of a return to an earlier stage of life. For instance, in reference to visiting

Greece, Robert Eisner rhapsodizes, "Perhaps the greatest benefit is the sight of things once more as you saw them in childhood, fresh and bright and exciting and alien."[7] This promise of renewed perception suggests that the travel experience can strip away one's own cultural baggage and the sensorially deadening effects of familiarity. The renewed vision that supposedly characterizes travel to exotic lands is seen as diametrically opposed to the quotidian experience of the already codified reality of our daily existences in our homelands. Thus, while a semiotics of tourism suggests ways that the tourist's home culture mediates the travel experience, the myth of authenticity as suggested by Eisner and Crichton situates travel to foreign lands as demediating—cutting through layers of expectation and language to deliver raw and authentic experience.

This conundrum of demediating mediation is not a tension that can be resolved or dismissed; rather, it remains a defining feature of touristic experience. This characteristic of tourism, in combination with the futility of defining authenticity (or even confirming its existence), renders moot the question of whether the tourist actually finds authenticity or, as Boorstin suggests, merely mistakes a commercialized imitation of it for the real thing. The conundrum of demediating mediation suggests a continual push and pull within which the tourist is neither a cultural dupe satisfied with touristic spectacle masquerading as authentic culture nor a resolute nihilist who has abandoned all hopes of finding the last remnant of authenticity in an otherwise artificial world. Both the traveler and the tourist—if the distinction between the two is not false to begin with—are equally vulnerable to this myth of demediation. More accurately phrased, the illusion of demediation casts doubt on the possibility of differentiating tourist from traveler or distinguishing authenticity from inauthenticity.

The tourist's relationship to authenticity mirrors a comparatively well investigated paradox of film spectatorship as an illusory form of demediating mediation. Like tourism, film—despite its undeniable filtering of the profilmic—paradoxically offers up the illusion of a more intense and plentiful reality than that which lies just outside the theater doors. While this phenomenon has been explored using various methodologies that have exerted their influence within the discipline of cinema studies (e.g., phenomenology, cognitive science, psychology, and semiotics) the most enduring vocabulary used to explain this conundrum comes from Christian Metz's employment of psychoanalysis. Like MacCannell's attempt to parse a particular cultural experience's relationship to reality, Metz's theorization of the same problematic in regard to film is foundational to the field of film theory. Metz positions film as an illusory return to the plenitude of preverbal experiencing of the world, a view of the world that, to recycle Eisner's words, is "fresh and bright and exciting and alien." Metz describes the filmic text as a composition of "short-circuited signifiers" whose resemblance to reality obscures their status as mediated and authored, thereby producing the illusion of direct access to a lost world, or at least to a lost way of directly perceiving the world. Metz borrows from Lacanian terminology to suggest that the short-circuited signifier collapses the traditional distance between signifier and signified, producing the illusion of a return to the presymbolic imaginary, a time when language as a layer of signification and cultural meaning did not interfere with pure experience.[8]

Continuing in the psychoanalytic tradition that has dominated much of film theory's history, Kaja Silverman has expanded upon Metz's theory to suggest that cinema acts as a fetish object used to disavow the fact of a lost access to reality. The absence of the profilmic reality, or the filtering of reality through the symbolic communication of film language, parallels the adult's loss of direct access to reality, which occurs with induction into language and the resultant, inescapable linguistic mediation of the world. Fetishization of the cinematic image is a disavowal of film's mediation and of the larger loss of direct access to the real. As fetish object, film denies its own mediation while contradictorily drawing attention to itself as a technological miracle of simulation.[9]

Cinema's ability to deliver the illusion of direct experience was not born with the invention of cinema, but was cultivated in other nineteenth-century entertainment forms, ranging from world's fair exhibits to natural history museum displays and furthered through the invention of precinematic technologies. Postcinematic entertainment forms have borrowed from filmic convention and have sought to develop their own version of immersiveness, at times sacrificing scale for interactivity, image quality for a sense of coextensiveness with reality, or movement for the experience of three-dimensional space. Yet cinema, while not the only technology to take advantage of representational media's perpetuation of the myth of direct experience, still remains the paradigmatic immersive entertainment form in its ability to bring together image quality, verisimilitude, scale, and movement.

—— Postmodernity and the Eclipse of Authenticity

The trope of shifting cultural logics, from modernism to postmodernism, provides a viable structure and strategy for categorizing and contextualizing certain developments in the evolution and transformation of the tourist gaze. This use of modernism and postmodernism as a theoretical armature is predicated on an understanding of the movement from modernism to postmodernism as an inten-

A naive view of global relations, within which tourism is seen as unproblematic, includes the belief that "peripheral" cultures benefit from exposure to American ways.

From an advertisement in *Century* magazine, November 1909.

sification process rather than a cultural rupture delivering us from modernist mastery into postmodern oblivion. The modernist debates around direct experience and the illusive entity of authenticity have merely been renewed and popularized through the employment of the vocabulary of postmodern theory. Rather than being confined to academic writings or buried in the subtexts of modernist writers like E. M. Forster, issues of authenticity have moved into the mainstream and taken on narrative forms, as is evident in the plotlines of such films as Peter Weir's *The Truman Show,* Josef Rusnak's *The Thirteenth Floor,* and Andy and Larry Wachowski's *The Matrix,* in which reality is presented as an illusion—a TV show, a video game, a digitally generated simulation. Even once that illusion has been peeled away through narrative revelation, faith in the reality that lies beneath has been irrevocably shaken, even replaced by a conceptualization of reality as a peelable onion with nothing at its core—a response designed to be shared by characters and spectators alike. Some would argue that postmodernism, while not responsible for the birthing of concerns around the eclipse of originality, coherent subjectivity, and authenticity (all issues that predate postmodernism), has been defined by some scholars as the acceptance of this eclipse and the disappearance of the traumatic effects of such a realization. Yet I would argue that the dramatic effects of films like *The Matrix* and our need to rehearse its revelations with new variations of the same essential plotline indicate a continuing struggle with the traumatic effects of a severed relationship to authenticity. Nor has the attempt to locate authenticity ceased, but rather the desire to fervently continue the peeling process to get to the core of reality persists as a compensatory effect. As Steven Connor has noted, "Alongside [postmodernism's incessant production of images with no attempt to ground them in reality], as though in response to the awareness of the fading out of the real, is a compensatory attempt to manufacture it, in an escalation of the true, of the lived experience; in other words, the cult of immediate experience, of raw, tense reality, is not the contradiction of the regime of simulacrum, but its simulated effect."[10]

Such observations may have particular implications for tourism, which paradoxically is seen as the last frontier of authenticity. While this understanding of tourism as the final reservoir of "immediate experience" is particularly relevant in a postmodern era, it is interesting to note that when MacCannell first explored this idea it was within an attempt to penetrate the nature of modernist culture. Even so, virtually the only change made in the 1989 reissue of *The Tourist* is a new introduction, in which he suggests that his theory of the tourist is as applicable to postmodernity as to modernity. Acknowledging the new cache of postmodernist discourse, MacCannell writes, "Perhaps 'the tourist' was really an early postmodern figure, alienated but seeking fulfillment in his own alienation—nomadic, placeless, a kind of subjectivity without spirit, a 'dead subject.'"[11] With the mass of the book unchanged, it is left to the reader to insert the appropriate posts into prior statements such as, "For moderns, reality and authenticity are thought to be elsewhere: in other historical periods and other cultures, in purer, simpler life-styles."[12] And further vindicating the search for throughlines between modernity and postmodernity—even before MacCannell's repackaging of the tourist as post-modern,—his oxymoronic terms such as "staged authenticity" seem part and parcel to the Baudrillardian concept of the proliferation of simulacra.

If the desire for authenticity—or the "cult of immediate experience," as Connor has termed it—has indeed survived the passing of a modernist era, then where does one locate the transition into postmodernity with greater specificity than simply the intensification and popularization of modernist questions around the issue of manufactured realities? I argue that the shift in cultural logics is most visible in the increased desperation of this cult's compensatory function and the more belabored nature of attempts to bring narratives about authenticity quests to a satisfying resolution. For instance, I explore the narrative trope of the repeat journey, a literal or metaphoric retracing of steps in the reenactment of a past journey marked by discovery. Such overlaying of the original time travel story (to the extent that the journey to a less industrialized locale is consistently figured as travel to the past) with yet another illusory recouping of times past often leads narratives to crumble under the weight of their own convoluted attempts to recapture authenticity, as in the case of the ethnographic documentary series *Millennium* explored in chapter 9. Another doubling effect within immersive travel stories is the mirroring of the filmic technology or other visual apparatus within the travel story itself; yet within more recent travel representations this diegetic technology becomes a focal point for profound textual ambivalence, thereby implicating the story's delivery medium within the scam of demediating mediation. To emphasize these most subtle of differences and the postmodern crisis of confidence in modernist visualizing strategies that such subtleties reveal, I juxtapose the travel/scientific fiction hybrid literature of Jules Verne and Michael Crichton and trace out their adaptations into subsequent media forms across chapters 5 and 8. Even in Crichton's recent novel *Timeline*, authenticity remains the object of pursuit, only Crichton's postmodern attempts to visualize the world are more belabored and tentative regarding their success. The technology that allows the recouping of authenticity is revealed to be the mechanism of corruption, as time travel risks becoming the equivalent of a masquerade party at which each individual pretends to be "the real thing" but firmly believes himself to be the only faker amid the crowd. Across Crichton's texts, the attempts to access lost worlds and untapped reservoirs of authenticity are structurally similar to Verne's pursuits, yet more elaborately woven, as if in hopes of burying the seeds of skepticism in a flurry of detail and complexity. The subsequent portraits of lost-and-found civilizations, undocumented species, and rare archeological treasures are hampered by an equivocation absent from Verne's texts.

My mapping of the terrain of the modern, the postmodern, their cultural shifts, and their continuity through the lens of the touristic gaze justifies the book's chronological structure and the comparative framework of chapters that juxtapose Verne and Crichton, or Claude Lévi-Strauss and contemporary anthropologist David Maybury-Lewis. However, the acceptance of the temporal continuum of modernity and postmodernity at times can threaten to leave us at a stalemate, an inability to move beyond its terms. Similarly, the rubric of a gaze suggests a decorporealization of the tourist, which may foreclose avenues of investigation pertinent to the postcinematic age. For these reasons, the final chapter breaks free of some of the constraints inherent in past uses of this particular methodology with its emphasis on the transition into postmodernity. This last chapter, with its focus on virtual reality, moves beyond this methodology as it draws on loose strands, particularly in reference to the body—a topic that, within earlier chapters, is never dismissed nor fully embraced, in part due to the blind spots of traditional film theory. In this way, chapter II tackles a pivotal issue within cross-media studies—that is, the initial rewards and eventual limitations of importing one media framework into the study of emerging media forms. Models of spectatorship borrowed from cinema are stretched out beyond recognition in grappling with complex interface issues, an area largely untouched by humanities-based analysis. In effect, within this final chapter, the subject matter outgrows the theoretical framework set up in earlier chapters, thereby giving way to a new paradigm of touristic possibility and a new definition of immersion. Interestingly then, within this work, the more decisive cultural shift is relocated from the seam signaling the transition from modernism to postmodernism to an inchoate terrain in which somatic experience is reconfigured. The virtual reality interface, insofar as efforts to effect complete transparency of its physical apparatus fail, suggests the possibility of a technology that does not externalize bodily experience but situates the crucial point of interaction at the point where technology and the body meet. Ultimately, the models constructed to confront the challenges presented by this new media form move us beyond assumption of authenticity and suggest new paradigms for conceiving of the spaces for "staging" cross-cultural contact.

—— Stakes of Investigation

Ultimately, several inquiries propel this study of constant and changing modes of touristic perception. The most essential question inherent in the analysis of the tourist gaze, however, is how individuals see across cultural difference in an era of increasingly commercialized and globalized culture. Undoubtedly, other models of global movement—nomadism, forced migration, military invasion, and colonialism—might similarly address questions of cross-cultural perception. Yet these other models lack tourism's power in expressing both utopic and dystopic versions of cultural exchange in a commercialized world. Leisured travel has been defined by some as the fatuous interaction between privileged "first world" tourists and an objectified class of "third world" people. Within this understanding of tourism, the latter group performs a degraded form of their native culture for a moneyed audience, and unknowingly participates in a perpetuation of economic dependence, stunted industrial development, and power dynamics reminiscent of colonialism. In a utopic view of tourism, however, the tourist is confronted with a radically different culture that confounds Western epistemologies while her tourism dollars simultaneously provide an economic impetus for preserving indigenous culture. Tourism, seen in this light, becomes a global form of the trickle-down phenomenon, leading to the strengthening of less economically established nations while staving off the approach of a homogeneous monoculture. Leaving questions of economics aside, my primary interest is in the political effects of representation, and in this way I echo MacCannell's query: "Does tourism and/or postmodernity conceived in the most positive way as a (perhaps final) celebration of distance, difference, or differentiation, ultimately liberate consciousness or enslave it? . . . [D]oes it trap consciousness in a seductive pseudo-empowerment, a prison house of signs?"[13] As an extension of the touristic, the commercialized multiculturalism of entertainment media raises similar questions. As American filmmakers and television producers direct their cameras overseas and foreign-made films receive global distribution, are domestic audiences being integrated into a "utopia of difference," to use Georges Van den Abbeele's words, or is it an epistemic colonization of outlying words that merely packages cultural difference in a reification of the West?[14] These questions drive the following study, and its recounting of the ways in which worlds outside the West are perceived, imagined, and commodified; of the tropes, visual practices, and narratives employed across media and social practices in the representation of cultural difference; and of the roles of various perceptual technologies in these representations.

PART ONE

Foundations

CHAPTER ONE

Defining the Tourist Gaze

THE NOTION OF THE "TOURIST GAZE" first came into currency with the publication of John Urry's 1990 sociological text, which takes the term as its title. Although Urry identifies the gaze of the tourist as "socially organised and systematised" and sets out to "elaborate on the processes by which the gaze is constructed and reinforced," his study never moves beyond tourism itself to study the gaze's social organization in other institutions.[1] Nor does Urry extend beyond his field of sociology to take advantage of theories of the gaze and of interlocking modes of perception and representation. In this way, despite the following of Urry's semantic lead, my understanding of the tourist gaze more closely resembles Anne Friedberg's concept of the "mobilized virtual gaze," with its cultural ubiquity and its ties to technological and capitalist development. Friedberg makes a conceptual move similar to my own in comparing the virtually mobile gaze of the static film viewer to the actually mobile gaze of the pedestrian, the window shopper, or the traveler. In the case of tourism, this continuity across the actual and the simulated, between the tourist and the armchair traveler, suggests a larger cultural source, a "tutoring" of the tourist gaze that takes place in other cultural forms and may long precede any actual immersion within a foreign landscape. Also important within Friedberg's work is her situating of particular visual modalities within cultural shifts linked to economic change, and the subsequent positioning of the public as ever-ready consumer when looks come to be organized in the service of capitalist consumption.[2] For the purposes of this study, the understanding of a gaze trained for consumerism is essential, as is the notion of the shaping and sharing of visual practices by the larger cultural and economic backdrop.

A compelling methodology for studying perceptual strategies can be glimpsed in Giuliana Bruno's *Streetwalking on a Ruined Map*. Bruno, along with Friedberg and a series of other film scholars, draws attention to the simultaneous development of cinema and another cultural practice and, consequentially, to the shared logics informing both. Such analyses have taken on the form of the simultaneous appearance of cinema and nationalism, cinema and imperialism, cinema and consumerism, and cinema and modernism. Bruno's study targets cinema in its first twenty years and coincident developments within medicine—specifically medicine's visual practices that tend toward spectacularization and theatricality, particularly in regard to the female body. She locates a particular desire at the core of both medicine and cinema and constructs a continuum that links the visual practices of scientific knowledge with those that characterize certain popular pleasures, particularly film. By excavating the Latin term *curiositas* to describe this motivational undergirding of both medicine and cinema's visual practices, Bruno extends this analytical technique of acknowledging cultural institutions' shared childhoods, so to speak, to unearthing shared parentage. As she goes on to describe, *curiositas*'s "lust of the eyes," as parent to film and to spectacularized medicine, seeks knowledge through vision, targeting such uncanny sights as the anatomically denuded body. Through her study of the spectacle of live, simulated, and filmed human dissections exhibited for popular and scientific audiences, Bruno makes evident the epistemologies cinema shares with scientific investigation, and the impossibility of divorcing these practices' analytic desires from the mechanics of power and sexual difference. Bruno's analysis of medical exhibitions and anatomical entertainments in turn-of-the-century Naples then continues through a detailed explication of parallel histories, shared tools, and points of intersection in order to further support this idea of the common perceptual strategies.[3]

Not only are the general contours of Bruno's methodology applicable to the study at hand, but my own study of the tourist gaze as an instrument of mastery could begin with the concept of *curiositas*. This same term was applied in descriptions of the prurient curiosity motivating travel during the medieval period. While travel for other purposes—the pursuit of food, shelter, and eventually wealth—is a prehistoric matter, the Renaissance's legitimization of curiosity reversed the consideration of curiositas as a venial sin by the likes of St. Augustine, St. Bernard, and St. Thomas Aquinas. Curiositas became an acceptable and even noble motive for traveling the world.[4]

Despite its initial usefulness, *curiositas* as a term lacks specificity for pinpointing the desires at the heart of tourism in its popular and scientific forms. Certainly, the pursuit of beauty, interest in geographical diversity, and the drive to record variation in flora and fauna became components of this newly legitimated wanderlust. Yet more interesting to me is travel impelled by a fascination with the exotic, with the exotic being best understood as a conflation of cultural, geographical, and physiological difference. A people's mode of occupying a unique landscape, their material culture, behavioral modes, linguistic peculiarities, and the particularities of their racial/ethnic type are "exotic" insofar as they differ from those of the traveler. In fact, "exoticized" is a more appropriate descriptor since it references the active process of seeking out, recognizing, and fetishizing difference.

At the heart of this fetishization is the basic presumption that the confrontation of difference involves a negotiation of boundaries in order to bolster a sense of self. Although most notably applied to sexual difference, this defensive response can apply to a variety of types of visual fascination. For instance, to return to Bruno's subject matter, since constitution of self and the maintenance of boundaries are also at issue in visions of corpses, evisceration, physical violence, and other cases of punctured bodily integrity, here lies another site for fetishization. While not described by Bruno in exactly this way, the viewer's response is an attempt to keep intact an illusion of inviolate borders between corporeal interiority and exteriority, life and death. Conversion of perceived reality into spectacle is a defensive recitation designed to build armor against the constant nettling of subjectivity's coherence. Whether in reference to bodily integrity or to the more commonly explored topic of sexual difference, sights that threaten to reveal the fragility of the material supports of selfhood become sites of visual fascination ripe for the application of the gaze as a tool of control and analysis.

Culture, like body, is a "propping-up device" integral to subject coherence; it structures subject formation and continues to brace it through articulations of the individual's place within culture and nation. (Here I assume a Western subject and, for the sake of simplicity, a certain coextensiveness between culture and nation). Revealing culture's constructedness, or its lack of inevitability, through the presentation of cultural difference as anything less reassuring than a variation of Western culture at an earlier stage of development casts light on culture's role in the individuation process and the inextricability of culture from self. In other words, the extent to which culture or nation constitutes the subject can remain unproblematic and even invisible in the face of radical cultural difference if the illusion of linear cultural development with the West as the spearhead of its forward thrust can be maintained. When the traveler's cultural position is no longer reified and culture is seen in the light of extreme relativism, the extensive and inextricable structuring of subjectivity by culture then becomes perceptible. When one's own culture becomes denaturalized through the experience of the wide range of diversity possible among cultures, boundaries of self appear disturbingly diffuse as one tries to separate self from the arbitrarily formed armature of culture. The traveler slips into the uncomfortable weightlessness of culture shock. The illusion of the autonomy of selfhood or the romantic notion of the soul as a self-contained, self-formed whole separable from body and surroundings suffers a blow, unless that blow is parried. Visual fascination is part and parcel of this dodging effort, the rehearsal of which is actually sought in order to strengthen the illusion of impenetrability, autonomy, and coherence. Exoticization is this fetishization process at work during the confrontation with extreme cultural difference. And the tourist gaze is the solidification of this process within the tourism industry; within ethnographic practice as informed by the methodologies of classical anthropology; and within the viewing strategies mobilized by the conventions of classical film and other immersive entertainment forms.

The suggestion that exoticization is a form of fetishization implies an act of denial through substitution within the process of exoticizing a landscape or people. This substitution remains hidden from view to the extent that ideologically inflected visual practices have been naturalized and are understood to be our primary tool for surveying and accurately accessing reality. We believe in a strong correlation between reality and the image that is a product of our perceptual strategies. In the case of the use of simulation technologies, a melding of fetishization processes occurs, as the demediating effects of the technology promise direct access to the object of fascination. Thus, the rhetoric of demediation further removes the filtering and distorting process of exoticization from sight by characterizing this uncanny position at the precipice of culture shock as unmediated experience. The tourist gaze is thus a largely invisible, transformative process replacing that which is seen with a touristic vision. The touristic vision is constructed by way of an oscillating series of objectifying strategies: reduction to surface spectacle; mystification; assimilation to Western structures of aesthetics, narrative, or scientific explanation; reduction to a simplistic surface/depth model demanding unveiling; totalization; essentialization; and synecdochic consumption, accumulation, and representation.

—— Classical Periods: Epistemological Roots
and Shared Worldviews

The institutions of cinema, tourism, and anthropology all began their processes of development in the late nineteenth century, establishing a classical form with standardized techniques and favored visual instruments sometime in the early twentieth century. These simultaneous processes of maturation were accompanied by various intersections among the cultural practices: tourists provided information for early armchair anthropologists; anthropologists used film as a data-collecting tool; popular films were financed by tourist bureaus and tourist footage was integrated into popular films; anthropological texts charted out new tourist areas; and anthropologists and tourists were protagonists in popular films.

While the first public film screening dates back to 1895, narrative paradigms and stylistic standards associated with a classical style did not solidify until approximately twenty years later. According to the dates and labels used by some film historians, the years 1895 to 1909 mark the "primitive period," followed later by the "classical period," from 1917 to 1960, with the intervening years forming a transitional period.[5] With the arrival of a classical period, narratives, genres, and stylistic tendencies appeared with considerable implications for the visualization of foreign cultures. This transition to the classical period, effectively marrying narrative to a series of privileged viewing strategies, involved a shift from what Tom Gunning calls a "cinema of attractions" to a narrational system that provides a position for the spectator within an unfurling drama.[6] In regard to the travel spectacle, cinema's process of maturation involved setting the spectator into motion through a series of conventions that seamlessly combined the two forces that Christian Metz describes as constituting the basic structure of cinema's spectatorial experience: primary and secondary identification.[7] Metz's primary identification can be defined as the acceptance of the camera's gaze as an extension of the spectator's own vision or as an identification with the act of looking. This kind of muscular perception—one strengthened by instruments acting like prosthetic devices, with the spectator's internalization of their extended visual powers—would already have been a part of the public's perceptual vocabulary with the advent of aerial photography, microscope technologies, and X-ray devices by the turn of the century. The invention of cinema was a part of this period's "frenzy of the visible," but unlike some of the above devices, cinema's technology provided a view on the world not totally unlike our own unaided view of the world.[8] Its power as a tool of muscular perception becomes evident when

The film *Latuko,* produced by the American Museum of Natural History, was distributed as ethnographic entertainment, with the superior quality of the technological delivery standing in for the power of "being there."

film is seen collectively with its ability to traverse the world and bring those imagistic souvenirs home. The power of cinema as an instrument for extending vision thus is often summarized as the ability to put the spectator in motion as a disembodied eye, fully unencumbered, allowing limitless motion through the spectator's identification with the camera.

As addressed more fully in chapter 4, this early stage of cinematic development spectacularized an exotic world in motion, offering it up to a static viewer. In other words, despite cinema's oft-cited power to put the spectator into "bodyless flight," these preclassical films placed greater emphasis on the movement of the diegetic subject matter without carving out a solid position in which the spectator could enjoy the illusion of travel. With the classical style came narrative, and a spectator position engendered by certain narrational and perspectival conventions. With classical film narrative's insertion of secondary identification into the spectatorial experience, the travel film's first-person perspective was set into motion through the mediation of an authoritative traveler-protagonist whose narrative movement across the globe thereby altered the dynamic of stasis and mobility and with whom the spectator could identify. Through the traveler-protagonist, identification with visual perspective was married to character identification.

Travel films of the early twentieth century formed a mutually reinforcing relationship with the burgeoning tourist industry of the period. While travel, broadly defined, undoubtedly has a long history, packaged tourism and mass tourism are more recent developments. Thomas Cook, often credited as inventor of the packaged tour, began organizing tours of Europe in 1841, making use of the new railroads for his group tours by 1845. Cook's advertising marketed the journey as a commodity to be purchased, and heightened public awareness of travel possibilities and of exotic cultures available to the average consumer. Eventually, the increased availability and visibility of the packaged tour and a greater number of companies offering such tours ushered in a period of mass tourism; this was marked not only by the accessibility of leisured travel to a large portion of the population but by the public perception of tourism as a standard, even essential, feature of modern society. Within the United States, the first phase of mass tourism took place in the 1920s and 1930s, as transportation costs dropped, tour companies expanded, leisure time increased, paid holidays became more common, car ownership expanded, and motel chains made lodging more affordable.[9] In successive stages, tourism became available to larger portions of the population and became more international in terms of destination; however, the character did not change significantly until the emergence of new, competing "styles"

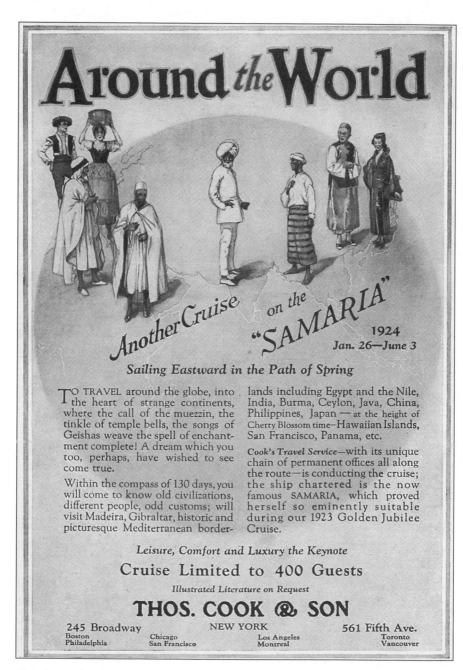

Around *the* World

Another Cruise on the "SAMARIA"

1924
Jan. 26—June 3

Sailing Eastward in the Path of Spring

To TRAVEL around the globe, into the heart of strange continents, where the call of the muezzin, the tinkle of temple bells, the songs of Geishas weave the spell of enchantment complete! A dream which you too, perhaps, have wished to see come true.

Within the compass of 130 days, you will come to know old civilizations, different people, odd customs; will visit Madeira, Gibraltar, historic and picturesque Mediterranean border-

lands including Egypt and the Nile, India, Burma, Ceylon, Java, China, Philippines, Japan — at the height of Cherry Blossom time—Hawaiian Islands, San Francisco, Panama, etc.

Cook's Travel Service—with its unique chain of permanent offices all along the route—is conducting the cruise; the ship chartered is the now famous SAMARIA, which proved herself so eminently suitable during our 1923 Golden Jubilee Cruise.

Leisure, Comfort and Luxury the Keynote
Cruise Limited to 400 Guests
Illustrated Literature on Request
THOS. COOK & SON

245 Broadway	NEW YORK		561 Fifth Ave.
Boston	Chicago	Los Angeles	Toronto
Philadelphia	San Francisco	Montreal	Vancouver

The advent of packaged tourism was accompanied by advertising, which helped disseminate the idea of experiencing other cultures as a leisure activity.

From an advertisement in *Mentor*, August 1923.

of tourism in more recent years.[10] To this extent, it is possible to identify a "classical" style of tourism emerging over the first part of the century with the seeds of mass tourism. The particular aspects of this travel style, established in the 1920s and '30s, including the purchase of postcards, the avoidance of places considered overly touristy, the photographic capture of sights and attractions, and the desire to see a location from within and above continue to be a part of this classical style.

Finally, yet another critical component of the backdrop for film's early development was a classical style of anthropology that emerged in the first two decades of the twentieth century, as will be explored in chapter 1. The professionalization of anthropology during the late nineteenth century occurred in two stages as anthropologists—educated scientists rather than the leisured hobbyists/collectors who made up the original group of "scientists of man"—first found employment in burgeoning natural history museums in the United States and later attained university positions. In this way, anthropology moved from a hobby to a profession intimately connected to popular tastes as the first individuals to call themselves anthropologists by profession engaged in packaging ethnographic visions for museumgoers as well as attendees of world's fairs. Eventually, the profession would scale the ivory tower and, through the legitimization of academe,

World's fair exhibits such as the reconstructed ruins of Uxmal celebrated not the Yucatan culture that produced these structures, but, as the caption for this photo suggests, the individuals who risked death venturing into the jungle to make papier-mâché molds of such ruins.

From *The Dream City*. St. Louis: N. D. Thompson, 1893.

enact an erasure of its roots in popular culture. The pioneering career of Franz Boas illustrates this repositioning of the anthropologist from world's fair and museum employee to academic figure, as well as the emerging centrality of the travel experience within the newly professionalized field of anthropology. Unlike the "armchair anthropologists" before him, Boas conducted fieldwork on the northwest coast of North America and among the Eskimos of Baffin Island. However, Boas's fieldwork was often conducted as part of a larger expedition, rather than as an individual enterprise, and typically for short periods of time. Thus, while Boas was a pivotal figure in the development of anthropology, the start of a "classical" ethnographic methodology is sometimes dated at 1922 with the publication of Bronislaw Malinowski's *Argonauts of the Western Pacific*, a text that disseminated a set of enduring standards for participant observation and prolonged fieldwork. With the popularization of Malinowski's ethnographic methodology and the academic authority granted the anthropologist through his university setting, the stage was set for the lionization of the lone anthropologist as a new kind of frontiersman. Once removed from the ranks of rich hobbyists and sideshow hucksters and set up as a noble figure pursuing knowledge in a mystically foreign landscape, the anthropologist could return to popular culture, but now in the fictive form of a hero.

To the extent that the historical development and solidification of classical anthropological, cinematic, and commercialized travel practices coincided, each of these cultural activities drew upon the dominant epistemologies, worldviews, and economic conditions of the early twentieth century. Broadly speaking, the establishment of these practices was enabled by Enlightenment thinking, which valorized vision as a mode of attaining knowledge and labeled the world as an appropriate object of knowledge. While the primacy of vision within film viewing could hardly be debated, travel, before the era of packaged tourism, was not viewed primarily as a visual activity. Judith Adler traces the ascendancy of vision within the history of travel, with "tourist" and "sightseer" becoming interchangeable terms only after 1800. The classical ethnographer shares this same post-Baconian and post-Lockean history and therefore the same associations between vision and knowledge to the point that, as Johannes Fabian has noted, "The ability to 'visualize' a culture or society almost becomes synonymous for understanding it."[11]

Beyond a simple emphasis on vision, however, is the suggestion that the *gaze*, a term now carrying with it a richness stemming from Laura Mulvey's work, involves a structuring and interpretation of visual data. The gaze understood in this way is a both a symptom of and a conduit to modes of knowledge and representation. It is transformative and epistemologically inflected in its perception and transformation of sight into representation. Like the explorer who not only sees but also maps the world, the tourist is distinguished not solely by sight-seeing activities but also by his camera or sketchbook, which allows for the visual reproduction of the sights seen. Martin Heidegger writes, "The fundamental event of the modern age is the conquest of the world as picture."[12] This "age of the world picture" is marked by a scientism that portrays the universe as a representable and therefore knowable object; a belief in the image as conveyor of truth; and technological developments that provide mastery through representation. To see the world as a picture is to "get the picture," to understand the world as a uniform totality, and to take up a subject position in relation to an objectified world. This scientism or drive to knowledge, as a mode of experiencing the world and as an orientation to one's surroundings, extends beyond science to leisure forms. To view the world as being of a "picture postcard" is to attain the illusion of mastery through vision and aestheticized representation.

The postcard collection, like a globe with its totalizing view, enacts a containment of and distantiation from the entity being represented; one takes up a cosmological position to contemplate the world in miniature and as an entity that represents the tourist's accomplishments expressed in material and visual form. Pierre Bourdieu, although specifically referencing anthropology, describes the objectivist approach in such pursuits. He writes, "Objectivism constitutes the social world as a spectacle presented to an observer who takes up a 'point of view' on the action, who stands back so as to observe it and, transferring into the object the principles of his relation to the object . . . . This point of view is the one afforded by high positions in the social structure, from which the social world appears as a representation (in the sense of idealist philosophy but also as used in painting or the theatre)."[13] Bourdieu suggests that objectivism is infused with the subjective to the extent that the observer's interpretation of the object bears the signs of its objectification; the interpretation always incorporates something of the observer's "relation to the object." Rather than this lie of objectivity—that is, the figurative shadow of the scientist cast over the object of investigation—being the product of accident or imprecise science, it is instead the unacknowledged central drive of scientific investigation. To put oneself in that towering position, to ascend to the high position that affords this particular point of view, amounts to the grounding of self through science, a formalized method of mastery through distantiation and objectification. Seeing the object through the filter of one's own shadow is assurance of one's dominant position and, metaphorically speaking, one's closer proximity to the light.

Scholars of tropes of exoticism suggest that the construction of bodies of knowledge about exoticized cultures participates in this process of establishing a Western-defined self in the world. While the self/other binarisms of such studies vary—occidental/oriental, West/East, civilized/primitive—among scholars such as Edward Said, James Clifford, and Marianna Torgovnick, accord is reached around the idea that the predominant truths found in Western constructions of the exotic, the Orient, or the primitive, are found in what they reveal about the West's crises of identity. For instance, James Clifford argues that the category of the primitive can only be understood as an "incoherent cluster of qualities that at different times have been used to construct a source, origin, or alter ego confirming some new 'discovery' within the territory of the Western self."[14]

Dean MacCannell's analysis of tourism returns to this same issue of establishing a relationship between world and self. For MacCannell, tourism is the search for a way to overcome the alienation and fragmentation of modern life. He compares tourism to a multi–billion dollar research project, directing tourists

The heroism of the explorers who were a part of the Greely Expedition into Arctic regions is re-created through the "being there" effect of this panorama at the 1893 Columbian Exposition in Chicago.

From *The Dream City*. St. Louis: N. D. Thompson, 1893.

across the world to conduct their own personal ethnographies of modernity. The museum becomes yet another means of grasping the total vision, and it is "by means of [the museum's] specificity that [it] can set the totality of the modern world in motion in the tourist's imagination."[15] Replicated in MacCannell's observations is this same structure of distantiation and totalizing vision. The tourist temporarily leaves the niche of home life, with its narrow view on the world, exchanging it for the ability to trace one's finger across the globe in a recounting of past journeys and in an illustration of a recently procured expansion of perspective.

This dynamic of distantiation and totalizing vision as a trope of mastery for affirming one's place in the world thus can be seen as a product of an era and as an enduring cultural component. Thus, its appearance within the tourist gaze is unsurprising. The paradox only emerges with a consideration of the appeal of engulfment or immersion that is at the core of tourism and central to many entertainment forms that deliver a sense of presence or "being there." The tourist gaze is characterized by the constant push and pull of distanced immersion, by the desire to be fully immersed in an environment yet literally or figuratively distanced from the scene in order to occupy a comfortable viewing position.

—— Proximity, Distance, and the Semiotics of Tourism

At the heart of the myth of direct experience, as described in the introduction, is the same kind of tension found at work within the desire for distanced immersion. In fact, the play between the intimacy of direct experience as mythological procurer of authenticity and the distance imposed through mediation closely resembles the dialectic between distance and closeness found in the tourist's distanced immersion. Examining the phenomenon of distanced immersion more closely, the distancing that comprises one half of this oxymoron should be considered as both figurative and literal, as sometimes intentional but more often unavoidable and invisible to the tourist. Consistently, we can point to a slippage between the optical point of view and more conceptual maneuvers, thereby making this movement between figurative and literal more seamless. For instance, the conceptual distantiation of the tourist-scientist from the object of study as a process of abstraction and extraction finds its more literal correlative in the tourist who seeks out a view of a locale from above. The tourist attempts to extract herself from the scene and views the location from a point of view that delivers an almost abstracted vision similar to that of the map. This type of movement, from immersive to distanced, is a continual fluctuation within the tourist experience, as the tourist stops to gaze at the guidebook's floor plan of the castle, for instance, before continuing down the staircase running her hand against the cold and worn stone of the castle wall. To highlight mediation as figurative distantiation is to acknowledge the continued presence of that floor plan and other organizing structures that filter and guide experience long after the guidebook is tucked back into the tourist's backpack. And the myth of direct experience is the promise of enduring cultural immersion leading to a puncturing of that wall of mediation.

Suggesting that direct experience is the stuff of myth and myth alone means sealing off any consideration of the effects of culture shock (or other self-knowledge effects resulting from exposure to cultural difference), and thus some problematizing of this notion is necessary. The quickest route to demonstrating the predominantly mythological status of direct experience's puncturing effects is to reference the knowledge that is passed off as a result of the intimacy of immersion. Traditionally, such knowledge has been the effect of abstraction and distance. For instance, in one of his travel essays, Lawrence Durrell writes about how to best extract some truth about "the spirit of place." Durrell suggests that a traveler can reduce a locale to a knowable entity through immersive sensory experience alone. He notes that "as you get to know Europe slowly, tasting the wines, cheeses and characters of the different countries you begin to realize that the important determinant of any culture is after all—the spirit of place. Just as one particular vineyard will always give you a special wine with discernible characteristics so a Spain, an Italy, a Greece will always give you the same type of culture—will express itself through the human being just as it does through its wild flowers."[16] Durrell advocates a method of communing with the land through direct experience. Such a mystical effect takes place as a result of a prolonged stay and an openness to total immersion. Traveling becomes a process of sensory exposure for the sake of knowing a place, "piercing her hard heart and discovering the landscape-mystery of her true soul."[17] Durrell suggests both that culture can be tasted, consumed, and judged by the traveler-epicure and that the traveler can master the landscape (and its people, who are not easily separated from the same landscape) by isolating its essence or discovering the "invisible constant." Such essentializing and the totalizing effects of a survey of Europe's different "characters" indicate a movement from immersion to the type of abstraction that can only be achieved through distantiation from place as object of study.

Parting with the romantic notion of direct experience is difficult. Indeed, it is appealing to believe that when the tourist sets down her guidebook to peer into the depths of a volcano or to climb the Tower of Pisa, she abandons textually mediated experience to commune with the real thing. The simplest way to debate this viewpoint would be to insist on the absolute ubiquity of mediation and the impossibility of escaping the filtering and transformative effects of our own mental structures and interpretative frameworks. For instance, one could cite Bill Nichols's supposition that unmediated, nonideological perception is impossible. Nichols suggests that much like our perception of visual media, "our perception of the physical world is also based on codes involving iconic signs," and thus "the environment becomes a text to be read like any other text."[18] Perhaps more useful, however, is a brief analysis of the semiotics of tourism, what Jonathan Culler has described as the reduction of all aspects of culture to signs of themselves.[19] Another semiotician, John Frow, notes, "A place, a gesture, a use of language are understood not as given bits of the real but as suffused with ideality, giving on to the *type* of the beautiful, the extraordinary, or the culturally authentic."[20] The kissing couple is a sign of the romance of Paris, just as the arguing merchants are seen as a sign of "Greekness." The tourist attraction as a sign of itself is perceived as an image seen previously in films and on postcards or as a potential image to be captured on film or videotape. The landscape or monument is judged according to standards of picturesqueness, framed by the tourist's viewfinder, and separated from its context and placement in a real world by the act of recording. Whether some rupture-producing experiences can actually penetrate the mediating effects of tourism's semiotics, thereby bringing to life some variant of the myth of direct experience, is a topic for further investigation.

Whether penetrable or not, tourism's interpretative mediation is not unlike the interpretive strategies employed by the cinemagoer; both the profilmic reality and the tourist attraction are reduced to a series of framed signs interpreted in a socially constructed manner. In short, if vision cannot be separated from the translation of sensory impression into meaning, then many of the differences that distinguish, for example, normal perception from the bracketed perception of a photograph disappear from view. Furthermore, the semiotics of tourism described by Culler and Frow can be considered as just one instance of purposeful perception, shaped by the particularities of the tourist industry and that larger cultural phenomenon, the tourist gaze.

—— Ethnographic Mediation and Classical Style

To the extent that the field of anthropology is the legitimized branch of a larger cultural touristic impulse, the ongoing critique of its classical style provides analytical tools for investigating some of the dilemmas of the tourist gaze. For instance, one aspect of the classical style that anthropologists have attempted to repudiate is their field's version of the myth of direct experience, which nonetheless remains operational within the mystique that surrounds the profession. Although anthropologists may choose to study a "home culture," this decision is noted as a departure from the basis of the discipline, which is lone fieldwork in a distant and foreign locale. Within the ethnographic monograph or film, the claim to authority is rooted in the anthropologist's implicit statement "I was there." The standard photograph that appears adjacent to a title page, or on the back cover of an ethnographic text, features the anthropologist in the field, thereby documenting her presence, not entirely unlike the tourist photographing herself in front of the Taj Mahal or at the base of one of the Great Pyramids.

The field-worker is first and foremost an eyewitness whose value increases inversely with the number of other Westerners who have witnessed this remote culture. Within this simple formulation, knowledge derives from vision. Yet from classical anthropology the field has inherited an almost mystical belief in a defining moment that results from prolonged exposure within the field. The ideal outcome of such an "ecstatic moment" is described metaphorically as a shift in visual perspective, the acquired ability "to see through [the] native's eyes."[21] This holy

Travel writer Thomas MacMahon includes with his article about his ventures into Australia's northern territories a photo of himself with indigenes dressed for battle as a way to declare, "I was there."

Photo illustration from Thomas J. MacMahon,
"An Adventure into the Never Never Country," *Travel,* May 1919.

grail of ethnographic pursuit is thus the attainment of a particular vision, a form of knowledge expressed in visual terms. Through immersion, the classical anthropologist hopes to undergo some kind of transformation, a virtual out-of-body experience that will place him in the position of the indigene, from where he may view the world as the indigene does. Direct experience acts as the catalyst for the conversion in this particular myth. Clifford Geertz suggests that anthropology's particular variant of the myth of direct experience is a legacy of Bronislaw Malinowski, who espoused the belief that "one grasps the exotic not by drawing back from the immediacies of encounter into the symmetries of thought [but] by losing oneself, one's soul maybe, in those immediacies."[22]

Of course, this belief in a conversion to a position of knowledge through the simple fact of "being there" is accompanied by an interpretive methodology employed as a mediating force. In this example of distanced immersion, the classical anthropologist's faith in the power of direct experience coexists with a reliance on an ethnographic methodology for decoding culture and extracting knowledge. The ethnographer's prefieldwork training is an induction into an interpretive method designed to translate encounters with individuals and material culture into larger statements about an exoticized culture. It is not only an overtly acknowledged practice of mediation—that is, the mediation of direct experience through the filters of one's training in the field of anthropology—but a formalized and documented field of inquiry. To the extent that we accept this science as a formal practice of exoticization motivated by the same desires as other cultural practices, such documentation provides a guide to the basic contours of the tourist gaze.

—— Anthropology's Bifocal Knowledge

Despite revisionist anthropologists' attempts to eradicate the mysticism of direct experience's conversionary effects, the dualism of proximity and distance remains intact within the language used to describe ethnographic method. This is most evident in the description of anthropology's requisite dual perspective. "Going native," generally looked down upon as a loss of scientific objectivity, is the substitution of one perspective for another. "Seeing through the native's eyes," however, leaves open the possibility for the scientist's objective point of view. In other words, "going native" involves a loss in perspective, while "seeing through the native's eyes" involves a dual vision; one is marked by intimacy and the other by the steady and distanced vision of the scientist. We find a convenient abbreviation of this bifocal knowledge in anthropology's term "participant-observer." A *participant* is susceptible to the powers of exposure to a raw reality, to draw on the myth of direct experience, while the *observer* inserts distance in order to maintain the larger picture.

The overlay of this second, scientific vision supposedly differentiates the anthropologist's authority from that of a member of the culture being studied. Otherwise, the ideal anthropologist would be the bilingual indigene who is able to directly translate "through the native's eyes" into written form. Consider Malinowski, who writes, "The natives obey the forces and commands of the tribal code, but they do not comprehend them; exactly as they obey their instincts and their impulses, but could not lay down a single law of psychology."[23] Thus, the rigor of scientific analysis must be added to the equation. In her critique of the arrogance of classical anthropology, Trinh Minh-ha writes, "Remember, anthropologists always set out to depict that which the natives live or carry on in their lives 'without their knowing it' and to see through the latter's eyes with, in addition, God's grasp of the totality."[24]

The position of the field-worker as participant-observer is not unlike Durrell's proposed traveler-epicure. With the comparative knowledge provided by ethnographic training combined with protracted immersion, the field-worker can discern the unique "flavor" of a land that, according to Durrell, is expressed equally in the wildflowers, the wine, and the people. In short, a latent meaning is already present in the land, and by extension, in the culture that has sprouted up on the land, a meaning that, as Durrell notes, "will express itself." This type of essentialism is another aspect of classical anthropology that revisionists have attempted to move away from; yet it too persists in the form of a specter forever suggesting a singular truth that can be derived through scientific method. Within classical anthropology, this is the case even when active scientific interpretation is emphasized over the direct experience model of a truth that expresses itself to immersed initiates. Within Claude Lévi-Strauss's statement, "Exploration is not so much a matter of covering ground as of digging beneath the surface," scientific mediation is the digging tool for unearthing the "truth" of a culture.[25] Exoticized culture is seen as having a hidden interiority or a deep structure that can be revealed using the anthropologist's conceptual tools.

—— The View from Above

Classical anthropological method as a practice for collecting information is marked by a progression of visual perspectives beginning with the view from above. This formula can be seen in the ethnographic film, which traditionally begins with aerial footage, often shot from the helicopter or small plane that brings the field-worker to his chosen site. In a text designed for anthropology students, John Collier Jr. and Malcolm Collier explicitly describe this distanced view as the first step of fieldwork, and the role of representational technologies as critical to the task of attaining a "holistic vision" of a culture. The Colliers begin their textbook with a statement reminiscent of MacCannell's thoughts on tourists as amateur ethnographers out to overcome the daily fragmentation of their own lives through a totalizing vision of the world and of a distant culture. "Generally, the fragmentation of modern life makes it difficult to respond to the whole view," they write. "Our cultural development . . . has been oriented to commanding nature by super-technology, carried out collectively through super-organization and specialization, making it difficult for us to accomplish holistic understanding."[26] Within Colliers' method, the first step is "orientation" through the view from above. The "super-technology" of aerial and panoramic photographs provides long views that "establish relationships of ecology and community" and help reveal "the basic form of a culture"—that is, patterns and relationships not visible from the localized perspective.[27]

In making patterns evident, the aerial gaze moves toward an abstracted knowledge, representative of what Fabian calls anthropology's belief in "geometry qua graphic-spatial conceptualization as the most 'exact' way of communicating knowledge."[28] For the ethnographer, this "mathematical-geometric" visualism motivates the translation of information and experience into diagrams and charts that place pieces of knowledge into spatial orders (such as genealogical charts, with their abstracted perspectives on familial relations). The abstraction of the literal or figurative map is thus a way of finding oneself within the maze of a foreign culture and of assuring oneself of a knowledge that is at least as authoritative as that of the resident, if not more so.

The identification of these same strategies of multiperspectival viewing, aerial vantage points, and mapping within film and tourism may hardly be necessary. Nonetheless, it may be useful to acknowledge that classical cinema makes use of a shifting visual perspective, jumping from a character's point of view to close-ups to more distanced views of a scene (omniscient perspectives independent of any diegetic character) and back again. Tourist attractions are similarly structured to give the sightseer multiple perspectives on a single object. Multiple viewing points marked on a Grand Canyon visitor's map channel tourists from vista to vista as they try to comprehend the canyon's vastness. In almost any tourist destination, sightseers can be seen circling a monument, viewing it from each side, in order to grasp the totality; helicopter rides may make an even better view available to those who can afford them. And the more affordable postcard makes available a multiplicity of views possibly not available to the casual tourist. Undoubtedly the tourist, like the ethnographer, delights in an immersive perspective, meandering through the bazaar shoulder-to-shoulder with Turkish buyers and sellers, sitting in a café looking out at the busy street like a native French person taking a break from the busy workday. Yet tourists also clamor to transcend this localized perspective and get a privileged view from above. To climb to the top of the temple at Chichen Itza, to retreat to the hills above a Melanesian village, or to look out from the top of the Eiffel Tower is to view the terrain as a unitary whole. Often a similarly commanding view from above or a sweeping camera movement mapping out a panorama of place serves as an establishing shot within classical Hollywood film. The aerial gaze places the viewer outside and above a locale, separated from the action and progression of the narrative. Following this moment of spectacle, touristic pleasure, and visual/geographical orientation, the viewer is then plunged into a more immersive or local perspective on the action.

—— The Distantiation of Framed Mobility

Distantiation can be seen as a product of a scientism that pursues a vision of the object of study as a unitary and separable whole; but it can also be examined as an incidental effect of travel, an effect obviously not unfavorable to but perhaps not always directly resulting from the objective/objectifying stance of the drive to knowledge. For instance, distantiation may occur through mobility's effect on perception; as Eric J. Leed notes, "In the prolonged and intensified motions of passage, the world becomes more objective, an array of things stripped of their subjectivity, while the self becomes more subjective and invisible as it is subsumed in the activity of observation and defined in terms of this activity."[29] The tourist and ethnographer—as well as the moviegoer, by virtue of the moving camera— become mobile subjects identified not as part of an environment but as distanced observers surveying the objectified components of a static locale.

Second, an environmental bubble—the notion of which is somewhat less applicable to the ethnographer—often separates these mobile subjects from the exotic locale.[30] An extension of this bubble has assured the success of mass tourism by replacing the risks of travel with the comforts of a home away from home. The cushioned tour bus and Western hotel place the tourist in a separate space from the exoticized other, protected from the dust and heat, the occasional wild animal, and perhaps even the pickpockets making the most of host/guest relations. This environmental bubble imposes spatial divisions while enabling vision (although the view through the sun-shaded, glass window of the bus will always be a distantiated view). In reference to the environmental bubble of train travel, Wolfgang Schivelbusch argues that both the framing of the landscape by the train window and the train's velocity removes the traveler from the space through which he travels by blurring the foreground.[31]

While the actual traveler perceives the landscape through the environmental bubble of the airplane or train, the virtual traveler finds himself in the air-conditioned environmental bubble of the movie theater. Similar arguments have been made by Mary Ann Doane, Lynne Kirby, and Margaret Morse, who have commented on the parallels between the distanced, framed vision of cinema and television and the viewing strategies associated with train or automobile travel. Travel vision resembles media spectatorship, as the space on the other side of the window becomes less real and less easily entered, like a painted canvas, a televisual depiction, or a movie screen.

This distanced vision is evidently a product of various factors: the spectator's (virtual) mobility, the environmental bubble's physical separation of sightseer and terrain, and, last but not least, the imposition of a frame. This frame could be considered incidental insofar as it may be inescapable during a plane trip, for instance. However, the ethnographer and tourist may purposefully reinsert the frame by looking through the viewfinder of a camera. In her work, Susan Sontag discusses taking photographs as another way of distancing oneself from an environment, recording and appropriating an image at the same time as refusing direct experience. She writes, "A way of certifying experience, taking photographs is also a way of refusing it—by limiting experience to a search for the photogenic, by converting experience into an image, a souvenir. Travel becomes a strategy for accumulating photographs. The very activity of taking pictures is soothing, and assuages general feelings of disorientation that are likely to be exacerbated by travel."[32] Photography provides an instrument for appropriation, collection, and orientation; by placing oneself behind the camera, the tourist or ethnographer confirms placement within the landscape while also symbolically removing herself from the environment through a Cartesian perspectivalism. The world is captured as an image circumscribed by a frame that "emphasizes that within its four edges the picture has established an enclosed, coherent and absolutely rigorous system of its own," a system imposed by the spectator-owner who stands outside of the frame.[33] Photography's monocular perspective presents the world as geometricalized space radiating out from the viewing eye. The tourist-photographer or ethnographer-photographer, like the moviegoer identifying with the camera and "the pure act of perception," is hailed as the singular spectator through her occupation of the apex of vision.[34] The world appears to come into being by virtue of the spectator's act of looking.

—— Conclusion

The areas of intersection among anthropology, film, and tourism, far from being coincidental, are the result of a modernist worldview infused into the classical forms of these practices and a shared, underlying fascination with and defensive reaction to cultural difference. I have used anthropological writings and the self-reflexive field known as the anthropology of anthropology to highlight practices formalized within anthropology but shared by film and tourism.

I have grouped these practices and viewing strategies as definitive of the tourist gaze. Instead, I could have referenced the "ethnographic" within filmmaking and tourist practice, or made note of the "cinematic" within the tourist's or field-worker's visual stance. In my labeling of this bundle of commonalities as "touristic" I emphasize some qualities over others; the imbrication within commercial practices, the assumed superficiality of cross-cultural contact, and the overriding goal of pleasure seem to take precedence over links to art and education. A certain value judgment is evidently being made. It should be acknowledged, however, that a cultural attitude that views *tourism* as a dirty word in comparison to the more accepted practice of "travel," whatever that might be, is also in operation here. Future chapters problematize this antitourism and provide a wider view of tourism and its diverse practices. Nonetheless, my persistent use of the terms *touristic* and *tourist gaze* to refer to these modes of seeing and knowing that surface in multiple practices highlights that which is most worrisome and most deserving of political analysis in these practices.

By referring to a generalized classical period within film, anthropology, and tourism, I have verged on presenting the tourist gaze as a single, unchanging entity. Undoubtedly, some aspects of this gaze are dependent on the nature of the apparatuses involved, from film and television to the visual tools carried by the tourist. Yet a wide range of determinants independent of such technological concerns shape the nature of any single instance of the tourist's gaze. The "American" tourist gaze has been reconfigured over time as national consciousness has sought out a vision of otherness to resolve shifting ideological contradictions. And in some instances, filmic/televisual codes of viewing have been manipulated to bring us new modes of touristic viewing that question our comfortable assessments of cultural difference. Thus, visual apparatuses, moments of reconfiguration, personal visions that challenge the tourist's stance, and the diverse implications of the gaze for various locales provide fodder for the ensuing pages.

CHAPTER TWO

Touristic Births

PLACING THE TOURIST

FASCINATION WITH IMAGINED beasts and fantastic human oddities inhabiting the globe's farthest corners stretches back centuries. However, touristic experience—whether simulated or actual—of the late nineteenth century brought the Western subject face-to-face with the spectacle of difference, the exotic landscape dotted with wondrously alien human and animal faces. A series of developments paved a course from the distanced and indirect apperception of foreign lands as enjoyed by readers of travel literature to the pleasures of "being there" as a notable, widely marketed cultural feature. The tourist-spectator position was the product of a burgeoning worldview that neared maturity by the turn of the century. As suggested above, this capitalist view of the world as a reservoir of products, raw materials, and experiential pleasures melded with scientific understandings of the universe and a technological confidence on the part of the West. One outcome was the learned pleasures of the touristic as defined by various tropes: the visual objectification or the conversion of cultural difference into spectacle; a series of dividing lines drawn out by the process of commodification separating the tourist from the toured; and the identification of the tourist with a figure of mastery such as the explorer, colonialist soldier, or anthropologist. In other words, touristic pleasure was made possible through the creation of a safety zone within which the exhilaration of geographical proximity with an exoticized stranger could exist without compromising other, less literal, forms of distance. The marketing of touristic pleasures in the precinematic era helped popularize a coherent set of strategies for viewing cultural difference, a set of strategies that can only be analyzed in the context of a

This collection of tobacco cards represents a double rhetoric of collection and accumulation, in that such cards were intended to be collected by consumers while the cards themselves depict the globe as a reservoir of raw materials to be collected and utilized by the West.

"Products of the World" tobacco cards, Player's Cigarettes, circa 1910.

culturally shared worldview and late-nineteenth-century developments, including the professionalization and popularization of anthropology, improved transportation, the consolidation of capitalism, and the cultural ascendancy of the mechanically produced image.

—— A Viewable, Purchasable, Pleasurable World

The ascendancy of touristic viewing took place against a background of unprecedented Western contact with the so-called margins of the earth. In the decades before the close of the nineteenth century, missionaries, surveyors, explorers, anthropologists, and colonialists vowed to fill in the few remaining blank spots on world maps and to close up the larger gaps in knowledge of the globe's various inhabitants. Traveling merchants negotiated the purchase of physical types previously unseen in Europe and the United States, and showmen, gaining possession of these human display items, collected profits from audiences eager to look into the dark eyes of the world's jungles and deserts. Natural history museums sprouted up in U.S. cities as expeditions and world fairs created the need for permanent warehouses to store and display the West's increasing collection of exotic booty.

It was primarily explorers with strong capitalist affiliations, like Henry Morton Stanley, who charted out remote lands in the name of mercantilism, empire, or simple publicity. Nearly twenty years after Stanley's rescue of David Livingstone, coverage of his 1890 Emin Pasha Relief Expedition was inescapable, with the major illustrated weeklies' news of the expedition pausing only to bring readers advertisements featuring Stanley endorsing "Congo Soap" or Livingstone and Stanley sipping a particular brand of tea inside their tent.[1] Other travelers, associated with the East India Company, the British South Africa Company, and the British East Africa Company, similarly reached eminence, as overseas capitalist ventures became synonymous with adventure. The actual accounts of long journeys, venturesome heroes, and the occasional battle inspired colonial romance and adventure novels, which enjoyed considerable popularity during this period.[2] In 1874, a new literary genre—that of the "ethnographic novel"—was born, with G. A. Henty's first boys' book on the Ashanti campaign.[3] More notable literary works followed. Rider Haggard's *King Solomon's Mines* sold 31,000 copies during the twelve months following its 1885 release; Rudyard Kipling published *Plain Tales from the Hills* in 1888 and *The Jungle Book* in 1895; and following a Thomas Cook tour of Egypt, even Arthur Conan Doyle experimented with foreign settings, as in his 1898 tale of intrigue aboard a Nile steamer, *The Tragedy of the Korosko.*

The marketing of Henry Morton Stanley and the capitalization of his image by producers of goods with an exoticized origin—such as coffee, tea, and tobacco—was a mini-industry unto itself.

The battles forged in the name of colonialism were promoted as making the world safe for travelers as well as for the retrieval of raw materials, while making good fodder for adventure tales and images of courage used to sell consumer goods.

Tobacco product illustration. Courtesy of the Duke University Rare Book, Manuscript, and Special Collections Library, Emergence of Advertising in America, #D0295, http://scriptorium.lib.duk.edu/eaa/.

However, travel was not reserved for fictional characters, nor for the boldest of real-life adventurers; each exploration opened up new routes for tourism. And although the most exotic of trails were reserved for the likes of Sir Richard Burton or Alexander von Humboldt (individuals of unusual means and fortitude), middle-class travel across national borders increased during these same decades with the rise of packaged tourism and improved transportation technologies. Middle-class single women and widows became the new class of tourists with Thomas Cook's organization of group tours using new railway routes. And finally, with more leisure time available to workers, tourism—even if only on a limited scale—became a possibility for a greater portion of the population than ever before.

A gradually developing conception of the world as pleasurable spectacle was linked to this growing awareness of distant locales. As historian Robert Wiebe has argued, during the last quarter of the nineteenth century, Victorian Americans were engaged in a prolonged "search for order."[4] The discovery of "unfathomable multiplicity in the universe,"[5] along with rapid industrialization, created a dual vision of an ever-changing world—what was seen as a developing center barely recognizable to inhabitants of the recent past and an expanding periphery populated by similarly unrecognizable human cultures. Ironically, the same feature that made modern society and its rapid rate of change threatening to some—that is, technology—also made the so-called primitive world less frightening and more available. Improved transportation carved out paths from this conceived center to its periphery, and the advanced weaponry of colonialist government helped assure safe passage. Meanwhile, recording devices captured, duplicated, and miniaturized chunks of distant locales and their inhabitants for the viewing pleasure of Western citizens in urban centers. The world appeared to be at the West's disposal for colonialists, travelers, capitalists, and popular culture consumers alike. What Jane Desmond calls "an aestheticization of imperialist expansion" occurred as the world's distant locales were seen as places from which to extract pleasure, whether through tourism, the visual spectacle of armchair travel, or even the taste of a banana or some other exotic product newly available to North American consumers.[6]

The world was a quarry of sights and sounds that could be mined by the enterprising few and put on display for the middle class, who attended world's fairs, toured museums, and collected stereoscopic view cards. Traveling photographers could now use paper negatives to capture images rather than gambling with fragile and cumbersome glass plates while on the road. Professional photographers like Roger Fenton, Francis Bedford, and George Washington Wilson combed the world for the unusual and the picturesque and eventually made names for themselves through their images of scenic Europe, Asia, and the Near East. Bedford published a collection of 175 photos of the Holy Land, a project that was the outcome of a royal command to accompany the Prince of Wales to Egypt and Palestine. Fenton, eventually named the official photographer of the British Museum, took photographs of England, Russia, and many locales in between. After his death, his photographs were purchased by publisher/photographer Francis Frith, appeared in tourist brochures, and were reportedly still in production as postcards as late as 1970.[7] While the photographs of Fenton and Bedford were in wide circulation and surely were put to touristic uses even during their creators' lifetimes, Wilson was perhaps the first photographer to fully anticipate photography's touristic implications, the postcard business, and its links to the growing travel industry. With the thought that tourists might wish to view photographs as

The "Picturesque People of the Empire" tobacco card series identified types from around the world by nationality or ethnic/tribal origin and sometimes by occupation, whether warrior, cowboy, or "rickshaw boy."

Tobacco cards, "Picturesque People of the Empire," W. D. and H. O. Wills, circa 1910.

One-half the world now knows how the other half lives

YOU sit in a comfortable auditorium, watching the Zulu in his native dance, while out in the Dark Continent the savage sees the Easter parade on Fifth Avenue.

Today each half of the world knows how the other half lives—the motion picture has taught it. And, as in all other phases of photography, the Eastman Kodak Company has contributed, in a big way, to the advancement of the motion picture.

It was Eastman film that made such pictures possible, and it is Eastman film that tonight thrills you with the emotion of the drama, convulses you with laughter, gives you the war news in picture and instructs you in the ways and the work of the world. Photography today is a part of life. It touches every human interest, holds fast the memories of the home, is the right hand of science, the scout in war and truthful chronicler of history.

And the story of photography, during the past third of a century, is the story of the growth and progress and development of its strongest advocate and ally, the Eastman Kodak Company, for whatever promises to broaden the scope and usefulness of photography in art or science or business, is fostered through the research work and broad experience of that company until it has been made practical—made of real use to the world.

If it isn't an Eastman it isn't a KODAK

EASTMAN KODAK COMPANY

Although images of the less industrialized world were far more ubiquitous in the United States and Europe than images of the West in less industrialized locales, this Kodak ad presents the wonder of the roll film technology as providing mutual dissemination of images between the two "halves" of the globe.

Advertisement from 1919. Courtesy of the Duke University Rare Book, Manuscript, and Special Collections Library, Emergence of Advertising in America, #K0337, http://scriptorium.lib.duk.edu/eaa/.

a way of remembering their travels, he sought out the sites visited by large numbers of tourists and recommended in travel guidebooks;[8] such photographic depictions could be purchased by former tourists recapturing the sights of their voyages as well as by the more common armchair traveler.

The sights of the world, converted into spectacle by artists and photographers, could be purchased by Europeans and Americans in the comfort of their own cities; such purchasable images were ubiquitous. For instance, in what could be considered the nineteenth-century equivalent of the mid-twentieth-century diner's sugar packet emblazoned with a postcard-like scene, one brand of cigarette cards produced by the Ogden tobacco company featured 8,000 picture cards that collectively offered a "panorama of the world at large."[9] American, British, and French tobacco brands followed suit with series of scenes, peoples, and agricultural products from around the world, sometimes as an explicit illustration of a growing empire. World's fairs featured postcards so that the visitor could take home a bit of exotica, and mail-order stereoscopic cards of the globe's people and places provided another form of home viewing. With the late 1880s came the introduction of Kodak's roll-film camera and the beginnings of amateur travel photography. Popular culture consumers who couldn't—or couldn't afford to—travel could buy images of the world as spectacle at home, while upper-class tourists viewed the world as commodity through their own viewfinders. Thus, not only were newly discovered locations on the globe dragged into the capitalist system through the crisscrossing of new trade routes and the drainage of raw materials by European forces, but a touristic vision of the universe further integrated distant locales into commodity relations by selling the less industrialized world as visual pleasure.

—— Picturing the World through Science

With the popularization of science during this period, tourism—perhaps the first form of "edutainment"—cannot be divorced from the pedagogical discourses of science and its view of a structured universe. In fact, I have suggested in chapter 1 that Martin Heidegger's concept of the "world as picture," with the central role it assigns to science, could be extended to include the phenomenon of the "world as postcard," a form of mastery available to the layperson outside of scientific communities. This individual as actual or "virtual" tourist not only views familiarity with the world as an educational goal but employs learned touristic strategies to derive pleasure from the spectacle of cultural difference.[10] Like the scientist, the tourist takes up a subject position in relation to an objectified world. Like the cartographer who represents the world as a uniform whole from an

Illustrations of Nadar's *Le Geant* were widely distributed in periodicals and in narratives that recounted the adventure and science of hot air ballooning.

Illustration from R. M. Ballantyne, *Up in the Clouds.* London: James Nisbet, n.d.

impossible aerial perspective, the tourist seeks out the highest vantage point in an attempt to grasp the unfamiliar land as an understandable whole and as a system uniform in its character as scrutinizable object. Unsurprisingly, this same era witnesses Nadar's unprecedented and photographically documented ascent above Paris in the hot air balloon *Le Géant,* followed by the publication of Jules Verne's *Five Weeks in a Balloon,* a tale that places both the austere man of science and the working-class tourist in the same balloon basket.[11]

—— Collecting the World

Even with the progression from hot air balloon to other forms of aerial photography, truly perceiving the globe as a unified whole was no easy feat. The Victorian solution to this dilemma was the collection. While the diverse parts of the globe could not be simultaneously perceived, experienced, and understood by any one individual, examples of tools from around the world could be housed by one museum, the flowering plant types of all known climates could be cultivated in one botanical garden, and animal species representing each part of the globe could become cohabitants within a single zoo. The expansiveness of the world could be represented by the ordered collection.

Such collections of photographs, cultural artifacts, botanical samples, or zoological specimens were typically neither the sole realm of private citizens nor the exclusive property of the academy. In a few cases, individuals did maintain private collections or "curio cabinets," many of which were eventually opened to the public, such as the Horniman Free Museum in England. More frequently, however, the responsibility of collection fell on the shoulders of the public at large, or at least on those who found themselves in a position to aid in the grand task of collecting. Academic communities often published guidelines for collecting objects and information overseas, guidelines that were explicitly directed at nonscientific communities.

Although most collections were open to the public, collection curators came from the ranks of the academy and were responsible for devising, in Susan Stewart's words, "the classification schemes which will define space and time." Thus, bodies of knowledge developed to make sense of these accumulations imposed classificatory rules of order on collections, and by extension, on the globe. To the extent that these organizing principles were manifest in the display of public collections, scientific notions of an ordered world (which may have already drawn upon popular thought) were shared with nonacademic audiences. As Heidegger points out in reference to science and Stewart points out in reference to the collection, such orderings always involve the self as a central term.[12] This is to say that the devised organizing principles help articulate the collector's own identity in relation to the world as synedochically represented by the collection. Or in the case of the public collection, a society's worldview may be articulated, communicated, and reinforced by the organized displays of museums and world's fairs. And indeed, nineteenth-century collections of primitive artifacts and racial types were used in the construction of a racial and cultural hierarchy that placed industrialized Western nations at the pinnacle of progress and evolution.[13]

This placing of self within the world involved elaborating classificatory rules that not only defined space and time but, in the case of ethnographic collections, defined space as time. Johannes Fabian's influential book *Time and the Other: How Anthropology Makes Its Object* is dedicated to critiquing anthropology's spatialization of time. Fabian writes, "When modern anthropology began to construct its

This juxtaposition of a "a performer of the danse du ventre" and a Hungarian dancer from the 1893 Columbian World Exposition in Chicago was accompanied by the caption, "The change from a study of the Cairo girl and her frightful tambours and Listz's music and Western beauty and grace, is the greatest that could be furnished by feminine youth. Only Darwin could expatiate impartially on these variations of taste in the human kind."

From *The Dream City*. St. Louis: N. D. Thompson, 1893.

Other in terms of topoi implying distance, difference, and opposition, its intent was above all, but at least also, to construct ordered Space and Time—a cosmos— for Western society to inhabit, rather than 'understanding other cultures,' its ostensible vocation."[14] Anthropology converted the world into a timeline, insisting that the savage could best be understood as existing in another time and that Western society could be found on the tip of that timeline leading all of humankind into the future.

Anthropology's construction of a home for Western society within an ordered cosmos thereby carved out a secure position for the sight-seeing spectator and a fixed site from which to perceive the world's diversity. Once this placement and order was assured, a revisitation of the foreign context became possible and pleasurable, with the individual tourist's experiences, souvenirs, and postcards then fitted into a personal collection that reflected the culturally constructed and scientifically buttressed worldview. Just as important, these discourses helped maintain the sense of an unbridgeable distance between primitive and civilized in the face of decreasing geographical distance. In short, the illusion of a global playground with discernible boundaries, rules, and leaders helped carve out a place for touristic pleasure by rationalizing the tourist's superiority over the toured.

—— Anthropology As Popular Culture

To say that anthropology or the popularization of anthropology preceded and enabled the flourishing of touristic pleasure within the nineteenth century would be to oversimplify. The phrase "the popularization of anthropology" implies that a body of knowledge derived from an established scientific method disseminated from experts to the larger populace. In actuality, lines of differentiation between science and popular knowledge or between objective fact gathering and entertainment were difficult to draw during the mid-1800s. Even after the professionalization of anthropology, a two-way path of causality linked the two realms, with popular culture and anthropology influencing one another and with political and technological changes affecting both academia and entertainment. We can see developments within anthropological methodology intertwined with corresponding changes in the nature of exotic attractions enjoyed by the public. For instance, a close scrutiny of the body characterized both areas of cultural activity, but an increasing concern for context was evident by the 1880s. The collection of measurable, visibly different body types was not so much replaced as supplemented by a contextualism that placed the so-called primitive within a particular space or habitat. Interestingly, this "placing" of the exoticized person, or the suggestion of foreign peoples' rootedness in a landscape as exotic as the indigene's jewelry or music made the concept of being able to enter this space more tangible. In other words, the distant ends of the earth were not just represented as a collection of curios but as visitable spaces. And while popular culture marketed simulated immersion experiences, anthropology was beginning to value the anthropologist's version of tourism: the cultural immersion of fieldwork.

In the decades before the establishment of fieldwork as proper ethnographic method, anthropologists—not recognized as professionals or academicians but as hobbyists or a new brand of naturalists—were not unlike their nonanthropologist counterparts. Both groups may have enjoyed exotic attractions in their own cities, and perhaps collected postcards of racially diverse peoples, although with varying degrees of seriousness. The true travelers or field-workers were not the men who would become anthropologists at major universities but missionaries, colonial officers, and merchants. The anthropologist-hobbyist found his greatest allies in circus people and traveling entrepreneurs who were equally anxious for the professionalization of anthropology as a way of legitimizing their activities.[15]

In the middle of the century, individuals pursuing what was loosely called the "science of man" took advantage of touring groups to measure and examine people of different races and regions. Anthropological photographers documented the facial features of various ethnic types by taking pictures of ship laborers borrowed from their homelands and of circus performers showcased as racial oddities. Other anthropologists collected photographs from travelers and from merchants of the popular carte-de-visite without ever leaving the comforts of their homelands. Thus, while a few individuals picked up amateur anthropology while living in colonial outposts, most mid-century anthropologists could be likened to armchair travelers. In fact, as late as 1893, references to "anthropologists and traveling anthropologists" implied that the latter constituted a select category while the unmodified anthropologist referred to the more common stationary "scientist of man." These immobile anthropologists were able to further pursue their studies with the assistance of eyes and ears overseas. In Britain, for instance, the Royal Anthropological Institute published *Notes and Queries on Anthropology* (1892), a set of guidelines for "Travellers and Residents in Uncivilised Lands" so that they might assist in the collection of ethnographic facts.[16] Until the turn of the century, anthropologists served primarily as curators and interpreters for the resultant accumulation of facts, photos, and artifacts. It was only with the coincident rise in business and touristic travel that anthropologists also left their armchairs, and traveling field-workers became a dominant force in anthropology.

Late-nineteenth-century anthropologists thus were not professional travelers financed by the academy but more commonly were xenophiles with the education, economic means, and leisure time to take their hobby more seriously than other visitors to the same exotic attractions. Showmen became increasingly eager to work with anthropologists as ethnological and anthropological societies were formed in the 1880s and marketed as indispensable to imperialist objectives.[17] With the perceived need for understanding colonially subjected peoples and the concomitant growth in anthropological authority, showmen clamored for anthropological affiliations and for the air of authenticity that these men of knowledge could bestow upon their exhibits. The commercialist R. A. Cunningham, for instance, brought nine aborigines from Australia and toured them in the United States in 1883, bringing the surviving seven to Europe the following year. In various touring locations, Cunningham invited anthropological groups such as the

Société d'Anthropologie de Bruxelles and the Société d'Anthropologie de Paris to examine, measure, and photograph the dwindling number of Australians in his troupe. By the time the Parisian anthropologists examined Cunningham's "Ranting Man-Eaters! Veritable Blood-Thirsty Beasts in Distorted Human Form" after their 1885 exhibition at Paris' Folies Bergere, only three of the nine remained.[18]

Anthropologists in Paris had more regular access to ethnographic exhibits held at the Jardin d'Acclimatation in the Bois de Boulogne outside of Paris throughout the 1880s and early 1890s. A parade of Ashantis, Hottentots, Cossacks, Lapps, Sengalese, Somalis, Dahomeans, and Sudanese passed through the Jardin and other Paris locations as the exhibitions increased in popularity attracting hundreds of thousands of spectators yearly. By this time, commercialists began using scientific terms and referencing the exhibitions' anthropological importance in order to lend their shows credibility and perhaps to defuse censure from middle and upper class publications. One showman, the "Great Farini," called in the discourse of science to bill a hirsute adolescent named Krao as "The Missing Link" and marketed a performance of Bushmen as an "anthropological levee."[19] With increased demands for authenticity and the rise of officially sponsored ethnographic exhibits in the 1890s, anthropologists would play a larger role in planning and implementing such displays.

The line between showman and scientist was harder to distinguish when commercially minded anthropologists proposed schemes for funding ethnographic research through the profit-generating mechanisms of popular culture. In an early example from 1850, George Catlin suggested the formation of a museum aboard the ship *Great Britain*, which would travel from continent to continent collecting human specimens. The public would pay entrance fees in exchange for gawking privileges, while the presence of European anthropologists would guarantee authenticity and scientific respectability. Catlin's floating museum of exotic peoples, though never realized, would have been a botanical garden for anthropologists or perhaps the Noah's Ark of zoos for scientists of the human animal.[20] In the absence of such comprehensive assemblages, however, photography provided a practical substitute.

—— Collecting Body Images

Anthropologists' interest in photography coincided not only with technical developments in photography but with a sense of urgency surrounding the constructed image of the primitive. Many cultures were revealed to European eyes, not coincidentally, just as they began to disappear. Cunningham's ailing aborigines were a visible example of the dangers of Western intervention as witnessed on

European soil. Across the seas, exposure to Western colonialism, disease, and environmental disruption spelled extinction for many groups of people and their ways of life. For instance, the last fourteen of some four thousand Tasmanian aborigines were beginning their decline at the time of photography's new portability. The few photographs of Trucanini, the last Tasmanian, taken before her death in 1876 seemed to freeze time. Both anthropological and popular audiences were swayed by this rhetoric of dying cultures—"see them, study them, photograph

One of the final photographs of the last Tasmanian Aborigine depicts an aging Trucanini.

Courtesy of the Royal Anthropological Institute of Great Britain and Ireland, #687.

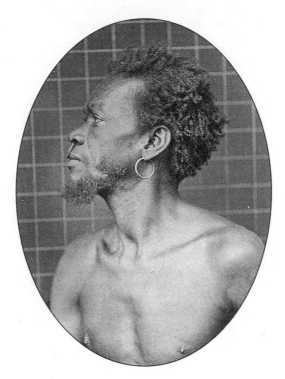

In addition to anthropometric measurements, subjects were photographed against a grid in order to study facial and bodily proportions.

Courtesy of the Royal Anthropological Institute of Great Britain and Ireland, #35892.

them before they are gone." In this sentiment were the seeds of the anthropologist's later public role as "a symbol of atonement," quelling collective anxiety over disappearing worlds and the onward march of history.[21]

Books like Carl Dammann's *Anthropologisch-Ethnologishes*, published in pieces between 1873 and 1876, took advantage of the proliferation of captured images to present a collection of photos that would illustrate the range of human appearances. Dammann, a German collector, photographer, and protoanthropologist, ordered these images in a hierarchical classification of race using European and non-Western portraits accumulated over several years. Dammann's "atlas of types" continued the work of Gottfried Schadow's 1835 *National-Physiognomieen* and J. C. Prichard's 1843 *Natural History of Man,* both of which had relied on the engravings of artists who had accompanied colonial expeditions. The so-called science of physiognomy provided anthropology with a method and justification for scrutinizing these images, and in the process gave birth to the typological methodology of anthropometry. As a system of measuring the proportions of the human body, anthropometry was used to distinguish human races and define their relationship to one another. Often anthropometry was employed in theories of human origin, tribal migrations, and mixed racial types. Although physiognomy and anthropometry date back to the late eighteenth century, the development of photography, combined with increased cross-continental contact, in the nineteenth century created a rejuvenation of the scientific surveying and registering of the physical body. Photometric techniques were borrowed from art traditions in order to create standardized systems for comparing data across photographs and societies. Photographers recording morphometric data for use by anthropologists were encouraged to disrobe their subjects, place them a standard distance from the camera, and capture certain poses that would best reveal bodily proportions. Subjects often held or stood next to rulers, or sometimes a grid was used as a background, from which measurements could be taken. Thus, through photography and the discourse of anthropometry, the human body as an amalgam of measurable and classifiable features became the object of anthropological knowledge. And the goal of anthropometry was tacitly defined as the collection and classification of the world's types as physiological evidence of the white European's placement within a world of less-developed peoples.[22]

This focus on the body and on the collection of bodies assembled for comparative analysis was mirrored in popular ethnographic interests. The best-attended exhibitions of exotic people were those that showcased physical attributes and even bodily oddities. In France, the most popular ethnographic exhibit of the 1880s was a test of the strength of West African Dahomeans. Competing against Parisian baggage porters (and perhaps anticipating the Dahomeans' future role in the global tourist industry), the Dahomeans carried sixty-kilogram sacks on their heads in a one-hundred-kilometer race. Coverage of the race relied on physical descriptions of strength, build, and color. Reporters called upon a vast repertoire of metaphors in their attempts to describe the exact shade of the Dahomeans' skin. Similar discourses accompanied world exhibitions as writers struggled to name the coppers, bronzes, or "well-done sweet potato" browns of the ethnographic villagers. For instance, the physical description of "Soudanese Village" inhabitants (who were actually from Senegal) that could be found in the official program for a 1901 British exhibit notes "the true ebony colour, their skin being jet black and highly polished, their faces . . . unrelieved by the customary red lips, and like the majority of African natives, they are as a rule quite beardless. As a rule, the men are finely made, their shoulders and arms being of the most magnificent proportions and their muscular development quite extraordinary."[23]

As Annie E. Coombes points out, the typical exhibit of Africans featured displays of brutish strength, with the public presuming a reverse correlation between bodily strength and refinement or intellect; dark-skinned males were applauded almost exclusively for their abilities in the areas of wrestling, acrobatics, and military exercises.[24] The close scrutiny of body applied equally to non-Western women, who found themselves on display at world's fairs and traveling exhibits. Their skin color, adornments, bodily movements, and facial features received extensive attention in unending accounts of dance performances and in comparative assessments of beauty.

The tradition of exotic bodily display is partly rooted in the long history of the freak show. In fact, the first examples of tribal peoples exhibited in the United States and Europe are hardly distinguishable from the freak show in terms of their shared presentation of bodily differences as abject objects of fascination. Saartje Baartman, or "the Hottentot Venus," is a well-known example from early in the nineteenth century. Exhibited to audiences across Europe between 1810 and her death in 1815, Baartman attracted crowds partially due to the fascination

The World's Congress of Beauties at the 1893 Columbian Exposition in Chicago converted beliefs of racial superiority into the format of a beauty contest.

From *The Dream City*. St. Louis: N. D. Thompson, 1893.

743 - La toilette.
La compostura.

Postcards of exoticized women followed tropes of erotic imagery, such as boudoir settings and the picturing of two women together in various states of disrobement, while purporting to depict ethnographic information in visual form.

French postcard, circa 1910.

with her protruding buttocks. The not-so-submerged subtext of physiognomy and anthropometric anthropology presumed physical differences to be signifiers of cultural and moral difference. For audiences familiar with unlikely stories of the eccentric sexual practices in the "dark continent," her buttocks were apparent proof of the primitive's assumed licentiousness.[25]

Individuals like Baartman were in high demand for circus shows and other places of entertainment due to their visible morphological differences from the

European-defined norm. Reportedly, medical advances caused a freak shortage that sent merchants and circus agents out into the world's peripheries scouting for deformed individuals or other oddities.[26] Such visual markers of difference could include medical conditions in conjunction with the added attraction of exotic origin, as in the cases of the original Siamese twins and the group of albinos from Madagascar who were displayed in P. T. Barnum's American Museum in New York in the 1860s; racial attributes, such as those demonstrated by the Batwa pygmies brought from the Congo to London in 1905; and cultural adaptations of the body, such as the artificially distended lower lips of the Ubangi women who performed in circus sideshows that became known as "Nig shows."[27] Often these individuals' curious physicalities were highlighted through photographs that

Two types of images of the Batwa pygmies were popular: those that demonstrated the pygmies' diminutive size through comparisons with Western figures and those that pictured the pygmies with cultural artifacts against a backdrop that suggested a natural setting.

Courtesy of the Royal Anthropological Institute of Great Britain and Ireland, #35827.

juxtaposed the odd and the so-called normal. The Batwa pygmies were photographed with members of the British Parliament on the front steps of the House
of Commons, while the Ringling Brothers Circus sold photographs of the Ubangi
women posing with attractive fair-skinned showgirls.[28]

Photography was a common means for documenting and exhibiting the surface markers of difference for the public. Some postcards of the Batwa pygmies
and of the Dahomeans sold as many as a quarter of a million copies.[29] Interestingly, because many of the same sources supplied photographs to both scientific
and nonscientific communities, and because the conventions of portraiture practiced in the mid- to late nineteenth century—the isolation of facial features
against an unobtrusive background—served the needs of anthropometry, few significant differentiations separated the collections of popular ethnographic photography from those of anthropological societies. Both groups of images
decontextualized the exoticized portrait sitter and allowed for the scrutiny of surface detail while a discourse of difference found its locus in the exotic body's colors and contours.

Both the proliferation of photographs and the assemblage of exotic peoples
were part of the previously described Victorian preoccupation with the collection.
For instance, the American Museum, the predecessor to American natural history
museums, consisted of a mass collection in which coins, birds, and human displays shared equal status. In Barnum's own words,

> The transient attractions of the Museum were constantly diversified, and
> educated dogs, industrious fleas, automatons, jugglers, ventriloquists, liv
> ing statuary, tableaux, gipsies [sic], Albinoes [sic], fat boys, giants, dwarfs,
> rope-dancers, live "Yankees," pantomime, instrumental music, singing and
> dancing in great variety, dioramas, panoramas, models of Niagara, Dublin,
> Paris and Jerusalem; Hannington's dioramas of the Creation, the Deluge,
> Fairy Grotto, Storm at Sea; the first English Punch and Judy in this country,
> Italian Fantoccini, mechanical figures, fancy glass-blowing, knitting
> machines and other triumphs in the mechanical arts; dissolving views,
> American Indians, who enacted their warlike and religious ceremonies on
> the stage,—these, among others, were all exceedingly successful.[30]

The ultimate collection of the era, however, was the world's fair. Barnum
himself presided over the New York Crystal Palace Exposition of 1853 and its displays, which ranged from the sewing machine and a Pennsylvania oil well to the
"Wild Man of Borneo" and "Fijian man-eaters." Subsequent American and British
expositions followed this formula of promoting nation through the juxtaposition
of national industry and alien cultures depicted as crude and antiquated. Yet

while this aspect remained relatively constant, between Barnum's fair and the Chicago Columbian Exposition world's fair of 1893, some significant changes had taken place in the field of anthropology and in the representation of foreign people.

—— The Importance of Place

According to some sources, 1884—when Oxford University granted its first appointment in the field of anthropology to E. B. Tylor—marked the discipline's coming of age.[31] Other aspects of this maturation are harder to pinpoint with a single date. The professionalization of anthropology and the establishment of extended fieldwork as the discipline's primary methodology gradually emerged in the decades surrounding the turn of the century. According to Bernard McGrane, these developments received their impetus from two other bodies of knowledge: geology and evolutionism. With new conceptions of time ushered in by these sciences, an altered breed of anthropological knowledge found its foundation in an understanding of cultural difference as temporal or genealogical difference. Charles Darwin's *Origin of the Species* (1859) theorized a progression of humankind over time, and anthropologists responded by suggesting an uneven evolution, propelling some societies into advanced development and holding some back at earlier stages. And geology's timeline, spanning millions of years, "gave anthropology the space it needed to account for the slow, progressive evolutionary rise of the human condition from savagedom to civilization" for some but not for others.[32] From the perspective of Darwinized anthropology, it appeared that to travel to the remote pockets of the world was equivalent to traveling in time.[33]

As Eric J. Leed points out, the theory of evolution is a form of what Clifford Geertz calls "local knowledge."[34] By suggesting that different regions took slower or different paths of development, evolution posits the importance of place in determining the character of a culture or species. Thus, while the human body was still an important marker for gauging development, geography took on new significance. Responding to this intellectual development as well as a number of other factors—the increased convenience of travel, large-scale government-organized expeditions, a younger generation of anthropologists trained in sciences such as geography that recognized the importance of region, financial support that became available with the institutionalization of anthropology, mounting frustration with the limited information provided by missionaries and travelers, and the hunger for artifacts created by the growth of museums—anthropologists abandoned their armchairs for the field. Frank Hamilton Cushing, for instance, was assigned to an "ethnological campaign" in the American Southwest in order to collect materials for Washington D.C.'s National Museum. When the other members of the expedition moved on, Cushing stayed on at a Zuni pueblo for another five years, eventually returning home in 1884. His choice may have been professionally motivated in part, but his sojourn with the Zunis has been described as the more personal choice of "going native." Cushing's participation in the field, which included his own initiation into the Priesthood of the Bow and baptism under a Zuni name, resulted in a detailed ethnographic portrait of the Zuni that in turn provided a new model of in-depth understanding, intensive cultural immersion, and extensive language skills.

Cushing became a figure of considerable notoriety upon his return to the east coast. He traveled with prominent Zuni men to introduce them to the ways of American life and performed ritual dances in Indian costume for American audiences. Between 1882 and 1886, Cushing wrote about the Zuni and his experiences among them in *Century* magazine and in various Boston periodicals. He became one of the first in a long line of highly visible ethnographer-heroes, which would soon include the likes of Franz Boas, Bronislaw Malinowski, and Margaret Mead.[35]

More than the fair's transported villages, the reproduction of Colorado's Battle Rock Mountain attempted to demonstrate the connection between geography and culture as mode of adapting to the environs.

From *The Dream City*. St. Louis: N. D. Thompson, 1893.

Although Cushing failed to achieve lasting respect within his field due to questions surrounding his objectivity in the face of an apparent conversion to Zuni ways, his experiences provide an early example of the anthropological rite of passage. Several writers have described an anthropologist's first fieldwork experience as the initiation period that defines the coming of age of the professional anthropologist.[36] This mystical form of authority gained from simply "being there"—in other words, the belief in the conversion induced by direct experience of the alien environment—is not unlike tales of mysterious conversion retold within travel literature or those experiences of epiphany marketed by the tourist industry. Within this romanticized vision, direct experience strips away ethnocentrism, paving the way for attainment of the holy grail of anthropological investigation: the unmediated vision of seeing through native's eyes.

In addition to the creation of this mystical form of authority, the rise of fieldwork helped establish various other anthropological tropes: objective knowledge, through the simultaneously engaged and disengaged experience known as participant observation; contextual understanding; and culture as a structure of signifiers and meanings accessible in part through language. This shift in the anthropological object of knowledge from the human body to the broad understanding of culture as religion, customs, folklore, and material culture was reflected in the ethnographic photography of the 1890s.

Whereas the indigene had formerly been cut off from his actual context through the use of studio-constructed backgrounds, portraiture, and anthropometric conventions and sometimes the blacking out of background with paint or varnish, indigenous environments now shared the frame with portraits of foreign peoples at work and play. Two photographs taken at the Stanley and African Exhibition in London in 1890 illustrate this transition within ethnographic representation. Both photographs depict two South African children, Gootoo and Inyokwana, who were displayed in native costume at the exhibition. Although the photographs were not taken in Africa, there is an obvious attempt to simulate a natural environment. What is perhaps supposed to be a dead animal (but which looks more like a half-unrolled leopard-skin rug, lies at the children's feet. One might presume that the rug conveniently hides the pots containing the palm-like plants that reach the children's waists. The first photograph, which was sold as a postcard to popular audiences, depicts the children with spear-like tools in their hands looking down at the animal in a pose that suggests a fresh kill; a hazy background shows what would appear to be an abode. For one willing to exercise imagination, the postcard gives the feeling of being "on the scene," witnessing the daily lives of these orphans, who must fend for themselves. The existence of a variant of this photograph, a second, slightly different depiction of these same two African children, suggests the start of a differentiation between scientific and nonscientific audiences as a result of the professionalization of anthropology. The second portrait displays one child in profile and the other in a full frontal position, providing the anthropologist still somewhat focused on physicality with two points of view. However, the children's bodily attributes are partially obscured by the palm fronds and the shield that one child holds, thereby reflecting shifting

The studio-constructed backdrop allowed for portraiture of regional types to take place under controlled lighting conditions while suggesting a picturesque background with some rough resemblance to the subjects' typical environment.

Postcard, circa 1900.

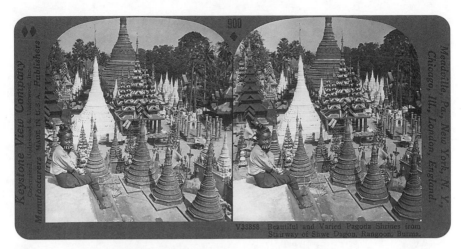

Although in this stereograph an indigene is depicted in her native environment, her status as a child and the commanding view, which she is denied as she poses for the camera, disassociates her from the land and the architectural accomplishments of the background.

Stereograph, Keystone View Company, Underwood and Underwood, Inc., circa 1910.

anthropological concerns between the measurable body and contextual understandings of cultural practices, material culture, and environment.[37]

It has been suggested that the previous decontextualization of the native might also have been a result of land ownership questions.[38] The unwillingness of European settlers and colonialists to accept indigenous people's claims to certain land may have contributed to the avoidance of representing a non-Westerner within his native landscape. This argument is particularly convincing in light of the Western tradition of representing the landowner within paintings of property. However, with the turn of the century approaching, a new set of concerns appeared. The decimating effect of colonialism on indigenous people was becoming evident, thereby requiring renewed rationalizations for colonialism and the suppression of visual signs of European intrusion. Contextualizing exoticized peoples within a lush, natural environment with crudely built shelters and minimal clothing denied contact with Europe and strengthened the presumed connection between the primitive and nature (if you ignore the fact of the presence of the photographer). Frequently, the minute material aspects of their supposedly untouched culture were focal points of the photos, and, as Brian Street notes, this "very attention to visual and surface detail militated against consideration of the role of European colonialism in their current condition."[39] Additionally, many photos appeared to appeal to a romanticism about "a simpler age," a discourse that of course was developing strength within the tourist industry.

Guidelines such as those found in the Royal Anthropological Institute's *Notes and Queries* were revised to reflect new expectations in photographic representation. In the influential article of 1893, "Anthropological Uses of the Camera," Everard im Thurn criticized anthropometric photographs as "merely pictures of lifeless bodies" and as "ordinary photographs of uncharacteristically miserable natives . . . comparable to the photographs which one occasionally sees of badly stuffed and distorted animals."[40] Alfred Court Haddon expanded upon im Thurn's critique, suggesting the abolishment of portraits as a model for anthropological representation. In his essay on photography in the third version of *Notes and Queries* (1899), Haddon discouraged the posing of subjects and called for the documentation of ethnographic details including the "common actions of daily life."[41]

—— World Traveling at the Fair

Anthropology's new approach to ethnography and ethnographic representation became popularized through various routes. Not only were successful fieldworkers like Cushing publicized in the media, but many photographs from the field reached large audiences as lantern slides. Perhaps more remarkable, however, was the attempt to popularize anthropology through Chicago's Columbian Exposition of 1893. While previous expositions had made use of exotic sideshows or displays of houses from throughout the world, for instance, the Columbian Exposition interwove anthropology's new interests in place and daily activity with entertainment, a synthesis that continues to characterize modern tourism. In fact, the fair's Midway Plaisance, despite some throwbacks to the exotic circus marvel (such as the nine-foot, ten-inch, 418-pound Bolivian Indian), offered nearly one square mile of commodified exoticism, marking a new phase in the marketing of touristic pleasure.

In 1891, Frederick Ward Putnam, director and curator of the Peabody Museum at Harvard University, was appointed chief of the fair's Department of Ethnology and Archeology to help realize the goal of turning the exhibition into "an illustrated encyclopedia of humanity."[42] With P. T. Barnum acting in an advisory capacity, the fair organizers were assured that it would be an entertaining and profitable encyclopedia as well. In addition to profits, the anthropological collection and the illustration of evolution were on the agenda; George Brown Goode announced that the fair would illustrate "the steps of progress of civilization and its arts in successive centuries, and in all lands up the present time."[43] Like Barnum, with his world "agents," Putnam deployed field-workers across the globe to bring back representatives of primitive cultures. However, these representatives were not supposed to embody primitiveness in their physical bodies so much as they were instructed to bring it along with them. These groups of non-Westerners were assisted in the collection and transportation of materials necessary to construct small villages along the strip of land known as the Midway Plaisance. These living exhibits were in addition to the Anthropology Building, which was more centrally located alongside the "high art" exhibits and which contained more traditional displays of relics and artifacts. The native villages, positioned alongside the Midway sideshows and amusements, far outstripped the Anthropology Building's more sober exhibits in terms of scale and appeal. The inhabitants of these temporary villages performed both the sacred and profane aspects of their life for audiences who delighted in the illusion of "being there." Thus, in the aisles of the Midway, the world yielded itself up as commodity and spectacle to the fairgoer willing to pay the price of admission.

The Midway offered both boundaries and invitations to direct experience. The village dwellings did create a greater sense of place than previous ethnographic exhibits designed to display only the exotic body or a culture's decorative

People transported to Chicago to be a part of these living exhibits were asked to carry on life as usual, without modification to their clothing, despite their relocation to very different weather conditions.

From *The Dream City*. St. Louis: N. D. Thompson, 1893.

Cairo Street, a hodgepodge of cultural fantasies offered up in the form of a city street, provided one of the most immersive experiences of Chicago's Columbian Exposition of 1893.

From *The Dream City*. St. Louis: N. D. Thompson, 1893.

arts. This was particularly true of exhibits that combined a native presence and traditional architecture with depictions of landscape, as in the case of the Kilauea Panorama. Additionally, many groups appeared willing to display, or at least simulate, the more intimate aspects of their lifestyles, including religious ceremonies and family life, appealing to the tourist's interest in "back regions," as described by Dean MacCannell.[44] Thus, these exhibits did create some sense of immersion in a foreign atmosphere as cultural exoticism was resituated from some distant part of the world to Chicago and as private affairs were dragged out of closed spaces into the open air in an example of staged authenticity. At the same time, however, these villages were still exhibits, and as such they were surrounded by ropes that blocked access and reminded spectators of the constructed nature of the display.

Midway's Cairo Street offered more direct and immersive experience approaching that of the tourist but at the price of even further compromised authenticity. A walk down Cairo Street might involve the varied experiences of watching harem sultanas, jugglers, dancing girls, and snake charmers; riding on the back of a camel, elephant, or donkey; participating in an Algerian bazaar; and consuming the food of various nations. The theaters, facades, merchants, and street performances created the illusion of being thrust into the chaos of the East—that is, the East of an orientalist's imagination. Even the more reserved exhibits associated with the Anthropology Building experimented with touristic illusion. For example, a model of the cliff dwellings at Colorado's Battle Rock was designed to make spectators feel as though they were climbing rocks alongside the cliff dwellers.[45]

Fairgoers walking down Cairo Street or hanging out among Battle Rock's cliff dwellers could fancy themselves tourists visiting the real locales suggested by the fair's attractions; or better yet, they could imagine what it might have been like to be the first explorer to happen upon a bustling native village or the first anthropologist to live among a particular tribal people. The 1890 Stanley and African Exhibition in London encouraged just such an imaginative identification with the men whose footsteps across Africa were so closely followed by an entire nation. The exhibition, with its portraits and expedition maps, not only paid homage to Europeans who charted the continent of Africa, but as Coombes observes, "The spectator was in fact constructed, through the narrative of the expedition, as an explorer. Through a vicarious intrepidation, they were thus able to gain the 'experience' of the seasoned traveller."[46] The exhibition entrance welcomed visitors with a palisade of tree trunks decorated with human skulls. This ominous entrance led visitors on a path through a simulated explorer's camp surrounded by a composite landscape of central Africa. After months of reading about Stanley's trek through dangerous territory, fairgoers could immerse themselves in a safe, make-believe Africa and partake in the illusion of seeing through Stanley's eyes. Being in the simulated land of the exoticized other thus brought spectators not necessarily closer to the experience of the indigene but more aligned with the conquering spirit of European explorers and soldiers. In short, the resituating of the indigene within his environment (or a constructed facsimile) after an era of representation based on isolating the exotic body was accompanied by the not only concurrent but mutually supporting placement of the spectator within a comfortable touristic position. Through a discourse of immersion, both spectator and indigene were "placed" within the highly structured relationship of the tourist and toured.

The notion of collections of measurements and artifacts as the best means for grasping cultural difference waned in the face of a growing popular and anthropological emphasis on environment and an increased utilization of immersive attractions that positioned participants as tourists. Exhibition goals as stated by

Some exhibits, such as this collection of boats paired with views of the water technologies in context, suggested a midpoint between understanding culture through context and through a comparison of collected, decontextualized artifacts.

From *The Dream City*. St. Louis: N. D. Thompson, 1893.

fair organizers bear evidence to these shifts, while demonstrating a continued emphasis on hierarchical, physically detectable, racial definitions, but now with the factor of environment figured in. An 1890 proposal to the U.S. Congress for the Smithsonian Institution's ethnological display at the Chicago fair, for instance, foregrounds the physicality of race in the stated objective "to show physical and other characteristics of the principal races of men and the very early stages of the history of civilization as shown by the evolution of certain selected primitive arts and industries."[47] By 1892, Otis T. Mason, curator of the Smithsonian's Bureau of American Ethnology, describes a concern for environmental issues as they affect culture and a movement away from evolutionism and toward cultural relativism: "The Chicago Exposition furnishes an excellent opportunity for testing the question . . . how far climate and the resources of the earth control the arts and industries of mankind in the sphere of language and race."[48] In reference to the 1904 Louisiana Purchase Exposition, one organizer touts the fair's "comprehensive anthropological exhibition, constituting a Congress of Races, and exhibiting particularly the barbarous and semi-barbarous people of the world, as nearly as possible in their ordinary and native environments."[49] Each comment insists upon a comparative framework and a comprehensive representation of the world's peoples, presumably hierarchically arranged; yet there is a subtle movement from isolated body to industry and culture as shaped by environment as detected through observation of the indigene in an authentic habitat.

—— Re-creating Context within the Museum

Although world's fairs were by nature transitory, many of the objects brought to the United States for exhibition found permanent homes in natural history museums, some of which were explicitly established to house the dismantled remnants of such expositions. Aided by colonialist thievery and fair fervor, the late nineteenth century brought an explosion in the establishment and expansion of natural history museums around the world. At this time, anthropologists' predominant support came from such museums, a fact that has led historians of anthropology to label the turn of the century the field's "museum period."[50] With the professionalism of anthropology and the growth of natural history museums, display techniques were suddenly at issue. International conversations ensued with particular attention paid to the viewing and learning experiences of the museum visitor. In 1899, the opening of the Bohemian Museum of Prague marked the beginning of a new kind of natural history display; visitors could view realistic exhibits that incorporated natural settings.[51] In the United States, both the National Museum in Washington, D.C., and the American Museum of Natural

History (AMNH) in New York established reputations for their similar use of "model habitats" or "habitat groups." Due to newly pioneered techniques in taxidermy, lifelike animals could be reconstructed and grouped with other animals found in the same geographic locale. In 1900, at the AMNH, Frank M. Chapman produced what some sources call the first habitat group display in a U.S. museum. As a profile in *New Yorker* magazine reported, "Dr. Chapman produced a Cobb's Island, Virginia, group which contained black skimmers and other indigenous birds against a setting of beach composed of actual sand and artificial seaweed, which merged with a painted background of ocean, sky and birds."[52] According to Nancy Lurie, Carl Akeley's 1890 habitat group at the Milwaukee Public Museum predated Chapman's in New York, depicting "a muskrat colony engaged in eating, swimming, and seeking food in a setting of a realistically simulated pond with accurately assembled marsh vegetation."[53] Moving to the AMNH, Carl Akeley began planning for the African Hall, which was okayed by trustees in 1912 but not completed until many years later. The African Hall became the museum's crowning achievement in terms of creating a fabricated setting that gave the sense of experiencing a region's animal life frozen in time.[54] Such displays, increasing in scale and executed with increasing technical precision over time, clearly created the illusion of immersion for the spectator who could stand at a particular point at which the curved background would fill the spectator's peripheral vision.

Concurrent with these developments in zoological display, parallel immersive environments appeared in other museum contexts. For instance, the concept of the "period room" emerged as a way of simultaneously displaying art, finery, and furniture from a particular era. The historically linked items were arranged in a room that could be entered by the museumgoer, who might imagine herself a visitor to the past. Similarly, designers of ethnographic displays took heed of the success of world's fair shows and tried to attract visitors with "life groups"— tableaux demonstrating dances or rituals, with mannequins standing in for the actual participants found at the fairs.

The life group was also a response to changing intellectual currents within anthropology. Undoubtedly, the intense fieldwork sponsored by the Bureau of American Ethnology assisted in the collection of artifacts that then replaced older specimens, which often lacked proper labeling as to place of origin and cultural uses. Previously, a Navajo tool might have been placed in a display with similar tools from other cultures. Without knowledge of tribal origin or use, not to mention sufficient artifacts to reconstruct a context, a life group would not have been feasible. With the ascendancy of fieldwork as a methodology, anthropologists had greater access to material culture and increased knowledge of context.

The period room was used to depict domestic living of a particular era and social class or to suggest the appearance of a historically significant space, such as the bedroom of Marie Antoinette.

From *The Dream City*. St. Louis: N. D. Thompson, 1893.

—— Franz Boas and the Life Group

Franz Boas's career demonstrates the above-described movement of anthropology from world's fair planning committees to natural history museums to university anthropology departments. More importantly, his writings about ethnographic museum displays evince the intellectual impetus toward the use of immersion strategies within the museum. Boas argued that the meaning of a cultural object could not be understood "outside of its surroundings, outside of other inventions of the people to whom it belongs."[55] As a way of "studying its productions *as a whole*," Boas prescribed a "collection representing the life of one tribe."[56] He himself conducted fieldwork among the tribes of the northwestern coast of North America to prepare a life group at the National Museum. In the final product, a group of mannequins were dressed and arranged to convey a sense of the Kwakiutl winter dance ceremony. In the AMNH, where Boas later worked, exhibits included a detailed model of native habitations on a scale of 1 to 20 to similarly communicate a sense of place, although in this case, without an appeal to immersion.

Boas continued to work on life groups at the AMNH, depicting a family or larger group conducting some characteristic work thereby demonstrating the use of a tool. In a letter dated 1896, he specifically described immersion as one of his goals: "It is an avowed object of a large group to transport the visitor into foreign surroundings. He is to see the whole village and the way people live."[57] Despite the esteem in which his work was held, Boas expressed disappointment in the life group's lack of realism. Specifically, he was dissatisfied with the distracting background, as other exhibits remained visible through the glass case that enclosed the life group, and with the life group's lack of motion, which he believed detracted from the efficacy of the exhibit. In his complaints, Boas anticipated both the use of film by museums and a method known as the "Milwaukee Style," which employed painted backgrounds and lighting effects borrowed from diorama shows.[58]

The habitat group, the period room, and the life group encouraged examination of the whole as opposed to fixing the gaze on a decontextualized object. Such arrangements drew on the pleasures of tourism, the joy of illusionistic immersion in a temporally or spatially exotic context. Boas acknowledged both the pleasure-seeking visitor and the power of ethnography delivered as spectacle in his article "Some Principles of Museum Administration": "The people who seek rest and recreation resent an attempt at systematic instruction while they are looking for some emotional excitement. They want to admire, to be impressed by something great and wonderful."[59] The interest of the museum-tourist could be piqued at the same time that the life group demonstrated Boas's belief in anthropology as contextual understanding and not merely as the collection, classification, and display of items severed from their place of origin.[60]

As Boas's work and ethnographic exhibitions of the period indicate, the outlines of touristic spectatorship were already being roughly hewn in the years immediately preceding the introduction of cinema. Exhibits and entertainment media offering glimpses at distant locales and their inhabitants straddled the sketchy line between science and popular culture as the Western subject learned to take a particular position in relation to a world understood as containable spectacle. For museum anthropologists, intellectual trends and the appeal to pleasurable exhibits happily came together in the emphasis on context and immersion. In other venues as well, representations of the world proliferated and called into action a consumerist gaze being honed by the burgeoning fields of advertising and product display, capitalism's bullhorns. The structure, the tropes, and the mode of viewing and understanding were already in place by the late nineteenth century. The pleasures of touristic immersion would simply reach a higher level of technological sophistication as perceptual technologies such as stereoscopy put immersive postcards within an arms reach or, with cinema's development, in motion.

CHAPTER THREE

Technological Identification
STEREOGRAPHY
AND THE PANAMA CANAL

ONE ROUTE TO INTENSIFYING a sense of immersion has been to increase the scale of the image or theatrical edifice in an attempt to extend the illusion into and beyond spectators' peripheral vision. The creators of panoramas and dioramas in the 1700s and 1800s, for instance, built specialized domes to accommodate increasingly vast paintings of cities or landscapes, thereby surrounding viewers by the illusion. Life groups and habitat groups within the better-funded museums of the early twentieth century also grew in size, incorporating naturalistic lighting and expansive curved backdrops not unlike dioramas. The cinema of the mid–twentieth century followed a similar route, as innovators expanded the size of the film negative and constructed larger theaters to house elaborate widescreen technologies. Yet in the latter half of the nineteenth century, immersive entertainments emphasizing scale experienced unprecedented competition for paying armchair travelers from a diminutive three-by-three-inch photograph, or more accurately, two three-by-three photographs in the form of stereographs. Nominally, the strategy of stereography and that of the diorama, for instance, was the same: to fill the spectators' ranges of vision with exotic imagery. Yet, the stereograph's implementation of this strategy traded image scale for proximity with the use of a single-person goggle-like viewer, not unlike that of contemporary virtual reality technologies.

While increased display or image size typically brought the added advantage of accommodating more paying customers, stereoscope use was limited to one spectator at a time. In contrast to the arc of a life group's backdrop or a domed diorama, both of which mapped out a wide range of ideal viewing positions, the spatial dynamics of stereograph viewing, even for the single spectator, were a matter of precise negotiation. The stereograph or stereoview's three-dimensional illusion derived from its creators' understanding of the short but significant distance, measurable in millimeters, between two important and distinct points of vision: those of the human eyes. The stereoscopic photographic process mimicked this aspect of human vision by capturing two separate images from two minutely different vantage points. The stereograph, as the juxtaposition of these two photographs, would have been viewed at a precise distance from the eyes in order for the illusion of depth to snap into place. This required the individual to adjust the position of the stereograph in order to bring the set up of the viewing apparatus into exact accord with the specifics of the spectator's body. This closeness and negotiated accord between the stereograph spectator and the adjustable representational device interestingly suggests a very explicit alignment between spectatorial body and technology.

To the extent that the basic structure of the technologically mediated tourist gaze resembles the more general formula laid out by Christian Metz in reference to cinema spectatorship—the overlay of primary and secondary identification—this notion of technological alignment is critical. Primary identification, or the spectator's identification with the act of looking, depends upon an anthropomorphicization of the viewing device. The representational technology must be assimilated, accepted as a prosthetic extension of one's own perceptual powers in a way that, say, a kaleidoscope as viewing device could not be. This process is made more explicit in the case of the stereoscope, with its need for adjustment, thereby making primary identification as a double alignment more evident. In other words, acceptance of the representational technology as akin to one's own vision is not enough. For successful primary identification, the alignment of body and technology must be extended to the alignment of spectator and photographer in a collapsing of time and space. The camera becomes an extension of or interchangeable with the stereoscope, as technology becomes the bridge for the spectator's alignment with the position of the photographer. More than with most other photographic technologies, the viewing of stereographs echoes the bodily comportment and spatial dynamics of the moment of image capture. The minute adjustments of the apparatus on the part of the spectator recall those of the on-site traveler perfecting the composition and focus of the image seen through the viewfinder. In short, within primary identification's double alignment, the stereoscope, with its links to the mechanics of the stereoscopic camera, simulates the role of transport device as the spectator adopts the position, posture, and lines of sight of the photographer.

(28) Wayfarers on a straight 30-mile road lined with stately poplars, Baramula to Cashmere, India.   Copyright 1903 by Underwood & Underwood.

Stereographic photographers often highlighted the three-dimensional effect of the technology by choosing views that emphasized perspective, such as this tree-lined road in Kashmir.

Stereograph, Underwood and Underwood, Inc., 1903.

The viewer of an ethnographic display, whether through personal bias or the structure of the exhibit itself, might also have been aligned with the viewpoint of the traveling showman or anthropologist associated with the exhibit. In fact, the prevalence of this very phenomenon may have been a precursor to the taking up of a touristic spectator position within subsequent touristic entertainment forms. However, in the case of a life group or a world's fair exhibit, the spectator's alignment with the ethnographer's viewpoint is not as explicit as in the case of the stereograph. In stereoscopy, spectator and photographer are linked by the technology that mediates their perception of the tourist locale. Despite the fact that the spectator employs a representational device while the photographer uses a recording medium, the stereoscope substitutes for the camera as the spectator assumes the same position as the photographer with his eyes stationed before the stereoscope that delivers the image. This idea of technological identification as a bridging force connecting the spectator to the space, time, and position of the photographer thus suggests a departure from prephotographic touristic entertainments. This becomes increasingly significant when we acknowledge the role of technological identification as more expansive than simply the glue that makes primary identification stick. Not only does the concept of technological identification allow us to integrate into the analysis of spectator positioning public discourses surrounding a technology's introduction, but it bears on the issue of secondary identification. Within Metz's formula, the fact that the technology remains relatively unproblematized means that the role that technological identification can play in bridging primary and secondary identification is at risk of being overlooked.

The collection of stereoviews of the Panama Canal that receive particular analytical attention within this chapter provides an opportunity to view three refractions of alignments, which illustrate nonnarrative bridges between primary and secondary identification through technological identification. To clarify, film historians tracing the development of classical narrative conventions within film have focused on ways that narrative and editing help to construct an immersed position for the spectator, a position that seamlessly shifts between a first-person perspective emphasizing primary identification and character (or secondary) identification. Such accounts typically rely on an assumption of the spectators' willing suspension of disbelief, which then allows the technology (understood within this formulation to be temporarily invisible to spectators) to be excluded from the analysis. In the stereograph collections investigated here, narrative does not exist as a desire-generating motor that fuels spectator identification with a diegetic figure. Thus, a precinematic touristic position that places the spectator both inside and outside the exotic space is dependent on some other way to bridge primary and secondary identification. Still, it is fair to say that although

Although Northern Americans and indigenous people are both pictured in souvenir images of Panama during the canal-building period, the former appear as anonymous placeholders for the tourist while the latter are posed for the camera and are meant to be noticed for their specificity.

Photograph from a souvenir book produced by I. L. Maduro's Souvenir Store, Panama.

stereograph travel sets were not narrative, a journey-like trajectory and, more significantly, some connection between the spectator and figures seen within the
stereograph frame can be identified. In fact, this connection, while perhaps only
a protean form of identification, is the third of the three alignments that I have
mentioned. This connection, as a further refraction of both the body-technology
and spectator-photographer alignments, is predicated on technological identification. Technologies of vision and of mastery over the landscape link the spectator, the creator of the photographic image, and Western figures who parallel the
position of the photographer (and by that count, the position of the spectator)
but occupy a position inside the image. Within the stereoviews of the building of

Within these souvenir collections, generic North American clothing items such as hats or
umbrellas, serve as markers for viewers to insert themselves and for marking the directionality of the gaze.

Enlargement of single image of stereoview, "South End of Pedro Miguel Locks,
Panama Canal" (21723). Courtesy of the Doheny Library Special Collections,
University of Southern California.

the Panama Canal, American surveyors and engineers represent the double of the photographers who, like them, have traveled to Panama with the technological tools of their trade in tow. Interestingly, these individuals are not always foregrounded within the image. In some ways, they are like the photographer, made anonymous by the presence of the technology, which either hides or dwarfs them. In contrast, exoticized figures within the frame are highlighted to demonstrate bodily and facial features, figuratively denuded by the absence of technology and made equally anonymous by virtue of standing for a racial type in the spirit of ethnographic synecdoche.

This doubled (or tripled, if we figure in the role of the spectator) structure of the traveler pictured within the landscape and the traveler-photographer responsible for the pictured landscape is far from unusual within documentary touristic texts. For instance, representations and descriptions of Henry Morton Stanley's location of David Livingstone often reconstruct this famous scene from Stanley's point of view, with Stanley as an unseen narrator. However, the presence of Livingstone within the frame acts as Stanley's double, creating the two acceptable positions for the Western spectator to insert herself. These two positions—that of the observer from which vision emanates and the fully immersed individual clearly within the confines of the represented exotic space—and the freedom to move between them are characteristic of tourism's distanced immersion.

More than simply a portrait of exotic contact, the stereographic depiction of the building of the Panama Canal is, like Stanley's recounted adventures, a tale of mastery, but with a more diffuse protagonist. The collection visually constructs a triumphal tale of American ingenuity and technological expertise in which nation is featured as hero. Thus, by taking into account the primarily American audience to which this collection was targeted, we can see how these alignments may have been generated along the lines of shared nationality and technological control, whether that technology be earthmovers, cameras, or stereoscopes. These alignments become even clearer within the following study of how technology operated visually and in combination with the text within this set of stereographs. This technological identification conceivably provided spectators with comfortable positions within and at the perspectival apex of the framed image, allowing for an oscillation between *amid* and *outside*.

—— From Concept to Household Item

Comprehension of the touristic positioning described above is dependent on a contextual understanding of the emergence of the stereoscope in the late nineteenth century. This historical account also connects back to previous discussions of the movement from collection to context as a strategy for representing distant locales, as witnessed within the museum phase of anthropology. Early stereograph distribution methods led to piecemeal accumulations of stereographs that were not unlike the same era's tobacco-card collections, with images of the world providing a scattered and superficial global view. Stereographs, often bought individually during travel, through the Sears-Roebuck catalog, or from traveling salesmen, became pieces in collections that represented the collectors' tastes and preferences. An image of the Parthenon might take its place between a scene featuring President William McKinley and a view of the Irish countryside, in a metonymic representation of the world. However, the stereoscope's popularity spanned over sixty years, and inevitably not only did the depicted locales change but the mode of marketing and collection underwent various developments. Most notable was a movement from the sale of individual cards to a fleshing out of a sense of place through organized sets of cards and lengthy descriptions—in other words, through "box sets" concerned with the re-creation of context through sequences of text and images. The cards were numbered to allow an orderly progression through the images, with a narrative of geographic movement or travel route linking each image to the others. Thus, the idea of a collection of stereoviews was not so much abandoned as supplemented by an emphasis on "being there" and on a multifaceted view of a place.

The box set was a rather late development within the history of the stereoscope. To begin the account at an earlier point, it should be mentioned that the optical principles behind the stereoscope were known to Euclid as far back as 300 B.C.E. However, the heyday of the stereograph only arrived with the development of photography and a portable, inexpensive stereoscopic viewer. In 1838, the English physicist Sir Charles Wheatstone made detailed drawings of the first stereoscope, which would allow each of the viewer's eyes to perceive an illustration drawn from a slightly different angle, thereby replicating the three-dimensional perspective experienced in actual human vision. Over two decades later, the affordable, hand-operated, hooded stereoscope invented by Oliver Wendell Holmes in 1861 set off a rage in the United States, making the stereoscope and a basket of view cards a fixture within the middle-class family parlor. By the turn of the century, the bookshelves of many families would have been filled with dark trompe l'oeil volumes laced in gold trim, volumes that opened up not to encyclopedia pages but to stacks of stereographs.

The Holmes stereoscope allowed the viewer to hold the apparatus in one hand while using the other to position the stereograph in one of several grooves carved into a wooden arm extending from the eye tubes. Variants on this prototype were soon offered to the public: a hooded stereoscope to block extraneous light; a stereograph holder that would slide forward and backward on the extension arm for proper focus; a revolving stereoscope built on the principle of the slide projector, allowing over one hundred stereographs to be viewed consecutively; and a revolving stereoscope that accommodated two viewers.

Few American professional photographers of this period did not experiment with stereoscopic picture taking. In France and Germany, many first-rate photographers shied away from applying their skill to stereoscopy, which was viewed as a popular fad more than an art form. However, in the United States, a number of quality photographers relied upon stereoscopic views as a steady form of income. During the early period of stereograph production, photographers would take two exposures from slightly different positions. Occasionally, as a result of the temporal separation of the exposures, the two images would differ in some respect. For instance, one of the two photographs might contain the ghost of a person or carriage that appeared in the scene for one brief moment during the long exposure, while the other image was without such a flaw. After 1854, stereoscopic cameras with dual lenses were manufactured, increasing the ease of stereograph production. By 1856, Sir David Brewster, a British physicist who invented the lenticular stereoscope a few years after Wheatstone's similar invention, wrote with self-congratulation about the stereoscope, "It is now in general use over the whole world, and it has been estimated that upwards of half a million of these instruments have been sold. . . . Photographers are now employed in every part of the globe in taking binocular pictures for the instrument,—among the ruins of Pompeii and Herculaneum—on the glaciers and in the alleys of Switzerland—among the public monuments in the Old and the New World—amid the shipping of our commercial harbours—in the museums of ancient and modern life—in the sacred precincts of the domestic circle—and among those scenes of the picturesque and the sublime."[1] Although Brewster's comments suggest the dominance of travel photography within stereograph card production, various types of stereographs were produced. In the United States, humorous domestic scenes, series of cards that depicted narratives, or scenes whose humor depended upon stereotypes of African Americans or the Irish were circulated. Nonetheless, in both Europe and the United States, foreign scenes were still the most popular and constituted a large majority of all stereographs produced. By 1870, the stereograph was so firmly associated with depiction of exotic locales that a writer for the magazine *Photographic Mosaics* wrote that the stereoscope "has become a necessary adjunct to the telescope and microscope, showing us the true form and configuration of the distant world."[2] Holmes called it "the card of introduction to make all mankind acquaintances."[3] In Europe, the sale of scenic stereoviews began with individual photographers such as George Washington Wilson, who took stereographic photos of Scottish locales romanticized in travel literature. Wilson eventually went on to find more remote and unexplored locations, which in turn led tourists on scouting adventures to witness the same picturesque views that Wilson had captured on film. Wilson established a network of retail agencies throughout Scotland and England in stationery, book, and fancy goods shops; hotel, steamship, and railway bookstalls—the same places where postcards are found today.

Although the first models of the stereoscope were built in Europe and exported to the United States, with the introduction of Holmes's stereoscope (an invention whose manufacture was widespread due to the fact that Holmes decided not to patent his design), the center of stereoscopic activity shifted from England and France to the United States.[4] Stereoscope photographers were hired to document the railway and the lush scenery its transcontinental routes offered. Such stereographs were then sold at each railway station along the route, and on the trains themselves. By 1872, five or six stereoscopic photographers had set up studios at Niagara Falls to cater to tourists' desire for vacation souvenirs.[5] Individual photographers came to rely on publishing companies for distribution. These companies eventually expanded and hired their own photography and sales staffs. Two particular stereograph publishers, Underwood and Underwood and the Keystone View Company, eventually rose to prominence and were the last two companies still producing stereoviews by the start of World War I. Underwood and Underwood came to dominate the market, with images of foreign locales and with a selling strategy borrowed from the less successful stereograph company Kilburn Brothers. Underwood and Underwood hired college students, who would spend their summers traveling between towns selling door-to-door and exchanging view cards for room and board. An intricate selling philosophy was developed, and stereograph salespeople were instructed to attend town meetings and church gatherings to penetrate the center of the community and gain access to its various members. By 1901, the company was publishing 25,000 stereoscopic views a day and 300,000 sterescopes a year.[6]

The golden age of stereoscopy had begun to wane by 1885, but several domestic and international events brought another surge of popularity for the stereoscope between the years 1898 and 1906.[7] Despite predictions of the stereoscope's obsolescence, which freely circulated among crowds struck by the new technology of moving pictures, Underwood and Underwood was able to prolong the stereoscope's popularity with the introduction of the Underwood Travel System, consisting of box sets covering particular locales and accompanied by companion books that often were written by degree-holding travel authorities. Between 1902 and 1910, more than three hundred different box sets were assembled into the Underwood Stereographic Library. However, by this time, the company's involvement in news photography had increased and the production of stereoviews was steadily decreasing. In 1920, production ceased altogether, and the company's negative archives were sold to its competitor, the Keystone View Company.

Entering the stereograph market a decade after Underwood's establishment, Keystone had followed their competitor's lead by imitating the Underwood box sets with the book-like slip cases. Keystone's hold on the market was secured by their educational department, which was organized in 1898 and purchased the rights to several other publishers' negatives for educational distribution. After 1922, Keystone was the only stereograph publisher in the world; it continued to market stereoscopic views in box sets until 1939, after which time the company only manufactured view cards for uses within the field of optometry.

—— Tour Guide in a Box

The advent of the box set was significant in many ways. First of all, the series of images sold as a set exemplifies the movement between fervent collection to re-creation of context. The first box sets were simple assemblages of individually distributed stereographs and carried names such as "A Tour of the World." The next series of box sets featured fifty to one hundred images of a single location, taking the viewer on a tour of the geography, culture, and nature of a single country or locale. While these box sets typically featured European nations, they were followed by a line of more remote and less industrialized locations, locations that increasingly experienced a parade of visitors with colonialists, merchants, anthropologists, and photographers marking out the trails for the tourists who would inevitably follow in their footsteps. Thus, middle-class Americans could sit in their parlors and examine the photographically captured lives of African pygmies, the Ainu of Japan, and the Indians of Tierra del Fuego. Unlike previous stereographs, the box set cards were frequently imprinted with lengthy descriptions on their reverse sides. Such descriptions frequently partook in a semantics of "being there" with lines such as, "You are on a country highway west of Dordecht . . . ," hailing the spectators and placing them on the scene and in the shoes of the photographer.

The stereoscope's illusion of reality received considerable publicity. It was reported that when children were asked to locate objects portrayed in a stereograph, they pointed to a spot beyond the stereoscope as if they were standing within the depicted location.[8] Holmes helped introduce the stereoscope to an

American audience with his praise for the instrument's reality effect: "A stereo-scope is an instrument which makes surfaces look solid . . . [and] produce[s] an appearance of reality which cheats the senses with its seeming truth."[9] In addi-tion to its context of home use, this reality effect also explains the common use of stereography for pornographic images. Regardless of the subject matter, however, the compositions of the images were characterized by background and foreground layering similar to that employed in natural history museums' habitat groups with sculpted foregrounds, less detailed middle grounds, and painted back-grounds.[10] In fact, curatorial advice articles and stereoscopic photographer trade magazines contained similar tips on the use of at least three planes of vision. Stereoscopic photographers were advised to exaggerate the illusion of the three-dimensional by composing in depth. Often an overhanging branch, a tree trunk, or an outwardly gazing person was purposively placed in the extreme foreground, just in front of the notable monument or land formation, with a distant back-ground that helped throw the whole scene into relief.

—— A Journey to Panama

Various scholars have remarked on the difficulty of studying stereographs due to the poor documentation of the details of their production. The same frustrations surround the collections stored by the University of Southern California (USC) Libraries. Both Underwood and Keystone, as well as some of the smaller com-panies, reportedly had photographers documenting the building of the Panama Canal between 1902 and 1914. However, the particular box set of Panama Canal views (one of about twenty box sets donated to USC by Cecil B. DeMille) bears the Keystone label on the outside while each individual card bears both the Keystone and Underwood names. Less than a third of the cards have dates, and none list the names of the photographer or text writer, if they were indeed different individu-als. Most likely, this particular set was the result of Keystone purchasing Under-wood negatives, either in the early 1900s before Underwood shut its doors or in 1920 during Keystone's outright acquisition of its competitor's stock.

One of the most interesting facets of this collection and others like it is its attempt to orient the viewer. For the stereoscope viewer as for any actual traveler, orientation—or the placing of oneself within a meaningful, navigable space—is an important first step, and perhaps a process that continues throughout the voyage in order to secure a pleasurable experience. It is possible to speak about various levels of orientation. The first involves this process of primary identifica-tion, the positioning of oneself as a spectator with the act of focusing inter-pretable as the establishment of a relationship to all that is viewed in the foreign environment, a relationship of spectator to spectacle. As evidence of this type of positioning even in a non–technologically mediated situation, Timothy Mitchell references a quote from Gustave Flaubert that first appeared in a letter sent home following Flaubert's arrival in Cairo, which reads, "'As yet I am scarcely over the initial bedazzlement . . . each detail reaches out to grasp the whole. Then gradually all becomes harmonious and the pieces fall into place of themselves, in accordance with the laws of perspective.'"[11] Orientation is conceived of as a visual operation or a uniting of the pieces into a whole, not unlike positioning the stereograph card and uniting the two pictures in an act of visual concentration that brings the illusion to life. The spectator thus appears to be at the site of the production of visual meaning, an active subject in the face of a static image of cultural difference.

The captions and companion books added another layer of meaning as well as assisted in the process of geographical orientation. For instance, the companion books that could be purchased with the Underwood Stereographic Library contained various maps and even utilized a copyrighted locator system. A camera icon for each stereograph indicated not only where on the map the view was taken but the direction the photographer faced while capturing the image. The descriptions on the cards themselves included the longitude and latitude of the depicted locales and further encouraged orientation by referencing directionality ("You are looking northwest across the river with the cathedral at your back"), by indicating a view's relationship to other views ("The north side of the castle, obscured from view here, is clearly visible on your descent from the surrounding hills as pictured in 10134"), and by providing elevated views that located environments in relation to surrounding land and sea.

Through the tracing of a geographical trail, the gaps between images were elided in the construction of a spatial trajectory. For instance, the companion book *Greece through the Stereoscope* by Rufus B. Richardson recommended a structured course through the view cards, providing historical and often anthropological tidbits for the vicarious tourist along the way. The map charted out this narrative path from image to image, as a sort of glue linking the various locations on the itinerary. The printed information on the back of each card anchored the viewer within the represented space while also reflecting on the path just taken and the path ahead. One inscription on the back of a view of Epidaurus reads, "The Gulf of Aegina is 8 or 10 miles away at our right and the Gulf of Nauplia twice far away at our left. Mykenae is 20 miles away directly ahead, in a straight line, though the actual journey by road would be considerably longer. This structure at our feet is the famous health resort of ancient Greece known as the Hieron of Aesculapius." The geographical instructions appear to place the parlor spectator on the scene and direct him or her on to the next location.

Another kind of orientation involves defining the nature of the viewer's relationship to the unfamiliar people whose images have been photographically captured. Western colonial perspectives would have already provided one possible orientation strategy: the world seen as a farmers' market, an array of material goods to be consumed. Thus, in the Panama collection, as in others, food as an important aspect of tourism is emphasized. For instance, the text writer/tour guide for the Panama collection calls attention to the island of Taboga as a health resort with freshwater springs visited by North and Central Americans alike. However, as important as the water is another Tabogan product: "A great many pineapples are grown on this island. They are very large and sweet. Many people think they are the best in the world" (20875). [12] Another view card gives instructions on how best to enjoy the coconut: "The traveler in tropical countries finds the milk and meat of this nut cooling and refreshing, even when taken from the shadow of the broad leaves in mid-day" (20858).

One of the most interesting stereoviews concerns the soursop fruit. On the back of the image card, our tour guide/narrator suggests, "The juice of the soursop in water, with a little sugar added, makes a delicious drink, something like lemonade flavored with strawberry sirup" [sic]. He adds, "The fruit when ripe contains an agreeable and slightly acidic pulp from which fine preserves can be made; but some foreigner would have to do this, for the natives of Panama neither can, preserve, nor make jelly" (20856). The fruit is described as "about as large as a boy's head," a comparison that is reinforced by the image's composition in which the head of a boy sitting next to a soursop tree appears at about the same level as the hanging fruit, with the symmetry of the two dark, oval shapes dominating the center of the view. The boy appears to have been placed in that particular spot as he turns his head slightly to the side replicating the large strawberry shape of the fruit, an effect that is intensified by the three-dimensional illusion. Such comparisons between indigenous people and food items, whether implicit or overt, are relatively common and lend new meaning to the concept of traveler as epicure.

—— The Sights of Panama: Picturesque Time Travel

Despite the "taste of the tropics" tour, the primary sensory modality of tourism is vision, as indicated by the term *sight-seeing*. Picturesque visions of remote locales, as well as photographs of well-known monuments that echo decades if not centuries of etchings and paintings of such architectural wonders are common in stereograph travel sets. At times, the text writer adds on another layer of visual description, perhaps implying that a still black-and-white photograph is inadequate in describing the wealth of detail, the visual saturation experienced by the traveler.[13] One card reads, "In the forest are always found flowers in blossom. Some in the soil and some hanging from the trees. Butterflies and humming birds, in all the colors of the rainbow are constantly on the move. Parrots whistle and monkeys chatter in the tree tops. Small lizards beautifully colored and absolutely harmless, dart under the leaves and over the ground. . . . Delightful it is to walk through a path like this. In addition to the varied plant and animal life there is the arched canopy of glossy green, the glittering spikes of golden sunshine, and glimpses of the blue eternal dome" (20860). In a contradiction of the stories of floods and earthquakes that plagued past efforts to cut from the Atlantic Ocean through to the Pacific, the emphasis on Panama's pleasant weather occasionally reads like a travel ad: "the average temperature of Panama is nearly ideal, for even the hottest days are tempered by its delightful breezes." On another occasion, the text writer, perhaps at least in this case the same person as the photographer, recounts the pleasantries of her or his own day trips as a possible suggestion to the would-be tourist, writing, "Across the bay southwest from the American village we find the interesting ruins of the old Spanish town [of Porto Bello]. Hiring a sail boat we enjoy a delightful trip across the bay. Although made at mid-day we

Panama Interior

During the building of the Panama Canal, the region was portrayed as the ideal tourist attraction, with its combination of historical significance, picturesque Spanish ruins, comfortable accommodations, exotic cultures, and lush tropical landscapes.

Postcard, circa 1912.

do not feel the need of a sun-shade. A gentle breeze tempers the rays of tropical sun. Soon we are walking in the streets of a city founded in 1584" (21700).

In this stereoscopic construction, Panama is a land fertile with pleasures ready to be plucked like the coconut that dangles from the tree awaiting the hungry tourist. In fact, Panama is positioned as the ideal tourist object with its natural wonders—tropical fruits, luxuriant vegetation, its great rivers, freshwater springs, and scenic bays—and its combination of an intriguing past, an exotic present, and a bustling future that lies ahead. In the evocation of colorful past, stereoviews of certain landmarks are a jumping-off point for the text writer's discussion of Columbus's explorations, Inca treasures, gold and silver brought to the

The indigenous populations of Panama were depicted as primitive cultures bookended by the glory of early Spanish settlers who left their mark on the land, as is evident in ruins still standing in the area, and the advanced technology of the new colonialists directing the building of the canal.

Photograph from a souvenir book produced by I. L. Maduro's Souvenir Store, Panama.

area from Peru, royal Spanish galleons weighted down with precious booty, and pirates who looted, tortured, and "committed all manner of debauchery and excesses" (20899). The trope of tourism as time travel is discernible on several occasions. On visiting the old Spanish town of Porto Bello, which now stands in ruins, our tour guide writes, "In visiting the ruins of the churches where hundreds of worshippers formerly attended religious services, one may properly stand with uncovered and bowed head. The old walls bring to our imagination the sound of the old bells in the tower, and the sonorous chanting of the Mass, but the faces of the brave men and beautiful women of centuries gone are not now seen in the auditorium" (20899). Even the present tense of Panamanian city-dwellers becomes an enjoyable jaunt into the past; one reads that "it seems almost like stepping out of the present into a bygone century to enter Panama and walk along some street of the older part. . . . [The balconied buildings] are built with no uniformity or regularity, but the result is wonderfully picturesque and ancient looking" (20866).

The term *picturesque* as used here is interesting in its referencing of the flat picture and the tendency to judge a locale's beauty in terms of the kind of picture it would make. The stereograph, as its proponents claimed, overcame the flatness of the still image to depict a spatial sense, a sense of immersion through depth. Yet, the distanced immersion of tourism, the desire to be immersed and to stand outside the space and perceive it as pure image emanating from the single focal point of the traveler, reintroduces the tug-of-war between immersion and flat, picturesque spectacle. The trope of picturesqueness not only involves a flattening effect but also a desire to reduce an environment to a digestible whole ruled by discernible structuring principles and a unifying visual harmony, as determined through Western standards of art. And finally, we might even see that the deployment of this trope of picturesqueness (to the extent that this judgment is shared by the viewer) further aligns spectator and photographer, this time not as fellow travelers immersed in a foreign space but as procurers of images sharing assessments of composition and aesthetics. Foreign spectacle is packaged as contained, imagistic surface for photographer and spectator alike.

Within the description for this same stereograph, the narrator makes note of a detail that might normally violate the visual harmony of this "picturesque" scene: a fire hydrant pops up on this otherwise "ancient looking" street. Instead of detracting from the location's appeal, however, according to the text writer, this process of modernization ignited by the American presence has helped make Panama a more attractive location for tourists. We are informed that while it was once difficult to get a good cooked meal in the area, now nineteen hotels serve visitors. A stereograph of the Hotel Tivoli, "a very fine hotel," we are told, serves as visual evidence. The narrator also brags about the area's hospitals for laborers (and maybe even the occasional traveler with a delicate digestive system), but adds that the hospitals have few patients because of the improved sanitary conditions in the canal zone. One hospital is even depicted in a picturesque manner, accompanied by a description of its beautiful walks lined with royal palms and other tropical trees. Evidently, to visit Panama's canal zone is to bask in the trop-

The caption for this stereograph depicts North Americans' presence as nonobtrusive and benevolent by drawing attention to the unchanged, picturesque streets altered only by the fire hydrant, a sign of U.S. improvements to the area's water and sewage systems.

Enlargement of single image of stereoview,
"The Quaint Balcony-Hung Avenue B of Panama" (20879).
Courtesy of the Doheny Library Special Collections, University of Southern California.

ical breeze without foregoing modern comforts; it is to glimpse a celebrated past and be a part of history, welcoming the future that the opening of the canal will usher in.

And as if this were not enough, to assure the tourist that she has really left home and traveled to an exotic space, the "quaint and picturesque" Panama City is complimented by the "crude and primitive" lifestyle of a racially exotic people living in the jungle. These indigenous people seem to require particular attention

Souvenir collections portray Panama as a region of contrasts between the crude housing and poor living conditions of the native populations, often represented by children, and the advanced technology of the United States.

Photograph from a souvenir book produced by I. L. Maduro's Souvenir Store, Panama.

and even a distinct tone of narration within the stereograph collection. An instructional mode takes over as ethnographic description dominates the captions. Examples of houses, ovens, sugar mills, and individuals are singled out by the camera and described as "typical" specimens for understanding the native way of life. Detailed explanations of cooking procedures, house-building techniques, and physiological characteristics impart anthropological knowledge of a people portrayed as lacking a history, and as racially and culturally homogeneous. In slightly over one-half of the stereographs of rural inhabitants, children stand in as picturesque and unthreatening representatives of the local culture. Throughout the ethnographic description of these inhabitants, a certain specificity as to their history and racial makeup is lacking. For instance, a single individual is highlighted as possessing the "typical" skin tone of the "native," effacing both the diversity of inhabitants, many of mixed Spanish descent, and the history of laborers brought into the area such as the many West Indians who came to work on the Panama Railroad in the 1850s and then settled in the area.

—— The Building of an Image

The viewer as a vicarious traveler gleans a form of anthropological knowledge from looking into the anonymous lives of a so-called primitive people, a worldliness that places the developed West at the center of that world. With Americans as the primary audience for such stereographic pleasures, the Panama Canal box set thus continues the process of orientation by positioning the United States, and by extension its individual members, in relation to a host of other nations whose people or whose legacies are perceptible in the canal region. In this construction of an American image on the rubble of other nations' supposed failures or inadequacies, a group of linked qualities becomes salient in a cross-cultural measure of worth; the enterprising spirit bolstered by corporate and engineering know-how and sprinkled with a bit of paternalistic benevolence for good measure becomes a way of defining the American spirit and its influence abroad.

The building of the canal functions as a centerpiece within the stereograph collection, a monumental endeavor next to which the sustenance economy of Panama's inhabitants inevitably pales in comparison. Card after card details with pride and exuberance the engineering feats and technological wonders of the American construction efforts. The not so tacit comparison is with the supposedly indigenous people, who are depicted as lacking the proper skills for making the most of their land, as already suggested by their egregious inability to make jam. One unnumbered card reads, "As we have already noticed in this journey through Central America, the native population in most of these countries is neither enterprising nor progressive." This viewpoint is continually referred to as a self-evident fact, immediately observable in the stereoscope images. Thus, the images of an unfamiliar culture and of foreign objects—the meaning or interpretation of which is not always evident—are given a singular translation by the caption, which insists upon an obvious meaning. In one instance, the narrator explains that Panama has the potential for becoming one of the great sugar-producing nations but "native production is hampered by poor methods of cultivating the sugar cane, and by poor machinery for pressing out the juice. Only the crudest methods are used . . . . A glance at some of the sugar machinery used by the

National pride is solidified not only through the comparison between American technological genius and the primitive conditions of indigenous culture but between U.S. efforts and similar efforts by the French that ended with failure as evinced by abandoned French equipment in the Canal Zone.

"Belgium Locomotive in Storage," reproduction from single negative. Courtesy of the Keystone-Mast Collection, Museum of Photography, University of California-Riverside.

Panama natives will suffice to tell the story" (20876). A similar sentiment is echoed in a later card of the same sequence : "From this typical home of the peasant, one can rightfully infer that there is no enterprise or successful agricultural operations among the natives" (21748). At times the comparison between American ingenuity and so-called indigenous backwardness is explicit. A card with a view of U.S.-built workers' quarters and the new town that has subsequently sprung up describes them as "different in almost every particular from the villages of the country around them for they are models of correct sanitation" (20890).

Long-standing structures built by the Spanish, such as the San Domingo Church, are contrasted with the temporary huts and bamboo structures in the region.

"Santo Domingo Church Arch," reproduction from single negative. Courtesy of the Keystone-Mast Collection, Museum of Photography, University of California, Riverside.

The comparison being drawn is of course not only between the U.S. and Panamanian ways of life but between U.S. efforts on the canal and those of the French. The high number of deaths from malaria, yellow fever, and other ailments related to poor sanitation during the French efforts to dig the canal received much publicity in Europe and North America. To avoid such a fate, the United States secured the right to enforce sanitary regulations even in Panamanian-owned land. Within the sequence of views, France's defeat in the canal zone is visually translated into the spectacle of abandoned equipment, strewn with vines, sinking into wet ground, or surrounded by encroaching rust and vegetation. Yet, there is an attempt to maintain a differentiation between the "civilized" West and the simple ways of the area's inhabitants. The text points out that the French equipment was top-notch for its time and probably could have completed the job were it not for corruption and extravagance at the upper levels of the French Panama Canal Company. Even the long-gone Spanish are praised for their formulation of a cement-like substance, which has for the most part stood the test of time. The engineering ability of the Spaniards is emphasized in the story of the freestanding arch in the San Domingo Church, an arch that had to be built multiple times before a design was hit upon that, by the time of the Canal building, had lasted close to three hundred years. Such accomplishments, not to mention those of the United States, are implicitly compared to the structures of grass, bamboo, and palm bark that lie outside of Panama's cities.

Indigenous Panamanians are again placed within a hierarchy of race and nation in a description of canal laborers. Creating a scale of workers rated by dependability and divided according to nationality, one card comments on the unreliability of the "natives," which led to the dismissal of all but 500 Panamanians out of 30,000 workers. The description continues, "A large part of the work is now done by Jamaica negroes, and while these are an improvement over the natives of the zone, they are far from satisfactory. Chinese labor is both cheap and efficient, but there are many reasons, both diplomatic and racial, which makes it undesirable to employ them." U.S. citizens found that canal work did not pay as well as jobs at home within the prosperous United States. In their absence, the best workers were supposedly found among the ranks of Europeans. We are told, "Of the various nationalities tried thus far, those from the agricultural districts of northern Spain have proven most satisfactory. They are rugged, intelligent, and work with determination. The compensation they receive is so much greater than what they receive at home that they consider the work a splendid opportunity. They are paid double the wages of the Jamaica negroes and earn every cent of it" (20881). Needless to say, Americans appeared on this scale only as supervisors, inventors, administrators, engineers, and doctors. Few Americans are in fact visible within this collection, apart from what appears to be the photographer's friends, a well-dressed bunch who pop up rather frequently. More common is a nameless, faceless reference to the United States, or occasionally to "Uncle Sam," as benefactor. We learn that the U.S. presence supposedly led to general improvement in the native population's work ethic and entrepreneurial spirit. And thanks to the Americans, the San Domingo Church had been cleared of trash and turned

The different national and racial profiles of the Canal workers provided yet another arena for comparison.

Enlargement of single image of stereoview,
"Spanish Laborers at Work on the Panama Canal" (20881).
Courtesy of the Doheny Library Special Collections, University of Southern California.

into a proper tourist attraction, a drainage system had been constructed to help clear the standing water where disease-carrying mosquitoes bred, a reservoir now provided fresh drinking water, and an opera house had been built out of part of the $10,000,000 paid to Panama in the U.S. purchase of the canal zone. In a rare mention of a specific individual, the text writer again lauds American benevolence: "Instead of being a hot-bed of disease, Panama has now become a healthful city and for this, its inhabitants, natives and foreigners can thank Dr. Gorgas and his employer, your Uncle Sam" (20859). All in all, as another card reads, Panama "has taken on an air of prosperity since Uncle Sam began his huge 'ditch' between two oceans" (20880).

—— Extending the Frontiers of Capitalism

As we know, the primary U.S. motivation for purchasing the canal zone was not altruism; it was more than simply lending a helping hand to our southern sibling, a nation practically of our own creation. The canal was both a new frontier and an international stage for proving that the United States as a leader of the New World could play in the same league with the long dominant nations of western Europe. On the eve of the canal's opening, author William R. Scott wrote, "Where the Spanish scoffed and the French failed, the Americans have triumphed. South America, like Africa, will soon become an island, and the heroic searchings after a passage to the Spice Islands, by Columbus, will reach fruition in 1913, by the hands of a nation, not of the world which he knew, but of that very new world which he discovered."[14] Yet by 1914, it could be fairly said that no "new" worlds were left to discover in the spirit of Columbus. On the international level, colonialism had passed its peak. The Spanish, once contenders for world ownership, had begun to lose their grip, as was dramatically illustrated by the Spanish-American War. Within the United States, manifest destiny had played itself out with the frontier's official closure before the turn of the century and what would become the country's fiftieth and final state had been annexed a few years before canal construction began. The Panama Canal as a symbolic new frontier in a world of dwindling expansionist possibilities was unlike the frontier that came before it. Instead of linking oceans through the ownership of land stretching from coast to coast, this watery frontier chipped away at a swath of land until Atlantic and Pacific met. The canal would be a gateway to new trade routes and Eastern lands. As one unnumbered stereograph reads, "Looking out over the Pacific one naturally thinks of the great eastern world that is just now awakening from centuries of slumber." At this juncture, the canal was considered an entryway, inviting not the frontiersman with his rugged individualism but the new American, the venture capitalist. One such trailblazer, the United Fruit Company, had already planted itself on Central-American soil.

The stereograph collection clearly depicts the canal and the land around it as ripe for capitalist conquering, with corporate control over the land's productive capabilities constituting the one true future for Panama. The only doubts concern whether the Panamanians themselves will be up to the task. The text writer notes, "The Panamanians are receiving an object lesson as to what is necessary for future development of their country" (20895). If an element of the natural landscape is not revered for its beauty as beholden by the tourist, then it is referred to within this collection by its money-making potential. In this spirit, the rubber tree receives special attention in light of the automobile boom within the United States. Turning his or her nose up at the small sugar mill employed solely for domestic use, the text writer notes that Panamanian sugar cane, if properly cultivated, can provide four times as much sugar as Louisiana cane. The fertile land will bring significant profits "as soon as the people of Panama can be brought to realize its possibilities in sugar cultivation" (20874).

What is missing from this touristic portrait is the sense of impending loss that inhabits many travel descriptions. A primitive connection with nature disappearing along with a whole way of life; a pristine landscape soon to be overrun by hotels, billboards, and tourist-filled cruise ships; indigenous people corrupted by incorporation into a global capitalist system; a moment in history soon to be lost. None of these tropes, common even in the early twentieth century, make their appearance here. Instead, a technophilia and celebration of corporate America pervades the sequence of cards, creating greater beauty out of efficient modern architecture, cultivated land, and sublimely intricate machinery than out of the wild verdancy of Panama's natural landscape. Imagery and description of turbines, generators, hydraulic dredges, wicket girders, and steam and hydroelectric plants reach a frenzied state within the collection. This monumental reshaping of the earth's contours is expressed in numerical terms, as the text writer draws upon fact and figure describing cubic yards of concrete, weights measured in tons, the heights of towering walls, and expected water velocities. The writer's apparent knowledge of difficult engineering concepts and of the workings of diverse machines align him or her with the engineers and machine operators hidden behind or within the machinery. And by way of the collection's educational bent, the stereograph viewer joins this elite club of knowledgeable technology operators.

After years of debate over who should complete the canal project, whether it would even be feasible, which route should be chosen, and whether the canal would be profitable, the impending completion allowed unflinching enthusiasm. In a celebration of science's ability to make the earth meet its demands, one author announced the canal's opening by remarking, "It is a literal fulfillment of the Scriptural promise to man that he should have dominion over all the earth."[15] Of course, this was not "man's" collective project but that of the United States.

As a nation, the United States was in the process of adapting to what Maury Klein has called "the flowering of the third America."[16] In the transition from an agrarian society to an industrialized nation, big businesses with large capital investments, using heavy machinery to produce large quantities of goods sold to mass markets, became commonplace. Figures like Henry Ford, the country's second billionaire after John D. Rockefeller, became national folk heroes. However, the amount of power wielded by a small number of corporate heads, the advanced technologies of an industrialized nation, and the profound changes brought by these developments was met with public ambivalence, even alarm. The building of the Panama Canal, deemed necessary for the expansion of American business into new markets, and requiring the deployment of unheard of machinery and new technologies for its completion, could have been used as a spark for the expression of such ambivalence. Yet, this is not the case with Keystone/Underwood's Panama collection. The contrast between two standards of living—the American way of life and the Panamanian lifestyle, described in less than glowing terms—may have served to legitimate the U.S. path of development. The consumer economy and its availability of a wide range of quality goods have traditionally been relied upon as evidence for the individual worker, assuring him that the system was working and that the good life could be achieved through dutiful participation. Thus, the positioning of Panama as a consumer good to be devoured by the tourist and the emphasis on its exotic goods soon to be available in the United States dispels any ambivalence within the stereograph collection. Simulated travel plays the compensatory role of constructing an international stage for displaying the merits of the "American way."

As frightening as any technology that changes the face of the globe may be, the canal project's huge scoopers and drills were domesticated by the stereoscopic card, which described their functions in simplistic terms and delivered them into the home as small images to be enjoyed by the family. Additionally, it must not be forgotten that the Holmes stereoscope, like the mechanical equipment used in forging the canal, was viewed by at least one generation of Americans as a new and peculiarly American technology that had not been available to past generations of farmers and rural inhabitants. The same capitalist society that looked to Central America for a passageway for commercial shipping marketed affordable

The "Invasion of the West" is typical of the invasion of the North, South and East by the

OLDSMOBILE

Here are the facts: We are to-day shipping Oldsmobiles to nearly every civilized country, and some half civilized ones. Russia for the last three years one of our best foreign markets, is taking more cars to-day than before the present trouble broke out. We have met European manufacturers on their own ground and have "made good."

Our Palace Touring Car, Model S, is the "top notcher" of 1906. It is a genuine American car, discounting European product at Wall Street rates. Send for booklet telling how we have packed more style, speed, stability and *brains* into Model S for $2250 than can be found in any car in the world for anything like the same money.

The Double-Action Olds is a car with two working strokes for every revolution of the crank. It's the "*latest*"—the "*new thing*"—in automobiles. It is free of valves, guides, cams, and other mysteries that usually terrify the uninitiated. It s motor has *only three working parts.* It's a giant for hill climbing and difficult roads. It s price, $1250. Write for our "Double-Action" Booklet.

OLDS MOTOR WORKS
Lansing, Mich., U. S. A.

Member of Association Licensed Automobile Manufacturers

Canadian trade supplied from Canadian Factory, Packard Electric Co., St. Catherines, Ont.

CATALOG COUPON	CALENDAR COUPON	MOTOR TALK COUPON
Kindly send me information regarding cars checked. I am interested. Model B____ Delivery Cars____ Model S____ Passenger Traf- M. M. Model L____ fic Cars____	*Enclosed find 10 cents, for which send your large Art Calendar (free from adver- tising and suitable for framing) for 1906. Design by George Gibbs* M. M.	*Enclosed find 25 cents, for which have MOTOR TALK, a magazine devoted to automobiling, sent to me for 1 year.* M. M.
Name_____	Name_____	Name_____
Address_____	Address_____	Address_____

In answering this advertisement it is desirable that you mention MUNSEY'S MAGAZINE.

The meeting of cultures was consistently portrayed as the ideal environment for seeing American technologies as items truly deserving of marvel.

From an advertisement in *Munsey's* magazine, 1906.

technological items for family entertainment in the form of stereoscopes, automobiles, and motion pictures. American stereoscope viewers could not only rejoice in the fact that they were members of the great nation behind the Victorian era's "Great Enterprise," and that they need not live in homes made of grass and bark; they could also take delight in the knowledge that they were among the few who could gaze out at the colorful inhabitants of the world, at less industrialized peoples who could not return that gaze. Their stereoscopes converted the parlor into part panopticon, part mirror, bringing into view a supposedly degraded other and an aggrandized vision of self. Immersion in a malaria-infested, primitive environment was made safe through two levels of technological innovation: the stereoscope, which collapsed time and space to place the armchair traveler in the jungle within the safe environmental bubble the technological mediation provides, and the sanitation efforts of American medical specialists and engineers, which banished those troubling, malaria-spreading mosquitos. It mattered not that the average stereoscope viewer was no Oliver Wendell Holmes or Dr. Gorgas. To own and use the technology, to cradle it in one's hand within the family parlor, to use it to educate oneself about America's other technological triumphs was enough to link the spectator to the nation's amazing endeavor in Central America. The spectator as a tourist is aligned with the out-of-frame tourist-photographer, who is a part of this American entourage on foreign soil and who, through his own mastery of photographic technology, occupies a secure position within this collection's spectacle of technological exuberance.

PART TWO

The Cinematic Tourist Gaze

CHAPTER FOUR

Moving Postcards

THE POLITICS OF MOBILITY
AND STASIS IN EARLY CINEMA

IN A SIMPLE HISTORY of immersive entertainment forms, the arrival of cinema as the next stop on the chronological tour would prompt a discussion of the addition of motion as a bold and promising step beyond the static pleasures offered by magic-lantern shows. With the advent of moving pictures, the illusion of immersion no longer risked feeling like stumbling into a wax museum, with all signs of life eerily frozen before the spectator. However, this is not a simple historical study of immersive media effects. The addition of exoticized subject matter and the operation of the tourist gaze within immersive entertainments introduce a dynamic of push and pull as the tourist tries to sate desires for both immersion and distantiation in the face of radical culture difference. The armchair tourist's desire for the sensation of being amid palm fronds and tiki carvings is accompanied by a compulsion to occupy an external subject position before an object that preferably has been essentialized, unveiled, visually composed, and conveniently summarized. This notion of distanced immersion is in some ways a unification of what Timothy Mitchell calls the "double demand" of tourism, the simultaneous delight in place as image separate from the tourist and as immersive space, with what Fatimah Tobing Rony calls "fascinating cannibalism."[1] Although Rony unpacks the term by explaining that the cannibalism refers to the consumer behaviors of ethnographic viewers, also implied is the danger posed by true cannibalism, the ultimate signifier of cultural difference and of a primitivism diametrically opposed to the collective rules of behavior known as civilization. Such threat is flattened or disarmed through a fetishizing and objectifying gaze that reduces difference to spectacle, thereby preserving the pleasurable aspect of "fascinating cannibalism." In the words of Dana Polan, this type of visual apprehension—the interpretation of people and their cultural events as spectacle—"offers an imagistic surface of the world as a strategy of containment against any depth of involvement with that world."[2]

This dialectic of distanced immersion suggests that the integration of cinema's reality effects into extant models for touristic entertainments did not occur without considerable negotiation around the issue of motion, with its detraction from static spectacle. Summaries of the privileged position of the cinematic spectator frequently reference the unencumbered, fluid movements of the film viewer, who can experience a multitude of locations in a matter of minutes without the difficulties of long travel times, unpleasant climates, or digestion-disrupting parasites. Yet to immediately cast the spectator into the role of the body in motion is to ignore the more obvious interpretation of cinema's innovation: film allowed the exotic bodies frozen in time within the museum display or stereograph to move, to run out of frame, or, most alarmingly, to rush the camera/spectator, like Auguste and Louis Lumière's train arriving at Le Ciotat Station. To return a state of repose to the restless natives and to instead put the spectator in motion would require alterations in filmic form and a tiptoed extension of the tourist gaze into this new media form.

—— Adjacent Media Forms

The suggestion that the existence of a relatively well-formulated touristic position had been established within other exotic entertainment forms, such as ethnographic exhibits at museums and world's fairs or Keystone's stereographic tours, lends weight to the argument that the tourist gaze appeared relatively early within film, even if with some necessary adaptation to the new cinematic form. However, a more appropriate starting point for such an argument is the more immediately adjacent entertainment forms that not only resembled filmic travelogues but would become the first forums for cinematic exhibition: magic-lantern shows, vaudeville, and travel lectures.

In material form, cinema most closely approximated its photographic cousin, the magic-lantern slide. And in fact, some of the first advertisements for motion picture projectors appeared in stereopticon catalogs targeted at lantern slide exhibitors.[3] Motion pictures in this context were touted as a profitable addition to the slide show. Even when films became the main attraction, lantern slides were often used to entertain audiences between films while the reels were being changed.[4] Considering their shared exhibition sites, it is not surprising that lines of continuity can be drawn between the subject matter of the two media and between the formats of their exhibitions. A magic-lantern show frequently consisted of a small number of slide series, with each series covering a single subject, whether biographical, travel-related, or fictional. Well-known stories were depicted using single images representing the primary dramatic moments, a strategy not unlike early silent cinema's attempt to condense stories such as *Uncle Tom's Cabin* on to a few minutes of film footage by representing key narrative moments. Many of the same stories, travel locations, and other subject matter covered within stereopticon screenings formed a repertoire from which cinema drew, although initially more mundane topics were also acceptable in cinema's early history, provided that movement was a primary component of the profilmic subject.

Looking solely at a list of travel locations represented by each of the two media, few distinctions would separate early cinema's depiction of world sights from that of the magic lantern. The Holy Land, well-known metropolitan areas in Europe, and America's western lands attracted the eager gaze of both media. Yet, the producers of lantern slides found an easy subject in quiet landscapes and architectural monuments, subjects with which filmmakers could hardly be content due to the stasis inherent in such subject matter. Thus, traveling filmmakers, while perhaps taking cues from the popularity of certain topics at magic-lantern screenings, ultimately had to seek out new ways of representing foreign environments in order to highlight film's potential to depict objects in motion.

In many respects, travel lectures were not too different from magic-lantern shows. Although the travel lecture predates the magic lantern, by the late nineteenth century most lecturers drew upon the visual accompaniment of slides. In fact, many of the images displayed as a part of the lecture may even have been identical to those viewed at lantern shows, since lecturers sometimes supplemented their own photographs with slides obtained from the same catalogs used by magic-lantern exhibitors. However, the single subject examined in depth, the venue of the grand lecture hall, high admission prices, and the air of respectability that were all a part of the travel lecture guaranteed a different audience than was attracted to the less extravagant stereopticon exhibition. And while narrators for slide shows spoke from scripts purchased from slide distributors, travel lecturers spoke with the authority of firsthand experience. Individual lecturers attracted followings, even achieving considerable fame through their lecture enterprises. One such lecturer was Burton Holmes, who reportedly crossed the Atlantic Ocean thirty times, made his way across the Pacific Ocean twenty times, and encircled the earth six times in pursuit of material for his eight thousand lectures given between 1890 and 1946.[5] His success was partially attributed to the beauty of his photographs, which he took himself and then had hand colored, initially by a group of Japanese women and later in his career by a team of American painters whom he had personally trained.[6]

While it is difficult to know if Holmes was actually the first travel lecturer to integrate motion pictures into the format of his lectures, as he claims, he was certainly the most well-known lecturer, and the most adept at self-promotion, to do so. In 1897, a leaflet promoting Holmes's *travelogue*—a word that he claims to have coined—advertised, "There will be presented for the first time in connection with a course of travel lectures a series of pictures to which a modern miracle has added the illusion of life itself—the reproduction of recorded motion."[7] Like his contemporaries in the stereopticon business, Holmes invested in this new technology as a kind of experiment. At first, the screened films were not connected to the material contained within the evening's lecture. At that first 1897 screening, for instance, the lecture's conclusion was followed by a trio of twenty-five-second scenes: members of the Omaha, Nebraska, fire department preparing for the day's inevitable exigencies; a police parade marching down the streets of Chicago; and, finally, Italians eating spaghetti.[8] Regardless of the obvious disconnection between the lecture and such footage, the overwhelming response convinced Holmes to eventually hire a motion-picture camera operator to accompany him on all his trips. Holmes continued to take his own still photographs, which made up the bulk of the show's visual material, and the films were displayed only at the end of the evening's lecture. Other lecturers reportedly modified Holmes's technique and alternated between slides and films. And although little documentation concerning the presentations of the lesser known lecturers exists, it is evident that such travel lectures were one of the primary contexts for the urban upper middle class' introduction to motion pictures.

The organizers of vaudeville shows integrated motion pictures into their format for the same reasons that motivated travel lecturers and magic-lantern operators: to attract audiences with this new entertainment form. While vaudeville theater—unlike stereopticon shows and travel lectures—did not routinely feature travel themes, another entertainment form that already occupied a privileged position within ethnographic exhibits was standard fare at vaudeville shows: dance offered the suggestion of continuity between cultures (even though the Viennese waltz, for instance, would have been considered to be a far more sophisticated cultural expression than ritual Native-American or Turkish dance styles that were collectively labeled "hootchie coochie" dances). At the same time that dance delivered spectacle in a familiar form, it could be read as a show performed solely for the benefit of a U.S. audience without forcing that audience to recognize the movements, postures, and music as components of a complex culture that may have been beyond audience understanding. From an ethnocentric standpoint, dance in such contexts could be read as a sexualized performance or as childish expressions of emotion—either of which would have reinforced traditional modes of viewing foreign peoples. For instance, while Native-American dance performances were compared to ring games for children, the "hootchie coochie" dance of a woman referred to only as Fatimah at the Chicago's Columbian Exposition of 1893 was covered in press reports as a scandalous and licentious exhibition unsuitable for family entertainment. Different cultural standards for the exposure of skin as well as sensationalism and stereotypes around the

The label *dancer* could be applied to any image of a young foreign woman as a way of explaining unusual dress, or often a lack of dress.

Postcard of northern African dancer, circa 1900.

sexual habits of foreigners, ranging from Middle Eastern harems to the alleged lasciviousness of African women also promoted a sexualized reading of exotic dance
styles. Whether viewed as the prelinguistic expression of a primitive culture or as
seduction performed to the rhythmic pounding of animal-hide drums, the dance
within this interpretive context would have helped to perpetuate the illusion of
an industrialized West surrounded by exotic cultures whose primary function was
to serve as a source of entertainment and wonderment.

Live dance performances within vaudeville shows would typically have consisted of dances from standard immigrant cultures within the United States: Ger-
manic folk dances, the hora, or clog dancing. However, once motion pictures were
introduced into the vaudeville theater, it could be expected that out of a series of
ten to twelve films fitted into vaudeville's traditional twenty-minute slot, one or
more would have continued this vaudevillian method of representing the exotic
through dance but with greater opportunities for representing little-known populations outside of the United States. Of course, while some dance films would
have been considered to have ethnographic value, many of them were characterized by the same kind of compromised authenticity that marked many vaudeville
acts. The 1903 film *Geisha Girls,* for instance, depicts three obviously Caucasian
women wearing kimonos and imitating a Japanese dance.

Scanty documentation concerning both exhibition venues and filming contexts make many dance films from cinema's first decade difficult to categorize. In
many cases, it is not known whether a vaudeville performance was captured on
film for documentation purposes or if the dance was performed with only the
camera as audience in the production of a film to be distributed to vaudeville
houses. Additionally, footage of dances by indigenous and tribal peoples captured
by traveling filmmakers, who intended such images to be projected for entertainment purposes, may have ended up in the possession of anthropologists, thereby
obscuring the context of the footage's origins. And of course, the growth of
tourism during this same period was rapidly erasing the distinctions between
dances performed as a part of traditional celebrations and the dances staged for
the benefit of tourists.[9] Thus, without reliable documentation concerning the
filming context, a film such as *A Jewish Dance at Jerusalem* (1903) could be either
labeled as an ethnographic moment or viewed as a staged performance within
one of the most popular tourist locations of the period. In either case, it is interesting to note that at this particular historical juncture, the same films could have
been screened at a vaudeville house, within a travel lecture, at a magic-lantern
show, or as part of an anthropologist's public lecture at a natural history
museum.[10]

—— Postcards in Motion

As indicated above, the sharing of exhibition outlets with extant attractions may explain some shared characteristics across cinema and these other entertainment forms. At the same time, the individuals who gathered images for showing off the new medium's capabilities must have sought ways of distinguishing motion pictures from its less technologically sophisticated rivals. And it was cinema's ability to represent movement, from the pounding of waves on the shore, to a train's rapid approach, to the delicate motions of a baby unsteadily drawing a spoon to her mouth, that truly differentiated motion pictures from the stillness of magic-lantern slides, stereoviews, and paintings. To use the motion picture camera to represent a static subject would have been an unheard of waste of the medium's potential. Thus, the exotic locale depicted on film could no longer be tamed in its stillness, no longer reduced to a picturesque place whose timelessness was confirmed by the frozen nature of the image. In the past, a Buddhist temple, for example, might have been captured with a long exposure that emptied it of all living persons with the exception of an unobtrusive blur here and there, thereby strengthening the illusion of a location patiently awaiting the tourist's visit, rather than depicting it as an integral site of a vibrant culture firmly set in the present tense. The pressure to represent a world in motion and the persistent appeal of distant lands thus forced traveling filmmakers to find strategies for adding movement to the exotic postcard.

During the first decade of the silent film era, a number of filmmakers made their reputation by crossing into lands that were just beginning to be documented via the movie camera. James H. White, employed by the Edison Manufacturing Company, was one such filmmaker. Examining White's work, a number of techniques for interjecting movement into the representation of exotic lands and foreign peoples become evident and can can be considered characteristic of the overall development of travel films shot for commercial exhibition in this period.

In the years immediately following the 1897 employment of White by Thomas Edison, White traveled extensively in the company of a camera operator, first William Heise and later Fred W. Blechynden, filming in the United States, Mexico, Europe, the Far East, and the West Indies. White's business alliances during this period clearly illustrate that from early on within the history of the film industry, cinema's potential for promoting tourism was duly noted and exploited. After American Mutoscope's success with the film *The Empire State Express* (1897), White pursued similar depictions of train travel. He facilitated ties with the Lehigh Valley Railroad Company, a corporate body that was eager to encourage domestic

Hotel Vendome, San Jose, Cal.
American Plan.   Morgan Ross, Manager

Postcards were originally sold at train stops and often advertised the same locations that were offered as parts of railroad companies' package tours.

Postcard, 1915.

tourism and thus waived the railway fares for White's trips. In the following years, White negotiated similar deals with the Southern Pacific Railroad, Mexican Central, and the Occidental and Oriental Steamship Company. At the time, many railroad companies offered tourist packages with predetermined itineraries and prepaid accommodations. Uncoincidentally, while White was on a Southern Pacific Railway—sponsored trip, his filmed stopovers, such as at San Jose's Hotel Vendome and Monterey's beaches documented many of the same locations included on Southern Pacific's advertised package tour.[11]

White's first camera-toting visit with a culture divergent from his own came in October of 1897, when he attended the American Indian Festival of Mountain and Plain in Denver, Colorado. The majority of the films shot at the festival depict Native-American dances, as indicated by the 1898 film titles *Circle Dance, Eagle Dance, Wand Dance,* and *Buck Dance.* Such dance performances and rituals obviously provided the requisite motion and, conveniently enough, confined motion to a relatively small space that could be framed by a static camera.[12]

When not focused on foreign subjects, film exhibitions of this time often included a double layer of technological celebration. Advertisements exalted moving pictures as the latest technological wonder, while the films themselves glorified labor saving machinery and advanced transportation technologies. In stark contrast, movement was introduced into depictions of foreign environments through training the camera on indigenes engaged in intense manual labor. For instance, in 1903 two films of excavation processes were exhibited in American theaters. In the first, *Excavation for Subway,* an elevated camera position reveals a large tunnel being dug under New York City's Union Square. Very few workers are visible as the film highlights cranes, electrical equipment, and sophisticated engines—the diverse machinery involved in an awe-inspiring project that would revolutionize intracity travel. The film *Excavating Scene at the Pyramids of Sakkarah,* on the other hand, provided a view of about fifty laborers carrying buckets of sand, tediously dumping their load on to a sand pile and returning for more. The pyramid visible in the background provided a picturesque setting while perhaps reminding viewers of the labors involved in the monument's construction centuries ago and of the fundamentally unchanged nature of the labor in the region. In such cases, this play of contrasts resembled the touristic pleasures of the Columbian Exposition and stereographic depictions of the building of the Panama Canal, pleasures that were secured through the assumption that a world of knowledge and scientific understanding separated Americans from these strange peoples that evolution seemed to have left behind.

This focus on overseas manual labor and its contrasts to the practices of industrialized nations are evident in White's films. In the 1898 film *"S.S. Gaelic" at Nagasaki,* Japanese men and women help unload the ship by passing baskets from one person to another. A similar scene is represented in *Native Women Coaling a Ship at St. Thomas* (1898) as the camera, positioned on the dock, captures a large number of women ascending the gangway carrying baskets on their heads. The camera's distanced viewpoint allows for a visual contrast between the impressive steam vessel populated by privileged individuals and the primitive loading and unloading methods employed by the darker-skinned locals. A number of other films shot by White on his 1903 honeymoon in the Bahamas and the Virgin Islands also target laboring women with a voyeuristic stance that penetrates those back regions of a culture that both tourists and anthropologists seek out. One film features a dark-skinned woman bathing a boy in a washtub, while another film shows several bare-breasted women washing their clothes by pounding them on a rock in a stream. In comparison to filmic portraits of towering steam shovels and ocean liners, such films brought the camera in for close scrutiny of laboring and often racially marked bodies.

The steamships and trains in White's films were part of a larger public fascination with transportation technologies. This public excitement, the demand for cinematic motion, and the financial contributions of transportation companies to the film industry made train and ship travel ideal subjects. The many depictions of transportation-related technologies and vehicles of all types included a fifteen-second film of a New York subway ride from City Hall to Harlem, automobiles delivering newspapers, a switchback on a trolley car, an electric car dragging a barge through a canal, a railroad mail car, rotary snow plows on the Lehigh Railroad, and a rock drill at work in a subway tunnel, to give just a few examples. Within White's transportation-focused films, the double-decker electric streetcar of *Street Scene, San Diego* (1898) and a Paris sidewalk conveyor belt featured in *Panorama of the Moving Boardwalk* (1900) contrast sharply with the oar-sculling boatman of *Japanese Sampans* (1898) and the rickshas of *Street Scene in Hong Kong* (1898). In terms of power and speed, the scurrying of human-drawn carriages and skiffs across busy streets and into crowded wharves undoubtedly existed in the shadow of the luxury liners that brought Western tourists to the docks and streets of the Far East.

While attendees of a travel lecture may have pictured themselves in the globetrotting shoes of the charismatic lecturer, many travel films of cinema's first decade lacked a similar point of identification. Occasionally within such films, however, Caucasian travelers could be seen in motion amid unfamiliar cultural environments. Thus, in White's film *Tourists Starting for Canton* (1898), six light-skinned travelers are seated on sedan chairs and carried on the bare backs of several Chinese men, while in *Shanghai Street Scene, Scene Two* (1898) Chinese coolies with one- or two-wheeled carts propel Caucasian men to requested locations. While brief, the presence of these white identificatory figures nonetheless prefigured the Western protagonists of later filmic travel narratives by suggesting a point of entry for spectators.

—— Technological Spectacle and Spectator Positioning

Due to the presence of the lecturer as tour guide, the travel lecture was quite amenable to a touristic positioning of the spectator. First of all, John Stoddard, Burton Holmes, and other lecturers explicitly promoted their performances as vicarious journeys for those lacking the time, money, energy, or courage for such adventures.[13] Many members of middle- and upper-class audiences would have previously traveled as tourists, or would at least have had the necessary leisure time and funds to thus imagine themselves making such a voyage at some time in their lives. Additionally, descriptions of "travelogues" and preserved photographs from lectures indicate that the slides typically presented a number of diverse viewpoints that facilitated the audience's placement in the position of the travel lecturer. For instance, photographic slides of the lecturer himself in the exotic space as well as slides taken of the lecturer's point of view from that same spot were not uncommon. Similarly, a photograph of passengers looking out a train window might have been followed by a slide of the scenery viewed from a position inside the train. In such instances, lecture attendees, by aligning their gaze with that of the camera, would have been placed in the position of the travel lecturer, an effect intensified by the accompanying words of the lecturer describing the sounds, sights, and smells that a visitor might expect to encounter on the journey.

The motion pictures that followed Holmes's lectures similarly included images of Holmes touring the featured location and also unobstructed views of the landscape and architecture. These latter images would have been interpreted as equivalent to Holmes's perspective (and in turn the perspective of the audience as vicarious tourists) in a conflation of several points of view: the camera's, the camera operator's, Holmes's, and the film viewers'. In the cases in which travel lecturers interspersed films and slides, it seems even more likely that such media were viewed using similar interpretive strategies.

The travel lecture, with the eventual similarity of film content and lecture subject matter, may have presented a context more amenable to a familiar spectator position than other film exhibitions that presented a jumbled combination of filmic material. In these latter cases, the connecting throughlines of shows would have been the representational power of the medium rather than filmic subject matter. Engagement with the image would not have been seamless due to audience fascination with the wonders of mechanical and chemical production of the moving image. As Tom Gunning points out, advertisements for film screenings gave top billing to the Cinématographe, the Biograph, or the Vitascope rather than to the titles of the films.[14] Such considerations become particularly important when examining new innovations such as camera movement. With a thorough acclimatization of the spectator to filmic images as a vicarious reality, and with a solid suturing of the spectator into the cinematic illusion of space and time, the addition of camera movement would be easily assimilated into an understanding of the spectator-tourist in motion.[15] If primary identification was in full operation, achieving an equivalency between spectator vision and the camera's gaze, then camera movement would be experienced as the virtual tourist's rickshaw being set into motion. Gunning suggests that this would not have been the case within the "cinema of attractions" stage of film's development. In reference to an early upward camera tilt revealing the length of a building's facade, Gunning writes, "Camera movement began as a display of the camera's ability to mobilize and explore space. The 'content' or purpose of this film is as much a demonstration of the camera's ability to tilt as it is the Flatiron Building."[16] In other words, amazed by the camera's powers to slice through space, audience members may not have automatically imagined themselves at the base of the building tracing its towering height with their eyes.

By 1897, when it become common to mount cameras onto trains, subway cars, balloons, and even gondolas, film reviews indicate some ambiguity over spectator identification with camera movement. The label "phantom train films," referring to film footage created by mounting a camera to the front or back of a moving train, appears to indicate not an absorption in the depicted movement but a fascination with the camera's and projector's capabilities and with the film's creation of unseen offscreen space, the space of the "phantom" train. Within this description, a metaphorical gaze seems to stare back at the space of the mounted camera and the "invisible" train, rather than enjoying the ride with one's legs dangling from the front of that speeding train. One reviewer wrote, about Biograph's phantom train ride through the *Haverstraw Tunnel* (1897), "The way in which the unseen energy swallows up space and flings itself into the distance is as mysterious and impressive almost as an allegory."[17] The film is described as an enigmatic spectacle that inspires awe as opposed to belief in the realistic illusion and a comfortable taking-up of the spectator position of passenger. On the other hand, another 1897 review of a similar phantom train film paints a picture of total immersion in the depicted space, of a spectator undeniably in motion, noting, "The spectator . . . was a passenger on a phantom train ride that whirled him through space at nearly a mile a minute. . . . Far away the bright day became a spot of darkness. That was the mouth of the tunnel and toward it the spectator was hurled as if fate was behind him. The spot of blackness closed around him."[18]

Whether the spectator position of passenger or tourist was from the inception of cinema an aspect of the filmgoing experience (perhaps even coexisting with this engagement with the technology itself) or solidified as the spectator's interest shifted from the projector in the back of the room to the immersive reality depicted onscreen, by the start of the new century this type of positioning was being more explicitly encouraged by the viewing context. At the 1900 Paris Exposition, the Lumière brothers devised the Maréorama, which photographically simulated a view of an undulating Mediterranean Sea from the bridge of a ship. The platform rolled to and fro like a ship tossed by the sea while sirens buzzed, a funnel poured out smoke, fans imitated the winds of an oncoming storm, and lightning and thunder rocked the sky.[19] At the same exposition, Raoul Grimoin-

Sanson's Cinéorama invited audiences to stand on a raised circular platform and enjoy the illusion of being lifted by air balloon into the skies above Paris. Ten synchronized film projectors cast hand-colored 70-millimeter film images onto a 30-foot-high, 360-degree screen.[20]

The American version, Hale's Tours and Scenes of the World, made its debut at the 1904 St. Louis Exposition. During the following year, George C. Hale redesigned the attraction and sold exhibition rights to entrepreneurs across the country. According to one count, about five hundred of Hale's tours were operating in different parts of the nation between 1905 and 1906, the attraction's most popular years.[21] The simulated ride, often included within summer amusement parks, consisted of a mock train with an open front and side through which rear-projected films could be seen. Between the images taken from a moving train, a belt of moving logs beneath the viewing compartment, sound effects, and a rush of air which swept through the seating area, spectators enjoyed the illusion of being on a moving train chugging its way around the base of Mount Vesuvius or through the city of Tokyo. At some locations, the entrance to the theater resembled a railroad depot, complete with a conductor to collect the ten-cent tickets. Programs would typically change weekly bringing images of the American West, Europe, and beyond.

—— The Politics of Movement and Stasis

Between the years 1899 and 1906, over fifty films from the Library of Congress paper print collection were shot from moving trains, most frequently from the front cowcatcher or from a train's rear platform.[22] Many may have been used in Hale's Tours exhibits, while most were exhibited in the less spectacular surroundings of local exhibition outlets. Yet mounting cameras on trains or other types of moving vehicles was only one way of creating the illusion of moving through a space. During this same general period, camera movements such as the pan and the tilt came into use. With audiences becoming more accustomed to equating cinematic vision to their own, these movements could be read as an anthropomorphization of the camera in a way that the front-train-mounted camera, with its depiction of an unlikely human position, did not. Spectators could imagine an equivalence between a slow turning of the head and a gradual pan to one side, or between the turning of one's body to view an entire space and a 360-degree turn of the camera.

While the use of the vertical camera tilt was less common and typically reserved for unusually tall subjects, panoramic views employing up to 360-degree camera pans played a large role within the second half of cinema's first decade. By titles alone, panning films were not differentiable from films shot from moving vehicles, with both types of film frequently entitled *Panoramic View of*——. However, with a few exceptions, panning films appeared later than phantom train films, perhaps due to the late development of smooth tripod swivel heads. Within James H. White's work, the first pan, or in this case a slight horizontal readjustment of the camera, was not conducted with forethought but rather was the result of a bull's unpredictable movement while White was filming a bullfight during his 1897 trip to Mexico. The film's slight pan is an exception, however, with more planned pans not appearing in White's work until 1900. In the meantime, White shot a number of films from ships and trains, such as *California Orange Groves, Panoramic View* (1898) and *A Storm at Sea* (1900), the latter film being shot on his way to the 1900 Paris Exposition. Charles Musser speculates that White and the photographer who accompanied him to Paris must have acquired an improved panning mechanism somewhere along the route to, or in, Paris.[23] Along with a number of films shot from moving vehicles—*Panoramic View of the Champs Elysees, Panorama of the Paris Exposition from the Seine,* and *Panorama from the Moving Boardwalk*—White brought back footage that included a camera-tilt's view of the Eiffel Tower from bottom to top and back to the bottom again as well as a to-and-fro panning movement executed in a vain attempt to keep two Parisian female fairgoers in view.

Purposeful camera movements to keep a desired subject visible would eventually be incorporated into narrative film, and were already becoming more common in newsreel footage and chase scenes during White's days. Yet—quite separate from this development—upon his return to the United States, White and a number of other photographers became enthralled with the camera's potential for 360-degree pans, a circular movement that resisted smooth integration into narrative film, the conventions of which were developing during this transitional period. In fact, the circular panorama films seemed to be a throwback in name and movement to the dioramas and panoramas of the eighteenth and nineteenth centuries.

Part of the attraction of the panoramic film may have been the same as that which attracted visitors to dioramas: placement of the spectator in the midst of a fully described space. The circular movement of the camera capturing everything in view with its sweeping gaze marked out a coherent space for the spectator. Rather than a landscape providing a flat backdrop to some theatrical action, the unfurling of space enacted by the circular pan *was* the theatrical action. Yet, just as in the case of the filmed bullfight, certain pressures must have prompted the camera's circular spin, pressures rooted in the profilmic subject. The general thrill of virtually occupying a space, or of the visual demonstration of the camera's ability to turn on a vertical axis, does not alone explain the appeal.

In general, two types of locations are depicted, both of which fit neatly under the rubric of the sublime. The first type consists of the beautiful landscape, whether Niagara Falls' torrents of descending water or a series of lofty mountain-tops. The second type of panoramic film represents not plush and verdant land-scapes but its antithesis, the devastating scene of a recent disaster. A number of panoramic films documented the near catastrophic effects of a hurricane and flood that destroyed much of Galveston, Texas. Other films surveyed the damage left by urban fires, with the swinging camera slowly revealing the full extent of the damage.[24] In these scenes' visual presentation of the power of nature and of an almost unimaginable geographic scale, not to mention their ability to evoke a strong emotional response from the dwarfed human subject, both the site of dev-astation and the beauteous landscape could be called sublime. The sublime, even when manifested in beauty, is laced with threat, the threat of a world that exceeds human understanding and overshadows the human ability to create. Some kind of meaning must be reinscribed in the face of the sublime. The individual sub-ject's placement in that overwhelming environment must be reasserted. The panoramic film replicates the human experience of these sublime environments with its circling movement, visually taking in the landscape's details and its scope. It represents on film the space that is too big or too awesome to be absorbed from a single point of view. At the same time, the circular panorama converts place into meaning. Its movement maps onto the space a series of co-ordinates as the camera makes a quarter circle or half circle and returns to an imaginary starting point. Its arc and the camera's anthropomorphized vision assure solid placement for the spectator, for the human enveloped by this space; the circle described by the camera always refers back to a central point at which the spectator is inscribed. Its translation of sublime reality into a containable and manageable image is in short a process of harnessing the threat and distilling spectatorial pleasure.

Although a date would be hard to pinpoint, it seems that with time the mov-ing camera—whether it barreled down a stretch of train tracks, traced out a cir-cular panorama, or imitated the subtle movements of an individual's surveyance of a scene—came to be associated with the illusion of the spectator put into motion. With this adjustment from moving subject matter to moving spectator, the vicarious tourist's position as a subject in relation to an objectified and immobilized world would have been highlighted by these powers of fluid mobil-ity. This privileged spectator position solved the dilemma of adding motion to the postcard. Instead of being placed in a position of stasis gazing out at a foreign world bustling with motion, the moviegoer was mobilized and transported across a globe whose minute motions are rendered insignificant in comparison to the limitless mobility of the armchair traveler.

—— Narrative Movements

With the grafting on of certain types of narrative to the cinematic travelogue, the equation of filmic elements setting the spectator into motion was strengthened. Through filmic convention, the camera's gaze and its movements were further anthropomorphized by intermittently aligning the camera's point of view with that of a character present onscreen, a character whose eyes the spectator was invited to look through. The character, as one component of narrative, became the vehicle through whom the spectator was transported to distant lands. Narrative absorption was combined with the immersive reality effects of cinema.

Of course, this overlay of narrativity on the spectatorial pleasures of the single-reel travel film was not instantaneous. In fact, a popular pastime within silent cinema scholarship consists of tracing the development of particular narrative conventions through certain so-called landmark films. Interestingly, the films that historians such as Philip Rosen and Charles Musser have analyzed as exemplary of this transition to narrativity through the wedding of primary and secondary identification are travel films. Both authors analyze the integration of documentary footage into a fictional form and categorize the ways in which the documentary spectatorial gaze becomes harnessed by filmic narrativity.

The tendency in such a methodology would seem to lionize the editorial practices of directors who recognized how spectators would string together meaning from disparate shots. Yet Musser points out that such editing practices had their roots in exhibition contexts, such as when a Hale's Tours operator may have sandwiched a narrative film such as *What Happened in the Tunnel* or Edwin S. Porter's *The Great Train Robbery* (both 1903) between a couple of reels featuring train travel through the American West.[25] The new sequence then grounded the narrative action by establishing a coherent location for the events. Additionally, such sequences illustrated the nonproblematic combination of the subjective vision of the phantom train ride and the objective observation through the invisible fourth wall of theatrically staged narrative films. Of course, considerable experimentation with subjective vision integrated into narrative forms was already in full swing with dream sequences and "keyhole" storytelling. Yet the narrative's harnessing of the tourist's point of view as structured by actuality travel footage was a new innovation preceded by a number of small steps in this direction.

When examining White's creations, which were primitive in terms of combining narrative and scenic footage, a shifting of visual perspectives within a unified space is best discerned by juxtaposing two or more of his films, as exhibitors may well have done. The fictional travel narrative in classical cinema delivers narrative pleasure and documentary spectatorial pleasure by seamlessly shifting the viewer's perspective from one visual modality to another, from the subjective gaze of the tourist to the objective gaze of the spectator. Such a transferal of the gaze is accomplished by providing a diegetic tourist whom the spectator can alternately watch and align gazes with. Seen in juxtaposition, White's films, which either watch tourists or watch from a tourist's perspective, create a unified space within which a spectator's point of view may be shifted within a number of specified locations. *Panorama of the Moving Boardwalk* (1900), recorded from a static position some distance from the boardwalk, represents a number of tourists being leisurely swept along a path through the Paris Exposition. With the camera's new position *on* the boardwalk in *Panorama from the Moving Boardwalk*, the spectator has, between the end of the last film and the start of the next, taken up the moving perspective of one of those very tourists glimpsed only moments ago.

In White's *Prince Henry* series, the single focal character missing from the moving boardwalk couplet is proffered. During the Prince of Prussia's 1902 visit to the United States, White documented a number of stops along the prince's tour of the country. A number of the films appear to have been produced with the intention of being screened together. For instance, *Prince Henry at Niagara Falls* (1902) shows a shot of the crowds gathering to witness Prince Henry at the falls, followed by a shot of a train on a bridge. Succeeded by another film documenting a later stop on the prince's itinerary, the train shot would appear to be a transition, showing his passage to the next locale. In a few of the films within this series, White's inability to get close to Prince Henry produces ambiguity within the film; the spectator does not know if the Prince is in the shot or if the shot documents the same views that the royal visitor witnesses. This confusion is intensified by the similarity in content across the films. Six of the eight films depict a procession of some sort, a procession that Prince Henry is a part of or that has been staged for his benefit. For instance, *Prince Henry at West Point* (1899) contains two shots, the first showing the prince escorted by West Point cadets to the reviewing stand and the second depicting the corps of cadets marching by the prince for review. This second shot approximately represents the prince's point of view, or at the very least, the camera directs its attention to the same object that attracts the Prince's gaze.

These shifts of perspective within a single space, whether it be the Paris Exposition or the space of the United States as seen by Prince Henry, erupted occasionally within the same film but more likely with the fortuitous juxtaposition of films by exhibitors. Yet with the greater use of cutting, such shifts were increasingly seen within a single film. For instance, *Shoot the Chute Series* (1899), a film that may have been filmed by White but at the very least was filmed under his auspices as the head of Edison's kinematograph department, is an early example of multiple perspectives utilized within a single film. A water flume at Coney Island is viewed from the bottom of the slide, from the top of the slide, from a boat sliding into the water, and finally from a crowd of people watching the boat ride.

The absence of a central figure again limits the extent to which spectators may have believed that they were taking up a specific person's point of view while sliding down the chutes to a splashy landing below. Understandably, then, Musser cites Porter's *Rube and Mandy at Coney Island* (1903) as a noteworthy film in this integration of travel sights into a narrative form. Musser notes that the film, which starred two vaudeville actors, combined the acted comedy of the vaudeville stage with the camera styles associated with scenic material. Rube and Mandy are at times framed to provide spectators with an optimum view of the actors' physical comedy, while at other points, the actors' movements across Luna Park are kept in sight through a camera pan that captures views of the park in a style akin to the panoramic film. Other scenes, which make use of a camera positioned over the actors' shoulders, allow the spectator to see a view similar to the one witnessed by Rube and Mandy.

Rosen makes similar arguments in regard to a later motion picture, *A Policeman's Tour of the World* (1906), which moves beyond the over-the-shoulder shots of *Rube and Mandy* to point-of-view shots. For instance, in one scene, a character on a studio set of a ship looks through a set of binoculars. The following shot, masked to appear as if seen through binoculars, shows the Suez Canal from a moving boat. Through the eye-line match, actuality material has been integrated into the film's narrative of a chase around the world. In this way, the film positions the spectator as a tourist through an optical point of view while also narratively facilitating identification with the diegetic tourist. In the spirit of classical travel narratives, the spectator is invested in the film's global and narrative movements, simultaneously soaking up the pleasures of touristic vision and narrative involvement.

Thus, by 1906, the majority of traditional methods for supplying touristic spectatorial pleasure through narrative film existed in one form or another. The transitional shot or the establishing shot with its all-encompassing view of a locale, shot from a perspective not necessarily rooted to any diegetic character, appeared with exhibitors' combination of travelogue footage and films with narrative actions that could have believably occurred within the space depicted by the actuality material. Similarly, views of Western travelers moving through foreign places and among foreign people appeared first within the nonfiction form and later within fictional narratives as companies such as Kalem brought their actors overseas to shoot on location in Germany, Ireland, and the Holy Land in 1910 and 1911.[26] In these films and in a number of earlier films, the exotic environs could be glimpsed over the actors' shoulders or seen dominating the majority of the frame as the actors became small figures within a wide shot. Through the use of optical point of view in late preclassical films, theater-seat tourists and the tourists occupying the screen could share the same views of distant lands. Alternatively, location shooting could be avoided all together by matting in stock footage foreign backgrounds during the post-production phase.

BY WAY OF CLOSING, it should be acknowledged that despite extensive scholarship in this area, some aspects of early cinematic viewing practices remain opaque from a contemporary standpoint. It does, however, seem clear that a touristic position did exist within early cinema, even if a clear starting date cannot be established. A more fully developed form of this spectator position grew out of the search for moving subjects to illustrate the wonders of the cinematic apparatus and out of the subsequent tension between documenting an exotic world in motion and retaining the mastery implied by a "frozen" vision of cultural difference. During these first years of cinema's history, cameramen deployed across the globe captured on film the contrast between privileged travelers who left home via luxurious ships or newly built railroads and non-Western peoples who awaited their guests with empty rowboats and unsaddled donkeys. An equally stark comparison could have been drawn between these foreign laborers viewed by their visitors as technologically backward and the theater-seat tourists who by their attendance became participants in the technological "marvel of the century"—moving pictures. In either case, technology, movement, and leisure drew clear dividing lines between the haves and the have-nots, the mobile and the static, the tourists and the toured. By the close of cinema's first decade, in a further elaboration of this politics of stasis and mobility, the spectator had been granted greater vicarious movement first through the anthropomorphized, moving camera and later by the movement of the travel narrative with its stand-in tourists and its many modes of integrating the spectatorial pleasures of its filmic predecessor, the single-reel travelogue.

CHAPTER FIVE

Jules Verne

TRAVEL AND ADAPTATION

THIS CHAPTER BEGINS with and continually returns to the opening sequence of the film *Around the World in Eighty Days* (Michael Anderson and Sidney Smith, 1956) in the same way that classical narrative film in many ways began with and has continually returned to the work of Jules Verne. In a day and age in which films invariably thrust spectators into the thick of narrative action even before the opening credits, the delayed introduction to *Around the World*'s fictional diegesis may seem strange. Instead of directly entering Jules Verne's fictional tale in medias res, audiences must first sit through close to ten minutes of introductory material narrated by news commentator Edward R. Murrow. In fact, the first fictional world we enter is not the home of Phileas Fogg rendered in brilliant color, but rather the standard format, black-and-white world of Georges Méliès's 1902 film *Le Voyage Dans La Lune* (*A Trip to the Moon*). Through the use of this clip as a lead-in to their own film, *Around the World* producer Michael Todd and directors Anderson and Smith construct an abbreviated history of cinema with the help of a film and a director conspicuously absent from my own narrow history of silent cinema.

To review for a moment, the chapter 4's brief chronology of silent cinema ended at the year 1906, with the film *A Policeman's Tour of the World*, a film that was released four years after the success of *A Trip to the Moon*. According to Tom Gunning, this same year, 1906, marked the endpoint of what he has termed the "cinema of attractions."[1] And according to Philip Rosen, *A Policeman's Tour* marked the beginning of a new level of sophistication in the fictional travel film, integrating actuality footage, narrative, and the alignment of the spectator's gaze with

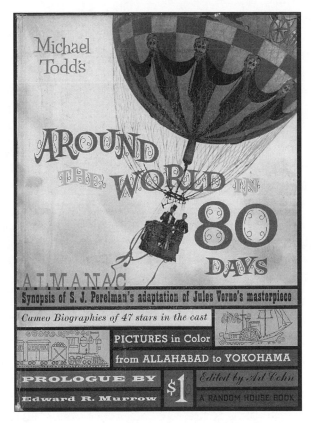

Supplementary materials that were sold in conjunction with the film documented the triumph of technology that the film supposedly represented, and the litany of actors and locations featured in the film.

Cover image, *Around the World in 80 Days Almanac*. New York: Random House, 1956.

that of the diegetic tourist.[2] The film itself tells a simple tale of a policeman chasing an embezzler around the world. In the end, the embezzler saves the policeman's life, returns the stolen money, and invites the policeman to go into business with him using the profits from the invested embezzled money. Despite this ending and a few other variations, the story is nonetheless borrowed from the pages of Jules Verne's *Around the World in Eighty Days*.

A Trip to the Moon, however, predated *A Policeman's Tour* not only in its borrowing of Verne material but in its construction of a fictional travel narrative (albeit one of a different nature) considering that documentary lunar footage would have been exceeding difficult to secure at this time. Verne, Méliès's contemporary and compatriot, had written two tales of lunar travel, *From the Earth to the Moon* (1870) and *Around the Moon* (1865), in the years preceding Méliès's new career venture as a film magician and animator. From the cannon-blasted rocket to the eccentric scientist-hero, the film's obvious inspiration is Jules Verne, although, like Porter, Méliès takes certain liberties in altering the original material; unlike Verne's characters, the protagonists of *A Trip to the Moon* are able to disembark, explore the moon, and encounter a strange tribe of moon dwellers with spears and painted bodies.

Returning to the year 1956 and to *A Trip to the Moon*'s reappearance on the screen, *Around the World*'s reference to film history as well as film's history of adapting Verne's work prompts a couple of issues. First of all, what in the Vernian oeuvre attracts filmmakers and encourages its usage in the retelling of the medium's own history? And second, in the wake of numerous recent adaptations of Verne's travel stories in nonfilmic media, an inquiry into the flexibility and persistent appeal of Verne's stories is called for. Even more interesting is the tendency to adapt Verne's work, whether in filmic or postfilmic media forms, using newly introduced technologies that enhance the medium's reality effects. This observation holds true across a range of texts: *A Trip to the Moon,* with its newly minted special effects techniques; *A Policeman's Tour of the World,* with its unique combination of fictional and documentary footage woven together with simulated point-of-view shots; *Around the World in Eighty Days,* with its wide-screen format and using a 120-degree lens, 70-millimeter film, a film rate of 30 frames per second, and stereophonic sound; the Cinerama title *To the Moon and Beyond* (Con Pederson, 1964); Walt Disney's first big-budget live action film delivered in CinemaScope, *Twenty Thousand Leagues under the Sea* (Richard Fleischer, 1954); the Disney amusement park ride based on the same story; Cyan's best-selling computer game Myst, with its captivating graphics that ushered in new expectations for immersion within CD-ROM titles; the short-lived HDTV television series *The Secret Adventures of Jules Verne;* Twenty Thousand Leagues: The Adventure Continues, a CD-ROM game promising continuous movement along a 360-degree field of vision delivered via SouthPeak Interactive's Video Reality format; and most recently, the fall 2001 opening of DisneySea Park in Tokyo, with Mysterious Island forming the centerpiece of the one-hundred-acre park, a new Twenty Thousand Leagues under the Sea ride, and Journey to the Center of the Earth, Disney's third attraction using enhanced motion vehicle technology.

—— Vernian Adaptability

The preponderance of adaptations of Jules Verne's collected works, *Voyages Extraordinaires,* cannot be explained by universal acclaim for his literary achievements. His biggest claim to fame is his status as one of the first writers of science fiction, a literary genre that has not typically garnered high respect among critics and other literati.[3] Although read by people of all ages, Verne is remembered as an author of travel adventure stories for adolescent boys, of fun tales with modest educational value and little intellectual depth. Thus, while some may hail Verne as a scientific visionary, few have gone to great lengths to call him a literary superstar.[4]

This tendency to divorce Verne from the world of lionized authorship, from the pure genius crystallized in the lines of the great poets, and from images of tortured writers struggling over word choice is one factor that has contributed to the liberal borrowing of his work. First of all, with over sixty Verne-penned novels in existence, borrowers have considerable material to draw upon. The pure quantity of Vernian literature also strengthened this appearance of "cheapness," like a series of romance novels published by its author whenever the cash flow starts to dwindle—a criticism that has followed Verne, labeling him a "manufacturer of marketable textual commodities devoid of aesthetic merit."[5] Verne's tarnished reputation for literary art has served to keep him separate from a notion of author as inviolate owner of his words. In fact, the power of Verne's work could be said to lie at the level of story or concept as opposed to in his writing style or eloquence.[6] His work thus gets passed on as mythology, rather than as quoted literature. The names, themes, story structures, and resonant objects from his novels appear to be handed down through history separate from the act of writing, as Vernian stories continue to be known by many but read by few. Thus, Verne's greatest contribution has been the recognition of enduring myths of travel adventure and their application to sites of fascination ranging from the cosmos, the deep seas, the center of the earth, and the farthest reaches of the earth's surface.

Both the compromised sense of literary authorship that surrounds Verne and his ability to pull together a timeless array of travel tropes derive in part from the reality of Verne's work as a nexus of intertextuality, borrowed concepts, and contributing voices. Verne liberally drew on authors of various nationalities including Edgar Allan Poe, Honoré de Balzac, James Fenimore Cooper, Victor Hugo, and Sir Walter Scott. Pierre-Jules Hetzel, Verne's publisher and mentor, radically affected the style and content of Verne's writing through a process of gentle persuasion and outright censorship. Additionally, Verne's son Michel added and deleted entire chapters of his father's work and perhaps wrote entire novels credited to his father. A single text's containment of multiple authors and multiple textual references is supplemented by another type of intertextuality: the referencing of Verne's work within other books written by Verne. For instance, a tour of a protagonist's library in one book is likely to reveal the titles of other Verne books resting on the shelves. In Verne's *The Mysterious Island* (1870), the story ends with the meeting of two protagonists, Cyrus Smith, the leader of the island colony, and Captain Nemo, the notorious eccentric whom Smith had read about in a book entitled *Twenty Thousand Leagues under the Sea.* And Verne, of course, would not be the last person to draw upon *Voyages Extraordinares,* referencing its characters and reworking its themes. Thus, to the extent that the name Jules Verne is "the call-sign of a plurality of writers" and the novels themselves consti-tute a cluster of references then referenced by a cluster of successive authors,[7] *Voyages Extraordinares* seem to belong to both no one and everyone.

—— Constructing Technological Histories

Returning once again to perhaps the most famous of Verne adaptations—Ander-son and Smith's film *Around the World in Eighty Days*—the introductory sequence provides insight into some of the themes interwoven throughout *Voyages Extraor-dinaires,* themes that in part account for the enduring appeal of Verne's travel stories. *A Trip to the Moon* is not the only film clip shown in the film's intertextual introduction. Murrow's voice-over is also accompanied by some dizzying views of the earth as filmed from a rocket. Through the juxtaposition of these fictional and nonfictional visualizations of space travel, a kind of continuity starts to build curi-ously around a topic that has little or nothing to do with Phileas Fogg's earth-bound adventure. Yet, one could say that the rocket footage does bring us closer to a theme within *Around the World* and many other Vernian texts. This footage taken from above earth looking down at the masses of land and water below moves toward an envisioning of the world as an integrated whole, as a sphere that can be circumnavigated, penetrated to its core, and seen in its entirety by the human equipped with the proper technology. Thus, through this introduction, cinema adds itself to the list of Vernian devices from the wondrous submarine *Nautilus* to the hot air balloon that grant individuals a privileged view of the world from above, below, and inside.

While Méliès's fantastical cinema neglected to actually show the world in the same way as did the documentary cinema of Auguste and Louis Lumière, to whom Méliès is often compared in a dichotomization of silent cinema styles, the Méliès films exhibit a certain joy in the unexplored potentialities of the cinematic appa-ratus, a whimsical pushing of the technological envelope not unlike that of the Vernian scientist-hero. For both Verne and Méliès, the science of a series of inter-locking mechanical, chemical, and electrical parts added up to a kind of magic that could transport the viewer, reader, or inventor-explorer to distant horizons.

Wide-screen processes were marketed with a similar discourse of magical travel possibilities; wide-screen images were advertised as breathtaking visions that transformed filmgoing from an act of simply watching to something infinitely more experiential. In reference to CinemaScope, cinematographer Joe MacDonald commented, "People will see things they've never seen before. When you look at CinemaScope it's like taking off blinders. It gives all the three-dimensional feeling that people want."[8] With wide-screen technologies used in combination with stereophonic sound, sound engineer Lorin Grignon declared, "The illusion of reality will be conveyed to a degree never before realized."[9] The revolutionary aspect of these technologies was compared to the earlier coming of sound. Of course, as in the case of sound, the technologies that made wide-screen cinema possible predated the widespread acceptance of these technologies by the film industry. The first thirty years of film history are dotted with odd names for obscure formats and devices that projected 360-degree images, used 70-millimeter film, or had aspect ratios that exceeded 2.5 to 1. Examples include the 1895 Eidoloscope; Raoul Grimoin-Sanson's 1900 Ciné, with its 360-degree view; the 1927 Hypergonar, with an aspect ratio that was beat out by only a few of the wide-screen formats introduced in the 1950s; and a slew of 1930s formats such as Magnafilm, Grandeur, and Realife that had 2 to 1 aspect ratios. In fact, when Michael Todd had his wish of "Cinerama outa one hole" fulfilled, it was by marrying a 12.7 lens to the design of a wide-gauge camera from the 1920s. This 65-millimeter image was then printed onto 70-millimeter film stock.

Despite the fact that the Todd-AO methodology and its retrofitted 1920s technology did not constitute a total break from the past, the promotion of the film *Around the World* unsurprisingly partook in the same type of hyperbole that surrounded the introduction of other wide-screen formats of the early 1950s. Promoters of *Around the World* presented the film as yet another breakthrough moment within the illustrious history of cinema, as a wide-screen epic unlike anything that came before it, but through its introduction declared a position for cinema within the history of technology and within the human conquering of earth and space. The promotional efforts took on a distinctive American flavor, even in spite of the multinational texture of this production—Verne as a French author, Méliès as a French director, Phileas Fogg as the British traveler, and a whole collection of international actors in cameo appearances. America operates as the primary referent within the film's condensed history of technology. Of course, the historical context for the film's production is a 1950s protechnology United States fighting to be the first into space and number one in technological weaponry. The nation, at the height of its superpower status, fighting the Cold

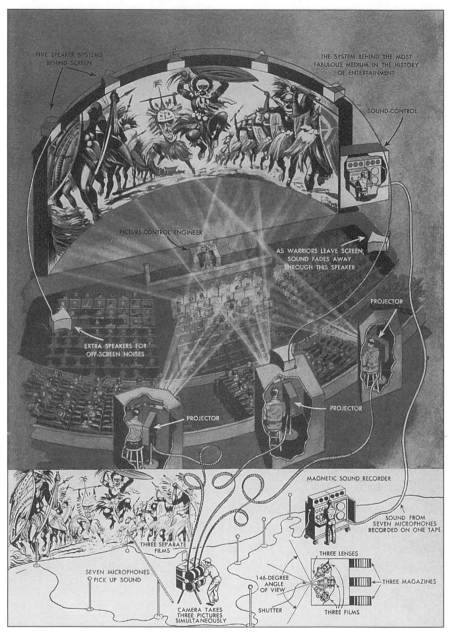

The complexity of projecting Cinerama films by synchronizing three projectors gave birth to Michael Todd's dream of "Cinerama outta one hole."

Diagram from *Cinerama South Seas Adventure* souvenir book.

Michael Todd's promotional campaign spanned the earth as well.

Photograph of promotional efforts in India.

War with nationalistic discourse and a program of science education, was understandably attracted to Verne's scientific didacticism so long as it could be suffused with Americanism.

Even if the United States was only pretending to be top dog in space, it really was dominant in the international filmmaking and distribution game.[10] The introduction of wide-screen technology was viewed as a crowning moment for Hollywood, although a hindsight perspective might not grant these large-format technologies the same revered position. And certainly, only the allure and high capital investments of Hollywood could bring together so many locations and stars within a single film. At the same time that *Around the World* was a filmic adaptation of Verne's story, it was a visual display of Hollywood's latest technological developments, its bottomless travel allowance, and its worldwide appeal that attracted actors and audiences alike. The introduction with its referencing of cinematic history and U.S. technological achievement encouraged this mode of viewing the film as a nationalistic moment to be witnessed by all in the same way that the latest shuttle launching would have been collectively witnessed. And the presence of Edward R. Murrow only enhanced the sense that something serious and newsworthy was transpiring.

—— Touristic Adventures

In both the film and the book, a group of characters sit around a table at the Reform Club and discuss how the world, as of 1872, was now accessible in ways heretofore unknown. Although the hot air balloon was one of Verne's obsessions within and outside of his literary work, it was the newly developed system of

A promotional shot features Michael Todd seen through his famous bug-eye lens.
Promotional photograph of Mike Todd with CinemaScope lenses.

railways crisscrossing the earth's continents that would make Fogg's eighty-day
adventure possible. The story of *Around the World,* set in the same year in that it
was written, mirrors the potentialities of Verne's world and the transportation
system that he witnessed sprouting up around him, from the opening of the
Suez Canal to a series of transcontinental railways. It would not be long until
someone of the nonfictional persuasion took up Verne's challenge. In fact, in 1890
Nellie Bly, a New York journalist, made headlines by circling the earth in just over
seventy-two days.

At the beginning of the film *Around the World,* Murrow brags that in the year
1956 it is now possible to circle the earth in less than forty hours. However, it was
not merely the development of commercial airlines that enabled such cross-
global adventures to be enacted by average citizens. Central to the plot of *Around
the World* is Phileas Fogg's inexhaustible supply of money and its questionable origins, money that allows Fogg to speedily navigate the earth even if it means buy-
ing a steamboat in order to command its dismemberment to feed the fire that
keeps the boat in motion. The United States in the 1950s was in a similar situation as Fogg in the 1870s. Enjoying an era of unprecedented affluence and increasing leisure time, middle-class America was in a position to travel. The end of
World War II and the U.S. role in negotiating a conclusion to these hostilities

helped propagate the appearance of a peaceful world ready to welcome U.S. tourists wherever the globe's waterways and plane routes might carry them. The economic and military dominance of the United States and the perception of the majority of the world lying in acquiescence were, in fact, not unlike the position of imperialist Britain during Fogg's day.

While the London branch of the Thomas Cook travel agency visited by the fictional Fogg was probably accustomed to a trickle of upper-class clients during Verne's day, the postwar American travel agency would have been just one piece in a firmly entrenched, far-reaching tourist industry that serviced a much larger portion of the populace. And although many people chose not to or could not afford to travel, by the date of *Around the World*'s release, tourism was recognized by all as part of the fabric of American life, as an appropriate counterpart to the hard-working lifestyle of American breadwinners and their families.

Due to tourism's establishment as part of America's leisure vocabulary and to the development of wide-screen technology, the filmic travelogue made a comeback. As in previous generations, this new stage of filmic innovation grew out of a series of special format screenings at U.S. world's fairs, events of spectacular proportion known for their highlighting of technological growth in the name of nationalism.[11] This tradition of portraying the exotic through simulated immersion continues with systems unveiled at more recent world's fairs (such as the IMAX Magic Carpet). However, in the 1950s, these special format screenings were not limited to extraordinary contexts such as world's fairs, amusement parks, and museums. With the idea that wide-screen films might replace older technologies, a number of theaters were refitted to accommodate large-format films. And to demonstrate the powerful effects of these new technologies, wide-screen travelogues were released, much in the same way that early silent cinema relied on filmed exotic environments to convey the powers of cinematic illusion to those first film audiences.

In 1952, the wide-screen process known as Cinerama made its debut with the appropriately titled film *This is Cinerama* (directed by Merian C. Cooper, Ernest B. Schoedsack, and Michael Todd Jr.), which featured a self-congratulatory introduction like the one that would begin *Around the World* four years later. The black-and-white, standard-format prologue featured newsreel commentator Lowell Thomas speaking on the development of art from cave paintings to cinema. He declared an end to artists' confinement to limited frames, and with his announcement, "This is Cinerama," the curtains opened to reveal a stretch of screen that dwarfed the former image, a literal image to accompany the claim that wide-screen technologies removed the blinders of previous film formats. The following

Widescreen technologies were marketed as experiential events rather than as mere movies.

Cover image of souvenir booklet from Japanese release of *This is Cinerama*.

cinematic whirlwind tour of the world brought together images of Old World Europe and New World natural wonders: Venetian gondolas, Scottish bagpipers, Spanish flamenco dancers, the Niagara Falls, the California coast, the fertile plains of the U.S. Midwest, Arizona's dramatic canyons, and a couple of U.S. amusement parks. The next few Cinerama films, including *Cinerama Holiday* (Robert L. Bendick and Phillipe de Lacy, 1955) and *The Seven Wonders of the World* (Tay Garnett, Paul Mantz, Andrew Marton, Ted Tezlaff, and Walter Thompson, 1956), continued the trend of travelogues presented from an American point of view delivering views of the world's best-known tourist sites. Initially, the addition of narrative was avoided, as producers opted to solely focus on what one publicist referred to

Promotional efforts around *Seven Wonders of the World* presented in miniature the diverse sights of the world, sights that could be viewed in large scale during the film itself.

Cover image of souvenir booklet for *Seven Wonders of the World.*

as Cinerama's "audience envelopment" effect,[12] or what film historian John Belton has called the "participation effect" cultivated by wide-screen roller coaster and airplane rides.[13]

Cinerama was plagued by a number of problems, including distortion within the picture, and by all of the difficulties inherent in projecting three separate images onto a single screen. When investor and collaborator Michael Todd voiced his concerns over such technical problems and was ignored by Cinerama's board of directors, he established his own company with the goal of creating a wide-screen image using a single camera. The result was the Todd-AO process, which debuted with the showcase film *Oklahoma!* (Fred Zinneman, 1955). *Around the*

World in Eighty Days was the second Todd-AO production, and the film combined two tendencies of past wide-screen productions. Like its Cinerama counterparts, *Around the World* was essentially a travelogue uniting footage shot in a number of foreign countries and the United States. With their company's first film, Todd-AO producers, however, had gone in a slightly different direction than the travelogue, recruiting songwriters Richard Rodgers and Oscar Hammerstein II even before the Todd-AO process was perfected. Such a move was in keeping with Todd's background as a Broadway producer. And although the film *Around the World* was not released as a musical in the spirit of *Oklahoma!* Todd's prior connections with the Verne material came in the form of a collaboration with Orson Welles on a Broadway musical version of the novel during the 1940s.[14] *Around the World* thus played a similar role as *A Policeman's Tour of the World,* combining documentary-style footage with narrative in a film format that previously had featured them in separate contexts only.

Whereas both *Around the World* and *This is Cinerama* situated themselves on the cutting edge of film technology, in the case of *Around the World* such emphasis on the present tense was followed by a fictional return to the year 1872. Many aspects of Verne's touristic stance, although situated within the nineteenth century, found a receptive audience among the moviegoing virtual tourists of 1956. Additionally, some deviations from the original story facilitate a fuller visualization of the exotic environment. The balloon, a virtual trademark for the film, was borrowed from another Verne title and so outraged France's Verne Society that they thoroughly objected to the film, until its international success changed their tune. Additionally, the novel begins with and remains more closely tied to the figure of Phileas Fogg than does the filmic version. Within the movie, audiences are first introduced to the character Jean Passepartout and learn of Fogg's character as Passepartout overhears a conversation about his exacting standards at the employment office. Only later and through Passepartout's perspective do viewers meet Fogg. The optical and emotional alignment with Passepartout allows for a greater view of the sights as this "gentleman's gentleman" embarks on adventures eschewed by the sedentary Fogg, an antitourist who declares his loathing of sightseeing. An alteration in Passepartout's character from its development in Verne's novel interjects another type of gaze within the film. While Verne's Passepartout yearned for a quiet life and an employer who avoided excessive alcohol and skirt chasing, the screen version of Passepartout has a lusty appreciation of everything female. Thus, the camera documenting Passepartout's misadventures and occasionally his optical point of view finds ample opportunity to fix an objectifying gaze on sexualized women purportedly of other nationalities. Passepartout's lasciviousness is treated comically within the film, but the visual depiction of women within *Around the World* is nonetheless complicit with Passepartout's project of tasting a world of diverse feminine beauty. In this way, *Around the World* is not unlike pornographic stereoviews of the 1870s or one of the first pans employed in James White's work as he nudged the camera to follow two female pedestrians. The expansion of photographic representation quickly becomes inflected with male desire as these enhanced viewing apparatuses are trained on the female figure.

One of the primary themes from Verne's work that is carried over into the film is a concern for comprehensiveness and for travel as an epistemological endeavor. Dean MacCannell has referred to tourism within a modernist age as an attempt to understand the world as a whole. And as argued in chapter 1, Martin Heidegger's concept of the "world as picture" points out the connections between this epistemological goal and the strategies for seeing and representing the world. For Verne, the globe could be seen from above and understood through travel to its core or beyond the strata of the earth's atmosphere; it could be mastered by rigorous classification and the creation of detailed taxonomies. Science, space, and time could all be controlled by the human hand and mind, and nature's chaos kept at bay.

Hetzel helped shape Verne's image as documentarian of the universe in its entirety, or as a "terrestrial and celestial surveyor."[15] The subtitle of *Voyages Extraordinaires*, "Travels in Worlds Known and Unknown," hints at this drive for comprehensive knowledge; so does Hetzel's introduction to the series in which Verne's work appeared, where Hetzel writes, "The goal of the series is, in fact, to outline all the geographical, geological, physical and astronomical knowledge amassed by modern science and to recount, in an entertaining and picturesque format that is his own, the history of the universe."[16] Verne himself once made a similar statement in an interview, noting, "It is my intention to complete, before my working days are done, a series which shall include, in story form, my whole survey of the world's surface and heavens; there are still corners of the world left which my thoughts have not penetrated."[17] Within the individual novel of *Around the World*, the drive for comprehensiveness manifests itself in the concept of circumnavigation. To girdle the earth is to grasp its wholeness, and to complete this project within a specified time allotment is to master the earth's vastness. The visual equivalent of such understandings of the globe is accomplished through the aerial perspective granted by the hot air balloon, the dominant image from the film. The airborne traveler gains a holistic perspective, a view that sees cities, land masses, and water bodies in their entirety. The movie *Around the World* grants this first-person perspective from a balloon perched high above Spain and from numerous moving ships and trains collectively encircling the earth. And even though portions of the story and of the voyage are left unrepresented by the film, it still presents the illusion of inclusiveness with its long running time and its incorporation of a slew of stars. Although by 1956, the globe had figuratively shrunk even further and the view from space brought a greater portion of the earth into view from a single perspective, apparently the theme of understanding the world as a whole had not ceased to hold appeal; the film's profits were more than healthy, as was its success, measured in terms of Academy Awards.

Both MacCannell and Heidegger argue that a placing of the self is an integral component of picturing the whole. MacCannell suggests that it is a loss in self-placement or an alienation from one's everyday conditions that drives the touristic project. Heidegger, on the other hand, is concerned with spatial position and its connection to mastery. In other words, the subject standing outside the world picture or lifted high above the world via an air balloon or space shuttle is in a commanding position by virtue of the subject's transcendence of all that is seen, by virtue of the separation of picturer from pictured, or of subject from object. Within Verne's work, man (but not woman) as an agent of invention separates the subject from the seamless envelopment of nature. Man is alone in his power to soar above nature, to harness the earth's powers rather than to solely be mastered by them. Man's inventive spirit and scientific knowledge endow him not only with the powers of movement but with the powers of precise, controlled movement. Fogg's navigation of the earth draws upon a codification of space into longitude and latitude, timetables, and time zones. He is in a state of utmost awareness of his position in space and time at any given moment, giving credence to one critic's assertion of a Vernian "narrative tic" of constant self-localization.[18] Additionally, the narrative is dependent upon the audience's continual knowledge of Fogg's location and his temporal position as those eighty days are quickly exhausted. In fact, the film's reliance on clichés and stereotypes may be in part attributed to this desire to keep the spectator oriented; bullfighters mean Fogg is in Spain, rickshaws spell the Orient, and peace-pipe-smoking Indians can only refer to the American West.

Unlike readers enjoying Verne's novel in 1872, audiences viewing the 1956 film version of *Around the World* experienced a time warp into the past. To the extent that the film could be considered a plunge into nostalgic, the introductory sequence provides a motivation for turning to a historical context to tell its pro-technology tale. In the year 1956, under the shadow of the atomic bomb and an ever-mounting stockpile of weaponry, accolades for American technological advancement could hardly be frivolously tossed around without acknowledging the more ominous side of the same coin. Indeed, this is the case in Murrow's didactic introduction to the film. In describing the "stretching fingertips of science," Murrow adds, "Man has devised a method of destroying most of humanity or of lifting it up to high plateaus of prosperity and progress never dreamed of by the boldest dreamers." A return to an age when the apocalypse was less conceivable (although not *inconceivable,* as evidenced by Verne's later writing) provides a safer context for singing the praise of human invention, speed, and scientific mastery. At the same time, the film's narrative drive and its movement toward a set of explicit goals establishes a framework for judging technology—that is, by its power to propel humans into space and around the earth at ever accelerating speeds, and affirming progress from a 1956 perspective.

Although none of Verne's fictional plots takes place in the distant past, Arthur Evans notes that over 90 percent of his stories are situated in the recent past in relation to the time of their publication.[19] Several explanations could be given for this consistency in historical setting; of these one possibility might be that this precarious positioning between past and present is the ideal context for indulging in two mutually exclusive fantasies that inhabit much of Verne's work. Within the Vernian travel story, security comes from confronting a finite and knowable world previously codified through naming and mapping processes. At the same time, Vernian heroes indulge in the fantasy of places still undiscovered. Andrew Martin points out this very tension in his elucidation of "an ambivalence that runs through all his work: the thought that there may already (or soon) be nothing left to discover or explore is scarcely less disconcerting than the prospect of an uncharted space, a gap in our knowledge of the world."[20] Fogg's peace of mind is maintained by adhering to a predetermined route, following the well-trodden path of the travelers, merchants, and railway crews who came before him. Not only is the world of Fogg's travels previously codified in map labels and cartographers' measurements, but Fogg prefers to access travel destinations indirectly or through the textual codings of maps and train schedules. In this way, through the figures of Passepartout and Fogg, the film combines delight in immersion and the tendency to experience the world through previously produced abstractions of place. Similarly, while the scientific conquering of the world is celebrated, the text also delights in stumbling upon an East Indian religious ritual witnessed by few white men or in invading Native-American territory visible on the map only as a sparsely labeled area circumscribed by European-derived civilization. Other compelling examples from *Voyages Extraordinaires,* pointed out by Martin, include a scene from *Five Weeks in a Balloon* in which one traveler comments, as they pass over the sources of the Niger River, that this would be a "wonderful opportunity to discover them, if only they hadn't already been discovered." Another traveler responds, "At a pinch, couldn't we find some new ones?"[21] Several Vernian voyages seem to be motivated by this desire to explore the unknown, or "to go where no man has gone before," as one Vernian character declares. Yet discovery often degrades into rediscovery as *The Journey to the Center of the Earth* is revealed to be a retracing of someone else's footsteps or as the island in the book *The Mysterious Island,* named on no map, turns out to house a previous explorer, an aging Captain Nemo living in a water cave deep inside the island's interior. This desire to discover unknown lands and the Verne-expressed anxiety that there may be nothing left to discover may not have dissipated into acceptance within contemporary entertainment so much as it has been further displaced into fantastical forms, from *Star Trek*'s repeated vow "to boldly go where no man has gone before" to Michael Crichton's retracing of Henry Morton Stanley's footsteps only to discover a lost city in the Congo.

—— Around the World with the BBC

In Edward R. Murrow's speech that introduces *Around the World,* he segues from Méliès's lunar adventure to a 1956 world in which "fact still lags behind fiction" as the moon remains untouched by human hand or foot. Such a statement could no longer be made in the current year, of course, but some things have remained consistent across the many decades since Verne's writing of *Around the Moon.* Scientists continue to send out extensions of themselves even farther into space, and the makers of cultural products continue to draw on Jules Verne for inspiration.

Within the past few years, I have come across several loose adaptations of Verne in nonfilmic media—the BBC TV series *Around the World in Eighty Days with Michael Palin,* Electronic Arts' educational CD-ROM Around the World in Eighty Days, Cyan's CD-ROM Myst, SouthPeak's DVD game Twenty Thousand Leagues: The Adventure Continues, and two television adaptations of *The Journey to the Center of the Earth* (1993 and 1999). In film, hardly a decade has passed without a cinematic depiction of Verne's work. With over fifty filmic adaptations, the most notable of these have included the 1916 *Twenty Thousand Leagues under the Sea,* Disney's 1954 Cinemascope adaptation of the same novel, 1961's *The Mysterious Island,* and the 1959 version of *Journey to the Center of the Earth,* followed by a campy 1989 remake. The intrigue with Verne has even extended to a 1990 Japanese television series called *Nadia: The Secret of Blue Water,* loosely based on *Twenty Thousand Leagues,* and to a 1995 *Mysterious Island* television series that aired in

Canada and New Zealand. A number of works referencing Verne's writings are particularly engaged with crossing the line that separates the facts of Verne's life from his fiction. In the game Twenty Thousand Leagues: The Adventure Continues, submarine explorers of the near future seeking out underwater food supplies happen upon Captain Nemo's *Nautilus,* thought to exist only in fiction. And the HDTV production *The Secret Adventures of Jules Verne,* which aired on the Sci-Fi Channel, is premised upon the idea that the adventures and characters Verne wrote about were real but passed off as fictional. Interestingly, while Verne is kidnapped in *The Secret Adventures,* he hooks up with a time traveler in *Mark Twain's Greatest Adventure* (Verne Nobles, 2002). And in Jeff Blyth's 1992 film *From Time to Time,* both themes are combined as the character Jules Verne is kidnapped by a time traveler.

Most likely these various productions did not invest research funds to ensure a match between their own line of thinking and Verne's political leanings and philosophical presumptions as they manifest themselves in his fiction. Had they, however, they may have discovered multiple meanings within his seemingly simple texts and enough ambivalence to support a number of diverse viewpoints. Literary critics engaged in such research have found evidence of heartily endorsed positivism as well as romanticism, didacticism but not to the exclusion of mysticism, imperialist bravura despite occasional condemnation of colonialist practice, and a firm protechnology stance as well as deep skepticism over science's destructive potential. Some of these strands faded, while others strengthened during the course of Verne's life as he became increasingly pessimistic; yet even in his earlier work an ambivalence is present that allows various interpretations of his work. Contemporary adaptations are thus able to extract different elements from this multiplicity of meanings, although faithfulness to the source does not seem to be a concern within most of the contemporary productions.

One element that does persist in some adaptations is Verne's engagement with the reality of his world despite his status as a writer of fiction. As a comparison between his own travel accounts and his fictional writing reveals, much of *Around the World* was based on Verne's own travels. Nearly all of his novels are dotted with references to historical events: the building of the Suez Canal, the assassination of Abraham Lincoln, the struggles of British imperialists within India. And his extensive technical descriptions of mechanical and chemical processes, which earned him the title of writer of not just science fiction but scientific fiction, are all based on fact. In short, Verne's fictional characters appeared to exist in the same reality as readers of that era, a reality that was insistently referenced by Verne. The filmic travel narrative (of which Todd's *Around the World* is one example), as it emerged in a classical form from the twin developments of documentary and narrative within the silent era, ideally reflects this union of documentary depiction and fiction. At the same time, it is not surprising to see *Around the World* rendered in a completely documentary form such as in the BBC series *Around the World in Eighty Days with Michael Palin.*

Whereas the 1956 film *Around the World* began with a statement of progress and a general enthusiasm over America's continued technological development, the BBC's *Eighty Days* acknowledges change while lamenting the loss of adventure in a modern world. The introductory sequence shows Palin in an airport gift shop, thumbing through a copy of Verne's *Around the World.* A voice-over recounts Palin's realization that in this day and age, adventures such as Fogg's can happen only in books. His desire to re-create the escapades of yesteryear within his own age thus motivates his decision to appear in the BBC program. For Palin, unlike Fogg, eighty days represents a leisurely schedule, and it offers him an opportunity he relishes: the chance to experience the globe's cities through more than airplane windows and hurried taxi rides. Palin speculates that eighty days is just about the amount of time required to really see, taste, and experience the world. Yet, he finds that his own time-constricted travel schedule often creates the same dilemma of superficial visits as he travels by cab trying to meet his next connection and barely glimpsing the city through the night's darkness and the fogged car window. Fogg, on the other hand, expressed no desire to see or interact with the locations through which he passed but nonetheless ended up seeing a number of sights by way of saving Passepartout from the Sioux Indians, looking for Passepartout within a troupe of Japanese acrobats, and getting entangled in an East Indian suttee ceremony.

As it turns out, eighty days still has some meaning as a duration of time for circumnavigating the earth. Palin discovers that a number of small seafaring vessels find it a challenge to complete the trip in under eighty days, and regularly compete for an "Around the World in Eighty Days" trophy. Palin's adventure is set up with certain restrictions; he may travel by land or by sea, but he may at no time make progress toward his goal by way of an airborne vessel. (He does take a hot air balloon ride, but not as a means of moving forward toward his next destination.) Like Fogg, the connections between boats and trains leave some exploration time, but missed connections threaten to sabotage his entire timetable. Thus, although at times it feels somewhat artificial, the show attempts to create a sense of urgency and suspense through Palin's adherence to his travel schedule. At one point, he nearly misses his ship, the next of which would not leave until several days later. He radios a request for the ship to wait for him, but when the request is denied, he must pull some strings and throw around of bit of BBC cash to arrange a fast boat to catch up to the already departed ship.

Palin's voyage reflects a nostalgia not only for the kind of colonial adventure that is no longer possible but for a particular type of privileged, class-inflected travel. The history of tourism has witnessed an enlargement of the tourist pool as greater numbers of people from the middle and lower middle classes have taken on the role of tourist. Although travel still demands a financial commitment, the "grand tour" is no longer reserved for the upper echelon of society. In front of the Parthenon and in the galleries of the Louvre, upper-class travelers can expect to hear their native language spoken by less prosperous backpacking college students and middle-class senior citizen tour groups. Thus, to mourn the passing of a nineteenth-century brand of travel and its replacement by something derogatively referred to as "mass tourism" is to yearn for a long-gone brand of class privilege and exclusivity in travel practices. By abandoning the most common form of long-distance travel, Palin is forced to use slower forms of travel that in many cases have been marketed to those who are financially endowed and can afford the more sluggish rate of travel in exchange for an escape from the tourist hoards and a chance to mingle with a select group of people en route. In this spirit, Palin enters the Guangzhou station and purchases his "soft class" ticket to Shanghai. His compartment is decorated with fluffy pink cushions, embroidered fabrics, lace curtains, and a reproduction oil lamp with a cut-glass shade. An army of cooks create an elaborate meal for Palin's consumption while the passengers in "intermediate class" and "hard class" coaches plunge into their bags and boxes brought from home, eating their meals in markedly more crowded conditions.

When not in transit, Palin takes up luxury accommodations reminiscent of the colonial opulence of Fogg's day. While in California, Palin stays at the Queen Mary hotel, an ocean-liner relic from another era anchored and refitted to make money in its new environment. In Hong Kong, he stays in the lap of luxury at The Peninsula, a remnant of colonialist Hong Kong. He reaches the hotel via a champagne-stocked Rolls Royce, and upon entering his hotel suite is offered yet another glass of bubbly. He quips, "Oh good. I haven't had any champagne for at least ten minutes," bringing to mind the champagne humor of the film version of *Around the World* as Passepartout scoops up a handful of snow off the Alps to chill Fogg's champagne as their balloon placidly floats between snow-covered peaks.

Within Todd's film, Fogg's exigencies force him to take alternate means of transportation that also serve to bring him into contact with the native culture, such as when a mix-up leads to a voyage aboard a red-sailed Chinese junk, or when he finds himself riding on the back of an elephant through India. Though more for the sake of variety than out of desperation, Palin also makes use of less traditional means of transportation, or those representative of a region's culture. For instance, Palin crosses part of Colorado, albeit a small part, by dogsled. A portion of his voyage takes place aboard container ships transporting cargo, but rarely passengers, across the ocean. On one occasion, he finds himself amid a Yugoslavian crew with its own ship culture, a combination of national culture and rituals developed to fight the monotony of life away from land. As this situation proves, Palin's easygoing nature and humor gains him acceptance among the most eccentric of travel companions, making him an entertaining tourist stand-in, with his combination of Passepartout's sense of adventure and Fogg's financial resources, punctiliousness, and gentlemanly ways.

From Todd's film to Palin's venture to another recent adaptation, the CD-ROM Around the World, an interesting transformation of the Passepartout character takes place. With the move from a classical fiction film to television documentary, a lack of direct acknowledgment of the audience by diegetic characters (except Murrow) gives way to direct address and recognition of the filming process.[22] Within this altered format, Palin's frequently acknowledged traveling companion is the cameraperson. The various members of the camera crew are in fact referred to by Palin as "Julian Passepartout," "Dave Passepartout," and so on. More striking is the transfiguration of Passepartout in Electronic Art's CD-ROM version. Instead of an accented manservant to provide comic relief for the audience and dedicated service for Phileas Fogg, a monkey named Sidney plays the role of Passepartout. Despite the alteration in species, the narrative role of the Passepartout figure is the same. Sidney is given language skills that do not lag far behind those of the filmic Passepartout played by the Mexican comic Cantinflas, and his acrobatic skills, curiosity and verve serve to alternately get Fogg into and out of trouble, as does his filmic counterpart.

For the most part, however, the CD-ROM's similarities to the film and the book are superficial. The concept of an around-the-world adventure is used to familiarize children with world geography and the diversity of different countries. The game is also designed as a reading tool juxtaposing written text and the spoken word in order to assist children with their language skills. "Hot words" give players the option of hearing or seeing a definition, while a "Fun Facts" option provides information about Fogg's current location. Scientific solutions such as mounting a sail on a railway car are replaced by a set of "paintbox pals" that invite children to treat the foreign environment like a canvas. Using a paintbrush, a zipper may be painted onto an Egyptian sarcophagus to supply the mummy with an escape route. The eraser can be employed to erase the villains' pants, strangely enough, or to eliminate an attacking shark's teeth.

While reading Verne's *Around the World* could convey a sense of one particular historical moment, the CD-ROM does not purport to teach any historical lessons. In fact, it employs creative temporality in the same way in that some films draw on creative geography. Playing footloose and fancy-free with history allows the CD-ROM creators to draw upon a larger reservoir of cultural stereotypes. Fogg, with his David Niven–esque appearance and nineteenth-century outfit, travels by way of a 1940s-style airplane to Zaire where he meets Dr. Livingstone, who died in 1873 when the Wright brothers were just toddlers. In Japan, a samurai barber left over from feudal Japan trims Fogg's sideburns, and in Australia, a loin-clothed aborigine asks for Fogg's help in finding an emu's stolen egg. Los Angeles appears to be historically ahead of the rest of the world as Fogg flies above the Hollywood sign and comes in for a landing in front of Universal Studios, where his studio tour turns into an audition for a part in a science fiction film.

Clearly, the lessons taught by Verne's texts and the educational content of the CD-ROM version of *Around the World* share little resemblance, unless of course, you take into account this class of software's goal of acculturating children to computer technologies. Much of Verne's early work was published in Hetzel's *Bibliothèque d'Education et de Récréation*, a positivist publication dedicated to scientific pedagogy. Arthur Evans comments on how Verne's didactic technique and his rendering of science was made palatable and easy to assimilate through a variety of techniques: technological change is combined with social stasis, transportation devices are demechanized and depicted as homes away from home, new apparatuses appear in the context of the recent past, and scientific devices are portrayed as understandable and user-friendly. Evans writes about Verne's work, "As a rule, the new is always embedded in the old, the strange is always anchored in the traditional, and the extraordinary is always firmly rooted in the ordinary."[23]

A number of software applications designed for the home similarly situate the new in terms of the old as a means of dealienating these computer tools. *Around the World*'s animated scenery viewed in the lid of a paint box and the interactive component that involves the use of simplistic items—an eraser, a pencil, a book, an hourglass—certainly constitute methods of drawing upon a child's repertoire of toys in order to familiarize this digital experience. The use of a well-known text, written in and associated with the past, further domesticates the strangeness of the computer by embedding the new in the old. It is very possible then to group some CD-ROMs and Verne's work within Lewis Mumford's category of cultural "shock absorbers."[24]

The re-creation of Captain Nemo's *Nautilus* at Tokyo's DisneySea extends Verne's original emphasis on enclosure by featuring individual sea-exploration pods as offshoots of *Nautilus,* replicated with a Vernian aesthetic of textured gadgetry.

Photograph by Marc Borrelli, www.TokyoResort.com/www.LaughingPlace.com.

—— From *Mysterious Island* to Myst

In the same way that Verne created a plush home of velvet chairs and homey wood paneling inside the dauntingly powerful vessel *Nautilus,* one could say that some CD-ROMs create an enclosed space with many of the accouterments of home encased within the high-tech shell of a computer. Yet, within that finite space of a CD-ROM's digital simulation—its limits determined by the CD-ROM's memory capacity—designers aim for the illusion of infinite richness and possibility. It is common practice among CD-ROM purchasers to seek out those limits, to explore comprehensively, to exhaust all of the possibilities. Like in global exploration, comprehensiveness is the goal in the exploration genre of computer games. Frequently, all spaces must be searched and all clues found before the game's goal can be achieved. With greater memory capabilities and improved screen resolutions, graphics are becoming more intricate and game environments more richly visual. This very tension between enclosure and detail texture is what Roland Barthes describes in relation to Verne in an essay entitled "The *Nautilus* and the

Drunken Boat." Barthes maintains that Verne is the ideal writer of children's fiction because of his consistent construction of "self-sufficient cosmogony"; he writes, "The compatibility between Verne and childhood does not stem from a banal mystique of adventure, but on the contrary from a common delight in the finite, which one also finds in children's passion for huts and tents: to enclose oneself and to settle, such is the existential dream of childhood and of Verne."[25] The environmental bubble of *Nautilus,* a self-sufficient floating home with a window on the world, is in some ways analogous to the home equipped with a television or computer. The tactile images of this cubbyhole-like space within the home is alternately a window to an exterior and another homelike space to crawl into. With HDTV and multiple CD-ROM games, the detail and complexity of such images increase and these simulated spaces become more enterable. Barthes describes a similar pursuit of richness within the enclosed spaces of Verne's work, noting, "Verne had an obsession for plenitude: he never stopped putting a last touch to the world and furnishing it, making it full with an egg-like fullness. His tendency is exactly that of an eighteenth-century encyclopaedist or of a Dutch painter: the world is finite, the world is full of numerable and contiguous objects."[26]

Two metaphors of enclosure have been identified within *Voyages Extraordinaires*: circularity and the island. The Vernian narrative is often predictable, with its route mapped out in the novel's title. Geographical journeys, the current within electrical circuit, and the diegetic state of affairs all come full circle within Verne's worlds. Within forty-two of Verne's sixty-three novels, one or more integral scenes take place on an island. In a story such as *The Mysterious Island,* a self-sufficient microcosm blossoms within the clearly demarcated contours of the island. And in a layering of enclosed spaces, Captain Nemo lives inside *Nautilus,* inside a cave that is entirely contained beneath the island's surface.[27]

Many of the recent digital-based adaptations of Verne's work mirror this same dialectic of enclosed, detailed space and exploration. *The Secret Adventures of Jules Verne,* produced by Voodoo HD, a Montreal-based visual effects studio, was shot in Sony's digital high-definition format, and for HDTV-equipped audiences, provides a television image full of rich detail, clarity, and spectacular special effects. The game Twenty Thousand Leagues: The Adventure Continues also promises immersion with continuous movement along a 360-degree field of vision, as provided by SouthPeak Interactive's Video Reality format, which breaks away from the convention of either a select set of angles of view or multi-directional vision only at predefined spots. Promotional materials boast of "the richest, most detailed environments anyone has ever played in a computer game,"

James Bond–type intrigue, and "wild places in uncharted territories," including the lost city of Atlantis, tropical destinations, Antarctica, and the Bermuda Triangle. In both adaptations, considerable time has been spent on the Vernian travel vehicles, which serve as homes away from home for the characters. Like the three-dimensional, interactive walk-through of the Disney version of *Twenty Thousand Leagues* currently being built on the web and billed as "an experience like no other," The Adventure Continues features a *Nautilus* built to Verne's exact specifications. In *Secret Adventures,* it is the hot air balloon used by Fogg, Verne, and Passepartout that steals the show, with its photorealistic appearance and its uncanny combination of skis, tail fins, the base of a houseboat, and side-riding rockets.

While success for either the makers of *The Secret Adventures of Jules Verne* or of Twenty Thousand Leagues: The Adventure Continues has still not been solidly secured, Myst, inspired by Verne's *The Mysterious Island,* has received the title of the best-selling CD-ROM to date. Myst's success has largely been due to its visual plenitude in the creation of an abandoned island environment. Called stunningly beautiful by reviewers, Myst uses detailed, often surrealistic environments that players can explore by clicking a mouse. Although the island has its high-tech touches including a generator, a missile, and a time machine, its overall look is more reminiscent of Verne's era. Marble, rivets, columns, aged books, wood panels, stone towers, and metal gears amid a forested island speak of the mechanical age. The only reference to the digital, other than the CD-ROM itself, is a video clip that plays with varying degrees of image disintegration through which the nature of the medium is clearly displayed.

The characters of *Mysterious Island* are castaways on what looks to be a deserted island but which, in fact, is inhabited by a more technologically sophisticated predecessor. Players of Myst similarly feel like castaways trapped on an island; however, signs of previous inhabitation are clearly evident upon arrival. The technical apparatuses scattered across the island, thanks to some unknown group of earlier inhabitants, are beyond the immediate understanding of the castaway players. In a Vernian text, these machines would require scientific explanation but within Myst this explanatory mode is conflated with another Vernian device—the cryptogram. The actual mechanics of the island's machinery are fairly simple, but the operation of such devices requires decoding; the right sequence of actions must be hit upon before the bridge raises, the door opens, or the electrical power switches on. There is a certain delight in the operation of such machinery and in the smooth clicking of gears engaging within this nostalgic, mechanical world.

It would not be fair to overemphasize the similarities of *Myst*'s mysterious island and Verne's *Mysterious Island* for the former is characterized by an atmosphere unlike any textually communicated by Verne. Exploring Myst's island, one has a sense of occupying a post-apocalyptic space. Instead of a verdant, untouched island, the Myst player enters a landscape of messages and machines, evidence of a way of life mysteriously suspended. Thus, while the central mystery of Verne's book is the identity of the person or people who saved the island colonists' lives on multiple occasions, the question behind Myst concerns the very absence of people on the island and the possible existence of some force of destruction. If Myst can indeed be compared to a postapocalyptic environment, then the player could be likened to an investigator remotely accessing the site, carefully proceeding, gingerly laying hands on certain objects through the dismembered hand icon, as if fear of contamination keeps the player from interacting with her or his entire body. As the search for survivors continues, the player becomes acclimated; the environment becomes less strange, and the limited tools of interaction, like the bulkiness of a toxic clean-up suit, become more bearable.

Today, in an age that postmodernists are eager to label as postapocalyptic, armageddons, or at least technologically induced armageddons, are perhaps more conceivable than formerly. However, Verne as scientific prophesizer embraced this possibility in his fictions. The idea of overheating, combustion, and total destruction inhabits a number of his works, although this vein of fatalism intensifies in his later work. (Verne was a prolific writer for almost half a century, but the most heavily adapted works were written in the first ten years of his publishing career.) Individual devices may be subject to overloading, such as *Robur the Conqueror*'s electrical flying machine that suffers an explosive death in an electrical storm. *Mysterious Island*'s narrative traces the development of Lincoln Island as a rich world unto its own until volcanic pressure builds to an uncontainable level. The entire island is demolished in an instant, bringing the characters full circle, floating back to the country they left years ago. In most Vernian texts, the miniapocalypse is an end in itself and serves to return things to the status quo. The short story "Eternal Adam," written during Verne's final years and published posthumously in 1910, however, is unlike his other fictions. The apocalypse is more total and is situated in the past as the story is told from the the future. Forces of destruction do not end the narrative; instead, apocalypse is revealed to be a serial and cyclical process. To the extent that the apocalypse returns the state of affairs to a status quo, that status quo is a state of human primitivism. Science and technology then prevail, repeatedly destroying everything but an island located at the exact geographical position of Atlantis.

It is suspected that "Eternal Adam" was written or partially rewritten by Verne's son, producing an entanglement of father/son authorship issues. In Myst as well, the external conditions of the game's creation and the buried narrative of the island's creation produce a confusion of fathers and sons and a continual rewriting of creationism. Myst's creators Robyn and Rand Miller, who are introduced on the CD-ROM's "The Making of . . ." creationist tale, are the sons of a traveling Bible salesman. The book, a constant theme in Myst and in Verne's work (both of which grant a central place for the library within their diegetic spaces) thus takes on various meanings. Like Michel Verne, the Miller brothers rewrite the work of the so-called father of science fiction. And in the brothers' acts of digital creationism, they rewrite the book of their religious father, the book of the Father. Their digitally rendered images are utilized within the game, popping up whenever the proper book is opened. In this way, they play the narrative role of the two sons of a lost father (who, incidentally, is looking for a lost book), the two Adams of a father who essentially created the island's microcosm and its mechanical life. It appears that in a world in which the union of a zero and a one can beget Myst the game and its digital empire, and electricity and steel can give birth to Myst the island, only fathers and Adams are required. As in the case of Verne's self-enclosed island with Nemo at its core playing God with the male colonists, self-sufficiency within the contained cosmos of Myst is achieved without Eve. Noah's wife has been lost in the rewriting of the apocalypse; and yet, digital life goes on.

—— The Adventure Continues?

At the heart of Verne's work is a commitment to a home base replete with detailed craftsmanship and wondrous, user-friendly technologies that allow this dream motor home to be set into motion in order to witness the rich texture and exotic details of a world only recently discovered and not yet spoiled. Each generation of new immersive media technologies—Méliès's optical effects within an adolescent filmic medium, *Around the World*'s Todd-AO format, CinemaScope as witnessed in Disney's *Twenty Thousand Leagues,* HDTV, SouthPeak Interactive's Video Reality, even the 1958 "Mystimation" visual effects of the Czech film *The Fabulous World of Jules Verne* and the Twenty Thousand Leagues under the Sea set of viewmaster slides released in 1957—have been employed in an attempt to recapture Verne's exuberant desire for pleasurable, eye-opening experience in a scientifically tamable world. The success of some of these attempts has been undeniable, and the nostalgic aesthetic implied by the use of Vernian levers, cherrywood surfaces, and metal gears has in many cases helped audiences to acculturate to a new home technology such as the computer. Yet the fecundity of this approach may be dwindling. The Canadian premiere of *The Secret Adventures* in June of 2000 was barely a blip on the press' radar screen in comparison to the hype given the project in 1999 while the show was still in production. In the United States, the series began uneventfully amid a media blitz concerning the torrent of new reality shows filling the airwaves. In the case of The Adventure Continues, the game's release date of fall 1998 was pushed back to fall 1999, and then three months before the arrival of the game's advertised release date of May 2000, SouthPeak Interactive mysteriously declared that the game would not be released and that no more games with the Video Reality format would be produced by the company. Clearly, the wish to re-create a Vernian world of adventure propelled by fantasy apparatuses and delivering exotic detail is still intact; the litany of Verne adaptations within even the past ten years bear witness to this fact. However, the lukewarm reception to these most recent adaptations suggests that these travel tropes and myths of adventure have just recently begun to strain under the pressure of promises to deliver ever more spectacular and immersive incarnations of Verne's world. The overuse of the nostalgic aesthetic reminds audiences of the undeniable past tense of Verne-influenced adventures, despite attempts to "kick it straight into the twenty-first century," to use the words of the producer of The Adventure Continues. While the magnifying glasses, wood paneling, brass bolts, and hand-drawn maps of Verne's world still have considerable visual appeal, they no longer resonate in an era of real-time vision technologies, global positioning devices, and advanced satellite communication. In an age in which claims to new discoveries and untouched corners of the world are increasingly hard to believe, authors and media producers have explored avenues other than adaptation in hopes of delivering those elements of Verne's work that still hold considerable appeal while wrapping them in new packaging. The model of adaptation, while providing a once predictable route to tapping into the excitement of Verne's exploration novels, has cramped the acknowledgment of altered world politics, the integration of new modes of viewing the world, and the elaborate workarounds to postmodern skepticism that recent travel texts have developed.

Interestingly, the one context in which Vernian adaptation still seems to hold considerable promise is within the world of Japanese tourism, with its particularly postmodern flair. While Disney World's Twenty Thousand Leagues under the Sea submarine ride quietly closed in 1994, Tokyo's DisneySea Park, with its reincarnation of the same ride and its various other Verne-inspired attractions, opened on September 4, 2001, with much fanfare. While the centrality of Mysterious Island as a park landmark and the scale of the two Verne-themed rides make

Seven years after the closing of Disney World's submarine ride, the Twenty Thousand Leagues under the Sea ride has been recreated and improved upon at Tokyo's DisneySea Park, which also features Captain Nemo's base as a centerpiece.

Photograph by Marc Borrelli, www.TokyoResort.com/www.LaughingPlace.com.

Jules Verne the park's dominant motif, other attractions include the Indiana Jones Adventure ride; a ride based on the Disney film *The Little Mermaid* (Ron Clements and John Musker, 1989); a ride that re-creates the Amazon River in the 1930s; an attraction featuring Sinbad's seven voyages; an Aladdin ride; and a *One Thousand and One Arabian Nights*–themed attraction.

Looking at the experiential rhetoric surrounding wide-screen technologies, the amusement park ride is the next logical extension of the quest for simulated immersion. For instance, in 1986, Showscan Entertainment, advertising "Don't watch movies. Experience them," combined its 70-millimeter image running at 60 frames per second (technology created by Douglas Trumbull in the late 1970s) with motion seating technology to create what it called the first simulator ride, although that claim could be debated. Showscan publicity materials boast, "Picture quality is so sharp and clear and 'real' that the sensation is almost like 3-D in reverse. Instead of popping out of the screen at you, the amazing depth pulls you in and you literally become an invisible spectator standing in the middle of each film scene."

The industry has come full circle, returning to the paradigm of George C. Hale's tours by combining film technologies with simulated vehicle motion. The roller coaster ride depicted within *This is Cinerama* has extended beyond the frame to become the experience itself, whether or not it uses film technology as some part of the simulation or borrows its exotic themes from film, such as the Indiana Jones Adventure ride. Yet, the Japanese context of the new Verne rides at DisneySea demands a closer look. Rather than coming full circle to return to the same place, as in one of Verne's novels emphasizing circularity, Japan's tourist attractions, including DisneySea and Awaji World Park's re-creation of the world in miniature from New York City to London's Buckingham Palace point to a certain exuberance in artifice that is not unknown in the United States but seems to reach a new high within Japan. Not only does this represent a new brand of tourism in its radical dismissal of the quest for authenticity, but the gaze has reversed, with the East not only turning its sightseeing eye toward the West but re-creating the West in 1:25 scale within its own borders.

CHAPTER SIX

Snapshots of Greece

NEVER ON SUNDAY
AND THE POLITICS
OF TOURISTIC NARRATIVE

WARM TRAVEL DESTINATIONS have a special place in the tourist's imagination. While some tourist spots seem to require only the surface involvement of a detached gaze accompanied by occasional intellectual contemplation, to head south (for those of us in the Northern Hemisphere) is to seemingly abandon the globe's areas of civilization and rationality in search of the sultry zones that linger around the earth's equator. Lounging in the sun of such locales, the tourist experiences an awareness of the body that becomes heavy in the heat and is revived by the ocean's waters. The physical boundaries of self are highlighted by the warmth of the sun on the skin, and these same boundaries of interior and exterior are penetrated with the intake of exotic food and drink. This comingling of self and foreign within the body's interior is taken to another level in what is considered the traveler's ultimate crossing of borders—having sex with an indigene. Such licentiousness appears to match or perhaps even be a direct product of the landscape, with its warmth, beauty, and fertility that requires little clothing and keeps the body in an unguarded state and the mind in abeyance beyond a sort of general aesthetic appreciation of the sensuous colors, sounds, and bodies that surround the tourist.

Within this tourist myth, travel to less developed nations with warm climates is thus envisioned as a heightened corporeal experience that takes place in an imagined geography that reproduces the globe as body. Of course, this metaphor only stretches so far, with tourists departing from the cranium and armpits of the Northern Hemisphere and seeking out the equator's "Torrid Zone." Referring to more than just a geographic area, the term *Torrid Zone,* borrowed from a 1941 description of Carmen Miranda, contemplated the area between Miranda's seventh rib and her waistline, a zone consistently left bare by her costumes.[1] In this context, the corporeal geography is also a gendered geography. This familiar metaphor of land as feminine body has been called into use particularly in reference to colonized nations or countries less industrialized than the United States. In keeping with the metaphor, the charting and exploring of such lands by armies, colonizers, adventurers, or tourists is compared to sexual intercourse, or in a less positive light, rape.

This chapter explores filmic narratives tracing the tourist's trek to the warm climate of Greece, a location that defies simple dichotomies of East versus West or "first world" versus "third world." As a country stuck between East and West, considered part of the first world despite its relatively recent emergence from the control of empire builders, and regarded as a rural, less industrialized nation at the same time that it once was the site of a civilization highly developed for its time, Greece confounds basic categories. However, within tourist narratives, the Mediterranean nation is depicted as feminized by stunted industrial development, a factor that has produced the happy side effect of preserving the country's natural beauty. Within travel films shot on location in Greece, the Hellenic woman, as a symbol of the nation's physical beauty, becomes a standard part of the tourist's corporeal rite of passage marked by ludic sexual amusement. The films discussed in this chapter demonstrate these gendered inflections of the tourist gaze, within which the prototypical tourist is often figured as male and the sights are marked by sexualized feminine beauty. This focus on Greece, in light of international events of the past decades, allows for an analysis of how the local politics of the tourist encounter have repercussions at the level of global politics. Specifically, this case study illuminates how a widely shared touristic vision of Greek history can conflict with Greece's own construction of a narrative of nation and with its political goals as a member of the present tense of international politics.

—— Facial Politics

In the film *Mediterraneo* (Gabriele Salvatores, 1991) a group of Italian soldiers are stranded on a Greek island during World War II. With the island's native male population engaged in war duty elsewhere, a Greek Orthodox priest, as a last resort, invites one of the Italians to restore the fading murals of the local church. When the job is complete, a slow pan across the church walls reveals that where the faces of Greek saints and historical figures once existed, now the likenesses of the Italian artist and his military buddies stare out at the congregation.

Within the film, this defacement—or perhaps *re*facement—of the church iconography is presented as a comic moment. Yet for Greece this scene has a certain resonance, a historical parallel that drains the filmic moment of its humor. A significant part of Greece's history as a civilization is physically rooted in the land east of the Aegean Sea, land now occupied by the nation of Turkey. Through the course of various hostilities and territorial disputes between the two countries, Turkey has often attempted to erase Greece's historical ties to the monuments and relics that stand on these eastern lands. For instance, where Greek Orthodox churches on Turkish land have not been destroyed, the Turkish have systematically chipped off portions of the frescos, leaving white plaster in place of the faces of Greek religious figures.

On the western front, another type of effacement has occurred. Due in part to its poor economic status within Europe, Greece's artistic and political communities often have failed to find strong voices outside its own national boundaries. As a result, spokespeople of various other nationalities have carried images and news of Greece to the international forum. Many of these modern Lord Byrons, so to speak, have been concerned with preserving their own cultural heritage rooted in ancient Greece. Yet, in many cases, the end result has been a cultural effacement of modern Greece, a representation of Greece painted by non-Greek hands.

Many representations of Greece are those circulated by a worldwide network of travelers and tourist industries that serve to popularize a particular image of the nation as the picture-perfect vacation destination. In his book *Balkan Ghosts*, Robert Kaplan has traced the history of this tourist myth back to the literature of Henry Miller and Lawrence Durrell and through the release of two popular films, *Never on Sunday* (Jules Dassin, 1962) and *Zorba the Greek* (Michael Cacoyannis, 1964).[2] These films helped propagate an image of Greece as a place of titillating contradictions, with its reassuring familiarity and exciting exoticism. For Kaplan, volatile political events may be significant in deterring tourists and tarnishing the tourist myth, but he does not investigate the idea that a nation's public image, seen through a tourist gaze, could have repercussions on international politics by promoting the illusion of a touristic locale existing in a different era or perhaps in a timeless pocket of the world. In Greece's case, the tourist gaze not only erases a political present tense but popularizes a view of history that differs from the historical narrative of nation that inhabitants of Greece have tried to promote. During a period in which the meanings of history continue to be debated among Balkan nations and in which Greece struggles to be heard within the shouting match of international politics, the implications of envisioning Greece through a tourist's gaze are particularly pertinent.[3]

Zorba the Greek is both a character study of the stormy contradictions that constitute one man's personality and a tale of the transformation of a straight-laced visitor.

Still from *Zorba, the Greek*, a Michael Cacoyannis production.

—— Narratives of Nation

Current literature suggests that nations should be viewed as "imagined communities" and national identity as process, as a construction that is constantly in flux and readjusted to meet certain political and economic needs.[4] In a narrative of nation, Greece's grandiose history certainly plays a significant role, but not always the same role it plays for the rest of the West. In fact, images of Greece—those that promote visiting history as a motivation for travel, those used by other nations in sketching out their own historical past, and those constructed by Greece itself in a discourse of nation—sometimes overlap and complement one another, while at other times they collide with one other in a contest over whose constructed historical narrative will prevail.

For most of the Western world, ancient Greece is a simple matter of shared heritage—a golden moment in Europe's collective past that provides a convenient historical justification for the constructs "Europe" and "Western." In fact, various Western nations' interests in preserving Greece's classical treasures have often overshadowed Greece's own relationship to its past. For Hellenes, the supposed descendants of the long-lost race of ancient Greeks, the legacy of classical Greece serves a complex function. Greece's insistence on continuity between its ancient ancestors and its modern citizens warrants the nation's membership in the elite European clique at the same time that it provides a means of defining cultural specificity apart from the rest of Europe.[5] More important, this tie to the classical past has served as a raison d'être for the nation-state, dating back to its use as the theoretical justification for breaking free from Ottoman rule.[6]

Today, links with the past continue to take on political implications, thus carrying struggles over national identity into the realm of semantics, symbols, and artifacts. In one such example from the early 1980s, Melina Mercouri, acting as Greece's minister of culture, attempted to return to Greece the statues originally housed in the Parthenon. The British Museum, however, responded by insisting that with the passage of time the Greek works of art had become more a part of Britain's cultural heritage than that of Greece. Appointed as minister of culture again in 1993 (for a term she would not live to complete), Mercouri renewed her campaign to claim the Acropolis artifacts, only to be met with the same response from Britain.

The past decade has witnessed another example of what Greeks consider the stealing of heritage: a formerly Yugoslavian population has chosen to call their republic Macedonia, a historically significant name used by Greeks for centuries to describe their northern region. From the Greek perspective, it is as if the Hellenic symbol of Alexander the Great of Macedonia were being repainted, obscuring his Greek identity in favor of a new Slavic face.[7] In their protests, Greeks displayed the symbol that once signified the Macedonian Dynasty of Alexander and his father, Phillip II, and that has since become a symbol of Greek pride—the Star of Vergina. During the summer of 1992, the Slavic republic in question adopted that very symbol for their national flag.[8]

As the Macedonian controversy quietly drags on, with Greek officials only gradually reopening their northern borders (which had been shut down in protest), the nation of Greece exemplifies the need to understand the political implications of national culture and internationally circulated images. Caught between the East and the West and its own past and present, Greece undoubtedly presents a unique case study made more challenging by our own national perspective. To Americans, a people prone to defining themselves primarily according to their modernity and assumed superpower status rather than in terms borrowed from their relatively short history, the Greek dilemma may be perplexing. This gap in understanding is widened by the very paucity of Greek voices reaching across the Atlantic Ocean.

The Star of Vergina, once used as a symbol of Greek pride, has been appropriated by the nation now called Macedonia, a name also claimed by northern Greeks.

Star of Vergina decorating Alexander the Great's tomb.

—— Envisioning Greece: Views From Across the Ocean

On a superficial level, American exposure to Greece may seem quite prevalent and diverse. Few people do not have some knowledge of classical scholarship, drama, and mythology. Many middle-class Americans have made the recreational trek to Santorini or Mikonos or at least know someone who has. Regardless, one need not have left American soil to have tasted baklava or glimpsed the brilliant blue and white images of the Greek isles that have become a staple of our visual vocabulary. Yet our vision of Greece rarely extends beyond romantic envisionings of "fair Greece, sad relic," or the tourist's gaze with its limited field of view. Nowhere is this more true than in the images of Greece that have reached American eyes via the cinema. The collection of films made in the past forty years using Greece as a backdrop make evident the clichés and stereotypes that have precluded a clear-eyed view of Greece. Within this collection, one film, Dassin's *Never on Sunday* (1962), breaks away from the pack to look steadily at Greece in a self-critique of the tourist-in-Greece theme, a first step toward a more incisive understanding of

Greece's cultural and political situation. Yet first we must examine this larger group of films, keeping a particular scene from Clare Peploe's *High Season* (1987) in mind. In this scene, a critic examines an American artist's photos from Greece published under the title *The Light of Greece*. He questions her romanticized vision, which neatly excludes modern Greece, asking, "Where is the light of Greece? This is the light of Kodak." In other words, we must approach these films with similar skepticism, asking about whose images they are, and who is being represented.

In answer to the first question, a surprisingly small number of these popular images of Greece can in fact claim Greek authorship. Perhaps the two Greek directors best known outside of Greece are Constantin Costa-Gavras and Theodoros Angelopoulos. Costa-Gavras has spent the majority of his life as a Greek exile, obtaining French citizenship in 1956. Only one of his films concerns Greece, and none of them uses his native language. Although Costa-Gavras has always acknowledged his Greco-Russian background, he has never been particularly concerned with tropes of "Greekness." While the narrative of his film *Z* (1969) ostensibly takes place in Greece (although filmed in Paris and Algeria), its depiction is most remarkable in its similarity to his other films that document hypocrisies of government in various nations, including the Czech Republic and Uruguay. In other words, instead of exploring national specificity, Costa-Gavras plucks out stories of misused power from international headlines in order to draw parallels across national boundaries. In fact, when *Z* was released, very few critics commented on the film's portrait of Greece, choosing instead to explore the similarities between the murder of Grigoris Lambrakis in 1963 as unraveled by *Z*, and two other crimes—the murder of Medhi Ben Barka in Paris in 1965 and the assassination of John F. Kennedy in Dallas in 1963.

While Costa-Gavras is better described as an international citizen and a humanist than as a nationalist or a philhellene, Theodoros Angelopoulos's work illustrates the director's concern with his identity as Greek. To date, each of his films has centered on Greek historical themes or issues concerning Greece as a modern state. Unfortunately, his films have not had a wide theatrical release in the United States, despite the recognition of Angelopoulos's work as a major component of a "new wave" in Greek cinema. In fact, if asked to name a Greek director, surely few American could respond with Angelopoulos's name, much less spell it correctly. A more likely response might be Michael Cacoyannis, the not Greek but Cypriot director made known in the United States by the popular film *Zorba the Greek*. To this day, *Zorba* remains one of the most widely known portraits of Greece, but sadly is not significantly differentiable from the "vacation" images of Greece popularized by Italian, British, and U.S. directors.

All in all, few widely disseminated films by Greek directors challenge the predominant image of Greece that has been popularized by travelogues, tourist
brochures, and the vacation film. Focusing on the latter of these three, one broad
plotline seems to describe the majority of films in this category: A visitor or group
of visitors arrives in Greece; during the stay, they are infected by the uninhibited
spirit of this so-called pagan land, and by the time of their departure, these vacationers have unearthed a part of themselves, an ability to enjoy life, that had been
otherwise buried in their rat-race lives outside of Greece. The most recently
released film adhering to this narrative pattern is the previously mentioned Italian film *Mediterraneo*. After being stranded on a Greek island, a group of World
War II Italian soldiers abandon their militaristic ways to sun themselves, drink
ouzo, and learn to dance the *zeibekikos*. In *Shirley Valentine* (Lewis Gilbert, 1989),
an unhappily married British housewife on vacation in Greece relocates the rebel-
lious and sensual young woman she once was before her marriage. In *Summer
Lovers* (Randall Kleiser, 1982), a repressed American woman vacationing with her
boyfriend discovers new potential in the relationship and in herself as they welcome a third person into their bed. Similarly, in *Zorba* a bland visitor learns from
his Greek laborer how to feel passion and loss and how to abandon these emotions in the fury of Greek dance.

Not known as one of Daryl Hannah's or Peter Gallagher's best films, *Summer Lovers* is a island
romp among three lovers supposedly influenced by the Dionysian spirit of Greece.

Promotional photograph for *Summer Lovers*, Filmways Pictures, 1982. Photo by Roger Jans.

The common denominator in all of these films is, of course, sex. Something about the air, the sun, or the sea makes these people want to take off their clothes and frolic in the sand. Nearly every one of these films contains the token nude bathing and lovemaking scene set against a luscious Greek backdrop, with the exception of *Summer Lovers* which contains little besides such scenes. It is easy to see how such films have popularized the portrait of Greece as the world's headquarters for skinnydipping and general sexual abandon. And Greeks, with their pride in the land and a belief in certain freedoms permitted by their relaxed culture, might be the last to deny the veracity of this stereotype. Furthermore, as one of the poorest countries in the European Union, they can hardly afford to contradict the image that keeps tourist money pouring in.

Many of these films push Greek characters to the margins of the script by tightening their focus on the internal change and growth of the vacationing visitors. *Mediterraneo*'s treatment of the indigenous people is somewhat typical. In the initial scenes, a strong Greek presence is implied as the Italian soldiers encounter the words "Greece is the tomb of Italians" scrawled on a whitewashed wall. Yet, within the narrative, this threat is quickly forgotten and any acknowledgment of Greece's political role in the war and its early defeat of Italian invaders is submerged by the Greek women's eager embrace of their Italian foes. And even these few horizontal appearances by Greeks play a small narrative role as the film concentrates on the shifting homosocial relationships between soldiers.

—— Products of the Land: *Kamakis* and Sirens

A few films do feature Greeks as primary characters, *Zorba the Greek* and *Tempest* (Paul Mazursky, 1982) being two examples. The well-known character of Alexis Zorba, played by Anthony Quinn (an actor of Mexican descent) has helped propagate the stereotype of the boisterously libidinous Greek male. Despite his volatile nature and skirt-chasing misogynism, Zorba is basically an affable worker who teaches his stuffy British boss how to laugh at life's misfortunes. The character Kalibanos in *Tempest* brings a less likable version of Zorba's simplemindedness and feverish temperament and a less imaginative rendition of Shakespeare's idincarnate, Caliban. Played by the Puerto Rican Raul Julia, Kalibanos is the hermit-king of a remote island that he shares with his animals until a Greek-American architect arrives. Dressed up as a doorman, Kalibanos welcomes the foreigner and quickly falls into a servile role reminiscent of Zorba's obsequiousness. He abandons a romance in progress with one of his goats to chase the architect's young daughter, attempting to impress her with his English language skills: "Double your pleasure, double your fun." Undoubtedly, few characters could be less flattering as a supposed representative of Greek men.

A variation of the Zorba/Kalibanos character frequently seen inhabiting the sidelines of the vacation film is the *kamaki*. Known to Greeks as a self-declared stud who tries to prove his masculinity by "picking up" on tourists, the kamaki exhibits his expertise in both *Summer Lovers* and *Shirley Valentine*. In the former, the teenage kamaki who fails at his attempt to seduce Daryl Hannah's character later emerges triumphant from the bedroom of a dowdy middle-aged tourist. In *Shirley Valentine*, a part-time tour guide/full-time kamaki endears himself to un-suspecting vacationers with his affected broken English. If the kamaki's running tally of one-night stands is an act of resistance against the tourism that engulfs his homeland, it is not apparent in these texts, which depict him as infantile and degraded. In these filmmakers' hands, the kamaki becomes just one more para-site of the tourist industry, joined by the kind-hearted Greek prostitute (*Mediter-raneo*) and the laughable Greek entrepreneur who sells out his heritage to erect a monument to the Unknown Tourist (*High Season*). With Greeks depicted in this manner and the only supposed experts on the indigenous culture being French archeologists (*Summer Lovers*) and American art collectors (*High Season*), it seems that Lord Elgin's stereotype of the Greeks' "uncultivated hands and indifferent minds" has come to life on screen.[9]

Despite the presence of these male characters, the prototypical Greek inhab-itant portrayed in these films is often the captivating Hellenic woman. In fact, in films and tourist guides, the beauty of the Greek women sometimes seems to merge with the beauty of the Mediterranean landscape. Thus, within the vacation narrative, it matters little whether the taste of the lotus or the song of the sirens is responsible for the tourist's love affair with Greece. This apparent interchange-ability of the women and the land allows us to see the feminine as a metaphor for Greece as positioned by these texts. Like an exotic woman, the Greece depicted on screen, with its undulating coastlines and inviting vistas, draws sailors and tourists to its shores. But similar to the prostitute in *Mediterraneo*, Greece's eco-nomic reality as an underdeveloped nation forces the country to depend on its physical beauty and a reputation of hospitality to attract these prosperous visitors and their foreign coins.

The importance of the Hellenic landscape, however, appears to extend even beyond its ability to attract foreign sunbathers and swimmers. Like the onscreen Helens of these vacation films, Greece's supposed essential qualities seem to be summarized by and inescapably rooted in its beauty and physicality. In other words, within internationally circulated stereotypes, meanings assigned to Greece and its people appear to be determined by the physical nature of its land. For instance, if Greece lacks the industrial developments of northern Europe, then perhaps the warmth of the Greek sun is to blame for the languid spirit that is believed by some to be the national character. If Greeks are frequently depicted as unrepressed, carefree, and even infantile, one can point to the womblike comfort of the Greek climate as a probable cause for this "Zorba syndrome." One is reminded of Lawrence Durrell's theory on "spirit of place" that reduces national character to a function of the land: "[T]he important determinant of any culture is after all—the spirit of place [that] will express itself through the human being just as it does through its wild flowers."[10]

This same type of logic characterizes many descriptions of ancient Greece. Tourism advertisements, for example, announce that Greece was "chosen by the Gods" for its "azure seas and majestic mountain peaks." Similarly, the Greek National Tourist Organization attributes the achievements of ancient Greece to the environment, claiming that "the landscape, the sea, the mountains and the light . . . . These are what prompted the first artisan to fashion a small clay statuette that differed from those made by the others before him; these are what inspired the first poet to forge verses in order to sing of beauty and love, of life and death."[11] Although the landscape may have contributed in some way to the apotheosis of philosophy, literature, and art achieved by classical civilization, it seems that the factor being effaced by such descriptions are the very people who authored the gods and built the civilization of ancient Greece. Uncoincidentally, it is this same pattern—the reduction of Greece to catalytic scenery and an accompanying obscurement of the Greek people—that characterizes filmic depictions of modern Greece. In these contemporary portrayals, however, the landscape casts its spell on foreigners not Greeks, and instead of inspiring poetry and democracy, the island vacation induces the inverse: a return to nature and raw sexuality.

Within these films, a visual emphasis on the landscape reinforces the narrative role of locale at the same time that it positions spectators as tourists drinking in the picturesque beauty of such a locale. The exotic culture becomes a postcard/object viewed by the subject/sightseer, and the person situated within that landscape is reduced to ornament. As James Buzard acknowledges, the trope of picturesqueness denies a notion of a culture as an ongoing way of life with its own historical placement and contemporary political realities and instead positions this culture as a timeless, consumable object.[12] Certainly, the Greece we see in these films is a picturesque one that focuses on timeless, unspoiled landscapes and interprets compromised industrialization as quaintness.

—— The Cross-National Voices of *Never on Sunday*

To this point, we have recognized the homogeneity of Greek images reaching American shores. However, one glaring omission in this rough inventory of films should be corrected. Absent from the list is a film that may have been the inspiration for the series of Greek vacation films produced in its wake. In 1962, the American-born Jules Dassin wrote and filmed *Pote tin Kyriaki* as an exile in Greece after being blacklisted in Hollywood. Due in part to Dassin's previous acclaim and to Melina Mercouri's successful American debut with the import of Cacoyannis's *Stella* (1954), Dassin was able to get funding from United Artists in order to hire a Greek film crew and start filming in the port of Piraeus. Since the plot concerned a bumbling American tourist played by Dassin (scarce funding prohibited the casting of his first choice, Henry Fonda), more than half of the dialogue was in English, with the remaining portion in Greek.

On first glance, *Pote tin Kyriaki* fits in quite well with the previously outlined pattern. As the starring actress describes, the project appeared to get studio approval based primarily on one scene:

> "Do you know at least how the story begins?"
> Julie (Jules Dassin) had an inspiration. He plucked it out of the air. "Men are working on the docks of Piraeus. A girl comes running down a pier. She undresses as she goes. Stark naked, she dives into the water. In a matter of seconds every man on the dock leaps into the water to join her."
> Smajda (of United Artists) said: "I love it."
> A few hours later, I received a telegram in Athens. "God bless Smadja. Clear the decks. We've got to be shooting in a month." [13]

So at the film's premier at Cannes, Mercouri made her splash running down the pier and taking the plunge into the cold waters of Piraeus, wearing only a black bra and underwear. Released in the United States as *Never on Sunday*, the film became instantly popular. Mercouri became known internationally, the film was adapted into a Broadway musical, and Greek restaurants across the United States cashed in on the public fascination with Greece. Dassin recalls estimates of an 800 percent increase in tourism in Greece during the year following *Never on Sunday*'s release. [14] Three years later, Cacoyannis obtained Hollywood funding to make the commercially successful *Zorba the Greek*, thus prolonging the hellenomania. Thus, as a result of *Never on Sunday*, not only did tourism soar but the following decades brought additional foreign film crews to these Mediterranean islands to reconstruct the exotica and erotica of a mythic Greece.

While it is true that *Never on Sunday* communicates a now familiar image of Greek beauty and sexual vitality, the film distinguishes itself from its successors in significant ways. While the films discussed thus far depict how the outsider (whether she be Italian, British, or American) views Greece, *Never on Sunday* integrates this viewpoint with the reverse perspective: a steady look at how some Greeks perceive their foreign guests. In this way, the film may be the most widely seen portrait of Greece that incorporates a Hellenic authorial voice. And yet it is debatable to whom we should attribute this voice. Jules Dassin is credited with the writing of the script, and undoubtedly, he was concerned with the integrity of his Greek subject. This concern even led him to insist on writing the script in Greece, amid "endless chatter, the click of backgammon dice and the strumming of bouzoukis." [15]

Andrew Horton has described Dassin as a multinational filmmaker who escapes the trap to which many American filmmakers fall prey—that is, the imposition of one's own national perspective within the depiction of another culture.[16] Horton argues that Dassin accomplishes this by borrowing from both Greek and American traditions in the telling of his story; however, at some point, Horton's analysis becomes somewhat reductionist and essentialist in his eagerness to define different aspects of *Never on Sunday* as "Greek" or "American." To modify Horton's observations, it seems more accurate to say that rather than somehow escaping his own cultural viewpoint, Dassin focuses on cross-cultural interaction with a degree of self-consciousness about his own perspective and limited vision. Thus, Dassin's success comes from admitting the impenetrability of Greek culture from an outsider's point of view, a realization paralleled within the film's narrative.

One could also assume that his collaboration with romantic partner Melina Mercouri helped him to glimpse himself and the American cultural position from a Greek perspective. This perspective intermittently takes hold of the filmic text due to the engaging character of Illya, the Greek prostitute played by Mercouri. The statements and implicit beliefs of Illya, however, so closely approximate Mercouri's own outspoken thoughts and political actions that it is difficult to separate the nationalistic voice of Illya within *Never on Sunday* from that of Mercouri. The result is a combination of two textual voices: Dassin's self-conscious American perspective and a Hellenic voice spoken through Illya Mercouri. Together they create a dialectical text that sets up polarities representative of the patriarchal imperialist position, only to prove their instability.

Simply stated, *Never on Sunday* concerns the meeting of two cultures. Homer Thrace (Dassin), an idealistic American, arrives in Piraeus to discover the secrets

In *Never On Sunday,* Homer Thrace's view of Greece, formed from his greater knowledge of the world at large, proves to be inferior to Illya's local knowledge.

Still from *Never On Sunday,* Lopert Pictures, 1962.

of ancient Greece. On meeting Illya, Homer turns her into a metaphor for Greece, the fallen woman who has lost her ties to ancient history. In his naive romanticism, Homer believes that if he can discover what caused Illya's alleged fall from grace he will have the key to understanding the decadent state of modern civilization. With the presumed superiority of an anthropologist, Homer begins to record his observations on the "restless natives" while the Greeks around him dance and drink.

The discrepancy between Homer's image of Illya and Illya's understanding of herself, or between Homer's conception of Greece and the Greek woman's vision of her own cultural identity, is immediately apparent. For Homer, modern Greece is only important as a bridge to classical Greece. He arrives eager to walk in the footsteps of Aristotle and pay tribute to "the beauty that was Greece." Illya, however, is firmly planted in the present tense. Her amused stance toward Homer suggests that she shares the same perspective as many Greeks—that is, that the Greek past is a more intricate history than is recognized by the nostalgia for the glory of ancient Greece. In the words of Melina Mercouri:

> To be born Greek is to be magnificently cursed. To a surprisingly large number of people, it means you personally built the Acropolis, you created Delphi, the theater, and you sired the concept of democracy. The truth is that you're poor, many of your people can't read, and the rare moments that you tasted of democracy and independence, foreign protectors and their Greek stooges snatched [it] away from you. It is infuriating to know how little the world knows about Greek history. Most people talk to you as if Pericles died only yesterday and as if Aeschylus is still writing plays. If now and then you meet someone who knows that in 1821, after four hundred years of Turkish occupation the Greeks rose up against their oppressors, the chances are that someone is English. And he happens to know about it only because Lord Byron came to fight at our side and wrote beautiful poems about us.[17]

Thus, what Homer's romanticized yearning for the past blinds him to is the Greece that feels a strong sense of continuity with its ancient past yet exists in the twenty-first century, the Greece that is politically and economically linked to Western Europe but culturally rooted in the Byzantine Empire, an Eastern religious tradition, and an assimilation of Turkish customs. In other words, in his respect for "the beauty that *was* Greece," he ignores the country's culturally rich present tense, with its unique combination of hellenic and romeic.[18]

Within *Never on Sunday*, Homer, as a representative of the more powerful or masculine nation, becomes the binary opposite of Illya, who is presented as the embodiment of Greece, a nation feminized by foreign domination, the power dynamics of tourism, and underdevelopment. Much like the stereotype of Greece, Illya connotes sexuality (by virtue of her profession) and natural beauty, whereas Homer is characterized by the arsenal of knowledge he brings with him ranging from philosophy and literature to psychoanalysis. He is rational and sexually restrained in contrast to Illya's volatile emotions and the lusty demeanor of her admirers. Despite being warned against following his Pygmalion fantasy, Homer attempts to raise Illya from her supposed sin and ignorance into respectability and the realm of culture. However, incorporation into his culture means isolation and alienation from her own.

On one level, *Never on Sunday* risks slipping into a romanticism that privileges nature over culture and genuineness of emotion over intellectualism without admitting the ideology of this binarism. Homer is a likable character but he is a comic hero who is often subjected to humorous ridicule, as are a number of the things that he represents. His knowledge frequently brings misery, either to his pupil or to himself as he gets beat up by an incensed Greek. He questions a Greek's musical talents because the musician does not know how to read music.

The musician, with his fractured self-confidence, refuses to pick up his instrument until Illya reminds him that the birds do not read music either. Homer's restraint, rationality, and moralism are revealed to be pretense as he moves from the inevitable question "How did a nice girl like you . . . ?" to admitting his sexual attraction for Illya and putting aside his prudery to get roaring drunk, then giving the Greeks some competition on the dance floor. At this point, *Never on Sunday* approaches the stereotype of Greece promoted by *Summer Lovers* and *Mediterraneo*, the myth that the beauty and magic of the Greek landscape will put the foreigner in touch with his natural self and will free him from inhibition.

Despite the threatened romanticism of *Never on Sunday*, the film ultimately stops short of sinking into these polarities of culture/nature, male/female, rationality/sexuality, knowledge/ignorance. First of all, the film asserts that a Greek culture does exist, and that national character cannot be reduced to the effects of nature and the beautiful Greek landscape. Second, Homer does not have the monopoly on knowledge; Illya actually speaks more languages than Homer (a necessity of her profession), and on occasion proves herself to be wiser than her instructor. If she does not pay Aristotle the same respect as does Homer, it is not out of ignorance but rather out of a distaste for his opinions on women.

Never on Sunday walks on the most fragile ground when Homer realizes that Illya's appreciation of Greek tragedy has been based on misinterpretation. According to Illya, both Medea and Oedipus live happily ever after with their families, as every tragedy ends with "and they all went to the seashore." The final curtain call, in Illya's eyes, affirms the hand-holding togetherness of the family at the story's conclusion, despite Medea's cruel practical joke of appearing to have killed the children. The film risks asserting that the modern Greek cannot be trusted to understand the greatness of ancient Greek culture. Not only are we reminded of Lord Elgin's remarks, but also of other scholars such as Jakob Philip Fallmerayer (1790–1861), who proclaimed to have solved the paradox of modern Greece's alleged backwardness despite the incredibly advanced state of its ancient ancestors. Fallmerayer posited that the contemporary people of Greece are not actually descendants of the ancient Greeks, but a less superior people of different origin who happened to settle in the former terrain of the "real" Greeks.

Ultimately, however, it is not question of a correct or incorrect reading of *Medea* but a competition between two interpretations. Homer, as his borrowed name suggests, represents an assimilation of classical Greek culture that has been adopted and reconfigured by the development of Western thought. And his interactions with Illya suggest how this influence of ancient Greece can double back on modern Greek culture in alienating ways. The debate over the essential meaning of the myth of Medea serves as one example of a particular pattern. Much harder to illustrate on film would be the way the Greek language has been used in new branches of knowledge that find native, non-Greek vocabularies limiting. The Greek words are given highly specific definitions at variance with their meanings in Greek. Native Greek-speaking scholars find themselves a step removed from their own language as these "new" terms become popularized. Classical Greek mythology has met a similar fate in its integration into literary theory and psychoanalysis. The polysemic myths, rituals, and tragedies that were once rooted in the culture, history, and people of Greece have been isolated, analyzed, and transformed within the monolith of traditional European intellectual thought.

Thus, in the debate over the interpretation of Medea, Homer's view of the mythological character as an incarnation of evil is based on a reading of tragedy that extracts Medea from her Greek sociohistoric context and transforms her into a symbol of the base woman. Homer's reading illustrates how Medea has been absorbed into patriarchal intellectual thought as the woman who commits the ultimate crime against nature by denying the maternal bond. Although Illya tacks on a happy ending, her interpretation is representative of the part of the play that most represents the Greek context that has been excised by non-Greek adaptations: the female chorus. Through the women's chorus, Euripedes' original play expresses an empathy for Medea. According to literary critic Emily A. McDermott, "Right from the start of the play Euripedes is at some pains to portray Medea not solely as a woman whose immoderate passion will drive her beyond the accepted limits of human behavior but as spokeswoman for the fears and pressures faced by ordinary fifth-century Athenian wives in a male-dominated world."[19]

Without the context provided by the chorus, Medea loses her status as a historical character faced with certain exigencies and instead becomes an archetype without a context. Thus, while Homer subscribes to Medea the archetype, Illya remains true to Euripedes' sympathy for Medea and, perhaps more significantly, to the text's criticism of marital confinement. In fact, Medea's lament over the condition of women is marked by the same concerns that motivate Illya's resistance to male control. In her entrance speech, Medea explains woman's predicament: "Of all the things that are alive and have sense, we women are the most miserable breed. First we have to buy a husband with an extravagant dowry, and so take a master over our body—the latter evil more painful than the former."[20] Illya's profession is a way of resisting a master, and even though she has a suitor who could provide her with a socially respectable title, she chooses her independence and effectively reverses the economics of the dowry system.

—— Prostitutes of the World Unite

The characters played by Melina Mercouri frequently espouse gender politics similar to that conveyed through Illya. In fact, *Never on Sunday* has been called a musical comedy version of Mercouri's previous film *Stella*, which critiques the oppressiveness of marriage founded on the Greek male need to possess and control. In the film, a nightclub entertainer rejects marriage to a man she loves in order to keep her freedom and consequently faces death at the hands of her suitor. Mercouri and Dassin clearly saw Medea within this same vein of critique. Sixteen years after *Never on Sunday,* the actress-director couple made a modern adaptation of *Medea* in the film *A Dream of Passion* (Dassin, 1978), at which time Mercouri was quoted as saying, "Medea is the only Greek heroine to fight against the male establishment. It is comfortable for us to call her mad. It lets us off. We call her a monster, but that is not how the play was written."[21]

Within the film *Never on Sunday,* Illya does finally give in to Homer's insistence that Medea's children were killed, but not to his overall point of view. Nowhere is this clearer than when Illya rejects Homer as her tutor. At this point politics, the repressed discourse, makes its entrance. As Mercouri describes, "As a Greek, I agreed only too well with Julie [Dassin] that American foreign policy inevitably led to support of regimes hated by its people. The parallel was made in the film with the relationship between No-Face, the Greek super-pimp, and the American, Homer Thrace. Homer wants Illya to quit her way of life because he knows what's best for her. No-Face wants her out because her independence might give ideas to the girls who work for him. They become inevitable allies."[22] Politics enters the text in a more explicit way when Illya allies herself with the other prostitutes. Illya's political awakening criticizes her earlier happy-go-lucky behavior and her desire to always see happy endings that blinded her to the inequities around her. If through Illya the people of Greece appeared to be irresponsible and childish, a reevaluation is in order as Illya leads the Piraeus prostitutes into a strike. The portrait of Illya as the happy hooker who only takes customers she likes and works only six days a week is obviously problematic, but her alliance with the prostitutes being economically exploited by No-Face adds a new dimension to *Never on Sunday*'s image of prostitution. Thus, though the film presents an aestheticized version of prostitution and does not find a problem with the woman who offers herself as a commodity, it does show the possibility for dignity, independence, and female solidarity within prostitution. It is not surprising, then, that Mercouri was well received by the "working women" of Piraeus: "They liked me. If I had become a symbol for outlaw women because I sang their sorrows in *Stella,* with Illya I became the mascot of the whores of the world. I received letters from everywhere thanking me for portraying their profession with dignity."[23]

Although some feminists might argue that a positive image of prostitution is never desirable, a more productive approach would be to recognize the prostitute as a multivalent image. For instance, on the opposite side of the spectrum from films like *Stella* and *Never on Sunday* is the work of Jean-Luc Godard, who uses the prostitute to illustrate the exploitative effects of consumer society. Alan J. Pakula's *Klute* (1971), on the other hand, uses the prostitute to critique heterosexual romance; Bree Daniels (Jane Fonda) must choose between the independence of prostitution and the loss of identity inherent in patriarchal romantic love, a loss made more palpable by the stylistic conflation of the two men in her life—one who wants to kill her, and the other who loves her.[24] *Stella* takes *Klute* one step further by making the two men one in the same, as Stella's suitor struggles to possess her if not through marriage then through death. Thus, *Stella, Never on Sunday,* and *Klute* juxtapose the promiscuous woman and the woman who has been "spoken for" to highlight the loss in autonomy that often characterizes monogamous heterosexual relationships in patriarchal culture. Within *Never on Sunday,* Illya's pedagogical union with Homer, like Medea's commitment to Jason, brings dependence, isolation, and unhappiness.

Never on Sunday also resembles films like *Marked Woman* (Lloyd Bacon and Michael Curtiz, 1937) and *Unforgiven* (Clint Eastwood, 1992), which recognize the political possibilities of solidarity among prostitutes. In fact, *Marked Woman* and *Never on Sunday* share a remarkable resemblance in the visual depiction of the prostitutes' commitment to one another. Both films use symbolic shots of the women's legs walking the streets in unison in a chorus of footsteps. In *Marked Woman,* this shot marks the film's conclusion and the prostitutes' successful effort to put a brutal gangster behind bars. Similar shots accompany *Never on Sunday*'s opening credits and reappear whenever the Piraeus prostitutes approach Illya for help. When Illya agrees, this metaphorical chorus is replaced by a more literal one as they sing in jail. Similarly in *Unforgiven,* the prostitutes' union incites the disorder that propels the rest of the film. The prostitutes of Big Whiskey, Wyoming, pull their resources together to rebel against the town's justice system that does not consider them individuals but property. *Never on Sunday* unites these films' themes as the prostitutes led by Illya wreak temporary havoc on the small town to protest the unjust power of the town's gangster-like pimp.[25]

Even within *Never on Sunday,* different understandings of the prostitute coexist (although one eventually wins out over the other). To Homer, the prostitute is the woman who has sacrificed her virtue, the fallen woman who comes to represent Greece. But as Homer is reeducated, the film endorses a very different version of the prostitute. If we accept Homer's simplified metaphor, if Greece can be compared to the prostitute, then she is not just an inviting feminine territory awaiting foreign intrusion in exchange for some loose change. Instead, she is like Illya, a country that may have been exploited by foreign domination but that nonetheless retains her integrity and a strong sense of a cultural heritage that is uniquely Greek.

The film concludes with Homer watching Piraeus recede into the background as he makes his departure by ferry. Instead of converting Illya from prostitute to scholar, Homer is the one who has been educated. Acknowledging his previous assessments of the Greek people to be invalid, Homer tosses the pages of his notebook over the railing to be scattered by the wind and waves. Homer departs with a new knowledge; it is not, however, of a carnal nature like that achieved by the Italians in *Mediterraneo*. In fact, the final scene of *Never on Sunday* is a far cry from the departure scene of *Mediterraneo*, in which the Italian soldiers leave as sexual conquerors with a teary-eyed, pregnant Greek woman waving good-bye from the shore. And while *Mediterraneo*'s prostitute is "redeemed" through her love for one of the Italians, *Never on Sunday* leaves it unresolved as to whether Illya will choose a so-called respectable life with her suitor or continue her autonomous life as a prostitute.

Granted, *Never on Sunday* could not be likened to a subversive trumpet call awakening Greek nationalism and defiantly announcing Greek resistance in the international scene. In many ways, it is a somewhat simplistic musical comedy produced roughly within the confines of classic Hollywood tradition. The film is not directly authored by a Greek nor does it completely refute the stereotype of the unproductive, carefree Greek man. It is only when we compare *Never on Sunday* to other widely circulated images of Greece that the film distinguishes itself as a sincere attempt to represent the Greek cultural position. Unfortunately, the film was released more than forty years ago, and few films screened in the United States since then have echoed its words or updated its message for American audiences of a substantial size.

During a time in which Greece is struggling for a political voice, the implications of this cultural muteness are particularly lamentable. As David Morley and Kevin Robins argue, "A given group recognises itself through its recollection of a common past."[26] Thus, Greece has traditionally incorporated a sense of its history into its cultural products, thereby articulating its "space of identity." It is this same "space of identity" and sense of heritage that Greece feels are threatened in the last decade's shifts of European power. But the lack of exposure to

Greek culture outside its own domestic boundaries has engendered, at least for many Americans, a murky understanding of the issues that mark recent Greek political crises. So while one million Greeks gathered in Thessaloniki in the spring of 1992 to decry the new Macedonian republic, probably the only images of Greece viewed by large numbers of Americans were those offered by the film *Mediterraneo,* made popular by its 1991 Academy Award. And while the Greek government responded to U.S. recognition of Macedonia by closing down its northern border in 1995, thereby blocking the former Yugoslav republic's primary trade route, few Americans were aware of the controversy. As these distant tensions continued to brew in the late 1990s, sounds and images of Greece of a different sort danced across American television sets as the new cover girl was unveiled against the background of Santorini and fast food ads announced the latest "gyro craze." It is in light of such unsatisfactory images of Greece that we can recognize *Never on Sunday* as a rare glimpse into a deceptively familiar culture of which we actually know relatively little.

CHAPTER SEVEN

Corporeal Geographies

E. M. FORSTER ON FILM

THE ISSUES OF TOURISM, simulated travel, and the tourist gaze target many of the central questions up for debate within the discussion of postmodernism. For instance, idealist talk of "multiculturalism," colliding with the more ambivalent dialogue on postmodernism, has brought the question of how individuals see across cultural difference to the foreground in an era of globalized culture. Interestingly, many of the various theoretical concepts developed to grapple with this question have evoked the metaphor of travel, although in very different ways. Referencing travel as a survival-motivated homelessness rather than leisure-bound bordercrossings, both Gilles Deleuze and Lawrence Grossberg have theorized the passing of modernism, using the idea of "nomadism" and speculating on the "nomadic subjectivity" required by postmodernism.[1] Drawing on travel's more positive connotations, Maria Lugones seeks a solution to the postmodern political conundrum in a pluralistic feminism that "world-travels" or identifies across cultures without erasing difference.[2] And Elspeth Probyn, utilizing a far less generous view of commercialized travel, warns against the potential epistemic violence of the postmodern by comparing the contemporary touting of diversity to the superficiality and Western ontologies associated with tourism.[3]

The prevalence of travel metaphors in theorizations of the new phenomenology of postmodernism is unsurprising considering the centrality of terms like *globalization, commodification,* and *simulation* in such discussions. Travel can be seen as the paradigmatic experience, a fact confirmed by the linked etymological roots of the terms *travel* and *experience.* In his discussions of both modern and postmodern culture, Dean MacCannell uses tourism as a window into the larger dynamics of culture when he writes, "Increasingly, pure experience, which leaves no material trace, is manufactured and sold like a commodity."[4] The commodification of experience is linked to structural shifts in our economy and technological change, both of which have contributed to a remapping of the globe and the way we experience the world. The ease with which MacCannell converts his text *The Tourist* from a commentary on modernism to a glimpse into the onset of postmodernism, as I mentioned in this volume's introduction, suggests the coextensiveness of modernism and postmodernism and the status of the latter as an intensification of certain attributes of the former. One such attribute, simulation, is central to MacCannell's concept of staged authenticity. While tourists may be motivated by a sincere desire for involvement and understanding, the desire to satisfy tourists' search for authenticity can lead to staged authenticity or "an infinite regression of stage-sets." As tourists seek out the regions where unstaged real life transpires, a series of front regions are designed to look like back regions with the "true" back region lost in the regression.[5] Noting that with the loss of distinctions between front region and back region representation and reality begin to merge, John Frow repositions MacCannell's work within canonical postmodern theory, noting, "MacCannell thus elaborates something like Baudrillard's theory of a historical regime of simulation in which the difference between original and copy falls away, and indeed where the very existence of an 'original' is a function of the copy."[6]

Although MacCannell primarily deals with the tourist attraction as stage set or as a "copy" of the real thing, it is also true that the practice of tourism often involves confronting various copies of the original in the form of postcards, tourist brochures, snapshots, and images delivered by film and television. With this flooding of images, the tourist may read the original, whether it be the Parthenon or Stonehenge, through the filter of these previous images, judging the sight according to its adherence to the copies. Experience of the tourist object is also accompanied by its translation into image through the practice of amateur travel photography; the object is thereby read in comparison to previous images and as possible future image. In the process, the image begins to subsume the original, which in turn is only valued for its ability to be represented in yet another copy.

Targeting the issue of commodification, Davydd J. Greenwood suggests that indigenous culture loses any authentic meaning as soon as it is commodified, or turned into a stage set, by the tourist industry.[7] This definition of authenticity as that which has not been commodified is also the standard employed by ethnic-art collectors and museum artifact purchasers: authenticity requires that the artifact must not have been constructed for foreign markets—including mobile foreign markets in the form of tourists. Thus, like King Midas's touch, the tourist searches for the heartbeat of local culture and the art collector's purchasing hands reach out but, with their transformative touch, contact only culture as lifeless commodity, inauthentic objects for sale. Such quandaries around the pursuit of genuine culture have elicited references to "the vanishing horizon of authenticity" to which the tourist endlessly defers.[8]

The cinematic apparatus's promise of demediating mediation pledges to succeed where tourism has failed. To the extent that the medium is celebrated for its delivery of the illusion of direct experience, directors of location-shot and epic films are lauded for their realization of film's potential for visual plenitude and simulated immersion in a temporally or geographically distant world. We are thus confronted with an interesting predicament when we view a collection of films by filmmakers considered to be masters of location shooting and of cinematic illusion in general, and when these same films are adaptations of literary works that attempt to critique tourism's myth of direct experience, questioning the tourist's access to cultural authenticity. While the films deliver the visual pleasures of tourism through cinematic plenitude, through their narratives they are also assigned the task of convincing the viewers of the impossibility of any authentic access to the culture depicted—a fact that seems to be denied by cinema's ability to deliver an illusion of materiality, of place rendered in elaborate detail, scale, and spectacle.

The ostensible subject of this chapter is tourism as seen through the eyes of British novelist E. M. Forster and the film directors who have adapted his work for the screen. Yet, with the addition of the consideration of intersections between film, tourism, and postmodernism, this study expands from a closely circumscribed look at travel practices depicted in Forster's novels and adaptations of his work to a study of the filmic medium's contribution to the postmodern mediation of reality. Essentially, the use of film as an analytical lens creates a double layer of touristic practice to be examined: the travel experience of the fictional character at the center of the novel or film in question and the "virtual tourism" of the reader or spectator positioned as armchair traveler.

As suggested by authors such as Anne Friedberg, the touristic gaze of the cinematic apparatus and its delivery of a simulated reality has been a dominant force in the heralding of a manufactured reality that, in its superb mimesis, goes so far as to question the relevance of any original profilmic reality. The meticulously constructed spectacle of classic Hollywood cinema evinces simulation in a heightened, postmodern form that takes on a life of its own separate from any conception of an original. However, despite cinema's collective contribution to postmodernism's frenetic mediation of reality, the individual film does not necessarily integrate a knowing recognition of its participation in the loss of faith in a pure and immediate reality. In fact, it is through their masterful artifice that many films seem to insist upon the accessibility of some form of authenticity and real experience. Film's promise of demediation is the fetish that lets us forget about the fading of the real and its layered causality—the absence of the profilmic, the disappearance of unmediated access to reality following the assimilation of language, and postmodernism's frenzy of simulation that denies the significance of an original. Thus, adaptations of E. M. Forster's work play out this process of disavowal; any questioning of the image's mediation of reality is submerged by cinematic brilliance that conflates the experience of the fictional traveler with that of the filmic spectator.

Forster's work in its original form closely approximates the theoretical position of postmodern scholars who have postulated on the fading of a tangible, reliable, and unmanufactured reality. His novels' insights echo sophisticated analyses of tourism and cultural commodification by scholars who postdate Forster by well over half a century. For Forster, travel entails the fruitless search for cultural authenticity and an unmediated reality, a search ultimately played out upon the body and frequently in violent terms. At one level, Forster submits to an epistemological failure at the heart of the tourist's search for knowledge. However, as the contexts for his films move further from cultures akin to his own, his description of this failure becomes more mournful. In David Lean's *A Passage to India* (1984), for instance, the intellectual tenor remains ironic and distanced while battling with emotional currents of the novel that suggest Forster's own unfulfilled quest for spiritual union. In the face of his most exoticized subject, this yearning on Forster's part is most apparent, despite his own acknowledgment of the futility of the tourist's romantic quest to become one with cultural otherness. For this reason *A Passage to India* has been singled out among Forster's novels as racist, for at the same time that he denounces the political and spiritual effects of colonialism, he constructs Indian culture as an icon of mystery in the process of admitting a failure of the author as tourist to escape his own cultural perspective. His own love of the imaginary exotic still smolders beneath an attempt to explore tourism's exploitative side.

This tension between touristic desire and an emergent postmodernist perspective that denies the possibility of unmanufactured reality, a tension that is at its height in *A Passage to India,* is deemphasized within filmic adaptations of

Forster's work. Forster's critique of the traveler's quest becomes submerged within filmic forms that appear to be more invested in delivering touristic pleasures to spectators than in translating into filmic form Forster's analysis of the collapse between tourism and a kind of antitourism.

—— Forster and the Collapse of Antitourism

E. M. Forster's stance toward the tourist's overseas search for genuine experience can only be described as conflicted and ironic. Forster was himself a dedicated traveler, yet he had unusual and critical insight into the practice of tourism. Long before his time, the distinction had been made between travelers and tourists— travelers supposedly seek meaningful, authentic interaction with the inhabitants of a destination while superficial tourists seal themselves in their environmental bubble, eschewing contact with the foreign space unless recommended by their guidebooks. Forster's attitude toward this discourse of antitourism, however, approaches the sophistication of contemporary scholars who recognize the negligibility of difference between tourist and traveler. The attempt to recognize one's own travel experience as distinctively meaningful and authentic in contradistinction to someone else's touristic practices has become part of the phenomenon of tourism. As Jonathan Culler explains, the tourist/traveler distinction has functioned primarily "to convince oneself that one is not a tourist . . . the desire to distinguish between tourists and real travelers [being] a part of tourism—integral to it rather than outside or beyond it"[9]

Through the figures of the sheltered mass tourist and the romantic tourist, who in the spirit of antitourism call themselves travelers, Forster first evokes the antitourist position and then shows the collapse of difference between tourist and antitourist. He uses the well-known stereotype of the uptight, upper-class spinster traveling abroad on an extended museum tour. This is the tourist who returns from her tour of classical ruins remarking that the main problem with Turkey is the Turks. She demands English food, English standards of comfort, English company, and all the rituals of home. Her tourism is distanced, sterile, and permeated with class discourse. And, of course, she spends most of her voyage complaining, except when content in the sheltered company of other tourists who share the same nationality and class status. Within this particular evocation of the sheltered mass tourist figure, sexual status and inferred frigidity take on larger meaning as the spinster refuses any kind of active engagement with the travel destination other than distanced observation.

Two women from Forster's novels stand out in their conformity to this stereotype. Harriet Herriton, in *Where Angels Fear to Tread*, travels to Italy to retrieve the baby of her deceased sister-in-law. Harriet is perpetually miffed at the inconveniences of her surroundings and would probably barely emerge from her hotel room were it not for the exigency of her mission. The similar character Charlotte Bartlett, from *A Room with a View*, views her expeditions in Italy as a chance to get to know other Brits of her social class. As a chaperone for her young cousin, Charlotte considers herself responsible for keeping the maximum distance between all Italians and her impressionable, young companion.

Within each of these texts, the stereotypical tourist is gently ridiculed through humor or through a generally unsympathetic depiction. Forster's critique of this brand of tourism also surfaces through the juxtaposition of another tourist type—the romantic tourist or the self-declared traveler. Unlike the sheltered tourist who despises the crude materiality of an "uncivilized land," the romantic tourist searches for authenticity and spiritual transformation. In *Where Angels Fear to Tread* (Charles Sturridge, 1991), Philip Herriton tells Lilia, "Don't, let me beg you, go with that awful tourist idea that Italy's only a museum of antiquities and art. Love and understand the Italians, for the people are more marvelous than the land." [10] He urges Lilia to get off the beaten path and allow the romance of Italy to seep into her spirit. She takes his advice to heart, eventually sending her family notice of her engagement to Gino, a young Italian she met in the town of Monteriano. In *A Passage to India*, Adela Quested and Mrs. Moore are also interested in more than the sheltered tourist's role. They are eager to see "the real India" and rub shoulders with real Indians, a discouraged practice in colonialist India. Meanwhile, "the real India" remains distant and removed in the figure of Professor Godbole, who is played, ironically, by British actor Alec Guinness in the film version.

Within Forster's novels, however, even romantic tourists fail to encounter the real, or at least not the one they expect. In *A Room with a View* (James Ivory, 1986), the comical character Miss Lavish demands that Charlotte put away her guidebook and experience the true Italy. In an amusing scene, she drags Charlotte around the back streets of Florence, insisting that they breathe in the smells of Italy and quickly getting the two of them lost. Miss Lavish later reappears as the author of a poorly written romance novel that uses Florence as a backdrop. As one of Lawrence Durrell's characters in *The Dark Labyrinth* observed about Southern Europe, "I think it is only in the south that they warm themselves at life instead of transforming it into bad literature," but as Miss Lavish's trashy novel proves, this does not stop the British from pretending to live life and then turning it into bad literature.

In *Where Angels Fear to Tread*, Philip's romantic view of Italy also proves to be the stuff of bad literature. His idealist fabrications crumble when he hears that

Gino's father is a dentist. "A dentist in fairyland!" Forster writes. "False teeth and laughing-gas and the tilting chair at a place which knew the Etruscan League, and the Pax Romana, and Alaric himself, and the Countess Matilda, and the Middle Ages, all fighting and holiness, and the Renaissance, all fighting and beauty! He thought of Lilia no longer. He was anxious for himself: he feared that Romance might die" (26). The collapse of romance hits Lilia even harder. She tries to marry a specimen of Italian simplicity and charm while still living and entertaining like an English lady. Instead she wakes up next to a chauvinistic, unfaithful, and often violent husband and a culture that can only accommodate her British customs with difficulty.

In this way, the antitourist or the romantic tourist craves experience in an explicit rejection of sheltered tourism that refuses involvement with an unfamiliar environment. Ironically, however, in trying to get off the beaten path the romantic tourist follows a well-trodden route. And what the romantic tourist holds up as authentic experience dissipates into mirage. According to James Buzard, the real emerges on only one front within Forster's work: "The representation of foreign cultural authenticity by means of an irrepressible human body is a characteristic Forsterian metonym: bodies assert themselves and their materiality throughout Forster's work, in opposition to the falsely spiritual and romanticized experience that is tourism's stock-in-trade."[11] Through the insistence of the body, Forster evokes a fantasy of cultural difference in which desire and difference are inextricably linked; yet he maintains that a price must be paid for this fantasy and that it be paid in corporeal terms.

If we liken the journey to Victor Turner's rite of passage, the tourist passes through three phases: separation, margin or limen, and reaggregation. Although the sheltered tourist circumvents the liminality of travel, many of Forster's characters do become liminars within this margin that Turner likens "to death; to being in the womb; to invisibility, darkness, bisexuality, and the wilderness."[12] The liminar's escape from traditional social structures is both liberating and dangerous. And it is the ambivalence of this liminality that erupts on the fictional Forsterian body. Across the three mentioned novels, an unnamed Italian suffers a bloody death, a baby is crushed in a carriage accident, a British woman has a nasty run-in with a cactus, and a British man suffers various physical injuries.

Yet there is a sexual edge to much of the violence. In fact, perhaps Forster's attraction to the eroticized marginality of tourism can be attributed at least in part to his own sexuality. Mirroring his personal life, desire in his novels comes bubbling to the surface only at a distance from the repressive atmosphere of urban England and is always linked to escape and transgression. Repeatedly, the boundaries among races, nations, and classes are crossed and the rules of English propriety broken. The tourist's voyage becomes a sexual passage racked with promise and peril played out in carnal terms.

One example of sexually inflected violence is the Piazza della Signoria scene in *A Room with a View,* which has been labeled by some literary critics as Lucy Honeychurch's "symbolic loss of viriginity."[13] She wanders unchaperoned into the square, gazing up at the looming Palazzo dei Medici, appearing "no longer a tower, no longer supported by earth, but some unattainable treasure throbbing in the tranquil sky." She witnesses an argument between two locals. One man assaults the other in a flurry of events, with Lucy virtually caught in the middle. The one man "bent towards Lucy with a look of interest, as though he had an important message for her. He opened his lips to deliver it, and a stream of red came out between them and trickled down his unshaven chin."[14] Perhaps no experience could be more authentic than death or orgasm, or in this case, a strange cross between the two that leaves Lucy swooning. The movement toward Lucy begun by the unnamed Italian but cut short by death is completed by George Emerson instead; the chain of events initiated by the Italian reaches completion in the moment of physical contact between George and Lucy as he catches her fall. In this chain of events, the real penetrates Lucy's touristic bubble, allowing the slow transformation ending with sexual initiation and a departure from expected roles.

The psychic violence enacted upon Lucy's delicate sensibility is symbolically represented by the blood splashed on her newly purchased postcards. Additionally, the postcards, like the broken binoculars that play a significant role in *A Passage to India,* are symbols of the tourist's attempted appropriation of the foreign destination. Thus, the epistemic violence of tourism seems to double back against Lucy, and in the process, the Italian body, Forster's sign of authenticity, is subsumed in the narrative's very wake. Nonetheless, the end effect for both Lucy and George is positive. With Italy acting as a catalyst, the symbolic loss of virginity is transformed into an actual loss of virginity by the end of the novel. Genuine crosscultural contact thus appears to be both violent and fleeting, with the true victim consisting of an anonymous dead man left in the piazza, his life consumed in this catalytic process.

This idea of tourism's power differential becoming visible as actual violence on both sides of the host/guest encounter is but one explanation. It is also reasonable to suggest that since the Forsterian voyage is a sexual passage and since Forster's sexuality, although displaced into heterosexual forms within some of his novels, was considered to be of a taboo nature during the time of his writing, these intertwining forces of desire and punishment are not so surprising. Other

Since Adela's rape was most likely imagined and the events immediately surrounding the moment of her trauma are not represented by the film, various moments of sexually coded interaction with the Indian landscape stand in for the imagined rape: Adela's penetration by cactus thorns, her entrance into the cave, and her hasty departure from the monkey-filled temple.

Film still from *Passage to India,* courtesy of Photofest.

psychoanalytic investigations of homosexuality have linked homoerotic feelings and masochism. For instance, Kaja Silverman locates a linked homosexual and masochistic content in the Freudian "a child is being beaten" fantasy. The desire to be loved by the father manifests itself in a fantasy of being beaten by the oral mother. This involves transference of power expeling the father from the symbolic order.[15] In Forster's work, the father is connected to the homeland that is left behind by the tourist's adventure into liminality. Britain and the father are replaced by the foreign landscape, often coded as feminine. Adela's rape by either the echo of the cave or the cactus thorns in *A Passage to India* could then be read as an act of the phallic maternal power of the land. Forster's textually repressed homosexuality erupts in displaced forms across the various characters, exposing them to the effects of this sexual discourse of masochism.

—— Films with a View

The bodily attacks in Forster's literature are carried over into the film adaptations of each of the three novels and remain an essential part of the narrative.

In fact, Sturridge's *Where Angels Fear to Tread*, Ivory's *A Room with a View*, and Lean's *A Passage to India* all remain fairly loyal to Forster's own words and story structure. However, it is almost inevitable that currents of meaning will shift as literature is converted into another textual system. In this case, the primary changes are brought about by filmic stylistics that position viewers as tourists at the same time that the narratives critique tourism and its complicitous partner antitourism.

Various factors encourage this positioning of spectators as tourists. First of all, the long history of cinema's claim to capturing the real is buttressed by the tradition of location shooting. Just like the tourist who seeks out the full range of perspectives, from the intimate inspection of ancient stone carvings to the commanding view from the temple's cloud-puncturing summit, much of classical film and location shooting in particular provide a variety of visual positions. Before the film dips into close-ups and other building blocks of a scene, an establishing shot provides a scenic panorama from an elevated position, the same position so feverishly sought by tourists.

Each of these films is ripe with such scenic moments, with lingering shots of the Florentine skyline or of the Marabar caves perched above the city of Chandrapore. Additionally, since the characters themselves are tourists, the camera occasionally takes up their position, allowing the spectator to view Italy or India through their eyes. What is more unusual is the prevalence of a number of postcard moments motivated neither by a character's gaze nor by the traditional purposes of establishing shots: the introduction of a new scene, the announcement of the arrival of daylight or nightfall, a cue to a change of location, or some other transitional function. These are moments of omniscience for spectators who glimpse the sights even before the characters are privy to the same views, or who view a location from a privileged vantage point unavailable to diegetic characters. For instance, in *A Passage to India*, Adela and Mrs. Moore are frustrated in their attempts to make contact with the authenticity of India, only witnessing Indians as decor in a ceremony celebrating British imperialism or meeting Indians of a higher class who have in part anglicized themselves as a means of social mobility within colonial India. Their disappointing sight-seeing tour, led by a British guide, includes only British sights: a war memorial, the barracks, the hospital, and a church. Yet on the women's train ride into Chandrapore, the audience sees several unusual views of India not visible to the train passengers. One such shot depicts a number of Indians sleeping beneath the railway overpass. As one coughs with the dust kicked up by the passing train, perhaps the moviegoer fancies that she has seen the "back region" of Indian culture so eagerly sought by Adela and

Mrs. Moore. A second sight-seeing tour seems more promising, as the women embark for the Marabar caves, this time with an Indian tour guide, Dr. Aziz. Yet, Aziz's Anglicized nature and his obsequiousness are suggestive of something other than the real India that the women seek. Their relationship with Aziz is marred by the economics of colonialism as a mediating factor that prevents any kind of meaningful cross-cultural contact beyond violence as an authentic response to British occupation.

The picturesque views of tourist destinations that recur throughout *A Passage to India* seem to function in one of two ways, either unhinging themselves from the narrative in a moment of pure spectacle or endowing the landscape with a narrative function. During the times when these views unhinge from the narrative, they create the effect of a travelogue interspliced within a narrative film. In *A Room with a View*, locales such as Santa Croce and the Piazza della Signoria spark brief "slide shows" within the film. Narrative progression slows to a halt while a montage of close-ups of sculptures and frescoes ensues. In the Piazza della Signoria scene, the spectacle's halting of narrative movement is visually rendered through camera movement, and the montage of images provides a brief respite before the outbreak of a quarrel. As Lucy crosses the piazza, the camera swings upward and away from her forward movement. She remains in view only thanks to the removal of her dark coat, making her a spot of color in a sea of movement. The details of the Loggia sculptures revealed in the following montage remain disassociated from Lucy's gaze and only retrospectively can any vague link be made between her disrobement, the passion and aggression of the nude figures of stone, and the following sexually nuanced violence. In a montage of fresco details in the church of Santa Croce, links between the narrative and the slide show–like montage are even more vague.

In *Where Angels Fear to Tread*, these moments of touristic pleasure existing outside of the narrative help to romanticize Italy despite the narrative current that attempts to deromanticize this land of dentists. For instance, at one point, the camera fails to keep up with the protagonists as it pauses to capture the quaint image of young Italian schoolboys running and giggling on the cobblestone streets of Monteriano. Similar images in *A Room with a View* are a bit more complex. In one scene, an Italian hanging out of a second floor window lowers a bucket by rope to another Italian below. On the sound track, lively Italian folk music seems to reinforce the quaintness of this scene. Again, spectators witness this image before the protagonists do, allowing it to be viewed directly rather than from a fictional character's point of view. When the comical figures of Charlotte and Miss Lavish do enter the depicted space, they are in the midst of a conversation about the "simple souls" of Italy, a nation of peasants. Perceiving the oversimplifications of Miss Lavish's proclamations, spectators could read in a retroactive critique of their own complicity in this trope of quaintness.

In the work of the Ishmael Merchant–James Ivory team and of David Lean, the masterful composition of images creates an appreciation of the image perhaps not unlike the sightseer's appreciation of a beautiful postcard. Lean's aesthetic sense tames the India seen in *A Passage to India* by imposing an order upon the environment, an aesthetic order that encourages the viewer to see abstract patterns within the foreign landscape. In *A Room with a View*, an alternation between an extreme symmetry in composition and more unusually balanced compositions similarly elicits an aesthetic appreciation. In this way, the alien becomes understandable through Western artistic tradition.

One such tradition is that of the picturesque. In her analysis of "monarch-of-all-I-survey" scenes in Victorian travel writing, Mary Louise Pratt describes the "relation of mastery predicated between the seer and the seen" in the perception of the picturesque.[16] The landscape is apprehended from a viewpoint that imposes a symmetry between background and foreground. The scene becomes a painting to be judged, appreciated and even purchased. Buzard further comments on this trope of the picturesque transforming foreign culture into mise-en-scène, quite literally doing so in film. The role of the spectator is all important as the act of seeing corrects and completes the landscape. With the discovery of the vantage point that provides this balance of foreground and background, a "sublime synthesis" occurs. According to Buzard, "The authenticity of effect takes place in the epiphanic moment in which the unified aesthetic essence of the place shines forth." However, this essence is not a quality of the place itself. As Buzard notes, "What occurs at the moment of sublime synthesis is a successful matching of images stored in the memory (from reading, listening to travellers' tales, viewing paintings and sketches, and otherwise preparing oneself for the object) with scenes as they are encountered. The 'original' becomes itself when the viewer perceives that it suits its representations. But to conclude this is to attribute a particular importance to the role played by the viewer in *making* the original become what it (potentially) is. The implication is that only when it comes within the purview of the properly appreciative witness does the site attain its full aesthetic value and the realization of its essence."[17] The filmmaker, as surrogate witness for the filmgoer, captures this moment of sublime synthesis in an image that conforms to audience's preexisting conceptions of India or Italy, while differing just enough from previous representations in order to claim authenticity as not just another canned image. In *A Passage to India,* Lean even provides some of the

David Lean's views of the Marabar Cave are reprisals of the touristic images of the caves seen by the film's characters.

Film still from *Passage to India,* courtesy of Photofest.

images that would become the standards for confirming the "original." Before boarding the ship to Chandrapore, India, Adela glances at paintings of India, and of the Marabar caves in particular, that decorate the walls of the travel office where she purchases her ticket. The narrative then carries us up the hills sheltering Chandrapore to these caves so that the viewers might glimpse the "original" in all its glory.

Lean's picturesque vision is also a mobile one. With moving shots from trains, boats, automobiles, and even elephants, Lean highlights the movement of the traveler, and conversely, the stillness of the locale. Upon the protagonists' arrival in India, an automobile carries them through a marketplace. India is delivered in all its tactile glory as a market where the tourist may not only witness but purchase the exoticism of the East. India's liminality is simultaneously represented when a corpse is carried past the automobile. During this car ride, two Indian bicyclists who are knocked off their bicycles as if to enforce the Westerner's monopoly on motion occupy some kind of middle ground in terms of class and privilege between the colonial subjects on foot and the British in their cars, ships, and trains. This theme continues throughout as the mobility of one of these bicyclists, Aziz, is circumscribed by British desires and demands; he travels to accommodate British patients and tourists, getting his Tonga stolen by two English women, and eventually being immobilized through wrongful incarceration. Indians of lower status experience even more negligible movement in contrast to the incessant motion of British characters. Adela and Ronnie walk by a static gauntlet of servants that line the path into Ronnie's home. With much pomp and circumstance, the viceroy and his wife drive through a crowd of Indians assembled for their arrival. A single Indian waves good-bye as Mrs. Moore's train departs. In short, the British, with the privilege of mobility, construct India as an immobile stage, a place of stillness outside of time awaiting the traveler's arrival. To the extent that this construction is aestheticized and the spectator is absorbed by the beauty of the image, the critique inherent in this portrait of stillness is obscured.

Viewing the landscape as picturesque or sublime serves to personify the land. In other words, although the filmmaker's or tourist's perception is required to make the vision come to life, the land with its "authenticity of effect" becomes a narrative character affecting spectator and diegetic character alike. The spectacular landscape may have a pleasurable effect on the spectator at the same time that the land's mysterious effects are foregrounded by the narrative itself. In *A Room with a View*, Miss Lavish says to Charlotte, "I have a theory that there is something in the Italian landscape that inclines even the most stoic nature to romance." This theory is communicated through visual and sound design as one of Giacomo Puccini's arias accompanies the nap of the Italian carriage driver, an individual who has already displayed his passionate temperament. If such passionate impulses are indeed a function of the landscape affecting those who are, as Miss Lavish says, "open to physical sensation," then their infectiousness is signified by the music that ceases whenever the less susceptible Charlotte and Miss Lavish come into view. The carriage driver directs Lucy to George, who engages her in a long and fervent kiss in the middle of a Fiesole poppy field overlooking the city of Florence. After the kiss is broken up by the frigid Charlotte, an unusually long and static shot of the Florentine skyline is accompanied by the final bars of the aria. The extended shot endows the picturesque landscape with an assumed significance, acting as a kind of wink from the filmmaker to the audience. However, the degree to which the film takes entirely serious the idea of catalytic scenery is questioned by the gentle ridicule of Miss Lavish and her idea for a second-rate romance novel: "a young English girl transfigured by Italy."

In *A Passage to India*, Lean as scenarist adds a scene to Forster's tale in keeping with this notion of land as transfigurative force bringing repressed elements of the tourist's character to the surface. In a precursor to the rape scene, Adela's bicycle ride leads her to a dilapidated, apparently abandoned temple strewn with erotic statues, an exotic locale seemingly frozen in time for the benefit of the

The beauty of the land has a catalytic effect as romance sparks between Lucy and George in a poppy field just outside of Florence.

Film still from *A Room with A View,* courtesy of Photofest.

tourist. Entranced by the impassioned embraces of the stone figures, Adela approaches until a troop of screeching monkeys scrambling across the temple ruins frightens her away. The incident's repercussions are soon evident as a stirred-up Adela takes back her rejection of Ronnie's marriage proposal and as her morning dreams are haunted by these same sexually entangled bodies immortalized in stone.

In Lean's film, as in *A Room with a View,* a place's authenticity of effect is communicated aurally as well as visually. While much of the visual material is of a pleasurable nature, the violence of Forster's novel is cinematically rendered through sound. The monkeys' approach in the temple scene is announced first through sound effect before the actual creatures are visible. The chaos of their screeching and clawing on rock, breaking the scene's relative tranquility, is perhaps more distressing than its visual counterpart—the monochromatic tan fur of the monkeys against carved stone of the same color. Similarly, the visual paucity of the cave's interior is no match for the echo that unnerves Mrs. Moore and later incarnates Adela's rape fantasy.

In the end, it is difficult to say which filmic elements have the stronger effect—the visual touristic pleasures or the violence rendered through sound and narrative action. Andrew Higson has argued that the concern for surface detail that we see in each of these films characterizes many of Britain's heritage films. He suggests that the heritage film converts nostalgia into spectacle, thereby draining the original work of its emotional and political content and delivering the past as "a museum of sounds and images, an iconographic display."[18] Undoubtedly, the skillful iconographic display of these films delivers a spectacle of place endowed with the illusion of authenticity, thereby in contradiction to Forster's political critique and his suggestion of the unreachable nature of direct experience within tourism. For Forster, only the genuine expresses itself in the unpleasantness of a violent culture shock that either attacks the tourist's body or consumes the indigene in a reminder of the exploitative effects of using the foreign locale as a catalyst for the visitor's self-transformation. Within the visual splendor of these films, this critique begins to short circuit, leaving conflicted film texts that position spectators as tourists with only a brief questioning of touristic aims.

CHAPTER EIGHT

Global Mappings
MICHAEL CRICHTON'S
POSTMODERN TRAVELS

POSTMODERNISM IS THE cultural response to the crisis of the failure of modernism's visualizing strategies, so deemed a failure because this visualization is at the same time not enough and too much. The world understood as a time-based reality continually in flux propels technological attempts to capture global change in real time to a feverish pitch. While the map or the globe provided a sense of completion and enclosure, the satellite-monitored world—marked by animal migration, changing meteorological patterns, the movement of contraband across borders, and perceptible ecological deterioration—is an exhausting sequence of images that draws attention to its gaps. The amount of information produced is more than the human mind can process but is still doomed to fall short of comprehensiveness. This world, delivered in moving image form, thus eclipses the real not because of its comprehensiveness but because of its fullness in comparison to the narrow range of sensory perception that characterizes human experience of the real. In other words, theorists of postmodernism assert that the proliferation of simulacra within contemporary culture makes reality harder to distinguish and even moot in its indistinguishability. I suggest that we elaborate on these dynamics by examining not how simulation technologies replicate reality but rather at how they replicate, exceed, and even alter human perception of reality.

In recognition of the limits of human perception and the vastness of the world around us, we attempt to assimilate technology as prosthetic extensions of our own sensorium. The technology becomes a fetish standing in for the missing comprehension of the real with its enormity and incessant variation, which confounds even technologically aided perception. The process of assimilation—the attempt to build technologies with interfaces that take into account the human as physical form and as information processing engine—also works in the opposite direction. The human mind becomes attuned to technological media's representational methods. The temporally accelerated meteorological map or the ultrasound image becomes a mental pattern for understanding realities that cannot easily be glimpsed. In our assimilation of such technological perceptions and a fetishization of their powers, they take on the aura of the real in a compensation for our own inability to directly experience the butterfly effects of weather patterns or the delicate contours of a developing fetus.

Jorge Luis Borges's oft-quoted tale "On Exactitude in Science," which recounts the comprehensive mapping of an empire, provides an encapsulation of a portion of the above-described phenomenon. In Borges's story, the exhaustive cartographic efforts of the empire's administration lead to the production of a map that is coextensive with the empire itself.[1] Jean Baudrillard writes, in contemplation of such comprehensiveness, "When there is no more territory virgin and therefore available for the imaginary, when the map covers the whole territory, then something like a principle of reality disappears."[2] Since my own formulation of the compromised reality of postmodernity extends beyond Baudrillard's assessment, I supplement Borges's story with another fanciful account of simulation's effects, David Cronenberg's 1983 film *Videodrome*, in which a television executive's attempts to tailor television to individuals' needs ranging from sleeping patterns to sexual proclivities result in a reverse assimilation as the protagonist develops a brain tumor that produces televisual hallucinations. Although the protagonist attempts to mold the medium to human needs and habits, the mind itself is reshaped by television, as the internalization of the televisual image becomes literal.

It is not the coextensiveness of the map with the empire that causes the disappearance of a reality principle; to blame instead is the map's extension of human experience and an overreliance on the map in a disavowal of the map's and the human mind's failings in the face of a vast globe forever in flux. However, with such a static medium, it is difficult to imagine individuals referencing the map to the extent that a mental image of it supplants direct human experience and takes on the illusion of the dominant referent for the real. Cartographers' drawings would seem to be glaringly evident as abstractions doomed to obsolescence, simplifications forever falling short of the world's fluid details and infinite color palette. On the other hand, *Videodrome*'s use of television's moving images—delivered through instantaneous broadcast as the simulation technology in question—constitutes a more probable start to a metaphorical account of perturbations of reality. And yet, it is a third fictional tale that in combination with these other tales comes closest to metaphorizing postmodernism's compensatory effects, or what Steven Connor calls "the cult of immediate experience," that arises in reaction to postmodernism's image-saturated culture.[3] The cult of immediate experience finds an ideal home in the company of touristic cinema's myth of demediating mediation and its illusory promise that authenticity is not stamped out by but rather is accessible through simulation, as suggested by Paul Verhoeven's film *Total Recall*. Based on a short story by Philip K. Dick, this 1990 film posits the possibility of simulated travel marketed in the form of memory implants. Instead of spending money on transportation and lodging and having no guarantees of good weather or good health during the voyage, memory implants allow the virtual traveler to have vivid memories of an idyllic vacation without the hassles and expenses of actually taking the vacation.

As fetish, the custom designed "Rekall" vacation serves within the film's story as a conduit to authentic memory and direct experience, rather than merely celebrating its own economical artificiality. The first attempt to retrieve authenticity comes in the form of an escape of the tourist trap as defined by antitourism. According to the Rekall, Incorporated, salesperson, "What is it that is exactly the same about every single vacation you have ever taken? You. You're the same. No matter where you go, there you are. It's always the same old you. Let me suggest that you take a vacation from yourself. I know it sounds wild. It's the latest thing in travel. We call it the 'ego trip.' We offer you a choice of alternate identities during your trip. Face it, why go to Mars as a tourist when you can go as a playboy or a famous jock?" *Total Recall*, a sort of *Fantasy Island* for the 1990s, lays bare the logic of tourism and antitourism. The desire to see the world without becoming the denigrated figure of the camera-toting tourist defines the antitouristic impulse that is integral to tourism rather than outside or beyond it. Each tourist differentiates himself from other tourists by taking on the title *traveler* and dreaming of even greater departures from the tourist role, to be traveling as someone else, someone who belongs in the midst of the foreign landscape performing a grand task like the archeologist who discovers a gateway to a lost world or the spy who diverts imminent world disaster, all the while getting a great look at the sights. Thus, the "ego trip" offers an escape from the label of tourist. In this case, the protagonist of *Total Recall*, Douglas Quaid, played by Arnold Schwarzenegger, chooses to travel as a spy, a category not entirely distinct from playboy or famous jock as we know from the globe-trotting, skirt-chasing spies of the *I Spy* television series and James Bond films. The spy identity also implies a tourist stand-in figure

marked by physical prowess, mental agility, and a ready arsenal of local knowledge, weaponry, and handy gadgets.

Within this particular story, the "ego trip" ends up delivering even greater
authenticity than anticipated by the Rekall sales team. Quaid is unknowingly
drawn to the spy option due to his former profession within the interplanetary
intrigue business prior to an unfortunate memory-suppression procedure, which
left him with his current mundane existence as a construction worker. The Rekall
experience returns Quaid to his prior heroic self and reconnects him to authentic experience as he embarks on a life-threatening mission to Mars. Along the
way, Quaid is plagued by only a few moments of *Videodrome*-like reality confusion,
which force him to decide whether his spy identity is authentic or the product of
internalized simulation. This particular plot twist, the reawakening of Douglas
Quaid the former spy, turns the myth of demediating mediation into reality as the
literal internalization of the simulation technology in the form of the memory
implant leads to a shedding of the sensorially deadening effects of daily life. The
tourist's virtual adventure awakens the hero and delivers an authentic experience
of Mars for this masterful spy who breaks through the politics of deception that
has governed the planet's settlement.

—— Verne, Crichton, and Scientific Fiction

Total Recall takes all the narrative licenses afforded it by the science fiction genre,
a class of stories unconstrained by the limits of present day or by the realm of possibilities presented by our own planet's specificity. Interestingly, however, Quaid's
journey as facilitated by Rekall takes a path characteristic not of science fiction
but of *scientific* fiction, with an introduction to the exotic space paved by claims
to authenticity and scientific authority. Quaid's preoperative procedures include
a slide show of images from the travel destination, with the most memorable ones
depicting relics of artifacts from Mars, presumably acquired by some astro-arche-
ologist during a golden age of interplanetary discovery before the settlement of
the red planet with tract housing and unsavory dive bars. The informational
introduction is clearly of a documentary nature, evoking the apparently known
history of the planet's colonization. Thus, while the science fiction story may
begin with a time and a place—Jupiter in the year 2200 for instance—that is
grounded in the unknown and in an acceptance of the distant future's unlimited
possibilities, the scientific fiction story uses claims of scientific authority and the
realm of known information to funnel the reader or viewer into a fantasy world.
While suspension of disbelief is all that is necessary within science fiction,
informed belief is essential within scientific fiction. And that belief on the part of

the virtual tourist is gradually earned through the text's presentation of historical detail, archeological fact, and scientific discourses that carry a level of authority that makes a location more real and its past more accessible. The "exactitude of science" provides distraction from the fact of simulation: this textual demonstration of scientific mastery serves as a disavowal of the remoteness of authenticity within simulated travel. It also elevates the position of the tourist to a height of knowledge, which secures mastery in the face of a dauntingly different location.

Jules Verne, labeled by some as the father of science fiction, has been reclassified as a writer of scientific fiction due to his reliance on established bodies of knowledge, including physics, geography, cartography, oceanography, and aerodynamics. This reliance explains his prescience; the technologies he depicted were believable and had predictive value because they were based on understandings of foundational sciences and on knowledge of the trajectories of technological development. Because his novels were grounded in reality and buttressed by the exactitude of science, they were fertile for advancing the touristic fantasy, with its pursuit of authenticity. They referenced a world that could be toured while evoking a fantasy of discovery, first contact, and circumnavigation unavailable to the average tourist. The only contemporary author to rival Verne's popularity within the genre of scientific fiction is Michael Crichton, whose works are the focus of this chapter. The comparison of these two authors and of adaptations of their works into moving-image form brings into relief the repercussions of this transition from the map-filled library at the center of Verne's work to the satellite-fed, video-surveillance control room of Crichton's oeuvre. Yet certain similarities remain. Both authors draw on the structure of the repeat journey in an enactment of historical retrieval or "total recall," as if some reservoir of authenticity is only accessible through the past. And for both authors, travel as depicted within scientific fiction is consistently an "ego trip," if only due to the position of knowledge occupied by the scientist-inventor-explorer protagonist, a position shared by the viewer/reader by virtue of the authors' conveyance of scientific knowledge.

In the same way that Verne has been called the Homer of the nineteenth century, one could call Michael Crichton the Jules Verne of the twentieth (and now perhaps, twenty-first) century.[4] Both men have been classified as writers of popular fiction, and the work of each man has been deemed ideally suited to cinematic adaptation, even if neither writer has been hailed as a literary luminary. Verne began his writing career before cinema was a reality and died in 1905, before the release of Edwin Porter's interpretation of *Around the World in Eighty Days* in his film *A Policeman's Tour of the World*. Crichton, on the other hand, not only writes novels with thoughts of cinematic adaptation never far from his mind but has directed films, produced television shows, and reportedly is now in the video game business. And like Verne's work, Crichton's novels are nearly always scientifically informed. His expertise as a medical doctor and his dedication to exhaustive background research are both evident in his writing. For instance, *Congo*'s detailed bibliography reveals extensive research in the fields of primatology, satellite technology, laser applications, African ecology, and the history of culture and exploration in the Congo region. The narrative events of other novels such as *The Andromeda Strain* and *Jurassic Park* have been credited with a semblance of plausibility due to Crichton's groundwork in epidemiology, paleontology, and genetics, some understanding of which he passes on to his readers in a marriage of entertainment and didacticism.

Whereas Verne began writing nonfiction scientific articles before moving into the realm of scientific fiction, Crichton has alternated his fiction and nonfiction writing, publishing informative books such as *Five Patients, Electronic Life,* and *Travels* in between his better-known fictional explorations of medical technologies, underwater relics, and Japanese conglomerates. The status of Crichton's writing as informed by medical/scientific knowledge is combined with exploration narratives to create a particular version of the touristic: the visitation of new and exotic spaces fictionally conveyed, but still with some claim to veracity. In many ways, this touristic formula, which is not unlike Verne's, hints at a universal combination of education and entertainment in the Western touristic confrontation with the new and the different. The exotic is understood and enjoyed by the leisured tourist who maintains the upper hand against the foreign environment through a process of knowledge accrual.

Crichton's borrowing of Vernian strategies in his stories of Old World challenges met with New World technologies is not surprising in light of his avid consumption of Verne novels as a child and his collection of old Verne editions as an adult. Homage to the master of scientific fiction is paid in Crichton's *Sphere*, in which a deep-sea voyage and an otherworldly encounter results in crew members' thoughts manifested in reality. The most ominous of the manifestations is a sea monster almost literally torn from the pages of Verne's *Two Thousand Leagues under the Sea*. The manifestation is traced back to a crewmember (played by Samuel L. Jackson) who as a child never moved beyond the fear-inspiring page of Verne's novel detailing the giant sea squid's attack.

In Verne's universe, reality might be understood and organized through the map, but the cartographer's drawings are nonetheless abstractions, simplifications unable to record the world's detail and protean shape. In short, the coex-

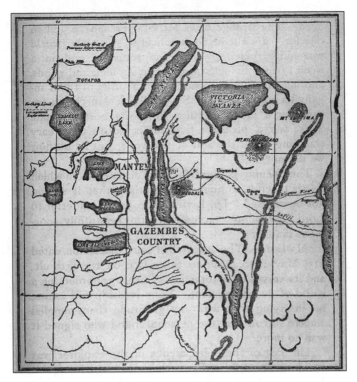

The map brings into tactile form personal experience, abstracted knowledge, and narrowing gaps in geographical knowledge.

———————

"Map of the Watershed of Africa,"
from *Doctor Livingstone: Life and Explorations in Africa*. John E. Potter, 1874.

tensive map does not exist. The true map of Borges's story comes closest to being delivered through more modern technologies such as cinema and video. A pixilated vision of the earth delivered by satellite and by multiple surveillance cameras moves toward a coextensiveness with and usurpation of reality through the maintenance of instantaneous temporal adaptation as the world shifts, rotates, and erodes. Thus, Michael Crichton is held up as a contemporary Jules Verne who replaces the yellowed and crumbling map with a postmodern mapping of the world through new technologies, a travel writer for the turn of the twenty-first century whose work elucidates the tricky status of authenticity within an age marked by new levels of simulated tourism. Appropriately, this travel writer for an era dominated by visual media is only secondarily a writer. First and foremost, Crichton is a creator of stories for the small and large screen, of original material that reaches the majority of audiences in cinematic, televisual, and interactive form.[5]

—— The Repeat Journey

In her book *On Longing,* Susan Stewart writes, "'Authentic' experience becomes both elusive and allusive as it is placed beyond the horizon of present lived experience, the beyond in which the antique, the pastoral, the exotic, and other fictive domains are articulated."[6] Souvenirs and relics help to bridge the void that separates past and present, documenting the authenticity of their points of origin and producing the illusion of the past's authenticity made accessible through the materiality of the object. The narrative structure that I call *the repeat journey* creates a similar illusion of past authenticity recovered through the present tense of narrative, a "structure of desire" aiming to realize a particular formulation of the world.[7] The journey as a spatial story is replicated in the retracing of footsteps as history and contemporaneity are conflated and a mythos of discovery and authenticity is woven.

The repeat journey, as an act of historical retrieval, also may draw on the power of a relic or artifact to propel it. The boat on which the journey was first made may be used in a tracing of the same path; the tale of the discovery of a notable museum piece may determine the structure of the travel itinerary; or an explorer's diary might serve as a map for the journey's geographic trajectory. The most notable relic from Verne's work is the volcanic rock given to Professor Lindenbrook that contains a message from a long-dead explorer on how to reach the center of the earth in the novel *Journey to the Center of the Earth.* But even beyond such explicit examples, Verne's characters seem to always be following on the heels of a notable explorer or referencing the cartographic charts of a recent pioneer traveler, with such explorers and travelers torn from the current events of Verne's day or even occasionally from the pages of his own fictional work.

Typically in Verne's stories, little time has passed between the original journey and the repeat journey made in its wake; but the same cannot be said of Crichton's travel fiction. First, Crichton's novels should be understood as repeat journeys to the extent that they duplicate the trail left by Verne's fictions, traipsing into space, beneath the ocean's surface, and across the earth. Thus, just as the paperback version of *Two Thousand Leagues,* which appears in *Sphere,* forms the link that explains the sea monster manifestation, Crichton's collection of old Verne editions are the relics that link the two authors' fictional journeys. They explain Crichton's writings as a manifestation of his childhood fascination with Verne, despite the century that separates the two men. Within Crichton's novels, the repeat journey may also be rather literal, as in the case of *Congo*'s explicit tracing of Henry Morton Stanley's path into the African interior. Or the relic itself may

Although contemporaries, Henry Morton Stanley represents a more modern traveler than David Livingstone in that Stanley was a journalist who aimed at bringing back knowledge of Africa and even transmitting it by telegraph while immersed in the African interior.

From an advertising promotion for Lion Coffee, circa 1890.

provide the conduit into a manufactured past, as in the case of *Jurassic Park*, the novel and film (Steven Spielberg, 1993) in which a return to prehistory springs from a petri dish. In this latter case, when the past is manufactured, as is also the case in *Westworld* and *The Lost World*, the simulation technologies within the stories mirror the virtual tourism of cinema spectatorship, providing an interesting reflection on the effects of simulation much like that in *Videodrome* or *Total Recall*.

—— In the Footsteps of Henry Morton Stanley

Some of Crichton's work sidesteps the problem of the apparent exhaustion of territories to be explored or of secrets not yet dragged into the light by combining earthly exploration with phenomena originating beyond earth. In *Sphere,* a voyage to the South Pacific reveals an alien spaceship resting on the ocean floor, while in *The Andromeda Strain,* contaminated space probes return to earth, setting off a chain of frightening biological events. In each case, an alien object plunged into earthly contexts forces a confrontation with the gaps in our knowledge of the universe beyond earth, without departing into the unbounded postulation of science fiction. Yet other books—*Congo, Jurassic Park,* and *The Lost World*—remain more firmly implanted in familiar terrain: planet Earth. Nonetheless, Crichton creates narratives of travel and discovery that engage in searches for origins. *Congo,* written in 1980 but not adapted into film form until 1995 (and directed by Frank Marshall) due to the difficulties of constructing believable apes for the screen, provides an interesting example in its use of the repeat journey as a device for resuscitating a belief in the existence of the as-yet undiscovered here on earth.

The book begins with an 1887 quote from Henry Morton Stanley and draws on Stanley's *The Darkest Africa* in a retracing of the explorer's footsteps into the past, into an unpenetrated Africa and an imaginary vision of the Congo. In his introduction, Crichton begins to sketch out this vision of a place on earth that exists in the past in its timelessness and in its reluctance to be pulled into the knowledge system and economic network of the present tense. Crichton limits the darkness of the "Dark Continent" to the Congo region in an insistence on some remaining mystery left to be unburied as he writes, "In fact, Africa is called the Dark Continent for one reason only: the vast equatorial rain forests of its central region. . . . This primeval forest has stood, unchanged and unchallenged, for more than sixty million years. . . . The great expanse of the forest remains inviolate, and to this day thousands of square miles are still unexplored." Crichton thus begins his trek into the imaginary by mapping out an untouched territory, a pocket suspended in time and surrounded by but disconnected from the Africa of the twentieth century. He continues to blend fact and fiction by comparing a 1979 American expedition to Stanley's search for Dr. David Livingstone and his voyage down the Congo River. It is this 1979 expedition that the next three hundred pages of fiction recount.

Like other Crichton novels, these three hundred pages are chock full of gadgets and high-tech tools that would have made Stanley green with envy. Yet, as most of these devices get lost, broken, or trampled by page 200, *Congo*'s characters find themselves facing some of the same difficulties that slowed Stanley's progress. The blending of past and present, fact and fiction continues as Crichton writes in reference to the American explorers, "And like Stanley, they returned with incredible tales of cannibals and pygmies, ruined jungle civilizations, and fabulous lost treasures."[8] He concludes the introduction with two sets of acknowledgments, one to the fictional characters of the book as if the company Earth Resources Technology Services or ERTS (known as Travi-Com in the movie), Project Amy, and Dr. Karen Ross actually existed, and the second to the actual people who served as Crichton's tour guides during his research visits to Zaire. (Like Verne, Crichton uses details from his own travels to embellish his fictional description.)

The lionization that has been showered upon Stanley has reached such a height that it is easy to forget that his journey was in itself a repeat journey in its duplication of Livingstone's travels. Stanley's fame has far outstripped that of Livingstone, who spent more time in Africa and attained greater knowledge of its people and culture as a missionary and medical practitioner. Undoubtedly, Stanley had the better lines of dialogue and was more proficient at self-publicity. As a

While David Livingstone's death was a media event of sorts—with the final words in his journal reprinted and illustrations of his final trip in search of medical help while ailing from malaria widely circulated—it lacked the media fanfare of Henry Morton Stanley's telegraphs and triumphant homecomings.

"The Last Mile of Dr. Livingstone's Travels,"
from *Doctor Livingstone: Life and Explorations in Africa.* John E. Potter, 1874.

correspondent for a New York newspaper, Stanley ensured that every leg of his trip was well documented, recounted in American and British newspapers, and retold in low-priced books that were often tailored to popular audiences. Livingstone, on the other hand, was so far outside of the West's communication network that questions concerning his possible death remained unanswered for quite some time. He also had the misfortune to never return to Europe to enjoy the kind of fanfare and exaltation experienced by Stanley. A retracing of Livingstone's path therefore would lack the nicety of a round trip for the virtual tourist.

If Livingstone had been tied into the dense network of satellite technologies and global positioning systems that characterized Crichton's protagonists' journey, a simple triangulation procedure would have been sufficient to locate Livingstone. What is surprising is not this technological disparity that separates Crichton's world and that of Livingstone, but the disparity that distinguished Stanley from Livingstone. Coverage of Stanley's expeditions was accompanied by lengthy expositions on the American press's penetration of the world and on the wonders of magnetic telegraphy, the technology through which Stanley's discovery of Livingstone was announced. One author pauses in his secondhand account of African exploits to report that thanks to the telegraph, "The inhabitants of Christendom were like next-door neighbors."[9] And in describing a dispatch from Athens, Greece, the same author writes, "The difference of time and the 'girdle round about the earth' put the inhabitants of the Mississippi Valley, as they took their suppers, in a situation in which they might have criticised an oration by Demosthenes before he had gone to bed, had Demosthenes belonged to this day and generation."[10] A discourse of instantaneous communication promised a quoting of "what these men have said of Africa on the spot."[11] The world was already beginning to be understood as an entity that must be tamed not only through static visualization, but also through the simultaneous conquering of space and time. And telegraphy was only the first step.

Current media expeditions often reflect a similar play between the desire for historical reenactment and a perpetual present tense afforded by real-time technologies. In 1995, thousands of American high school students returned from a vicarious voyage into Africa, a 6,000-mile yearlong trip that retraced Stanley's search for the sources of the Congo and Nile Rivers. The students never left the classroom, of course, but rather were electronically linked to a team of sixteen explorers in Central Africa. Twelve selected high schools participated in live interactive teleconferences with the explorers at various points along the route, while schools outside of these central twelve could pick up the down-link signal from the satellite as well as communicate one-on-one with explorers via the Internet.

Crichton's fiction shares in this celebration of instantaneous communication and the technological conquering of space as well as exhibits this play between immersion and separation. In fact, the Congo expedition for high school students could have even been an educational project sponsored by ERTS, the fictional organization in *Congo*, a group that uses the most sophisticated of technology to maintain a high-resolution satellite link with a finely knit web of locations across the globe. For ERTS, the world is a combination of material resources and information. The company's field teams are deployed to study "uranium deposits in Bolivia, copper deposits in Pakistan, agricultural field utilization in Kashmir, glacier advance in Iceland, timber resources in Malaysia, and diamond deposits in the Congo."[12] An array of cameras continuously records information using "conventional and draped aerial photography, infrared photography, and artificial aperture side-looking radar."[13] In short, while individuals of Stanley's era represented the continent as a mapable totality with the blanks now filled in, within the control room of ERTS, the world, lacking any kind of fixity, is reducible to a flow of information, of images that can be digitally deconstructed or reconstructed. The crunching of material reality into data is accomplished through a number of devices described by Crichton, who writes, "Instead of cameras, ERTS used multi-spectral scanners; instead of film, they used CCTs—computer compatible tapes. In fact, ERTS did not bother with "pictures" as they were ordinarily understood from old-fashioned photographic technology. ERTS bought "data scans" which they converted to "data displays," as the need arose."[14] On the one hand, ERTS functions as a library, as a storehouse of information much like the centering space of the library within many of Verne's texts. Yet, the goal of "picturing the world," theorized by Martin Heidegger to sum up the epistemological project of Verne's scientific age, seems to have shifted as anthropomorphic vision has been supplanted by "data scanning," the extraction of information without reference to human vision. Within the ERTS control room, knowledge of the world is fractured and immense. The narrative, however, quickly leaves this space to engage in an old-fashioned exploration account; yet this interpretation of the world as data continues to inflect the characters' experiences.

Several incidents within *Congo* emphasize the departure from the Enlightenment equivalence between seeing and understanding. The novel begins with an attack by a group of gray apes that is captured on videotape. The sounds and sights of that video clip are dissected and reworked to come up with an answer to the question of the animal's general species category. The questions "Does it look like an ape?" and "Does it sound like an ape?" cannot be trusted to human perception. Later in the novel, the lost city of Zinj is located, but the bas-relief paintings of the city walls cannot be read without technological assistance. Crichton describes the process: "By shining infrared light on the walls and recording the image with the video camera—and then feeding that image via satellite through the digitizing computer programs in Houston, and returning it back to their portable display unit—they were able to reconstitute the pictures on the walls."[15] One character comments on the peculiarity of looking directly at the walls and seeing only dark moss and lichen, while the computer screen displayed elaborate painted scenes: "There we were in the middle of the jungle, but we could only examine our environment indirectly, with the machines."[16]

Despite the novel's emphasis on technological vision, the immediacy of the jungle is given equal weight. The stifling heat of flowing lava, the pain of flesh-penetrating leeches, the dizzying sensations of parachuting—these and other strange tastes, smells, and sounds of the jungle are given a pungent tactility as descriptions of narrative events experienced through the human sensorium serve to convince readers of presence and immersion within the Congo. This bifocality—the touristic dual perspective of immersion and distanced perception—is even reflected in the movie poster for *Congo,* which features an image of immediacy in the face-to-face encounter with a gorilla, breaking the smooth surface of computer-generated text representative of the technological conversion of world into data.

It is through this dual perspective of technological and human vision that the characters of *Congo* are able to detect a lost world. While early explorers in Australia and other locations eagerly documented hundreds of new species, it is assumed that all species have now been detected and named and that we are now in a period of decline in which species are slowly disappearing. Similarly, excavations in long inhabited lands have nearly exhausted the earth of new finds. Sophisticated forms of radar and aerial photography have pinpointed many of the last undiscovered structures. Yet Crichton creates a tale of the last such discoveries as his characters happen upon the ruins of an ancient city built up around a diamond mine and protected by an undocumented species of gray ape. Interestingly, the African voyage is punctuated with laments about disappearing ecosystems and endangered species, while at the same time, Crichton depicts the Congo environment as inviolable and the race of gray apes as so abhorrent as to justify its extinction by human intervention if necessary.

The basic idea for *Congo* was formed in 1978, when Crichton suggested the idea of a "modern-day *King Solomon's Mines* with high technology and signing apes" to a producer at Twentieth Century Fox.[17] A gorilla named Koko, who became an animal celebrity of the 1970s because of her ability to communicate in sign language, had been Crichton's inspiration. Within the novel and film, Amy, the signing gorilla modeled after Koko, serves as a counterpoint to the gray apes. Collectively these primates fill in for the so-called primitives of *King Solomon's Mines,* with Amy representing the good indigene, the loyal if sometimes cowardly native who helps the Western traveler with flawless instinct, luggage carrying, and occasional translation. In contrast to the good natives who bow to Western superiority in such African exploration narratives are the warrior tribesmen whose cultural ways are marked by barbarism alone. Interestingly, the coloring of the gray apes, which fill the traditional narrative role of the barbaric natives, would seem to connote old age and the physical debilitation that such maturity brings. Yet, the grayness of this fierce species of apes is far more evocative of white pigment applied to a black surface, of white war paint smeared on to dark skin, that signifier of dangerous exoticism represented in Western cultural forms ranging from *National Geographic* magazine to the TV series *Gilligan's Island.* The only signifier that exceeds this image in its evocation of the perils of the primitive world is that of shrunken heads, necklaces of teeth and bone, or the discarded skulls that hints at the nature of the savages' last feast. Such a symbol also appears in *Congo* as the expedition crew encounters a pile of countless primate skulls, indicative of violence, cannibalism, and the lack of civilization implied by the absence of ceremonious disposal of the dead.

In the face of the disappearance of "untouched" tribal peoples and with the recognition of *primitivism* as a term marked by more fantasy than anthropological veracity, the monkey and its primate variants have come to fill the role of the primitive in re-creations of the exploration narrative. At the same time that this substitution—whether in reference to the substitution of a talking monkey for the manservant Passepartout in Electronic Arts' educational CD-ROM Around the World in Eighty Days (see chapter 5) or of a signing gorilla for the baggage-carrying native in *Congo*—indicates an effort to move beyond racist representation, the narrative pattern retroactively highlights the narrow divide that separates "missing link" depictions of African indigenes from monkeys within Western racist epistemologies, the traces of which stubbornly persist within exploration narrative paradigms.

Although the gray apes are the primary source of resistance impeding the expedition team's progress within the film, little screen time is dedicated to these warriors. Amy, on the other hand, is a consistent focal point of the narrative. In the transition from novel to film, her unaided signing described in the book is transformed into signing combined with an intelligent glove and voice box, which translate signs into spoken language. In addition to this cyborgian mix of machine and animal, Amy is perched between childhood and adulthood as she comes to terms with the traumatic events that led to her adoption by human parents. Her communication abilities have facilitated a partial assimilation into civilization, but her primitivism is depicted as an essential and inextricable component of her nature, despite her frustration with and alienation from nonsigning gorillas. The secrets contained within Amy's homeland—which concern the rise of civilization, the intricacies of the evolutionary chain, the elusive distinctions between human and animal, and the tentative balance of power between the two—also tell a larger story of human origins. The Congo expedition is thus the anthropological fantasy par excellence; it is the search for our past and for some human universal glimpsed in the eyes of a "primitive," defined as that which is not quite civilized, our footstep on the evolutionary chain. And with Amy in tow, the expedition members have the benefit of an informant, a translator who can communicate with the gorillas of the Congo and convey the "native's point of view" in the ultimate bridging of anthropologically defined difference.

—— Lost Worlds

In *Congo,* Crichton hatches a lost world seemingly from nothing more than Henry Morton Stanley's memory, in an act of spontaneous generation with little indication as to how the lost Atlantis of Zinj would have remained undetected for so long amid an overdeveloped, overexploited globe. *Jurassic Park* and its sequel *The Lost World* (Steven Spielberg, 1997) similarly utilize undeveloped pockets of the world for technological treks into a past-like context. In fact, the title *The Lost World* could fit *Congo* and a few other Crichton novels equally well. The difference is that in this case the diegetic universe has not actually been lost and found, as Crichton would have us believe in the case of Zinj. As the novel recounts, the not-lost world of *The Lost World* has been created in an act of scientific authorship. The remote island of the 1995 novel offers significant geological barriers to would-be trespassers, except for the Nemoesque characters who discover the water caves that lead to the island's interior. Nonetheless, this Central-American island has been mapped and drawn into the loop of contemporary economic relations by way of being purchased by a private citizen. Far from being a pocket of timelessness, the island contains the remnants of cutting-edge experiments in genetics. Its lost world has been reborn through the identification and reconstruction of dinosaur DNA found in naturally-preserved mosquitoes that stored blood drawn from their large Jurassic-era companions, a process detailed in *Jurassic Park.*

Visitors to the remote locations of *Congo* and *The Lost World* are tempted by scientific curiosity, but more often by the desire for economic gain. Two other

Crichtonian narratives, however, depict another motive for dropping in on these re-creations of the past: touristic pleasure. Both *Jurassic Park* and *Westworld* (the 1973 film directed by Michael Crichton) mirror the cinematic spectator's attraction to filmic simulations of exotic worlds and the distant past through the figure of the diegetic tourist who knowingly visits a technologically engineered past. *Jurassic Park*'s chain of causality is initiated when the amusement park owner invites his grandchildren to be the first tourists to visit his dinosaur safari. The dinosaurs are, for all practical purposes, real except for one significant alteration to their normal path of development: it is an all-female society. The threats of males fighting for access to mating partners and the dangers of overpopulation have thus been defused. In the case of *Westworld*, three pleasure parks have been designed to return tourists to the exotic past of feudal Europe, classical Rome, or the Wild West. Crichton's signature use of high technology makes its entrance in the parks' use of robots to simulate the inhabitants of these self-enclosed reincarnations of the past. Each robot is programmed to please, whether that means showing a cowboy a good time in the upstairs rooms of the saloon or challenging a hotshot tourist to a duel in which the robot will inevitably lose.

The functioning technologies of these tourist parks parallel the cinematic attraction in that pleasure is delivered to the tourist so long as the illusion is convincing. *Westworld* is particularly interesting in that role-playing and a willful suspension of disbelief are necessary to secure touristic delight in the charade, yet entrance into this world does not appear to have been guaranteed through signs of authenticity or references to an actual world. Within the films *Westworld* and *Jurassic Park*, however, the parallel between the smoothly running park technologies and the cinematic apparatus breaks down as a displaced form of authenticity returns with the technological glitch. In *Jurassic Park*, this glitch involves the overcoming of the all-female safeguard system and restoration of normal dinosaur behavioral patterns as the park is overrun by a reproductive, dinosaur-eat-dinosaur set of species relations. A similar state of turmoil erupts in the fantasy park of *Westworld* when the robots, like the dinosaurs, decide to do their own thing. In both cases, the semblance of a more authentic return to the past is accomplished through the dramatic fight to survive in which the tourist-turned-hero must engage while on her ego trip. *Westworld* thus proves the rule that the best adventure is a misadventure, as the safety of the environmental bubble bursts and the Wild West's kill-or-be-killed philosophy takes over. In short, the tourist may be precluded from visiting the actual frontier as it was in the late 1800s, but the theme park gone awry provides an authentic taste of its dangers.

—— Crichton's Success and Failure

As a seasoned traveler, Crichton is engaged in the search for immediate experience amid the planet's final reservoirs of authenticity. As a writer, he has tried to deliver the unique travel experience fitted into the story structure of traditional narratives of discovery made almost plausible through the insertion of scientific detail and technological spectacle. His writings evince an awareness of the receding horizon of authenticity and the use of scientific discourse in combination with the logic of the repeat journey to overlay geographical travel with an evocation of chronological backstepping. This metaphorical time travel is an effort to glean a sense of authenticity, a commodity far more abundant in the past than in the twenty-first century. This strategy and these terms are made most explicit in Crichton's recent work *Timeline,* which features a massively funded research institute conducting experiments in the area of time travel. The novel begins with a seemingly inconsequential argument between a husband and wife over the authenticity of Navajo rugs sold at a desert trading post versus those sold in Sedona tourist shops. The characters are extraneous to the story outside of their encounter with a dying man, a returning time traveler suffering from serious transcription errors as a consequence of miscalibrated time-travel technology. However, the issue of authenticity returns when Robert Doniger, the research institute president, reveals the financial wisdom behind investment in time-travel research. Doniger explains to potential investors, "In other centuries, human beings wanted to be saved, or improved, or freed, or educated. But in our century, they want to be entertained." He traces out a developmental path for this entertainment mania leading from film and television to participatory activities. He continues, "And what will they do when they tire of theme parks and planned thrills? Sooner or later, the artifice becomes too noticeable. This artifice will drive them to seek authenticity. *Authenticity* will be the buzzword of the twenty-fist century. And what is authentic? Anything that is not devised and structured to make a profit. Anything that is not controlled by corporations. Anything that exists for its own sake, that assumes its own shape. But of course, nothing in the modern world is allowed to assume its own shape. The modern world is the corporate equivalent of a formal garden, where everything is planted and arranged for effect. Where nothing is untouched, where nothing is authentic."[18] Doniger finds authenticity in a single location: the past. He muses to his audience, "The past is a world that already existed before Disney and Murdoch and Nissan and Sony and IBM and all the other shapers of the present day. The past was here before they were. The past rose and fell without their intrusion and molding and selling. The past is real. It's authentic."[19]

Crichton's belief in his own character's sales talk is only partial. As author, he uses the allure of the past to attract readers within this book and its predecessors. And, as has been mentioned, he has dedicated much of his life to the entertainment industry. However, the irony of the presentation's anticommercialist bent while delivered to an auditorium full of potential check writers is undeniable. Doniger's intention is to devise and structure an experience of the past to make a profit. While the book began with a contemplation of a castle's ruins as a signifier of authenticity, it ends with a relic, a statue with the visage of one of the time travelers, a sign of the past molded and shaped by one of Doniger's colleagues. Additionally, the assumption that the characters that populate the past are authentic is shown to be naive as several historical personages are revealed to be time travelers themselves. In other words, authentic experience in feudal France of 1357 risks being nothing more than an encounter between two time-traveling tourists appropriately costumed to fit in with the medieval crowds.

The wild success of *Jurassic Park* and the marginality of some of Crichton's other works, such as the film adaptation of *Congo,* ranked by some critics as one of 1995's ten worst films, illustrates the tenuousness of Crichton's strategy for delivering touristic fantasy. Judging from the success of *Jurassic Park*—both book and film, with their many differences—the formula for success is not singular. Scientific authority and cinematic spectacle play similar roles in the rerouting of a skepticism that detracts from the illusion of direct experience and from the belief in a return to a lost world marked by authenticity. The book's careful foundation of scientific fact with its protracted forays into genetics follows the route of scientific fiction. It builds up the tourist's ego trip by placing him in a position of knowledge—knowledge that makes plausible the narrative's recovery of historically situated authenticity. The film, while not totally dispensing with this technique, saves itself from an overly didactic and imbalanced narrative by exchanging the power of scientific description for technologically generated cinematic spectacle. The oscillation between an engagement with the spectacle as part of a seamless narrative and a fascination with "The Making of *Jurassic Park*" stories, which detail the efforts of puppeteers and special-effects wizards, indicates the presence of a fetishizing process. An acceptance of the dinosaurs' realism during the viewing experience is coupled with an overengagement with the splendors and mechanics of the simulation technologies behind *Jurassic Park.* This involvement with either the book's genetics lessons or the film's methods of computer-generated imagery is a necessary distraction from the absence of direct experience and from the possible pooling of skepticism around this miraculous recovery of authenticity. It is this gilded surface of science and technology that makes the illusion of demediating mediation convincing within an age marked by acute awareness of mediation and artifice. This celebration of technology paradoxically suggests that the very representational devices that are partially responsible for the decline of unmediated vision can enact the wonder of demediation. According to the myth of demediation (see chapter I of this volume), the devices that would seem to put us at a remove from an unfiltered reality by capturing and decontextualizing appearances can deliver spectacles of such grandeur and verisimilitude that we are brought closer to reality.

This formula only partially explains the failure of *Congo*. In this case, the book's dispersed scientific discourses actually work against the narrative's claims to an undiscovered world. Crichton's ecological, historical, anthropological, and geological description of the Congo suggests a fully probed and understood African interior rather than an opaque region with hidden treasures and perils; and the cinematic version suffers from a lack of originality in its special effects, causing the spectacle to fall flat. Similarly, the novel *Timeline* is plagued by the complexity of quantum physics, which blocks instead of facilitates the reader's entrance into informed belief in relation to the possibility of time travel. One chapter aptly begins with a quote from Richard Feynman: "Nobody understands quantum theory." Unlikely plot points are met by similar comments on the part of the book's scientists. Typical refusals of explanation include "Different world. Old assumptions don't apply" and "Quantum events are all counterintuitive." The reader does not absorb sufficient understanding of quantum physics to abandon old assumptions and intuition.

In short, although Crichton's formula for resuscitating a sense of discovery within a postmodern age has proven its promise, it frequently strains under the pressures of a questioning of the real. His successes reveal audiences' willingness, when given appropriate fodder, to believe in a world that has not yielded its most tightly held secrets. And Crichton's failures suggest that his technology-crowded pages and mise-en-scènes are sometimes better at demonstrating new ways of digitally mapping the world than they are at convincing readers and spectators that Captain Cook may still walk among us undetected by surveillance cameras and heat-sensing, satellite-triggered data scans.

PART THREE

Beyond Film

CHAPTER NINE

Millennium

TOURIST STAND-INS AND HYPHENATED ANTHROPOLOGISTS

ANTHROPOLOGISTS Deborah Gewertz and Frederick Errington describe a conversation overheard between tourists traveling to the Sepik River area in Papua New Guinea, where Gewertz and Errington do their fieldwork. The conversation eventually turns competitive as two of the tourists compare their prior visits to the river in terms of number of visits, duration of visits, and the degree of closeness to the area's indigenous people that they experienced during their visits. At first, the anthropologists listen with bemused distance, recognizing the familiar construction of a continuum of touristic achievement. On one end is the shuffleboard-playing cruisegoers, willing to skip the bus tour to finish their cocktails and, on the other end of the spectrum, rugged adventurers who pride themselves on getting as far off the beaten track as possible for as long as possible. The criteria for traveler-explorer accolades on this continuum were also familiar to the anthropologists, who long ago had integrated the study of touristic activity into their analysis of the changing dynamics of the Sepik River area. Particularly deserving of points within this evaluative scheme were the escape from all commercial structures and the ability to approach and build relationships, however short-lived, with the area's people in a spirit of respect and fair, nonmonetary exchange. At some point, Errington and Gewertz recognized their own position on the continuum, not as anthropologists whose pursuits were wholly unlike those of tourists but as glorified tourists who stayed a little longer, learned a little more of the language, and developed somewhat stronger relationships with the area's inhabitants. But nonetheless, the difference—for them and anthropologists in general—was one of degree, not kind.

The primitive is understood to have receded from view by way of extinction or compromised authenticity, such as when primitivism is a mask donned for the paying tourist-spectator.

Illustration by J. D. Crowe published in the *Los Angeles Times,* November 14, 1993.

Gewertz and Errington's questioning of their motivations as just another incarnation of touristic curiosity and desire is a consequence of one of the two major blows suffered by the discipline of anthropology in the last thirty years. Both have been gradual processes forcing anthropologists to reconsider the precepts of the field, as the "primitive" has disappeared from our world and our vocabulary and as a postcolonialist, postmodern critique of anthropology has questioned the discipline's ethics and integrity as a body of knowledge. To begin by addressing the former, the authenticity that the anthropologist traditionally has sought has been embodied by the idealized image of the primitive: the raw material of humanity, uncivilized, untouched by the "unnaturalness" of the modern world. Yet, the existence of the primitive, past or present, is at best dubious. Within an analysis of Claude Lévi-Strauss's search for a "natural" society, Marianne Torgovnick writes, "The primitive, like some grail, recedes before the observer. It may not exist and probably does not—but it is essential to act as though it does."[1] Twenty-six years after the publication of Lévi-Strauss's *Tristes Tropiques,* Jean Baudrillard writes of the state of the primitive in his recounting of the Philippine government's 1971 decision to protect the Tasaday tribe from the corrupting effects of industrial life by returning them to the remote jungle where they had been discovered. He notes, "Of course, these particular Savages are posthumous: frozen, cryogenised, sterilised, protected to death, they have become referential simulacra, and the science itself a pure simulation."[2] As if the eclipse of the primitive or the confirmed conversion of our final hope for authenticity into pure simulation were not troubling enough for the individual whose career depends upon the primitive, anthropologists have also been besieged by a questioning of their very ability to experience the authentic and bring word of it back to eager audiences. A body of critical thought has shot holes through the anthropological creed as stated by Bronislaw Malinowski, "to grasp the native's point of view . . . to realise *his* vision of *his* world."[3] Critics of anthropology from within and outside the discipline have addressed the impossibility of understanding a cultural difference in the indigene's own terms. Trinh Minh-ha, noting not only this dilemma but the power inequities of ethnographic knowledge states, "The anthropologist, as we already know, does not *find* things; s/he *makes* them. And makes them up."[4] Although few individuals within the field are willing to follow Trinh's lead and dismiss anthropology as total fiction, many agree that it may indeed be impossible to truly see from another person's point of view, particularly when the two individuals are separated by a number of consciousness-determining factors, not the least of which is a power differential that has outlived the administrative structures of colonialism.

In this chapter, both the heroic image of the anthropologist in the age of the primitive and the recent collapse in ethnographic authority is explored through the consideration of three cultural anthropologists who provide historical stepping-stones through a period of faith, the questioning of that faith, and finally the attempt to recapture authority and authenticity through the structure of the repeat journey. The first of these three anthropologists, Bronislaw Malinowski, is a fallen hero within the troubled discipline of anthropology. Through his work, the construction and downfall of the "chameleon field-worker" mythology can be witnessed, with all its implications for the authenticity-hungry tourist who looks to the anthropologist for an idealized version of herself. David Maybury-Lewis is a contemporary anthropologist and field-worker who struggles against two sets of tensions: the difficulty of bringing anthropology to a popular audience via a commercial medium and the dilemmas created by a sustained poststructuralist critique of anthropological practice and epistemologies. His trip into South America, enacted on television within the series *Millennium: Tribal Wisdom and the Modern World,* attempts to recoup a belief in anthropological authority and in an authenticity that lies outside of modernity. His strategy is the repeat journey; his voyage is explicitly a repetition of his own fieldwork experience and of Christopher Columbus's journey to the Americas. Like the Philippine government retracing the jungle path that once led to the "discovery" of the primitive in an attempt to reinvent the untouched savage, Maybury-Lewis charts a path through the jungle, covering past footsteps in the creation of a myth of first contact.

Maybury-Lewis's filmic trip down the Amazon perhaps most closely approximates the textual journey into memory of yet another anthropologist who trekked into the Brazilian Amazon: Claude Lévi-Strauss. While neither Lévi-Strauss nor his travel account *Tristes Tropiques* is referenced by the television program or by the program's companion book, Maybury-Lewis is clearly involved in the active construction of his own image as anthropologist in the model of Lévi-Strauss, the hyphenated anthropologist who straddles two worlds, at home in neither. In Maybury-Lewis and in the distorted mirror of Lévi-Strauss that he holds up, a reflection of the alienated tourist of the contemporary age becomes clearly distinguishable.

—— Anthropologist As Ideal Tourist Stand-In

As tourism and commercial relations penetrate the isolated islands and the inland jungles of the earth's continents, anthropologists, like authenticity seeking tourists, scurry to find those last "untouched" areas and the "unstaged" cultures situated there. Anthropologists, devoting their careers to such pursuits, have the tools necessary to locate those places that seemingly exist outside what is believed to be the polluting arm of modern culture. Thus, the antitouristic tourist eagerly follows in the footsteps of the anthropologist, hoping to beat other tourists, hotel developers, and the inevitable wave of commercialism. Such commercialism, Davydd J. Greenwood postulates, brings the gaze of the tourist greedy for glimpses of back-stage life. Allowing the tourist to purchase such glimpses transforms the host culture, eventually dissolving the culture's original meanings for the indigenous participants.[5] Anthropologists, on the other hand, presumably arrive on the scene before the original motives and meanings behind rituals and certain patterns of behavior are upstaged by an economic factor.

The anthropologist's training, language skills, length of stay, and supposed separation from the commodifying practices of tourism appear to guarantee the anthropologist's ability to secure an authentic vision of cultural difference. This notion of the anthropologist as the one individual who can extract truthful knowledge of a foreign culture is verbalized by Kenneth Read, an anthropologist known for his fieldwork in New Guinea. Two years before the discipline would be rocked by the publication of Malinowski's field diary, Read wrote in the preface to his 1965 monograph *The High Valley,* "The field-working anthropologist undergoes a unique experience; no one else knows quite so personally what it is like to live in an entirely alien culture. Missionaries do not know; government officials do not know; traders and explorers do not know. Only the anthropologist wants nothing from the people with whom he lives—nothing, that is, but . . . an understanding of and an appreciation for the texture of their lives."[6] Read's words, however, fail to communicate a certain mythology that has build up around the anthropologist. More than just education, a thirst for further knowledge, and assumed altruism separates the field-worker from other visitors; an aura of mystique surrounds the ethnographer, and Malinowski himself referred to it as the "ethnographer's magic." The Western anthropologist, as we will see in the case of Maybury-Lewis, goes through some mysterious rite of passage and, in the ideal situation, emerges from the trial by fire with the amazing ability to "see through native's eyes." Clifford Geertz describes this once common belief in the ethnographer's capacity for transcultural identification as "the myth of the chameleon fieldworker, perfectly self-tuned to his exotic surroundings, a walking miracle of empathy, tact, patience and cosmopolitanism" who possesses "some sort of extraordinary sensibility, an almost preternatural capacity to think, feel, and perceive like a native."[7] Geertz also notes that the man who had to a large extent created this mythos was the first to deliver a resounding blow to its foundations. In fact, tentative dates of birth and of the start of the myth's long, slow death can be sketched in using the dates of publication for Bronislaw Malinowski's *Argonauts of the Western Pacific* (1922) and his posthumously published *Diary in the Strict Sense of the Term* (1967), respectively.

—— Malinowski: Chameleon to Kurtz

If the repeat journey is indeed an attempt at historical recovery, then *A Diary in the Strict Sense of the Term,* experienced by readers as a revisitation to or a repeat journey of *Argonauts of the Western Pacific,* stands out as an exception to the rule. Rather than holding up the original voyage as a paragon, the *Diary* dismantles the myth set in motion by *Argonauts.* The 1922 monograph, published in the years following Malinowski's extended visits among the Trobrianders between 1914 and 1918, has been called "a kind of founding charter for the twentieth-century discipline of anthropology."[8] Following a period during which anthropologists relied on travelers, missionaries, and colonial administrators for information about distant cultures, individuals such as the physicist-turned-anthropologist Franz Boas and the former zoologist A. C. Haddon began to accompany—or organize, in

Haddon's case—official expeditions in the years immediately preceding the twentieth century.[9] Malinowski's fieldwork, on the other hand, initiated a new era of lone anthropologists living among the objects of their study for extended periods of time.[10]

Not only the fact of his prolonged solo sojourn among the Trobrianders established Malinowski as the "European Jason who brings back the Golden Fleece of ethnographic knowledge."[11] The monograph, which was the eventual outcome of his fieldwork, translated into text the ethnographer's experience and fully elaborated the nature of ethnographic authority. In the construction of this authority, *Argonauts* makes explicit the overlay of two gazes combined with a scientism grounded in the visual, a formula to be endlessly mimicked by successive fieldworkers. The primary gaze is, of course, that of the author. Insisting upon the authority of the eyewitness, Malinowski foregrounded his own firsthand experience, even including a list of events and rituals witnessed during his stay. Yet Malinowski is careful to bring the objects of his gaze into the sight lines of his readers. Photographs, which include among other things an image of his tent among the dwellings of the Trobrianders, solidify his "I was there" claim to authority and re-create for the reader scenes witnessed by Malinowski. His writing style similarly evokes what James Clifford calls the predominant mode of modern fieldwork summarized by the phrase "You are there . . . because I was there."[12] Malinowski relays this "ethnographic present" through his use of the active voice and the present tense.[13] Additionally, through his employment of the pronouns *we* and *you* he overlays his own gaze with that of the reader. The now famous line from his opening pages, "Imagine yourself suddenly set down surrounded by all your gear, alone on a tropical beach close to a native village" provides an apt example.[14] The reader as vicarious tourists is invited to engage her imagination, to place herself in Malinowski's shoes, and to enter an adventure communicated through what Mary Louise Pratt identifies as the familiar imagery of the castaway narrative.[15]

George W. Stocking Jr. similarly makes note of Malinowski's use of narrative tropes, and additionally, calls attention to his thick description of atmosphere that further serves to place the reader-tourist in an exotic environment of Malinowski's verbal creation. Skipping between the pronouns *I, you,* and *we,* Malinowski alternately becomes visible and then invisible to the reader. He may parade his own authority through the "I" of the "I-witness,"[16] then shift into a mode that allows the reader to see through the eyes of the effaced author. In the following example, concrete description of locale is combined with the use of a "we" that takes the reader hand-in-hand with the author into a tropical village: "When, on a hot day, we enter the deep shadow of fruit trees and palms, and find ourselves in the midst of wonderfully designed and ornamented houses . . . ."[17]

As Malinowski reminds his readers, the field-worker is no ordinary eyewitness. Afterall, the formula as described to this point could apply equally well to a good travel writer.[18] The ethnographer's perspective, as evinced by Malinowski, is marked by a remarkable duality. Malinowski, speaking in a how-to mode within *Argonauts,* encourages the field-worker to become not only observer but also participant. The scientist views and interprets from a distanced vantage point, one that enables a surveyance of the whole. The participant joins in, learns through direct experience, and comes to glimpse the world as the essentialized indigene sees it. Thus, while the abstracted vision of the scientist prevents absorption into the indigene's way of being, the participant, through empathy and identification, comes closest to an authentic knowledge of how the native perceives, understands, and experiences life. Malinowski, an apparent master of this careful oscillation between "outside" and "inside," thereby authored the mythos of the "anthropologist as pilgrim and as cartographer."[19] Unfortunately, over forty years later, it was discovered that this image of the heroic anthropologist was a work of fiction, or at the very least revealed only one small piece of a much larger portrait of the field-worker.

The story of the 1967 publication and reception of Malinowski's field diary is an oft-told tale. Discovered and published by his wife following his sudden death, *A Diary in the Strict Sense of the Term* sparked uproar within the anthropological community due to its portrait of the seamier side of fieldwork. Malinowski's scribbled remarks in Polish and English paint a portrait of a man in anguish, prone to depression, crankiness, and shockingly disparaging thoughts about his informants. He recounts his own escapism through novel reading and his battle to contain his sexual fantasies. His frequent use of the term "nigger" and his exasperated statement "Exterminate the brutes" (a self-conscious mirroring of the character Kurtz's words in the book *Heart of Darkness* by compatriot and fellow exile Joseph Conrad) radically alter our vision of the ethnographer who strikes the perfect balance between sober objectivity and empathy.

Other "confessionals" by field-workers published before and after the *Diary,* although without the same impact, continued to chip away at the mythos of the chameleon field-worker. Questions concerning the anthropologist's motives and the grounding of the discipline within the colonialist project similarly plagued anthropology. Books such as Johannes Fabian's *Time and the Other: How Anthropology Makes Its Object* (1983) and Bernard McGrane's *Beyond Anthropology* (1989) critiqued anthropological epistemologies and techniques of distantiation. The

Western, masculinist voice of anthropology received further scrutiny from the feminist, non-Western Trinh Minh-ha. Field-workers continuing to undertake ethnographic projects searched for alternative methodologies with varying success. Two such field-workers—Deborah Gewertz and Frederick Errington—grappling with the ethnographer's dilemma in the preface to their 1991 fieldwork account, summarize the critique conducted by postmodern critics, writing, "They ask: With what understanding and by what right do anthropologists speak for those among whom they have worked? They contend that ethnographic convention permitting anthropologists *because they alone were there* to speak with substantial authority about particular groups, no matter how different from their own, describing them as if presenting fixed and uncontestable facts, can no longer be taken as epistemologically acceptable. Nor can this convention be regarded as politically justifiable: to assume that one has the authority to speak for another is ultimately an act of hegemony."[20] Any other science relies on corroborating evidence, and measures accuracy through repetition of an experiment by others, but anthropology holds in esteem the lone field-worker, the first observer on the scene who recounts cultural detail from this early moment, which precedes inevitable contamination. Although anthropologists like Gewertz and Errington have arrived at personal solutions to the political dilemmas of fieldwork, the dominant models of anthropology continue to be questioned. Comparing the anthropologist to the tourist is yet another way of doubting the ability of the professional field-worker to escape her cultural framework and grab hold of an authentic or unmediated knowledge of cultural difference. Like tourists, ethnographers can not outrun the baggage of cultural prejudices nor sets of economic relations that forces anthropologists to exchange goods, even cash, for information and gawking privileges.[21]

—— Anthropology for Popular Audiences

While these discourses have clearly shaken the academy, the effect on the popular front is less measurable. As in the case of evolution—used as a framework for popular understanding long after the academy's dismissal of the concept—a "lag time" may separate popular and academic audiences. *Millennium,* a television series featuring noted Harvard anthropologist Maybury-Lewis but marketed to a popular audience, is intriguing due to its positioning between the popular and the academic. The makers of *Millennium* were undoubtedly aware of their dual audience: curious academic colleagues and members of the general public tuning in to a bit of educational—but involving—programming. Thus, a careful compromise between reviving the mythic heroism of past anthropological adventure and acknowledging current debates within the discipline had to be maintained.

Defying expectation, *Millennium* and its ten-part meditation on "tribal wisdom" is only one of several documentary series that have brought anthropology to television audiences in the midst of the current crisis in anthropological authority.[22] In fact, it seems quite unusual that in light of ongoing struggles to retain distinctions between popular, purchased pleasures and scientifically grounded knowledge, *Millennium*'s Maybury-Lewis would seek popular audiences via a medium noted for its solid imbrication within consumerism, a medium that has been compared to *One Thousand and One Nights* in its attempt to capture attention only to secure a stay of execution for corporate profit margins.[23]

Perhaps the tensions stemming from the ethnographer's dilemma[24]—as well as those generated by adapting pedagogy into a televisual/commercial form[25]—help explain the strangeness of *Millennium,* and in particular, the uncanny nature of its first episode, "The Shock of the Other," which aired in 1992.[26] The supposed anthropological object of this episode is the Mashco Piro, a tribe of Indians living in the Manu National Park in the Amazon rainforest. However, instead of learning about the Mashco Piro way of life or seeing examples of their material culture, viewers only get a partial glimpse of three members of this tribe and only during the last four minutes of the program. The rest of the episode is dedicated to the resuscitation of ethnographic authority through an odd mix of acknowledging contemporary ethical dilemmas and appealing to the traditional figure of the anthropologist as popular hero and ideal tourist stand-in.

As a tourist stand-in, Maybury-Lewis is one of a cast of characters who serve as intermediaries or buffers between a privatized television audience and an exotic "out there." The tourist stand-in delivers touristic pleasures to insulated, sight-seeing viewers often while differentiating himself from the denigrated figure of the tourist. The stand-in, with his privileged entrance into a distant culture, eases the viewers into exotic arenas through what Margaret Morse describes as television's logic of passage and segmentation.[27] A series of interceding passages connect disparate realms of the world as experienced through television. Aiding this process of transport are the tourist stand-ins, with their varying degrees of cross-cultural savvy and their use of incremental transport. For instance, the travel-show host may draw viewers into the intermediary space of his library before a final passage to the distant travel destination. Or in an instance involving a less authoritative tourist stand-in, during the TV series *I Love Lucy*'s season abroad, the outside world is mediated through the alternative domestic sphere of Lucy and Ricky's hotel room.

Not only traveling personalities but also objects often launch the televisual transport with the authenticity of the object guaranteeing passage.[28] The piece of folk art initiates the travel host's excursion, the tang of Italian-style pizza sauce transports the imaginary consumer to the top of the Leaning Tower of Pisa, or the stolen antique cross propels Remington Steele's journey to Malta in search of missing facts. In the case of *Millennium,* Maybury-Lewis holds the privileged object that propels the journey: a photograph of two women belonging to the Mashco Piro tribe, which has retreated into the Peruvian jungle and severed contact with the outside world. In what could be considered an act of wishful thinking, Maybury-Lewis interprets this photograph taken by a Peruvian neighbor as a sign that the Mashco Piro may be ready to reestablish contact.

Several intermediary spaces ease the viewer's passage to the nether regions of the Amazon. And like the host standing among bookshelves teeming with volumes, Maybury-Lewis gleans authority through these various intermediary spaces. The first such locale is Maybury-Lewis's original field site, the place of his rite of passage into anthropology; a crowd of Xavante Indians waits for him to step out of a helicopter and on to Brazilian land. His voice-over informs us that the Xavante Indians were known as a ferocious people who killed or drove away missionaries, government agents, and adventurers, but, a young Maybury-Lewis they accepted into their ranks as one of their own. He was given a Xavante name, adopted by Xavante brothers, and allowed to live in the chief's house. This acceptance by the indigene is reiterated as the new chief and adopted brother greets Maybury-Lewis. The subtitles translate the Xavante chief's words as, "We want only good people here. That's why we want you here, David. . . . We accept you, welcome." The implication is that the chief—who represents cultural otherness—accepts the good David and so we too should assume an underlying morality in his anticonquest.[29] Not only does Maybury-Lewis go through two rites of approval—the first presented as a memory of his first welcomed entrance into Xavante society and the second witnessed in this filmed arrival scene—but approval for the television series is also garnered. The reason given for this brief stopover is to get advice from his Xavante "brother" on whether to embark on the *Millennium* project. Presumably speaking for tribal peoples in general, a single Xavante Indian provides the consent Maybury-Lewis seeks.

The opening sequence similarly establishes the authority of the camera as unobtrusive witness through the use of self-effacing techniques common to ethnographic film. According to the narrative order implied by the sequence of images, the camera and its operator appear to already be on the scene, anticipating the arrival of Maybury-Lewis. The camera as window on the world presents images of a Xavante ritual, supposedly unstaged and performed in the absence of any non-Xavante witness (if we ignore the question of who operates the camera).

Only after these images is there a cut to Maybury-Lewis flying by helicopter to the village. When he climbs out of the helicopter, he is not accompanied by any camera equipment nor by a camera operator. The effaced camera is already on the ground, ready to witness the welcome scene.

The camera works in a manner similar to the way in which language works within Malinowski's *Argonauts*, enabling an alternation between the ethnographer's visibility and an invisibility. The camera at times provides an unmediated view of the Amazon and its scenery as seen through Maybury-Lewis's eyes. It entreats the viewer, "Imagine yourself . . . ." It suggests, "You are here . . . because I was here." However, most ethnographies combine some form of personal narrative, an insistence on the "I" of the author in order to establish ethnographic authority. Similarly, Maybury-Lewis steps in front of the camera, occasionally even directly addressing the audience. His visual presence frequently inhabits the screen, and a voice-over delivers further interjection of the ethnographic "I."

Maybury-Lewis's direct address contrasts with the Xavante's lack of acknowledgment of the camera. One is reminded of the 35-millimeter photographs taken of the Xavante by Maybury-Lewis in 1958. The photographic subjects appear to be at ease, hardly aware of the camera's presence. Interestingly, Maybury-Lewis implies that the journey depicted on *Millennium* is his and his wife's first return to Brazil since the original fieldwork. Actually, several short visits with the Xavante had occurred during the intervening decades. On a 1982 trip, the Maybury-Lewises were accompanied by William Crawford, a professional photographer. Crawford noted, "The Indians had all seen photographs and many owned photographs of themselves or of members of their families. Yet I found that they were often uncomfortable when a camera was around, far more uncomfortable than David had remembered from two decades before. Now they made it clear that they would only be photographed as they wanted to see themselves, at their best, in their best modern clothes, but still looking like Shavante."[30] This adoption of a certain savvy concerning their own representation on film is completely indiscernible, perhaps purposively effaced, within the sequences shown on *Millennium*.

Maybury-Lewis's editing out of his 1982 voyage is part of a larger rewriting of the past. The change in spelling from "Shavante" to "Xavante" is thus symbolic of a general reshaping for the popular eye of the Xavante image, past and present. Mary Louise Pratt, in her article "Fieldwork in Common Places," foregrounds the process of writing within ethnographic work by illustrating how arrival scenes self-consciously mirror the tropes of travel writing. Maybury-Lewis conveniently provides us with three such scenes of arrival. The one that takes place in the present tense of the television series resembles the welcoming of an old friend. A similar welcoming in the past tense—referring to the first fieldwork trip—is evoked by the voice-over. In the companion book to *Millennium,* this original arrival scene is further fleshed out. The Maybury-Lewises flew into an airstrip located near the Pimentel Barbosa post (named after an expedition leader killed by the Xavante) located on the Rio das Mortes. Climbing out of the plane and viewing their gear, they worried that their presents to the Xavante now looked "puny and insufficient."[31] The winning stroke, however, came with Maybury-Lewis's first words spoken to them in their own language. His ability to communicate with them amazed the Xavante, while his unusual accent brought them considerable amusement. At any rate, the Maybury-Lewises received their welcome into a supposedly fierce and feared tribe.

Oddly enough, a third and different arrival scene is described in Maybury-Lewis's *Akwa-Shavante Society;* it is a scene that Pratt includes under the category of "degraded versions of the utopian arrival scene . . . first contact in a fallen world where European colonialism is a given and native and white man approach each other with joyless suspicion."[32] Apparently the Xavante, who had become accustomed to the gifts brought by visiting Brazilian army officers, greeted the Maybury-Lewises solely to see what goodies would be handed them from the anthropologists' many trunks and bags.[33] Pratt views this as a symbolic prelude to the many problems that Maybury-Lewis goes on to describe in his monograph, including "his informants' hostility and uncooperativeness, their refusal to talk to him in private, their refusal to leave him alone, his problems with the language, and so on."[34]

It seems that in the same way that Malinowski's 1967 publication provided an altered vision of his first fieldwork experience, so does Maybury-Lewis's portrait within *Millennium* provide a different image than the troubled anthropologist of his 1967 fieldwork write-up. Yet where Malinowski's return to his site of professional conception debunked the hero image of his earlier text, Maybury-Lewis's return is an attempt to revive that image of the heroic field-worker.

—— The Making of the Hyphenated Anthropologist

In addition to being a repeat journey of Maybury-Lewis's past trips to Xavante territory, the first *Millennium* episode also resembles a return to Lévi-Strauss' *Tristes Tropiques,* the text that Susan Sontag argues establishes the model of the anthropologist as popular hero for a modern, alienated age.[35] The myth of the chameleon field-worker who becomes the indigene in order to see through native's eyes may have been born with Malinowski's *Argonauts of the Western*

Pacific, but Lévi-Strauss elaborates on the process or the epiphany that provides the anthropologist with this unusual insight. In his chapter "The Making of an Anthropologist," Lévi-Strauss also returns to his original field site, among a similarly missionary-murdering tribe of Brazilian Indians. He describes the experiential factor of fieldwork as the crucial factor that induces "that psychological revolution which marks the decisive turning point in the training of the anthropologist."[36] The mysterious ordeal of fieldwork, with its psychological revolution, appears to create a split subject, the hyphenated anthropologist caught between two worlds—or in this case, a Maybury-Lewis who returns to Brazil, to, in his words, "my other half, my other world."

The hyphenated anthropologist could be considered a close variant of the seemingly untroubled chameleon field-worker, the myth put forward by Malinowski's 1922 work. The hyphenated anthropologist, like the chameleon field-worker, straddles two cultures and can therefore serve as translator, conveying information about a tribal people to Western audiences. He learns to speak and, as Maybury-Lewis would have us believe, think like the people he lives among. Yet, he never loses the distanced perspective of the scientist. This duality is evident in the opening shots as Maybury-Lewis approaches the Xavante village by helicopter. Traveling with his Western accouterments and looking down from above on the gathered Xavante people below, Maybury-Lewis is the distanced observer, granted a privileged aerial perspective on the object of his study, a metaphorical reenactment of his past attempts to grasp the whole, to understand Xavante culture as a cohesive picture. This perspective soon collapses into a more intimate gaze and an attempt to convince the viewers through a visual equivalence granted Maybury-Lewis and his Xavante counterpart that the anthropologist-participant is as much a part of this world as the one he left behind.

The hyphenated anthropologist as embodied by Lévi-Strauss is an entity of complexity. Maybury-Lewis's rendition, a more transparent borrowing of past traditions, rises like the phoenix from the ashes of Malinowski's deconstructed *Argonauts.* He insists upon uncanny powers of transculturation but stands apart from the myth of the chameleon field-worker to the extent that the mental costs of his oscillation between two worlds are foregrounded. Such alienation or split-consciousness is not registered within Malinowski's *Argonauts,* but his *Diary,* on the other hand, illustrates a crisis of identity that has been compared to Kurtz's unraveling within *Heart of Darkness.*[37] With Lévi-Strauss and Maybury-Lewis, the alienation has reached new heights and is in many ways a reflection of modern alienation in general, although intensified in the figure of the intellectual. The hyphenated anthropologist suffers from what Georg Lukács has called "transcendental homelessness," a loss of groundedness in place, an alienation from one's home culture. Lévi-Strauss as field-worker, intellectual, and Jew in exile has lost sight of any firm concept of home, as has Maybury-Lewis, who spent his childhood in transit as the son of a British engineer deployed to various British colonial holdings in order to inspect canal construction. Now, as Maybury-Lewis laments his inability to feel at home in British culture or in his adopted American culture, he frames his journey to the Amazon as a quest to answer the same questions that plagued Paul Gauguin: Where do we come from? Where are we going? This alienation has become part of the heroic myth of the anthropologist, since alienation from one's home is presumed to reduce the mediating effects of viewing a foreign way of life through the lens of a rigidly held cultural standpoint.

In the repeat journey to his first field site, Maybury-Lewis tries to link his two worlds, his two halves, through the brief line segment that marks out his path from the United States to Brazil. The show's opening introduces us to the hyphenated subject as it shows Maybury-Lewis's Xavante self—known as Apawing—engaged in an intimate conversation with his Xavante brother while presumably his Western half uses a voice-over to espouse his philosophy on cultural difference and presumably the show's philosophy. The camera lingers above the heads of the two men laying side-by-side on the ground and intently conversing, apparently unbothered by the camera, while the voice-over drowns out their voices: "We are the two extremes of our world, yet we live together. Brothers, other and other—two mysteries to each other, yet joined by respect. So respect the mystery. Sometimes let the mystery be and maybe we'll be brothers still in a thousand years."

In this instance, *Millennium* does reflect some of the current debates within anthropology. Maybury-Lewis backs away from what has been called the epistemic violence of ethnographic knowledge,[38] the need to discover a society's essential core, to distill and translate a people into genealogical charts and exhibits of material culture. He seems to echo Trinh Minh-ha's words, "respect [a culture's] realms of opaqueness."[39] However, at the same time that Maybury-Lewis admits the irreducibility of culture, he retreats from science's domestication of cultural difference only to back up into the arms of the linked practice of fetishizing difference as mystery. Mystery attracts the curious Western eye; the tourist's gaze is allured by the promise that the obfuscating surface can one day be stripped away to reveal some deeper structure that puts all questions to rest. In one example of such a process, Maybury-Lewis, at points during his journey, struggles with two conflicting thoughts, that of his rational mind and that which is rooted in the unexplained intuition of his Xavante half. Such knowledge possessed by the transculturated anthropologist is elusive, even impenetrable to Western logic. It remains a mystery to the viewers but not to the man weaving more of that "ethnographer's magic."

—— Birth, Death, and Regret

Our introduction to this man of science and product of mystical initiation, however, is not over. Sontag has described anthropology as "necrology" so perhaps *Millennium*'s fixation on birth and death is appropriate.[40] Our little jaunt to Brazil is only one of several repeat journeys or passages to sites of conception. Maybury-Lewis transports viewers to the Catholic school in Spain where he first decided to become an anthropologist. Conveniently located there is a statue of Columbus, which Maybury-Lewis dutifully contemplates. He stands at the point of his own anthropological birth to ponder his next journey, a journey that mirrors Columbus's, the most legendary of contacts between the "civilized" world and the hidden realms of so-called untouched primitives. Maybury-Lewis mourns the loss of the moral certainty that motivated Columbus and the field-workers of another age, better known as missionaries. He states that *Millennium* will be "a series of films which will try to capture the wisdom of tribal peoples before it is all gone, before they are all gone." Maybury-Lewis's tropics sound as sad of those of Lévi-Strauss, who wrote, about his 1935 voyage, "Journeys, those magic caskets full of dreamlike promises, will never again yield up their treasures untarnished . . . . The perfumes of the tropics and the pristine freshness of human beings have been corrupted by a busyness with dubious implications, which mortifies our desires and dooms us to acquire only contaminated memories."[41]

MAYBURY-LEWIS'S SIMILARLY sad tale combines words and images. In a somewhat heavy-handed sequence, a funeral in a Peruvian town that the anthropologist calls a "halfway house" between two worlds is intercut with scenes that represent for Maybury-Lewis the evils of technological change and the slow death of what he calls the "web of life."[42]

For Lévi-Strauss and Maybury-Lewis, the anthropological journey is the construction of a narrative of loss and nostalgia, a cathartic appeasement of Western guilt over "our own filth, thrown in the face of mankind,"[43] and a race against time to find the last "untouched" human beings before they are gobbled up by a homogenizing monoculture. At least in the case of Maybury-Lewis, the anthropologist's funeral march comes at a time when many of these ideas, from the unequivocal belief in monoculture to the notion of pristine cultures, have been exploded.[44] But Maybury-Lewis's search for tribal wisdom marches on, driven by a nostalgia for "authentic human differences," "a sense of belonging," and "a harmony with the natural world," but most of all it is motivated by a nostalgia for ethnographic authority and an older, more dignified image of the anthropologist.[45]

The anthropologist of another era would have followed the path already cleared by conquerors and colonialists. Maybury-Lewis's route, however, has a few more roadblocks. Eventually, the episode moves forward from his soul-searching and vague contemplation of "first world"/"third world" relations to bureaucratic problems. An Indian council has restricted the film crew's access to the land where the Mashco Piro had been sighted. Apparently, "the Amazon's last secret" will not be revealed. Nonetheless, the boats loaded down with camera equipment still complete the journey, and as they float by Mashco Piro land, although prohibited from mooring, they glimpse three female faces from between the trees. No contact with the Mashco Piro beyond this exchange of glances ensues, and the excursion ends in disappointment. Maybury-Lewis laments that he was not given the chance to prove to the Mashco-Piro that he is different from the exploitative travelers who have come before him. He regrets that he was unable to prove to himself, to the viewers, to the Mashco Piro that he is something other than a souped-up, camera-clicking tourist floating down the Amazon.

In the spirit of Scheherezade, many anthropology shows try to fashion their material into narratives. In this episode, the structure of the journey provides the narrativity, and the many unknowns swirling around the Mashco Piro engage the audience's thirst for answers. However, Maybury-Lewis, like the tourist who travels to Memphis only to discover that Graceland is closed, meets with anticlimax. In an attempt to save this aborted narrative and to cover over the anticlimax, these glimpses of cultural difference are visually fetishized as the telephoto lens captures their every movement, and the final shots appear to be frozen in time. In the absence of any newly found anthropological knowledge, these images symbolize the journey and serve as trophy or souvenir.

Lévi-Strauss's journey was a similarly anticlimactic attempt to comprehend the authentic primitive who repeatedly eluded his grasp. He believed he might have discovered a "natural" society in the Mundi people, but he eventually left exhausted, unable to communicate and unable to learn anything about them. Maybury-Lewis similarly seeks an "untouched" people, but in a world that no longer believes in the undiscovered primitive. However, through the repeat journey's reanimation of inanimate past, Maybury-Lewis has helped us to forget that the Mashco Piro once experienced contact with a modern world but have now retreated back into the jungle in an attempt to recover (or simulate) their former way of life. By forgetting about past contact and constructing narrative as time travel, Maybury-Lewis creates a myth of first contact; however, as in the case of Lévi-Strauss and the Mundi people, the observer never gets close enough to validate or invalidate his claims. In the absence of any meaningful exchange, the frozen, fetishized image thus conceals a certain lack, the disappearance of the primitive and of the materiality of the past.[46]

John Frow has described tourism as a continuous circle of image production, with each new image deemed authentic to the degree that it adheres to previous images, with the actual object or locale diminishing in any importance beyond its ability to be visually reproduced.[47] Maybury-Lewis appears to participate in this loop and in the logic of tourism with his trip, which is incited by a photograph, and an ending that duplicates the original photograph. The visual image seems to take precedence over the profilmic reality as it provides a backdrop for another of Maybury-Lewis's *Tristes Tropiques*–like flashback voice-overs. Renato Rosaldo has suggested that often de facto imperialism has merely been replaced by a discourse of "imperialist nostalgia" or a "yearning for what one has destroyed that is a form of mystification." How do we read these final images, then—as responsible respect for the irreducible other, or as the "legal voyeurism" of anthropology that re-infuses the indigene with mystery for its own nostalgic purposes?[48]

Looking at this episode of *Millennium,* we can say that if traditional anthropology is indeed guilty of looking at the world's periphery (as defined by the so-called center) only out of a preoccupation with the self, then perhaps David Maybury-Lewis is justified in his indulgent self-contemplation. Leaving out the Mashco Piro is a way of eliminating the anthropological middleman, so to speak. Additionally, in the wake of cries for ethnographic accounts presented as subjective constructions,[49] Maybury-Lewis certainly could not be accused of being an invisible authorial voice. On the contrary, he thrusts himself in front of the camera even if it blocks our view of cultural difference.

However, if we judge *Millennium* on the criterion that David Turton has proposed—that is, by "the degree to which it is able to represent or 'translate' an indigenous viewpoint"[50]—we must admit that this episode does not cross cultural boundaries in a meaningful way; it only peers across that line from a distance. Trinh Minh-ha writes about anthropology's conversation among white men concerning the primitive: "A conversation of 'us' with 'us' about 'them' is a conversation in which 'them' is silenced. 'Them' always stands on the other side of the hill, naked and speechless, barely present in its absence."[51] *Millennium* shows the difficulty in changing the terms of that conversation and instead fetishizes the silence from the other side.

CHAPTER TEN

Narrativizing Cybertravel
CD-ROM TRAVEL GAMES

WHILE 1995 WITNESSED the introduction of the Cyan's computer game sensation Myst, consumers of 1997 could purchase Palladium Interactive's Pyst, a parody of the 1995 game offering a trek through a litter-strewn, tourist-ridden island plagued by overcommercialization. Pyst played upon one of the Myst phenomenon's central ironies: despite the game's commercial success and the millions of computer game players who have made their way across the island's alluring landscape and through its mysterious portals, the island remains perpetually deserted. Like a modern archeologist unsealing an ancient tomb, each consumer of Myst finds an uninhabited island and a series of undisturbed clues that unlock the secrets of its past. Thus, while various sectors of cyberspace are shared spaces where virtual communities burgeon, cyberspace also offers new frontiers for journeys of a highly private nature. The territories of Myst and of other computer games with exploration or colonialist narratives are infinitely renewable as every visitor at her own computer is positioned as a lone trailblazer amid an untouched landscape.

Antitouristic desires to consume touristic pleasures while assuming a loftier identity than that of the degraded mass tourist are granted in a postmodern world ripe with simulation technologies and commercialized forms of armchair travel. The age of discovery is long gone, but marketers of new technologies are reviving the past in simulated forms offering consumers pristine, unexplored landscapes and beckoning horizons. As Caesar II, a computer game by Impressions (1995), invites players to build an empire, and Interactive Magic's game Exploration (1995) offers a chance to race Christopher Columbus and Vasco da Gama across the ocean in pursuit of establishing a New World nation, the new frontiers of contemporary computer technology appear to be borrowed from the pages of history and brought to life for the joystick tourist.

—— Into Orbit with Our Hands on the Controls

The computer in its earliest embodiments was not an armchair traveler's companion but a scientist's tool for computing and storing information. Only with the last decade's technological developments has the personal computer been transfigured into a device of mobility, delivering the user to cyberspaces and virtual destinations. Actual locations become tangible either through link-up capabilities or through their interactive representations. These newly acquired powers of virtual mobility have been recognized in a variety of metaphors including the term *information superhighway,* which has spawned a host of corollary analogies ranging from discussion of Internet highway patrols to jokes about roadkill and wrong exits. The meaning of a computer's speed, or its ability to quickly complete procedures, has converged with the idea of getting from one place to another in a short time—traveling the World Wide Web, navigating cyberspace, barreling down the highway in a high-powered machine. One ad in *PC Magazine* reads, "386MAX runs Windows so fast you'll need a seatbelt. With QEMM, you may need something else." The accompanying photograph features a home computer with an inflated air bag protruding from the screen. Another ad bragging about quick acceleration shows a personal computer with red flame detailing and dual, fire-shooting tail pipes of polished chrome.

Advertisements for computer technologies also highlight alluring destinations and enterable spaces. Ads for high-resolution monitors, for instance, routinely show exotic locales from Barbados to Hawaii to Paris displayed onscreen. One such ad features a cartoon of a monitor displaying a blissful, tropical beach scene, but the computer user is drawn sitting on this beach wearing a flowered shirt and leaning outside the screen to manipulate the mouse that sits on his desk next to the computer. It has, however, been the marketing of CD-ROM games and other applications that have most consistently appealed to the consumer with entreaties of "enter," "explore," or, as ads for Microsoft's CD-ROM encyclopedia *Encarta* inquire, "Where do you want to go today?"

While some computer games simply use exotica as eye candy, other CD-ROMs more explicitly marketed as travel games are entirely situated within a single locale rendered in textured, three-dimensional graphics. Ancient Sumeria, the African veldt, the Amazon, the American West of the 1850s, medieval Europe, Antarctica, the Australian outback, and ancient Egypt are just some of the environments depicted on CD-ROMs. Often such games create cartoon-like universes that simply replicate the popular imagination's envisioning of such locales with little or no claim to authenticity: medieval castles filled with armored knights, Egyptian slaves building pyramids while high priests record their secrets in hieroglyphics, and gun-toting cowboys borrowed as much from the silver screen as from history books.

An equal number of CD-ROM applications do boast of some kind of engagement with the actual world, past or present. Photography is still the most surefire way of delivering the distant locale to the computer monitor and satiating the home tourist's desire for authenticity. Games like Broderbund's Where in the World Is Carmen Sandiego? (1992) and Luminaria's Wrath of the Gods (1994) intertwine still photographic backgrounds taken from actual locations and animated figures. Some games, on the other hand, employ the strategy used by Africa Trail (MECC, 1996), an educational adventure game whose not quite photorealistic graphics were nonetheless created from footage taken on actual expeditions to Africa. A number of CD-ROM applications designed to educate as well as entertain combine photography with an appeal to an authoritative body that endows the application with the air of authenticity. For instance, the music and photos for Where in the World Is Carmen Sandiego? come from two renowned experts on the non-Western world: the Smithsonian Institution and *National Geographic* magazine. Voyage in Egypt (EMME, 1994) is advertised as having been developed from the internationally renowned Scala Group archives. Antarctica: The Last Continent (Cambrix Publishing, 1994) cites connections to the International Antarctica Research Center, just as Material World (StarPress Multimedia, 1994) foregrounds its links to the United Nations. *Scientific American* magazine and the Discovery Channel have both used their established authority in popular science to sponsor CD-ROM applications. And Robyn Davidson has used the publicity and adventurer status garnered from her trip across Australia, documented by *National Geographic* photographer Rick Smolan, to compile From Alice to Ocean: Alone across the Outback (Claric Clear Choice, 1994).

As is apparent in this amalgam of CD-ROM games, a wide range of strategies exist for representing place and space—that is, actual photographed places from around the world and spaces that may be modeled on actual places but which are rendered in computer graphics and are more amenable to three-dimensional illusion and player movement through space. At this point in time, fairly clear differentiations between the depiction of place and space can be maintained since the technological capability for rendering photographed place as navigable space is very limited. Some golf and flight simulation games have come the closest in replicating actual spaces, with graphics that approach photorealism and in simulating the movement of an aircraft or golf ball through that space. For example, Looking Glass Technology's Flight Unlimited (1995) is one technologically sophisticated example of this merging of place and space with its flight simulation using actual footage from Arizona sites mapped onto three-dimensional terrain. And strides continue to be made in the area of 360-degree, wraparound panoramic video offering fluid user-controlled movements, making the full-frame slide shows of games like Myst look primitive.

—— Defining Movement through Space

Most CD-ROM games that depict three-dimensional spaces provide some means of simulating movement through space using a first-person perspective. Interface controls allow the player to determine the direction and speed of simulated movement delivered through continuous or discontinuous changes in perspective within a graphically depicted space. However, this illusion of motion through a simulated three-dimensional space is only one type of movement found in CD-ROM games. Another type stems from CD-ROMs' unique history within the development of home computer technologies and their ability to bring together disparate materials with increasing sophistication. From home publishing software, the development of which has brought a greater ease in creating and importing nontextual items, to the World Wide Web, with its similar combinatory possibilities, computer applications have incorporated photographic representation, animation, text, voice annotation, music, sound effects, and visual depictions of information in the form of graphs, charts, and maps to a greater extent than commonly employed in any other medium. Thus, interactivity and movement within CD-ROM games often involve a scurrying between media, between experiential modalities. With a single command, immersion within a simulated space may be temporarily abandoned while a map screen is consulted or textually conveyed information is sought. The virtual traveler thus pauses to become reader or alters his interpretation of flat image as three-dimensional space in order to engage in the type of spatial interpretation required by map reading.

These brief respites from three-dimensional modeled spaces within travel games that promise above all else the pleasures of "being there" are yet another example of distanced immersion, those behaviors designed to counteract disorientation and culture shock by giving travelers a sense of mastery over space and culture. Within CD-ROM travel games, the use of maps, the translation of space into picture or photograph, and the pursuit of elevated and/or aerial perspectives all involve a flattening process that reduces signs of difference into consumable spectacle. At the same time that tourists perceive foreign culture as spectacle—a play of surfaces without depth or meaning—they, almost in contradiction, view foreign culture as a layered structure requiring decoding and demystifying. Foreign culture is experienced as an accumulation of tastes, colors, and textures at the same time that it is viewed as hieroglyph awaiting translation. The tourist gaze thus seeks a vision of the foreign site as annotated spectacle. Guidebooks, maps, translators, tour guides, and labels provide the annotation, a ready supply of information about the unfamiliar culture that transforms puzzling foreignness into a knowable entity seen from a point of comprehending distance.

These touristic processes of extracting pleasure and defusing the threat of unfamiliarity are perhaps most evident in CD-ROM games, as maps and a ready flow of information provide spatial mastery, control, geographical orientation, and an assurance of the objects' and locations' knowability. For instance, games like Where in the World Is Carmen Sandiego? foster touristic mastery by straddling two modes of experience: the belief in image as immersive three-dimensional space and the distanced understanding of place as a flow of information. Although the game's featured photographs are foregrounded as static images or as postcards that tame, appropriate, and capture the world's sights, animated sequences suggest that these images constitute real space through which one could pass, or at least through which a cartoon character, Carmen herself or one of her cohorts, could pass. Folk music appropriate to the locale accompanies the player's voyage and continues for the duration of the visit, contributing to the illusion of immersion and authenticity. The player might visit eight locations around the world in the course of tracking down a single criminal, all the while linked to a steady flow of information about the locales and the pursued thieves. A portable videophone, a criminal database with a robotic interface, and a computer readout with constant information about the destinations and the ongoing crime-fighting efforts occupy the majority of the screen and provide this stream of information. These technological tools are aligned with the player and stand in contrast to the less industrialized cultures portrayed by the game as picturesquely exotic.

A similar formula is played out in multimedia atlases. Within Electronic Arts' 3-D Atlas (1994), a technologically aided omnipotent visuality allows users to view the earth as abstracted map, to manipulate the flat geographic image through nine zoom levels, and to access satellite images. The thousands of statistics contained within the software converts countries and locales into facts, numbers, hard data. The more than eight hundred color photographs, or country postcards, occupy a middle ground between the distanced perspective that renders the world as a flat, manipulatable image and the immersed, first-person perspective provided by the software's three-dimensional flights over world terrains.

The vacillation between the illusion of being there and separation from an image world is even more apparent in games within which the player is positioned as tourist-photographer. In From Alice to Ocean, for example, the invitation to feel like a fellow traveler on Robyn Davidson's seven-month journey across the Australian outback is clear and redundantly referenced. The written materials included with the CD-ROM offer the words of the publisher: "The enclosed CD-ROM lets you join Robyn in her travels." A letter from photographer Rick Smolan appearing in the same pamphlet reiterates, "With this interactive CD-ROM, imagine yourself joining Robyn . . . I wish you good luck and Godspeed on your own journey." Spoken journal entries, videotape clips, still photographs, and a map that allows the home traveler to join in on the trip at any point are designed to flesh out a sense of place and communicate the excitement of the journey. The photographs serve as entryways into the represented space and as documentation of Smolan's and Davidson's presence in the exotic space. Yet the artifice of the photograph is simultaneously foregrounded through Smolan's commentary on photographic technique. In an effort to educate the player and prepare the tourist for her next adventure, Smolan doles out advice on how to capture action and how to create silhouettes, dissecting his own images and revealing the tale of their creation. A similar background story inhabits Material World as the dominant discourse on the lives of the world's families is accompanied by narratives of the photographers who captured the game's images.

Such behind-the-scenes looks exhibit the photographers' expertise and remind CD-ROM users of Smolan's and others' presence on the scene, and therefore, of their authority to deliver the world to users. In the absence of any other Western character, the highlighting of the photographer as traveler also provides a figure for identification, positioning the game player as a looker and an image capturer rather than as an indigene. To the degree that this incorporation of the photographers' stories into CD-ROM narratives details cross-cultural contact, its inequities, and its awkwardness, such discourses can be helpful in revealing the constructed nature of a CD-ROM's cultural depiction. Yet when the photos themselves become prized items or virtual souvenirs that can be downloaded, as in Material World, or when the artful compositions and silhouettes romanticize and objectify indigenes who then become less important than the successful capture of a Kodak moment, the image world then takes a dangerous precedence to the actual world, with its political realities.

—— Animated Worlds: The Tomb of Qin

While 3-D Atlas, Material World, From Alice to Ocean, and Where in the World Is Carmen Sandiego? all rely on photographic representation to deliver touristic pleasures within the format of a primarily educational game, it is important to note that a similar manifestation of the tourist gaze can be found in less educationally directed games that simulate exotic spaces using computer graphics and three-dimensional animation rather than photographs. One game in this category that is worthy of a more sustained analysis due to its interesting content and unusual blend of fact and fiction is the game Qin (Time Warner Electronic Pub-

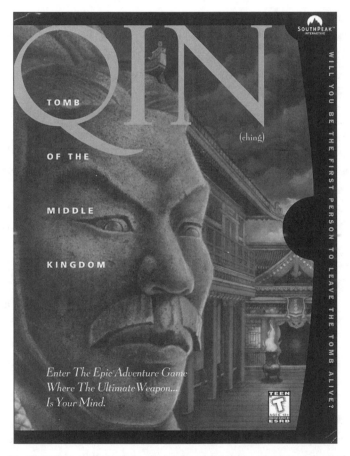

The game Qin advertises realistic three-dimensional graphics, a "score performed on period instruments in a full stereo soundscape," a "seamless integration of historical adventure play and educational content," and an integrated encyclopedia of ancient Chinese history and culture.

Courtesy of South Peak Interactive.

lishing, 1996). Qin focuses on a single location using a lush graphic style and a highly atmospheric feel reminiscent of Myst. In fact, the game has been accurately described by one reviewer as "Indiana Jones meets *Myst*." The game's title refers to Qin Shi Huangdi, China's first emperor and occupant of the subterranean tomb available for exploration by the game player. Players of Qin are simultaneously pulled into the future and the past as they learn that the year is 2010 and that they have volunteered for the excavation of the tomb of Qin, buried deep in the earth for the past two millennia. As happenstance archeologists, players witness what no one else has seen for centuries—if they can outwit Qin's booby traps and locking devices.

The game begins with an animated opening sequence emphasizing an illusion of depth, inward movement, and passage through space, a convention within the CD-ROM travel game that provides entry into the game space. This sequence sweeps players across the excavation site, interrupted only by a dizzying drop through a deep crevice, which leaves players bruised and shocked fifteen stories beneath the surface, locked inside the tomb of the man who united China and began the construction of the Great Wall.

Due to the efforts of a team of fifteen artists, Qin's graphics are remarkably engaging. Of equal noteworthiness is the music that, according to the accompanying documentation, is an original soundtrack based on traditional melodies using so-called authentic instruments in an attempt to replicate the spirit of Qin dynasty music. However, the CD-ROM publishers admit that many of the instruments and melodies postdate Qin's era. The music changes to match the various environments, which form not just a tomb but a virtual empire constructed underground. In the spirit of the puzzle-adventure game, doors and gates to new realms remain impassable until certain puzzles are solved. The resolution of puzzles and the resultant movement through space bring players closer to the game's final goal: to discover the secrets of Qin Shi Huangdi, a powerful man obsessed with the possibility of immortality.

Qin provides a couple of orientation tools to help direct player-controlled movement: a compass in the bottom right of the screen and a map that charts player progress. The view of the game space is letterboxed with these tools and others accessible in the black areas above and below the image, areas referred to by the game documentation as the DataVisor. Through the DataVisor's Archive tool, the illusion of spatial immersion is abandoned while textual information on ancient Chinese history, culture philosophy, and science is sought. One of the Archive's two functions, the Room Index, provides contextualizing information on Chinese culture related to objects or puzzles within that particular room. For instance, one environment includes a number of waterwheels and the ruins of other machinery. When invoked, the Archive's Room Index provides information on Qin's efforts to build roads and aqueducts and on irrigation methods during the Qin dynasty. The information proves to be useful in triggering the gate-opening mechanism that then leads the player to the realm just beyond this system of wheels, bridges, and waterways. The second Archive function, the Encyclopedia, contains a list of categories and related subcategories that link to illustrated text and can be searched using the Find function. The various categories of information include among others: Myths and Rituals, Science and Technology, the Afterlife and Occult, and Manufacturing and Crafts. And finally, the last element of the DataVisor, the Interpreter, activates a gray box that drops from the DataVisor and a light gray grid is imposed over the view of the game space while an inscription or Chinese character is translated.

The past tense of the Qin Dynasty effectively framed within the technologically advanced future tense of 2010 allows for an ideal touristic arrangement. The mystery and splendor of the past, or at least a fantasy version of it seeped in orientalist imaginings, is abundantly accessible to the tourist-turned-explorer enjoying a private journey through Mount Li, China in 210 B.C.E. The game documentation tells us that Qin's tomb actually exists and still quietly rests beneath Mount Li due to insufficient excavation funds. But within the world of Qin, excavation has begun, and, luckily for the player-tourist, technology has dispensed with the need for a bilingual tour guide. One only needs to strap on a handy DataVisor and embark on a sojourn through uncharted territory, with all exotic spectacles conveniently explained and translated.

This unexplored world is designed to be appreciated for its richness of texture and color as artifacts such as sculpted dragons and exquisitely crafted musical instruments can be examined in isolation. When the cursor is passed over an object and changes from its neutral marker to a yellow squiggle, the object can be scrutinized in detail with a click of the mouse. While the art object or historical artifact is magnified and isolated against a black screen, the arrow keys can be used to rotate the object as if circling a museum case to see all possible views of a particularly curious or beautiful object. Each perspective on the interior of the tomb is also generated with concerted attention to aesthetics and balance. The gray grid of the Interpreter function dividing a view into a series of perfect squares furthers this sense of a beautiful and ordered environment despite the strangeness of its splendors. Yet at the same time that this empire is presented as exotic spectacle and the culture presented as surface beauty, the game promotes the interpretation of Chinese culture as mystery. The game, however, provides a set of guiding principles for deflating its perplexing nature. Animals are invested with mythical meanings and environments are perfectly ordered through the rules of feng shui. Culture is boiled down to a set of meanings and rules that can be used to decipher the game's puzzles and to unlock the protected realms of Qin's underground resting place. The DataVisor thus acts like a decoder ring for the adventure.

—— Constructing Travel Tales

The relationship between the player and an unfamiliar culture is constructed not only through spatial orientation and a gaze that separates viewer from viewed but also through narrative. Michel de Certeau has described narratives as "spatial trajectories" that regulate changes in space, placing locations within a linear series.[1] Based on this sparse definition of narrative structure, the player, traveling through represented space with its illusion of three dimensions or through the more inclusive game space with its various information resources thus maps a trajectory and engages in the spatial weaving or narrative. Jurij Lotman's concepts supplement Certeau's notion of narrative by defining character types: "Characters can be divided into those who are mobile, who enjoy freedom with regard to plot space . . . and those who are immobile, who represent, in fact, a function of this space."[2] Applying this rule to CD-ROM games, it is possible to differentiate these two categories of characters. The player consistently enters the narrative as a character in the former group, as one who possesses the ability to move or navigate through the game space. When the game does not provide a subjective point of view accompanied by the illusion of the player's own movement through space, an identificatory figure is often provided. The player as puppet master may direct the movements of a young man in Wrath of the Gods, a female fish in Freddi Fish (Humongous Entertainment, 1995), Phileas Fogg in Around the World in Eighty Days (Electronic Arts, 1995, or two high school girls in Hawaii High (Sanctuary Woods, 1994). In such cases, the player might not be an actual character within the game but is aligned with a mobile character. Belonging to Lotman's second category are the game's obstacles or antagonists, "immobile enemy-characters fixed at particular points in the plot space."[3] Although a number of exceptions exist, for the most part the appearance of certain obstacles and enemies are anchored to particular points within the game space. For instance, each time a player visits Spain in the game Around the World in Eighty Days, a charging bull will have to be dodged, and each visit to France will bring the unfortunate encounter with a rude waiter.

Working from Lotman's character groups as applied to the story of Oedipus, Teresa de Lauretis theorizes that "the work of narrative, then, is a mapping of differences, and specifically, first and foremost, of sexual difference into each text."[4] Within the oedipal tale, the male, mobile hero is differentiated from the female Sphinx or mother who serves as "an element of plot-space, a topos, a resistance, matrix, and matter."[5] In a similar spirit, Eric J. Leed describes the "spermatic journey" as a travel tale that mirrors the narrative of reproduction. The traveler's journey from place to place, encountering stationary women in each locale, leaves a trail of descendants in every port. This path replicates the dichotomy of female immobility and male mobility as witnessed in the spatial trajectory of sperm into the female body or in the spatial trajectory of the baby subject's "escape" from the female bodyspace.[6] Ella Shohat has similarly written about the travel film, noting the preponderance of gendered narratives of military and epistemological conquest over female-obstacle-boundary-space and the sexualized unveilings of the immobile exotic woman.[7] Although each of these analyses focuses on narrative plucked from very different realms—history, film, literature, and biology—the conclusions converge at the paired binarisms of female/male and stasis/mobility.

Gender, thus differentiated via levels of mobility, can be a difficult category for analysis within the CD-ROM narrative in that the primary mobile character is often the player, whose gender is not determined by the game but by the gender of the person who sits down to play the game. In other words, in cases in which a game's subjective perspective creates the illusion of first-person travel, the player's gender is designed to be irrelevant to the game's actions. Nonetheless, gender cues are often still apparent. For example, in Gadget (Synergy, 1994), the first-person traveler's suitcase is switched for a case full of mysterious gadgets, but not before the player glimpses the contents of the original piece of luggage: men's clothing. In Myst, the player's gender is not represented within the game in the same way as in Gadget, but the trail charted by the island's former explorers/time travelers, who are explicitly coded as male, serves as the text's founding movement that the player retraces.

While a comprehensive gender analysis conducted in the same spirit as de Lauretis' study of oedipal narrative would contribute significantly to an understanding of the story patterns that may characterize CD-ROM games, the limits of a conceptual framework grounded in the oedipal narrative should be noted. Various travel narratives could indeed be considered oedipal to the extent that they involve a search for self, a visit to the birth place of civilization, a return to the site of one's ancestry, a confrontation with the primitive seen as the origin of modern culture, or a journey to one's death in a kind of cyclical return to one's origin.[8] However, the oedipal narrative, with its long journey only to find a place of unrecognized familiarity followed by blindness, hardly seems to account for the manifest content of the sight-seeing journey: the search for the strange. Or at the very least, the travel tale seeks out not solely a gendered strangeness but a strangeness defined by cultural difference. Nonetheless, it is possible to apply narrative theory to travel tales and to investigate the unevenly distributed privileges of mobility within such stories.

Certeau describes the search for the space of cultural difference as the motivating force of the travel account, noting, "This a priori of difference, the postulate of the voyage, results in a rhetoric of distance in travel accounts. It is illustrated by a series of surprises and intervals (monsters, storms, lapses of time, etc.) which at the same time substantiate the alterity of the savage, and empower the text to speak from elsewhere and command belief."[9] The outbound journey serves as a frame for the encounter with foreignness, and the length of the voyage, its hardships and distance traveled, authenticates the alien nature of the people and objects of that distant place. Only some CD-ROMs, which choose to include some element of the outbound journey, rely on this rhetoric of distance to assure the strangeness of the foreign other. In other CD-ROM applications, cultural difference is experienced as abundantly and instantaneously available. Digital atlases, Material World, and Where in the World Is Carmen Sandiego? to name a few, are characterized by easily accessed exoticism; views of cultural difference can be triggered with a simple click, and glimpses of various parts of the world can be had by the dozens. The framing of the exoticism in these cases is accomplished through the CD-ROM's introductory material. To provide an example, Voyage in Egypt requires the player to enter the game through an animated sequence that serves as a lengthy introduction or passageway and that cannot be bypassed. The player experiences the illusion of being sucked into the game as a small picture frame features a moving image against a black background. The white outlines of a pharaoh on either side of the picture frame appear to push themselves to the foreground, increasing the illusion of depth. Due to its dynamic movement within an otherwise static screen, this central image box quickly becomes dominant as it features movement through the complex architecture of an unnamed Egyptian structure. The player is visually pulled through corridors and deep into the recesses of the monument until entrance is finally announced by the slow opening of heavy stone doors and the scattering of light into the deep interior that lies beyond those doors. This passage initiates the viewer into the space of cultural difference where travel down the Nile River is instantaneous and a click on any map label elicits an immediate image of exoticism and accompanying text.

Regardless of the nature of the passage into game space, from Qin's precarious drop into a dark crevice to Voyage into Egypt's feeling of being sucked into a tomb, the mouse-clicking tourist pursues the expectations that were formed in reading the CD-ROM box's promise of strange, secret, distant worlds. The player's own mobility is counterpoised against the immobility of those objects and individuals encountered in the space of cultural difference and defined by their placement in the world on the other side of the CD-ROM's passageway. Thus, the difference mapped out during the course of the player's narrative construction is *cultural* difference. The Australian aborigine is an anchored image bound to a single locale within From Alice to Ocean. And Qin himself will not be found wandering randomly through the tomb's various levels; he awaits the player in the most secret recesses of his underground empire.

In Where in the World Is Carmen Sandiego? a world in transit is more accurately represented as an Asian helper character can be encountered in South America and an Italian in Africa. Within a single game, these characters appear to be stable, but after multiple solved cases, the same characters reappear in different parts of the world. The villains, who are definitely mobile as in any traditional chase story, are of various ethnicities and nationalities. However, the goal of the game is to curtail their mobility, to imprison them with the help of a police officer and a judge, both of whom are white American males regardless of the location of the arrest or trial. While it is worth mentioning that the title character Carmen Sandiego, presumably a Latina, seems to be forever on the loose within the logic of the game, the immobility of the photographically depicted individuals of the world should also be noted. Only the cartoonish characters and the player have powers of mobility, while the more material people of the world are photographically captured in all their exoticism and are rendered immobile by the mechanics of the camera and of the game.

The game narrative is marked by more than a player's movement through space. A set of goals propels movement and determines the results of the game. These goals contain the narrative possibilities by rewarding certain spatial paths and actions while responding to other choices with the disincentive of death and aborted narrative. The variety of game goals is vast: build the Great Pyramid, unravel the ancient mystery that has fallen upon an Indian village, help rescue a law student's time-traveling fiancée, get the inhabitants of Zarg to dig up precious stones faster than your opponent, destroy a doomsday machine, outwit the master computer in a game of psychological warfare, find the stowaway, defeat the Chinese emperor. However, often the means to the goals are relatively similar involving comprehensive spatial exploration and accumulation, two pastimes none too foreign to the tourist. Movement toward the goal can often be spatially plotted, and successful transversal of a space is often awarded through the discovery of some item or clue that can be virtually acquired by the player and may become necessary at some later point in the game. Or in a game such as Diggers (Millennium, 1993), the movement is downward into the earth, and the accumulation of precious gems allows the purchase of more sophisticated equipment that facilitates even greater movement and accumulation of precious gems. Although a certain order or itinerary may not be described by the game, the failure to explore a certain space and add a certain object to a player's bag of tricks may prevent further movement through space and thus prevent the goal from being achieved. In Gadget, the train may fail to depart on time unless the player has explored the destination thoroughly and added any new gadgets to her suitcase. The player proceeds in a "gone there, done that" fashion, with the acquired objects punctuating the player-spun narrative in much the same way that souvenirs serve as instrumental launch points for the narratives of the tourist's overseas adventure. As Susan Stewart concludes, the souvenir authenticates experience and documents achievement: "Removed from its context, the exotic souvenir is a sign of survival—not its own survival, but the survival of the possessor outside his or her own context of familiarity."[10] The intangibility of experience is converted into the tangibility of possession. However, within the game, possession is as intangible as experience, and thus souvenirs are easily traded in for the perpetuation of the game experience.

A similar materialist gaze even inhabits many CD-ROM applications with more educational leanings. In Material World, each family's prized possessions are displayed in front of their place of abode in what could be called the spread-eagle style of exterior decorating. A family's home appears to be turned inside out, exposing the interior and its inhabitants to the gaze of the passer-by. At times, the manner of display is even suggestive of a yard sale, evoking in these cases a consumerist gaze on the part of the user. The CD-ROM user can peruse the items and even use a magnifying glass icon to go in for a closer look. Unsurprisingly, many educational trips through past cultures focus on the valued treasures that have been left behind, allowing the CD-ROM user to view the past in material terms, much like the museum effect experienced through Qin's artifact examination function. CD-ROM games such as Ancient Lands (Microsoft, 1994) add to this museum formula a certain fictionalization that makes possible a voyeurism that is otherwise foreclosed in dealing with a past emptied of its inhabitants. Ancient Lands reincarnates and repopulates the past, beginning with an overview movie featuring a living mummy who plays the very same game on his computer. He exclaims, "Finally, I've found a way to discover ancient lands without ever leaving the tomb." The reincarnated mummy is only the first tour guide or informant. The user may choose between several guides, including a coy slave girl who promises to provide the native's point of view, a glimpse at the "back regions" of Rome. The tour guide can be abandoned at any point so that the player may pursue an alternate path or a closer look at a particular aspect of Egyptian, Greek, or Roman life. The interactive, multileveled structure of Ancient Lands and other CD-ROM applications facilitates this kind of penetrating gaze, as people's personal objects are made available for scrutiny. Icons such as the magnifying glass in Material World or the eyeball in Freak Show (Voyager, 1992) invite players to click their way to an intimate perspective that may bring a new level of information visually or textually conveyed. Whether rifling through a circus member's diary hidden in his trailer, shuffling through the prized belongings of a Brazilian family, or scrutinizing an Egyptian woman's cosmetics, the world's people, past and present, fictional and actual, are accessed through a voyeuristic perusal of their material possessions.

—— The Digitalized Past

While the assignment of goals to a player or a motivating question such as "Where in the World Is Carmen Sandiego?" helps to direct the player's movement and to contain the narrative possibilities provided by interactivity, the use of an extant narrative or the placing of the player in the shoes of a historical figure also acts as a force of containment. To the extent that most players are aware of the exploits of Marco Polo, a narrative and a set of goals suggest themselves to the player of the CD-ROM game Marco Polo (I-Motion, 1995). The supranarrative of history provides a model for the player's spatial path down the Silk Route and contextualizes the game's places with meanings borrowed from history.

In their analysis of Nintendo games, Mary Fuller and Henry Jenkins comment on the use of colonization narratives and new-frontier metaphors in new game technologies. Jenkins speculates that the re-creation of a New World open for exploration represents a desire to return to "a mythic time when there were worlds without limits and resources beyond imagining."[11] Tourism, to less industrialized nations and to geographical locations seemingly untouched by the passing of centuries, is often motivated by the desire to capture the romance long since drained from the more industrialized nations, to catch sight of an unspoiled world in much the same way that figures of the past must have seen it, to find unpopulated, undeveloped expanses of land where one can imagine that he is the first to set foot. With the disappearance of such destinations, the antitouristic notion that tourists participate in the despoliation of land and culture by their presence has gained currency over the past years. The goals of tourism thus get shifted into simulated forms of travel in which a denial of this loss is enacted and historical recovery through retroactive environmentalist control over the land and vivification of past events appears feasible.

While film may offer a past captured on celluloid or re-created through the historical epic, the CD-ROM game offers an opportunity to enter the past as something more than a spectator. Such digital re-creations of the past may be poor visual imitations, but their very pliability, the opportunity to explore, and the illusion of infinite possibilities in terms of space and action nonetheless act as compensation for any lack of photorealism. Additionally, the material nature of the CD-ROM does not change; its encoded possibilities and the mapped-out spaces are forever renewable. Actual tourists may lament that their visits may be the last time they witness a certain locale in its current state or that a place is simply not the same as before, now crowded with scenery-blocking hotels and overrun with tourists. Meanwhile, the CD-ROM game, as the home tourist's personal playground, may be saved or continually returned to its pristine starting point. Digital realities being unfurled through CD-ROM technologies present the illusion of coming into being, almost like reality, where nascent possibilities are brought to life by a player's decision making. The allure of the past delivered with a lack of fixity, pouring out like the present tense but forever renewable through the restart button, is clear; loss is negated as the past is experienced as enterable and changeable.

The promise of the past resuscitated is realized with varying degrees of satisfaction and at varying levels of technological finesse in actual CD-ROM games. Wrath of the Gods is interesting in that it almost accomplishes the tricky task of photographically depicting ancient history within an interactive game. The temporal placement is clearly in the past, with references to kingdoms, costumes from ancient Greece, and revitalized myths from centuries long gone; yet they all find a place within contemporary photographs of classical Greek monuments emptied of indications of their true time period. In a similar act of historical recovery, Voyage in Egypt invites players to "[v]isit the most important archeological sites and view photographs of the ruins accompanied by three-dimensional reconstructions that will allow you to enter the buildings as they once were." And Qin promises that it is possible to reconstruct the tomb of Qin Shi Huangdi from accounts of its construction and evidence from other archeological sites. Furthermore, the game suggests that undiscovered sites still exist, that the world's mysteries have not been exhausted, and journeys into the past are still possible.

As another example, Where in the World Is Carmen Sandiego? illustrates how CD-ROM games and other contemporary armchair voyages may also serve the function of atonement, of easing historical anxiety over lost ecosystems, decimated tribes, and the more general disappearance of unknown lands and secrets left to unearth. Within the game, lost items, items of authenticity that seem to defy the feared tides of an encroaching monoculture, are consistently recovered and returned to their proper owners. This narrative of loss and recovery seemingly reverses the past flow of artifacts, prized possessions, and historical items from indigenous hands into European museums and private collections. Additionally, through the game's crime information network, cellular phone, computer database, and the always-accessible robotic warrant issuer, Where in the World Is Carmen Sandiego? accomplishes something akin to the effect of a series of IBM commercials that ran in the late 1990s. These commercials, filled with Greek fishermen, Italian nuns, Japanese dancers, and elderly French men all bragging about their computer technologies, suggest a world conveniently linked by compatible computers; yet the picturesque images of these unique cultures, within which virtually no computers were actually visible, imply that this technological globalization can take place without moving toward worldwide homogeneity and the obliteration of local culture. Similarly, in Where in the World Is Carmen Sandiego? the player/crime fighter can experience all the advantages of a global communication system while the exotic images remain pristine, free from any signs of industrialization and Westernization.

Other CD-ROMs are focused on environmental concerns and atone for the loss of delicate ecologies and the species they once supported. The 3-D Atlas, in command of not only space but also time, offers views of the earth using time-lapse photography to observe urbanization, pollution, and deforestation. In a kind of *fort-da* process of loss, mourning, and mastery, these time-lapse sequences can be repeatedly returned to their starting points and reobserved. Mirroring the recent surge in ecotourism, many CD-ROM games embark on exotic expeditions in the name of environmental caretaking. The most popular CD-ROM trek through Africa to date has been a game called Eco East Africa (Viridis, 1995). A player still experiences the touristic: "three-dimensional animals, stunning landscapes, and changing seasons all in unbelievable photorealistic detail." In fact, one of the game's options involves a choice between being a tourist or a game warden. If the player chooses the latter, the beauty of Ethemba, Eco East Africa's fictional game park, may be fleeting unless the player effectively manages the game park's precarious ecosystem. However, even if poachers, disease, drought, and park mismanagement ravages the environment, the forests, grasslands, savannas, and highlands can be instantaneously restored by restarting the game.

By way of closing, it seems appropriate to ask exactly what the armchair tourist will discover in looking to CD-ROM travel games to fulfill whatever kind of yearning impels touristic exploration. Some software will undoubtedly be purchased for its markers of authenticity, and much will serve some educational function that should not be overlooked. Yet, in other cases, the structure of the game will encourage a viewing of the globe as a "material world," a world defined by the products available for collection and consumption, a world defined by the logic of accumulation yet infinitely renewable. Rather than taking advantage of the role-playing elements of such games in order to position a player as an inhabitant of a distant land, most games continue to deliver mobility and promote identification with Western travelers. Thus, the virtual tourist, aligned with technologies of both mobility and information retrieval, will stand out in counter-distinction to the static inhabitants of touristic destinations, frozen by photographs or viewed as tools (or maybe impediments) to the continued collection of booty and to the conquering of terrain. In short, in a world that according to Fredric Jameson is no longer mapable, travel CD-ROMs will provide environments that can be comprehensively mapped, explored, understood, and consumed from the privileged position of the tourist.

CHAPTER ELEVEN

Virtual Reality and the Challenges of Reembodied Tourism

VIRTUAL REALITY (VR) would seem to be the ideal culmination of a volume on the history of immersive entertainment technologies. (Some critics have suggested that when André Bazin dreamed of a "total cinema," he must have had something like virtual reality in mind.) Its immersion, spatially speaking, is total, extending from the ground beneath to the space overhead and including 360 degrees around, creating a sphere of immersive illusion around the VR user. It has a three-dimensional appearance, it moves, and it offers full color. But VR's primary claim to fame is its interactivity, the powers of movement that the apparatus grants its users in addition to mechanisms for responding to the simulated environment. Yet the very nature of virtual reality demands a more specific definition of immersion.

Within this present volume, analyses of prior media forms has relied on an assumption of some form of realism that provided a smooth transition between terms like *immersion, reality effects,* and even *authenticity.* Native villages at world's fairs, life groups at natural history museums, stereoviews, and museum displays all pointed to some connection to the distant locale whether that consisted of a person or artifact culled from the locale, photography's indexical link to the environment, or the anthropologist's field experience and desire to visually imitate a dance, craft, or ritual witnessed while in that remote environment. This connection to the exoticized environment has promoted the illusion of authenticity while simultaneously delivering visual mimesis. Even in computer-based travel games, the frequent use of photography and video in combination with more abstract references to organizations and bodies of knowledge with claims of access to authenticity has allowed the same terms of analysis to be employed with passing reference to the added issue of control through interactivity. These new features of computer-mediated interactivity— control and the infinite renewability of the game space—contribute to touristic pleasures with narratives of colonialist discovery, conquest, and acquisition while simultaneously allowing for an atonement, a sweeping away of the effects of colonialist exploitation, and historical recovery through reenactment, but the addition of interactivity has not forced a revision of analytical paradigms. Virtual reality, on the other hand, while growing directly out of the technologies, aesthetics, and game structures of CD-ROM applications brings to light heretofore submerged questions.

One such question targets the role of a realism that extends beyond the pursuit of visual mimesis within the definition of immersion. The focus on vision within tourism, with sightseeing as its synonym, lends itself to narrow definitions of realism focused on the visual depiction of actual sights. But the illusion of spatial immersion may exist independently of resemblance to an actual environment. This distinction was hinted at with the discussion of space versus place within chapter 10. While depiction of place relies on visual resemblance to a particular location, the depiction of space suggests an illusion of three-dimensional immersion and of the potential to inhabit or move through the location. For instance, a photograph of the Eiffel Tower may realistically document place. And a VR application may convincingly simulate the space of a Giorgio de Chirico painting and the experience of passing through its arches and alleyways, even if the environment is unlike any place the VR user has seen. The lack of detail may make the VR user feel like she is within a cartoon world, but nonetheless, the illusion of spatial immersion may be uncannily believable. Thus, we can separate out representational realism—whether a simulation looks, feels, or sounds like the audience thinks the represented object or place should—from an experiential realism that references not what we experience but how we experience it and the particular mechanics of our perception. Photography presented through the stereoscope, for instance, could be said to be experientially realist, or more specifically, optically realist, in its rough mirroring of human vision's doubled optical apex. Likewise, cinema's use of focal lengths that most resemble human vision evinces optical realism—again, that subset of experiential realism that relates to the single perceptual register of vision. In an example targeting a different perceptual register, developments in surround sound could be said to be attempts at enhanced experiential realism as it relates to auditory perception. However, such technological developments, barring audio static and other forms of distortion, remain distinct from whether the sounds delivered through a surround-sound system are judged by the audience to resemble the event or place being depicted, whether it be a jungle setting or the rumble of an approaching earthquake. In short, experiential realism refers to how a phenomenon is experienced via the apparatus rather than the way it is staged for the recording device. If we hear a nearby turkey's gobble in the way that we would normally hear a sound from a low-to-the-ground animal near us is a matter of *experiential* realism. Whether it sounds like a typical auditory representation of a turkey or more like an old man's muttering is a question of *representational* realism.

To this point, immersive technologies' portrayals of exotic locations have been explored with a tacit emphasis on the confluence of experiential and representational realism. The IMAX movie Grand Canyon: The Hidden Secrets (Keith Merrill, 1984), for instance, depicts this national monument as it has looked in prior representations. At the same time, it fills the spectator's peripheral vision, thereby appearing to surround the viewer as if it were a spatial environment. The primary emphasis on VR applications built to date has been on experiential realism, which can be created far more economically using digitally generated images as opposed to photographic images. Although it is tempting to claim that representational realism has been compromised for the sake of experiential realism, some VR developers suggest that no compromise has been made, that it is the very combination of experiential realism and a purposeful deviation from representational realism that explains VR's appeal. In the words of VR programmer Mark Bolas, "The more abstract, the more elsewhere the world, the more people felt 'in there' than anything else. I feel that elsewhere represents the true nature of the VR medium."[1] Nonetheless, representational realism in regard to actual travel destinations has been speculated on as one potential route for VR development. Kay Keppler, a columnist for the magazine *Virtual Reality* writes, upon returning from a Mediterranean vacation, "If what I wanted to see was churches, I could have done that faster, not to mention cheaper, in VR. A narrative could have supplied the historical and architectural history, and the visuals perhaps could have shown even more than I saw, given what was removed or covered for restoration when I was there."[2] The issue in which Keppler's article appears has on its cover the prototypical, Hawaiian-shirt-wearing tourist with camera, map, and oversized sunglasses. Dean MacCannell has also joined the conversation with his suggestion that VR is "the logical next step beyond tourism and the movies."[3] And anthropologist Christopher Pinney suggests that VR travel will replace tourism, thereby saving the world's tourist sites from ecological destruction at the same time that developing countries will lose an important revenue stream.[4] Despite such speculation, most VR games available to the public utilize science fiction or fantasy themes that justify creators' deviation from the demands of representational realism. Within actual VR implementations, the fun of an M. C. Escher–like game space or the eerie desert-like surface of Mars has replaced the touristic pleasures of simulated visits to Polynesian beaches or China's Forbidden City.

In travel films, a sense of authenticity and "being there" have derived from a belief in the existence of that "there" and from a faith in the technological apparatus's ability to illusionistically represent the environment and place the spectator in the midst of it. The reality effects of VR, with its representation of "elsewhere" rather than "there," on the other hand, have been relocated to a realm in which authenticity, if considered at all, is not judged by visual verisimilitude nor by indexical links to reality.[5] For instance, reminiscent of a scene from *The Lawnmower Man* (Brett Leonard, 1992), in which the VR apparatus is demonstrated for its ability to deliver the bodily sensation of floating, an exhibit at Disney's Epcot Center in Orlando, Florida, uses computer-generated scenes to promote the illusion of flying on a magic carpet. In the case of *Lawnmower Man*, the floater drifts through an abstract, bubble-filled space, while the Disney exhibit presents the town of Agrabah based on the animated film *Aladdin* (Ron Clements and John Musker, 1992). Despite Agrabah's exotic trappings, the referent is unhinged from any actual travel destination as VR users search for Aladdin's lamp and are hosted by a real-time computer version of the Disney character Iago. In this way, the technology is still introduced through the touting of its reality effects, but it is the experiential realism of VR's simulation of floating or flying that is evaluated rather than an illusion of being in an identifiable location.

Despite the disappearance of authenticity as pursued through cultural difference within this next generation of immersive entertainment technologies, travel metaphors and aspects of the tourist gaze can be identified within VR games. Yet, to the extent that there is no attempt to believably represent another culture, the political questions around the deployment of the tourist gaze within VR do not carry the same weight. The corpus of theoretical writing on VR culture, however, suggests that the political stakes of media analysis in this case has merely shifted into another terrain, that of the body. Such a paradigmatic shift from a politics of representation to corporeal experience could still be contained within a study of simulated tourism, with one adjustment: the tourist's departure from home and from quotidian experience in order to encounter some form of difference must be redefined to specify the inclusion of departures from everyday experience of the body and of difference experienced at a corporeal level. Arguably, actual travel has always involved different forms of corporeal experience that help to mark departure from the home environment. It may involve the sensations of undulating waves beneath the ship's hull, the vibrations of railway travel, or air turbulence. Differences in altitude, weather, atmosphere, and pollution levels may be immediately perceptible in addition to having cumulative effects on the body. Sickness, sun exposure, the extremes of indulgence, physical exhaustion, jet lag, unusual food and drink, and engagement in atypical physical activities may also produce an unusual combination of bodily sensation as a direct result of the travel experience. However, beyond certain rarities—changes in theater temperature, neck strain, the jostlings of a George C. Hale tour experience, CinemaScope-induced motion sickness, or the acceleration and centrifugal force of Disneyland's Indiana Jones Adventure—it is difficult for simulated travel to produce significant corporeal changes. Virtual reality, or at least the promotional discourses surrounding the technology, make a very different promise. Images of VR users are not of static bodies with eyes unblinking in rapt attention, but of human forms in unusual postures as they interact with unseen digital worlds. At the very least, their heads and necks strain under the awkwardness of the heavy VR helmet. By taking into account this interacting body and the expanded experiential realm of the VR simulation, we shift into a new terrain of embodied tourism.

—— Virtual VR

Virtual reality is unlike the media forms explored in this volume in that its depiction in popular culture exceeds the role of reality in defining public perception of the technology. For instance, magazines like *Mondo 2000* and *Future Sex* depict lush digital worlds and sexual fantasies enacted with digital partners via VR; yet VR exhibits available to the public barely extend beyond computer games coupled with vibrating chairs or a game of virtual Frisbee. The hyperbole surrounding VR generated within computer culture periodicals, science fiction literature, and academic pondering makes it necessary to differentiate between current VR applications and what I call "virtual" virtual reality: the goggle-and-senso-sheath technologies or the mind-penetrating devices that seem virtually real in popular discourses but have yet to enter the realm of actuality. To date, even scientists working hard to realize these VR dreams admit that the most fascinating work is still on paper and that current applications continue to be plagued by awkward interfaces and severe limitations in simulating sensory input beyond the visual and aural.

While the conflation of truth and speculative fiction within mainstream discourse may be a product of the assumed predictive value of science fiction, this same conflation within academic discourse warrants a closer look, in part because the divergence between my own analysis of VR's embodied tourism and that of other media scholars is a consequence of my effort to separate out virtual and actual VR. Academics often place VR-based entertainment forms currently in existence and entertainment texts about VR's future on the same analytical plane for a couple of reasons. First, on the surface, the implications of virtual VR appear to be far more revolutionary than those of actual VR studied in isolation. Second, the tradition of viewing such speculative portraits as indicative of some underlying cultural truth has led to a confusing collapse between the fiction and the reality. Certainly, futuristic VR portraits offer the same kind of fodder as films like *Videodrome* and *Total Recall* for finding metaphorical equivalents of the effects of technology. In this case, the temptation is particularly strong due to virtual VR's animation of issues central to debates around the changing nature of subjectivity. Cultural theorists in search of tangible manifestations of postmodern, decentered subjectivity have attached themselves to the cultural fantasy of virtual VR, an apparatus that will supposedly foster a split consciousness, straddling the here and now and a world that can only be located in strings of code and chains of signals passed through labyrinthine circuitry. Through the technological filtering of corporeal experience, the virtual VR subject appears to have stepped away from the foundations of his own identity, constructed through the body as a source of knowledge. Impressionable writers have suggested that VR, when fully realized, will indeed transform us into postmodern beings. They suggest that instead of being merely a pumped-up version of 3-D, scratch-and-sniff, or widescreen cinema, full-blown VR will bring a cultural revolution by imploding various forms of distance, breaking down self/other polarities in its path. The more typical position held by postmodern media theorists, however, is that this cultural revolution has already snuck up on us without the aid of virtual reality. Yet in the absence of a concrete image pulled from our own present tense that summarizes the radical effects of this stocking-footed revolution, another image has served the same purpose. Despite its fictional status, the image of the science fiction hero strapped and wired into the futuristic world of virtual VR has served not as a harbinger of things to come but as a metaphor for the cultural effects of postmodernism currently upon us.

One element of continuity in such uses of virtual VR as a symbol of the postmodern revolution and the subject's final absorption into a simulated world is the assumption of disembodiment as a fundamental component of the VR experience. Stated more precisely, virtual VR, as used in metaphorical portraits of postmodernism, is depicted as illusionistically embodying through the neurological interface, which short-circuits somatic experience by feeding signals directly to the brain. The simulation of bodily sensations that are neurologically communicated suggests a severing of traditional bodily experience for the duration of the VR experience. The most common examples of virtual VR referenced within musings on the new disembodied subjectivity are those filmic and televisual representations that first introduced the concept of VR to audiences. These VR depictions foreground their illusion of embodiment by using the sexual encounter as the ideal content for testing out virtual VR's reality effects. From the prerecorded orgy in Douglas Trumbull's 1983 *Brainstorm* to the kiss from a Miss America contestant in Oliver Stone's 1993 TV miniseries *Wild Palms,* virtual VR boasted of its power to simulate sex, the ultimate embodied experience. The bodily abandonment that this kind of simulation requires is most unequivocal in the cybersex scene in *Lawnmower Man.* During the encounter, the two bodies are separately strapped into VR stations like discarded coats on their hangers, for all practical purposes absent from the libidinal event.

This type of virtually embodied simulation must be examined more closely, not just in its divergence from the capabilities of actual VR but in its filtering through the logic of another media form. Sex has the convenience of being universally understood as a tactile experience while still enjoying unwavering popularity as a vicarious event delivered through aural and visual means alone, thereby making it a perfect candidate for displaying virtual VR's potential by way of a medium limited in its sensory bandwidth. The redesign of the virtual VR apparatus to suit the needs of cinematic spectacle is apparent first of all in the shift toward neurological interfaces within filmic depictions of VR. The cover of an issue of *Future Sex* from the early 1990s, for instance, features a man and a woman wearing goggles and full-body suits or senso-sheaths designed to deliver sensory input to the body with particular emphasis on the genitalia. This fictional envisioning of VR's use of a bodily interface can be contrasted to the direct brain downlink, or neurological interface, depicted in the film *Strange Days* (Kathryn Bigelow, 1995), an image of virtual VR that is currently far more common in film than senso-sheath implementations of VR. In *Strange Days* and other recent cinematic depictions of virtual reality, lightweight headgear delivers sensory information directly to the brain, thereby circumventing the body entirely while still simulating embodied experience. Interestingly, this goggleless redesign of the VR apparatus serves cinema's agenda of visual communication by providing the audience with an unimpeded view of the VR user's facial expression. The VR interactor is portrayed with all the visual stylistics conventional to the filmic depiction of a sex partner. The use of the facial expression in close-up at the point of climax, for instance, is a trope common to pornography as a means of visually underlining a tactile pleasure that almost defies visual representation. Or within the more closely regulated depictions of sex in mainstream film, the facial expression is the perfect cut-away shot for suggesting that which can not be directly shown.

In such examples, the cinematically depicted VR apparatus mirrors film itself in its movement toward a transparent interface. In reference to interfaces, transparency typically refers to a lack of intrusiveness and to the easy translation of intuition and desire into computer-facilitated action triggered by the user. The more transparent the interface the more similar the media experience is to direct experience. For instance, classic Hollywood cinema aspires to transparency by providing an anthropomorphic view on the action and by using changes in perspective to anticipate and sate spectators' desire to see the best view, thereby minimizing the recognition of their own inability to move within or affect the cinematically depicted space. The weighty and constraining contraption of a VR apparatus that makes use of a bodily interface is far less transparent than a direct feed into the brain. Equally important for its cinematic depiction is the VR apparatus's more literal transparency, providing spectators with a clear view of the jubilant interactor and the spectacularly well paid actor who plays the interactor.

The cinematic depiction of virtual VR also parallels film in its fantasy of disembodiment. Or, more accurately, the disembodied simulation of embodied experience suggested by the brain-interface versions of virtual VR may be a product of the same cultural fantasy of corporeal transcendence that underlies the theorized pleasures of cinema spectatorship. Despite film theory's recent developments that reinsert the body, such as in phenomenological understandings of spectatorship, theories of bodily repression, of vision liberated from the flesh, remain dominant within film studies. According to such theories about spectatorial pleasures, the corporeal transcendence of film, which puts bodyless vision into unencumbered flight, holds considerable appeal for members of a society that indulges in the fantasy of a cohesive Cartesian subject confined only on this earth by a bodily container. It is not much of a stretch to compare cinema's theorized repression of the body to a brain-interface technology that converts thought into action and supplies a constant flow of sensory data to the brain. The physical body disappears from view as the brain is wired into a digital universe otherwise inaccessible to a body of the flesh and blood sort. Sometimes within these virtual worlds extended avatars resembling bodies are provided for purposes of navigation, communication, and entertainment, thereby making the framework of desire not entirely unlike that of cinema, within which the actors' bodies operate as vehicles for our ideal egos reflected within the cinema's mirror-screen. In both cases, entry into the fiction demands a forgetting of the actual body and projection into the perspective granted by a virtual body. Repression of the body remains consistent; only the sensory bandwidth and level of interactivity differs.

In another suggestion of similarity between virtual VR and the medium that depicts it, one could compare psychoanalytic film theory's understanding of film spectatorship to virtual VR portrayals that suggest the medium as a conduit for thoughts, dreams, and unconscious mental processes. Cinema has been theorized as a phenomenon that lulls the spectator into a dreamlike state tantamount to regression to a pre-oedipal, prelinguistic state in which what Jacques Lacan references as the imaginary, not yet harnessed by the symbolic, reigns. Virtual VR has been similarly depicted as a play space for the unconscious mind, with personal demons, repressed thoughts, and primal desires erupting from the fabric of the VR experience. Once again, this may be the assimilating wand of cinema likening virtual reality to its own structures of fantasy. Yet, the neurological interface of virtual VR distinguishes itself from film in its more direct tapping of the mind. To some extent, every form of artistic expression allows for the representation of the mind's work, thereby justifying the use of psychoanalytic method to explore the symptoms of the unconscious mind that spill out on to the page, canvas, or screen alongside the artist's more conscious endeavors. Virtual reality depicted as a multiuser environment marked by infinite interactivity and controlled by the mind in a kind of visualization process removes the paintbrush as a middleman in this process. Thought is instantaneously translated into an environmental change via the neurological interface's direct connection to the brain. Such an arrangement, however, suggests the possible influence of the unconscious mind on the VR space. For instance, in *Lawnmower Man,* the 1999 television movie *The Cyberstalking,* and the 1995 television series *VR5,* despite the user's conscious control over VR as a kind of waking dream, elements of the VR experience—images, stories, and desires—appear to spring uncontrollably from the user's unconscious, turning these virtual worlds into fantasy lands rippled with psychic land mines.

In the case of cinema, the filmmaker's fantasies as expressed onscreen have been suggested to have particularly poignant effects due to the susceptibility of the darkness-enshrouded spectator transfixed by the light and temporarily regressed into a pseudo–pre-oedipal state. Such theories also rely on the existence of a collective unconscious to explain how films' repressed subtexts can operate similarly on multiple spectators. Virtual VR, with its thought-induced interactivity, on the other hand, indicates the potential of this imagined apparatus to allow each of us to experience her own dreams and fantasies, as is suggested in the film *Until the End of the World* (Wim Wenders, 1991). No burdensome conduit, such as someone else's film made relevant through a shared collective unconscious, is necessary; the mind and the VR apparatus form a closed circuit. When the virtual VR environment is shared by more than one person, it takes on the shape of a conversation unconfined by the narrow expressive potential of language and its imprecision. In this way, virtual VR is shown as another technology of demediating mediation. For the artist, the need for channeling expression through a physical medium is removed. Likewise, the film spectator no longer has to rely on film's roundabout route to the unconscious; he can tap directly into a fantasy world of his own making. And with VR-mediated interpersonal exchanges, language no longer has to be a mediating force. Thus, in *VR5* and *The Cell* (Tarsem Singh, 2000), the female protagonists can rendezvous with criminals in a virtual space and experience the horrors of these men's twisted minds, while in pursuit of critical information. While *VR5* and *The Cell* feature police interrogation turned into surreal adventure, *The Cyberstalking* does the equivalent for the music video. The recording artist exercises her voice and her fantasies in order to create a virtual environment, which music lovers can "jack into" instead of attending a concert. As a demediating technology, virtual VR within such portrayals is sometimes even discussed with references to direct or authentic experience. For instance, in the British TV miniseries *Cold Lazarus*, a media mogul asks, in reference to VR-accessed memories from the cryogenically frozen head of an eccentric writer from four hundred years ago, "Who would want made-up stories from a hack when you can mainline into the real thing?"

At the same time that film depictions of virtual VR render the wonders of VR into visual forms appropriate to cinematic depiction and film's own dynamics of pleasure, such portraits go to some effort to distinguish the dangers of a virtually embodied media form from the safety of cinema spectatorship. Some of these strategies of depiction, suspiciously similar to those employed in filmic portrayals of television, portray VR as mind altering and dependence inducing. Like an ever-available drug that delivers either mellow distraction or exhilarating intensity, VR becomes addictive in films like *Strange Days*, while in *Lawnmower Man* it brings about mental collapse in one case and a gradual personality change for the worse in another. *Brainstorm* suggests a different detrimental effect—the possibility that experiencing a VR-recorded death will induce the same effect in the VR user. Cinema insists that while a violent murder on the silver screen may make spectators squirm in their seats, death in VR may bring far graver consequences. When the interface becomes too transparent, or when the environmental bubble is compromised, simulated experience may be more immediate but the pleasure may be mixed with pain, and vitality coupled with fatality.

—— Virtual Reality as We Know It

Actual implementations of virtual reality stand out in distinction to virtual VR in at least two ways: they tend to be marketed with touristic discourses in the tradition of other media forms, rather than with sexual scenarios such as in the case of virtual VR, and—again in contradistinction to virtual VR—they make use of bodily interfaces rather than the far more scientifically dubious neurological interface. At the same time that such interfaces do not seem to present a revolution of disembodiment in that bodily interfaces rely on the normal relay of bodily sensation, they do suggest a logic of dual embodiment or of a bodily overlay. And while extant VR applications are too primitive to explore the more radical potential effects of dual embodiment, they are suggestive of the lure of a path of technological development that deviates from the pursuit of transparency and instead promotes corporeal dissonance within VR's capacity for dual embodiment. Dual embodiment, as explored below, suggests a break from the continuity that links VR to its media predecessors and a point at which theoretical models borrowed from film theory are stretched beyond their breaking point. But before reaching this point of rupture, we must trace out the continuity, which in terms of this study begins with the use of a touristic rhetoric to introduce the wonders of virtual reality.

Although the spaces for exploration are not always typical tourist locales, virtual reality nonetheless consistently has been marketed as a journey. In the announcements of alternative universes awaiting exploration, and in calls to adventure issued to all willing-and-able "cybernauts," VR games continually conjure up travel metaphors, such as one ad's announcement, "Welcome to the world of virtual reality. Please select your destination." Even the more science-oriented VR applications are referred to as "journeys" through virtual spaces, whether they be intimate voyages among the atoms of a complex molecular form or strolls through the unbuilt structures depicted in architectural blueprints.

Interestingly, at the same time that VR proponents insist that this technology will be something entirely new, attempts to describe VR experience tend to link it to familiar tropes of exploration and discovery torn from the past. Howard Reingold's tour through virtual reality, for instance, slips at times from technical talk into sentimental musings characteristic of the age-old genre of travel literature.[6] Even William Gibson's interface "cowboy" of the novel *Neuromancer* conjures up images from the American past when trailblazers charted paths through the Wild West for the rest of the population to follow. This trope of discovery is

This poster was commissioned to commemorate the 1993 opening of the first Virtual World site, which was promoted as the world's first digital theme park.

©1993 Virtual World Entertainment, LLC.
Conceived by Jordan Weisman, realized by Jordan Alvin.

also used in *Lawnmower Man,* as one scientist expresses his excitement over his VR experiments by declaring himself to be a Columbus figure discovering a new world and his latest breakthrough to be the equivalent of the "sighting of a new continent."

Perhaps the best example of this attempt to situate current forays into virtual territories in terms of the history of global exploration can be found at a chain of VR "theme parks" called Virtual World (VW).[7] Next to the company's logo, which resembles a compass, VW's motto announces, "A New Age of Discovery." On the company's poster an antique parchment map blends into a neon blue grid stretched out over a black mass of presumably unexplored outer regions in space, time, and virtual reality. The antechambers of Virtual World are filled with photographs of Sir Richard Burton, Amelia Earhart, Howard Hughes, and other historical explorers who all presumably belonged to the same Virtual Geographic League that VW players join before their maiden voyage. Yet such references to more earthly exploration immediately drop away upon entering the VR simulations of Mars—a world of robots, spaceships, and hollowed canals.

—— The Touristic Pleasures of Virtual Reality

As I have argued in chapter I, immersion in a new environment, simulated or real, can feel threatening at the same time that it presents an exhilarating feast for the senses. In a familiar environment, objects and scenes launch a myriad of recalled mininarratives, each reaffirming the subject's placement within that space. On the other hand, a world that you do not recognize is a world that does not recognize you. Its objects may not present themselves as immediately namable, and its inhabitants—human, animal, or bacterial—may not peacefully yield to the tourist's presence.

Within actual travel, the extension of the environmental bubble—the intervening space between a tourist and the foreign terrain—has helped mitigate such threats and transform travel from a perilous undertaking to an enjoyable packaged adventure for families on vacation. However, the insulation of this intermediary space cuts both ways; it protects at the same time that it blocks direct experience, which is why tourism and simulated travel both attempt to make the environmental bubble as invisible as possible. Thus, in addition to VR's use of historical exploration narratives to promise a return to a pristine past with dark continents unmarred by tourist traps and gift shops, VR strives for an illusion of direct interaction. Some VR enthusiasts speculate that it will bring about the ultimate breakdown of barriers between traveler and destination; the virtual tourist will be able to become a part of the environment, to enter the hillside, to become the Leaning Tower looking down upon the city of Pisa. Of course, in this area, existing VR technologies are a little disappointing. Most VR games do not provide direct interaction but rather place the participant once again in an intervening space that significantly filters experience of the destination environment. For instance, in the VW game Red Planet (1992), players are encased in a cockpit-like space, which is then "translocated" to another dimension. In other words, the cockpit monitor is turned on and the pod's functions are brought online. Interaction with Mars' surface is then limited by these functions accessed via the pod's control panel (Shoot, Accelerate, Brake, Reverse) and vision is similarly limited by the cockpit's small window/screen.

In a game such as Red Planet, not only the physicality of the environmental bubble but the rules of the game determine the nature of one's experience of a virtual world. Due to the warfare mentality of the game's design, interaction with a locale resembles a form of mastery associated with very early travel—in other words, with the military invasions that preceded the parade of anthropologists and missionaries, who were then followed quickly by the tourists. With such VR games developing out of military simulation technologies and being designed mainly for audiences accustomed to shoot-'em-up video games, environmental mastery can be quantified in terms of vehicle speed, body counts, and minimal equipment damage. Nonetheless, we can still see similarities between the surveyance of environments in VR games and what I describe as touristic strategies: mastery through acquisition, orientation within space, and the imposition of language onto landscape.[8]

Returning again to the examples of VR provided by *Lawnmower Man*'s fictional portrait and by VW's games, emphases on acquisition, identification, and orientation are evident. In *Lawnmower Man*, a chimpanzee with a VR helmet has been conditioned to play military games. When he escapes, the world appears to be a continuation of the game. His vision is framed by the goggles' screen, which contains information about the immediate surroundings and occasional suggestions like "ACQUIRE" if some useful item is nearby. The helmet also contains its own built-in tour guide, or DataVisor, which searches its databank to identify the names of objects and buildings that the chimp encounters.

In this case, actual and virtual VR bear some resemblance to one another. Like the chimp, VW players work toward the goal of survival; they too are assisted by the technology in identifying surrounding objects. A text screen provides a readout of any approaching vehicle and the "call sign" of the pilot inside. Little information, however, is given on the layout of the locale and a pilot's exact placement within that space during the game itself, presumably due to the time constraints of a short playing period. In an attempt to alleviate this temporary disorientation, maps are provided both before and after the game. A Basic Operations Primer, given to players upon signing up for a mission, maps out the two spaces that will be occupied by participants—the pod cockpit and the canals of Mars. And after the game, an aerial view of the "death canals" and the players' progress through them is mapped out on a pilot's log, which each player takes home. Although this log constitutes a souvenir, as of yet VW pilots cannot physically acquire souvenirs or planetary samples during the actual game. However, outside the playing pods, subtle "ACQUIRE" suggestions abound; visitors can purchase postcards, bomber jackets, or even videotapes of the games just played so that each pilot may remember his journey.

—— Death and the Embodied Tourist

The violent military themes of VR games, which clearly derive more from the video-game tradition than from safari films and widescreen romps through the South Pacific, would seem like an unlikely terrain for foregrounding the pleasures of embodied travel. Granted, embodied experience within a game like Red Planet is limited to the sensations of the bouncing pod reacting to simulated accleration, collision, and vehicular damage. Nonetheless, while the experience of velocity is coveted by go-cart speedway and sports car enthusiasts, sensations of speed have not always been considered entirely pleasurable, as nineteenth-century occurences of neurasthenia associated with railway travel attest to. As it turns out, most VR games exploit the spectacle of vehicle collision while suggesting a life-saving extension of the environmental bubble, a kind of protection against the trauma of collision, or "railway brain," as it was called in the case of train crashes. Just as film depictions of VR emphasize bodily impairment, psychological damage, or death as potential drawbacks of embodied entertainment, VR games deny death or bodily harm as a possibility while still retaining a win/lose game dynamic. Returning to the example of Virtual World, a briefing tape shows an expert pilot dropping into a race among slaves on Mars. Surprised at the stranger's sudden entrance into the race, a slave-participant inquires as to her business there. The pilot responds, "I'm just a tourist." According to the rules of the race, the winner earns freedom and the others get the booby prize of death. Our pilot-tourist finishes in second place but is "translocated" out of the game before enduring the consequences of defeat. This death-defying logic is continued in VW's fictional history and in the rules of the game. For instance, Amelia Earhart probably plunged to a watery death, but according to VW, she was the first pilot to translocate into another dimension. And within the game itself, death is virtually meaningless; the primer announces, "Don't panic if your vehicle explodes, your pod will automatically remorph facing in the right direction to continue the race."

In Magic Edge's virtual flight simulations, the pilot's visual perspective separates from the aircraft when it has been hit by enemy fire, and he watches the plane crash to smithereens below. Seconds later the pilot is zooming along in another aircraft. The same kind of temporary out-of-body experience followed by reincarnation occurs in Virtuality's Dactyl Nightmare (1991), a game explored in more detail below. At any point in the game, a flying pterodactyl might scoop up the player and cruelly drop him on the checkerboard floor below. Yet, at the moment that the pterodactyl releases the player's body from its grip, this falling rental body comes into view as the player's own perspective remains static, perched above this fatal scene. In fact, if one does not dwell on the trauma of death, it is a pleasurable experience to be lifted high above the game board and given an elevated vantage point. This seems to be VR's way of having it both ways—the fun of embodied experience without the threats that embodiment brings.

—— Becoming Someone Else

At Virtual World, consumers are encouraged to play make-believe. With their membership in the Virtual Geographic League and new names to match new heroic identities, players can feel like renegade explorers in cyberspace. Similarly, at the game center Magic Edge, the consumer might assume the illustrious role of a fighter pilot flying over Arizona's Monument Valley; at the competing VR center Cybermind, even greater departures from everyday identities are offered as players become pool balls knocked and rolled about in a fierce billiards game.

This idea of traveling as someone else or traveling in order to become someone else is a well-worn theme in personal narratives, in travel literature, and even in the marketing of tourism. Travel ads suggest that the rejuvenating effects of vacationing can bring out a "new you," while one strain of travel literature portrays the journey as a process of self-discovery or the unearthing of parts of the psyche either heretofore unknown or simply forgotten. In cinema, too, films from *Now, Voyager* (Irving Rapper, 1942) to *The Passenger* (Michelangelo Antonioni, 1975) have played with this idea of assuming a new identity for the duration of

For decades, many packaged tours have included as part of their entertainment masquerade parties and formal dress events allowing for tourists to become the natives seen on their tour, as in this photo from a formal dress party aboard the *S.S. Cleveland* in 1910.

Photograph by John T. Withers, published in *Around the World on the Cleveland* by William G. Frizell and George H. Greenfield. Copyright held by authors, 1910.

the trip. Actual vacation role-playing may amount to merely lying about one's real occupation back home, or for some it may be about "going native." Travelers often don different clothes and pursue altered physical appearances, whether it be sun-darkened skin or the weight loss of a spa vacation. From James Boswell to Pietro Della Valle, and perhaps we can even include Jan Morris, many notable travelers have experimented with the fluidity of identity allowed within travel and have experienced territorial passage as a shape-changing process. Travel, with its separation from familiar identity-grounding structures such as family and work, and the tourist attraction, with its encouragement of role-playing activities, appear to offer a liminality that fosters flexible identity and temporary escape from one's "home" identity. However, barring certain extraordinary events—spirit possession, death, reincarnation, out-of-body experience—there are certain limits to the body- and identity-altering experiences of travel. In short, chances are that wherever you go, there you will be, and most likely physically located in the same body.

Fictional portraits of virtual reality, on the other hand, suggest that, even beyond the role-playing games of VR, we will be able to choose to travel in certain bodies while occupying virtual spaces. Even current VR devices hint at an expansion of the traditional limits of body occupation by providing players with altered, albeit generic, appearances within the game space. Science fiction writers, however, would have us believe that the appearance alterations possible within VR could involve radical changes and infinite choices. A VR traveler might decide to experience her adventure in the virtual body of Arnold Schwarzenegger or to venture out as Marilyn Monroe's twin sister. While such drastic and temporary changes are nearly impossible outside of virtual reality, it could be suggested that this ability to be a tourist within a temporary virtual body is an extension of the contemporary world where not only is tourism one of the fastest growing industries but our bodies and appearances seem to becoming more malleable. Anyone with adequate funds can bring a photo of Michelle Pfeiffer's nose or Kirk Douglas's chin to a plastic surgeon and walk home wearing a celebrity body part. The use of steroids, liposuction, tattooing, prosthesis, reconstructive surgery, estrogen injections, hair dye, implants, and weight-loss drugs all construct the body as a surface to be painted and sculpted in more radical ways than have ever been possible. This inscription of bodily surfaces has been described by some cultural theorists as a process of "self-production" and by others as cultural commodification of the body. The Prozac rage, however, suggests that this self-production or consumerist self-reconfiguration does not have to use external surfaces to bring out or express some internal vision of the self. Instead, one can reshape from the inside out. Popular discourses around the drug seem to send out the message, "Depression? Poor self-confidence? Reclusiveness? Strap on a new Prozac personality. Become someone else, a better someone else."

The technologies that have immediately preceded virtual reality could be said to facilitate more temporary appearance and identity adjustments by removing the body from the social field or by providing new bodies. The phone-sex industry and Internet communication, for instance, strip users of physical appearance and allow them to reconstruct their image through words according to their own fantasies. We should expect enhanced forms of such disembodiment, cyber-transvestitism, and multiple identities as Internet technologies conjoin with virtual reality and avatar-based communication forms. The realization that the bodies and identities that we claim within these paraspaces may bear little resemblance to those parked at our monitors brings various questions to the foreground. For instance, if subjectivity is shaped by embodied experience, then will these electronic experiences of traveling in someone else's cybershoes constitute a difference in kind or only in degree from the temporary identity adjustments of tourism? Such a question points out the need for a greater understanding of the becoming-someone-elseness of tourism.

The rethinking of identity and the role-playing games common to tourism could be considered traditionally pleasurable and privileged forms of mobility rather than an instance of postmodernism's radical fragmentation of identity. Just as the tourist moves from country to country knowing that the journey is bookended by home, the role-playing tourist can playfully don various masks, often without questioning the original identity that lies beneath. This is not to say that the absence of the comforts of home does not sometimes threaten to question cultural and personal identity in significant ways. Yet, touristic strategies—societally learned behaviors and ways of viewing unfamiliar cultures—have been developed and fine-tuned in order to fend off such threats while far from home.

These touristic visual and orientational strategies, as discussed in prior chapters, can be employed to make sense of foreign and sometimes daunting virtual spaces and to maintain a stable subject position in the midst of this unfamiliar world. The attempt to understand a space as a framed and representable whole; the placing of oneself outside Martin Heidegger's "world as picture"; enhanced powers of mobility; the near-divine perspective of the cartographer; alignment with sophisticated technologies of mastery; the flow of information about the foreign environment; and the reduction of landscape to either picturesque spectacle or quantifiable facts and statistics—these touristic strategies help prevent the onslaught of culture shock, the feeling of a loss in self-placement, a multileveled disorientation that ruptures touristic pleasure. Yet this notion of the touristic or of the world as postcard only deals with external space and reduces the body to a disembodied eye positioned in space. While to date the body within virtual reality is first and foremost a seeing body—or what we might call a sight-seeing body—we should acknowledge the body itself and not just the surrounding environment as a potential object for touristic exploration.

—— Disembodiment versus Dual Embodiment

A corporeal tourism that involves a forgetting of the actual body and projection into the perspective granted by a virtual body seems to be in keeping with recent cultural fantasies of occupying someone else's body, what I call "body hopping." For instance, in Anne Rice's novel *The Tale of the Body Thief,* a character with unusual psychic fortitude can push people's minds out of their bodies and enter in their absence. Television's *Quantum Leap* offered a similar fantasy as a quantum physicist traveled through time occupying the bodies of temporarily dislocated subjects. William Gibson's cyberpunk novel *Neuromancer* differs from these two depictions in that its special brand of body hopping, "simulation-stimulation" (otherwise known as "sim-stim"), an effect made possible by neural implants, does not require that the original occupant leave her body while the visitor enters. The body hopping depicted in these examples represents a kind of reverse spirit possession in which the male protagonist becomes the spirit possessing someone else's body. Most important, this fantasy of body hopping, like cinema spectatorship and neurologically interfaced VR, involves a presumed transcendence of one's own physical body.

Such tales of body hopping seem to have acquired greater complexity with the release of the film *Being John Malkovich* (Spike Jonze, 1999), which recounts the discovery of a portal that facilitates entrance into actor John Malkovich's body. This body hop, however, does not imply a simple separation of mind from body. The original occupant is not forced out entirely, banished to some antechamber, nor is the bodily space easily shared with one mind piloting the body and the visitor simply along for the ride. Instead, a struggle over corporeal control ensues. The awkwardness of visitor-controlled bodily movement suggests not just this struggle but a readjustment, a recalibration of body image. In such a scenario, the mind is not entirely separable from body, but is corporeally contoured, inextricably linked to the body by body image. The mismatch between the mind's corporeal projection and the new body is played out in the struggle to control movement in a naturalistic way. The film's portrayal of shared corporeal occupation risks being reducible to the physical comedy that results from the battle of minds in *All of Me* (Carl Reiner, 1984), a comedy of reincarnation within an already occupied body. However, *Being John Malkovich* is saved from such a fate in part by its subplot involving marionettes. The operation of marionettes employed as a metaphor for bodily occupation makes clear the logic of dual embodiment, the combined mental and physical effort of projecting oneself into a very different body in order to control precise bodily movement. Both bodies are present in effect, but the one marked by otherness initially resists. Movements of the "home" body need to be recalibrated and precisely controlled in order to project oneself into the other body and bring this resistant body into abeyance. In short, dual embodiment differs from the fantasy of body hopping in that it does not rely on disembodiment and in that it recognizes the mind as shaped by and attuned to a particular body.

This distinction between dual embodiment and a reembodiment that relies on an initial escape of the body is at the heart of the difference between VR technologies with bodily interfaces and those with neurological interfaces. I have suggested that the neurological interface is a product of fantasy, a technological development characteristic of virtual VR but entirely distinct from the reality of current VR technologies. Likewise, the disembodiment and separability of mind from body supported by such neurological interfaces is a fantasy of escape from the body's burdens of pain, sickness, and mortality. In short, virtual VR as an abandonment of the body as "meat" is the cultural fantasy of travel without motion sickness, sex without AIDS, culinary indulgence without flatulence, dramatic conflict and adventure without death.

While contemplation of virtual VR fantasies assists in the analysis of a culturally shared ambivalence toward the body, it neither moves us closer to an understanding of actual VR apparatuses and how they play upon mind/body relations. Although it is not my intention to summarize the various theories concerning the importance of body to subjectivity, some reference to this theoretical terrain is necessary to explore the experiential realm of VR that extends beyond the protective sphere of the tourist gaze that defuses all it sees. That is to say, if travel is defined as the departure from quotidian experience in order to confront the unfamiliar, then those aspects of unfamiliarity that are experienced through perceptual registers other than vision should not be overlooked. And unfamiliar somatic experience through a disruption of the normal operation of the body image becomes most significant in light of understandings of how subjectivity is constituted through lived bodily experience.

A short list of theories concerned with the body's role in identity formation would include Sigmund Freud's notion of bodily sensations and libidinal drives

that activate ego formation; Jacques Lacan's mirror stage theory, which postulates a coincident recognition of defined bodily contours and individual subjectivity; and Michel Foucault's system of surveillance and discipline within which
bodies are made, not given, and within which social identity is contingent on
self-knowledge of the body. We could also add to this list existentialists and phe-
nomenologists who break away from René Descartes's body-as-object to acknowledge the body not as a useful appendage to the thinking subject but as the very
fabric of self. Each of these theories acknowledge such body-subjects as socially,
culturally, and technologically determined such that the tools we use as extensions of the body and the machines we use to alter bodily experience become sites
for interrogating the possibility of transforming body-based subjectivities.

—— A Realism of Positionality

With a renewed interest in body-technology intersections, we return to VR's bodily interfaces, which do not involve hurling the sighted mind into the lights and
flashes of William Gibson's datasphere but rather align the real body with a kind
of rental body provided upon entrance into a virtual space. In this sense, contemporary VR does not transcend or forget the original body but synchronizes the
two bodies, one on either side of the interface. In some cases, body is loosely
defined to apply to the simulated aircraft, walking robots, and other virtual vehicles in which the user appears to be encased during the VR game. More interesting applications, however, attempt to achieve an equivalence between the
user's body, equipped with a head-mounted display, and the body that moves
around in the virtual playing field. In such setups, the headgear typically combines goggles that deliver streaming images to the user's field of view, and a tracking device that detects head movements and prompts appropriate changes in the
perspectival orientation of the streaming images. A handheld gun or mouse picks
up on activity commands such as "walk" or "shoot." The example of this type of
goggle-and-gun interface that I draw upon is from the game Dactyl Nightmare,
which can be played at Cybermind VR entertainment centers in the United States
and Japan.

At the same time that science fiction writers are describing technologies that
would allow users to shape their own appearances in VR paraspaces, researchers
are a few steps behind working on "image extraction" technologies that would
project one's actual image into a virtual space using video cameras.[9] Thus, current applications like Dactyl Nightmare place the VR user in virtual reality using
a standard-issue body. Regardless of how the player actually looks or would want
to look within virtual reality, other players see him or her as a thin, slightly

androgynous white man in jeans and a T-shirt color-coded to correspond with the player's Virtuality SU 1000 unit. All virtual players have short brown hair, with any facial features obscured by a virtual helmet similar to the one the player's "home" body wears.

This body, however it is defined, is essential to the realism of virtual reality, a realism that, of course, has little to do with photorealism or visual resemblance. Maurice Merleau-Ponty has cited the body as the very condition for our access to and conception of space.[10] In agreement, Henri Lefebvre relates understandings of space to subjectivity, noting, "One relates oneself to space, situates oneself in space. One confronts both an immediacy and an objectivity of one's own. One places oneself at the centre, designates oneself, measures oneself, and uses oneself as a measure. One is, in short, a 'subject.'"[11] Virtual reality as an imitative form of reality grants users access via temporary bodies, and these same bodies are what endows a simulated space with a realism of positionality and a sense of subjecthood within this space. VR users' ability to occupy and negotiate space in these bodies, however, is a learned skill. In fact, the process of acculturation to this corporeal overlay is not unlike the developmental stages of human understanding and motor control. First of all, a period of adjustment is required to master the use of certain triggers in order to move forward or change directions. Concurrent with the ability to control movement comes an understanding of what in the visual field is a part of the self and what is foreign, what moves with the VR player and what remains impervious to her movement. In the case of most Cybermind games, an outstretched, gun-toting arm is the only visual reminder of a player's own virtual presence.[12]

According to psychoanalytic developmental theory, differentiating the self from the surrounding environment and developing motor skills often forms the background for the mirror stage. The rules of Dactyl Nightmare prepare players for such a confrontation, with images similar or identical to their own. Multiple users equipped with guns occupy the same virtual space. To win, the interactor must find and shoot these other players. However, preceding any such confrontation, players find themselves alone and exploring the immediate environment and their own movement capabilities. Of course, no actual mirrors pop up in this sparsely decorated environment, but as Lacan would remind us, the mirror stage can be prompted by an encounter with another person. In Dactyl Nightmare, recognition of a moving figure as another player sparks the realization, "Oh, I must look something like that, too." For infants, the mirror stage also brings an understanding of space as a social or intersubjective field and of the transitivity of the gaze—"I can look but I can also be looked at." Within Dactyl Nightmare the gaze's transitivity is undeniably apparent; if a player were not visible to others, then she would not be a target for other players' gunfire. Thus, in the world of Dactyl Nightmare, the subject is inducted into a hostile space ruled by the edict "I shoot, therefore I am." Interestingly, in this violent VR world, only one instance provides an actual view of one's virtual self—the moment of death.

While waiting to experience the irrational violence of roaming gunmen and swooping pterodactyls, the VR player begins her induction in the space of Dactyl Nightmare by watching a series of monitors from the sidelines. These monitors reinforce a realism of positionality by providing the perspectives of multiple players in the same space. Thus, even though the images provided by the monitors are two-dimensional, the multiplicity of moving viewpoints and crossing visual paths encourages a belief in the simulated space. The monitors serve as a physical equivalent to the player's mapping of an intersubjective space via what Lacan calls "kaleidoscopic" vision. He writes, "Let us say that animal psychology has shown us that the individual's relation to a particular spatial field is, in certain species, mapped socially, in a way that raises it to the category of subjective membership. I would say that it is the subjective possibility of the mirror projection of such a field into the field of the other that gives human space its original 'geometrical' structure, a structure that I would be happy to call *kaleidoscopic*."[13] A realism of positionality or a kaleidoscopic understanding of social space determined by reversible vectors of vision is intensified within the game itself as players gain a strong sense of their virtual bodies as a source of vision.

Echoing Lefebvre, Elizabeth Grosz emphasizes the importance of recognizing your body and its position in space, noting, "For the subject to take up a position as a subject it must be able to be situated in the space occupied by its body. This anchoring of subjectivity in its body is the condition of coherent identity, and, moreover, the condition under which the subject *has a perspective* on the world, and becomes a source for vision, a point from which vision emanates and to which light is focused."[14] Extending these ideas to virtual reality, it would follow that the successful occupation of space and the fixing of a coherent identity within a virtual environment are thus dependent on the acceptance of the VR body as an overlay. Yet, seeing one's hand and gun rendered in the same digital graphics as the rest of the environment, or looking down at one's feet to see only simulated ground (as is the case with many VR programs), threatens the feeling of distinctness from the surroundings, a distinctness that is a precondition for subjectivity in the actual world. Founded upon the misrecognition of the mirror stage, the belief in a unitary body and the ego's anchoring in this body is always precarious. Thrust into VR, where bodies dissolve into the background or do not appear where they should, the belief in bodily unity may be shaken. Like a pixelated chameleon amid a universe of pixels, the VR user may be confounded by a mirror image that fails to discern self from surroundings. This type of disorientation could be likened to temporary "legendary psychasthenia," the psychotic "depersonalization by assimilation to space" theorized by Pierre Janet, or a kind of severe culture shock. Roger Caillois describes the psychasthenic condition as a loss of "connection between consciousness and a particular point in space."[15] He writes, "To these dispossessed souls, space seems to be a devouring force. Space pursues them, encircles them, digests them. . . . It ends by replacing them."[16] Without the cues provided by gravity and with the occasional lag time between head movement and a reorientation of the field of view, the unacculturated VR user may feel on the edge of crisis and must struggle for an alignment of his two bodies in order to comfortably occupy the strange space.

Successful alignment comes with the acceptance of the gun and virtual body as "auxiliary organs," in what Freud calls "man as prosthetic God."[17] Freud, drawing on the ideas of nineteenth-century psychophysiologists, describes a tiny mannequin or visual image of the body registered in the cerebral cortex. Grosz, combining the ideas of Freud and neurologist Sir Henry Head, describes this image as a "postural model of the body . . . a three-dimensional image that both registers and organizes the information provided by the senses regarding the subject's body, its location in space (i.e., its posture or comportment) and its relation to other objects."[18] The body image, or cortical homunculus, as it was referred to in the nineteenth century, is also characterized by a plasticity, an ability to incorporate tools into its imaginary anatomy or to gradually adapt to bodily changes such as weight gain, growth, or amputation. In VR worlds, the body image must similarly adapt; it must extend itself in order to take into consideration the size, movements, and auxiliary organs of a prosthetic virtual body.

It is useful to note here that the cortical homunculus is not a point-for-point projection of the body's surfaces; certain points and regions are salient. For instance, Freud describes a typical imaginary anatomy that is overdeveloped in oral, manual and genital representations.[19] Warren Gorman's elaboration of the homunculus likens this entity to a little monster, which, without too much stretching of the imagination, almost resembles the creatures we might witness running around fictional VR worlds. He writes, "Their visual appearance is that of distorted little male persons, whose deformities are arresting to the studious as well as the curious. The face and the mouth of the homunculus are huge, his forehead is barely present, his hands gargantuan and his genitals gross. He has a respectably large intra-abdominal area, but he possesses not even a trace of a brain area."[20]

In Freud's later theories, the cortical homunculus merges with the ego, defined by Freud as a distorted bodily cartography mapped through the registering of libidinal intensities. The ego, in its augmentation of itself through the incorporation of tools and instruments, may experience libidinal cathexes that could alter the psychophysiological mappings of the ego. It seems reasonable that the ego's constituent points of intensity and their plasticity may carry over into virtual worlds, that these anatomical libidinal investments influence the design of game systems, and that virtual bodies may create their own regions of salience through software and hardware design. To the extent that virtual bodies may differ significantly in areas of intensity or regions of particular investment, it may require a longer period of acculturation to stretch and adjust our body images. The body image as a neurological function keeps a record of these past postures and sensations associated with various auxiliary organs.[21] Or, to use Merleau-Ponty's set of concepts, the individual's corporeal schema has a motor memory that gradually naturalizes body movements and the use of external tools. Thus, it is possible that the memory of such corporeal overlays could serve to denaturalize current socially inscribed, internalized anatomical imagings.

The corporeal overlay presents a new way of experiencing difference—not cultural difference in this case, but nonetheless a form of difference with the same potential to temporarily break the tourist's frame of reference. In the case of the encounter with cultural difference, tourists seeks out renewed vision through difference, teeter on the brink of culture shock, and finally brace themselves through mechanisms of visual distantiation. The touristic experience, in a protective measure, is collapsed down to a phenomenon of the visual register alone. It is then framed, tamed, and consumed using a set of well-polished Western strategies of visualization, strategies tied to epistemological mastery. This distantiating and objectifying process is a process of positioning oneself, confirming a personal and cultural position in relation to an exoticized culture. The VR experience similarly demands taking up a position in relation to the unfamiliar environment. While alternative positions marked by distance and visual objectification are made available on either end of the VR experience, while within the virtual world the tourist's pursuit of a firm position in relation to the foreign environment forces an accelerated acculturation to the corporeal overlay. A transparent interface will facilitate a smooth transition in the taking up of this dually embodied position. In the case of an interface in which the corporeal overlay's points of salience are ill-matched to the libidinal investments of the

Western subject's body, a form of culture shock may be experience as the tourist struggles to adjust.

In a combating of culture shock, VR worlds may provide a terrain for developing skills for dealing with such corporeal adjustments as bracketed experiences that do not spill over into the home environment. In other words, VR may be a training ground for developing protective strategies like the tourist gaze, but applied to the experience of corporeal difference. To date, the Western preoccupation with disembodied knowledge and a persistent visualism has impoverished the skills set for converting nonvisual, embodied experience into knowledge and for accommodating to corporeal change with resiliency. Thus, if we acknowledge that VR could exploit a weakness of the Western subject by targeting a realm of experience for which insulating strategies have not yet been fully developed, then the question becomes, For what purpose? The uncomfortable reembodiments of VR interfaces that fail to achieve transparency may create effects limited to a physical level, like the awkward walk of the long distance cyclist who readjusts to the resistance of the ground against her feet. To extend beyond physical effects alone, reembodied experience must be coupled with challenges to both our phenomenological and epistemological foundations. Yet VR worlds are constructed universes, built from cultural biases and assumptions converted into code, and perhaps even the most antisocial and ethically questionable impulses incarnated through data strings, if current applications are seen as indicative of future routes of development. In short, even as we acknowledge the potential of the reembodiments of VR's dauntingly strange spaces to spark a reappraisal of the world, the bodies in which we conduct our daily lives, its epistemologies, and our own identities within that world, we must remind ourselves of the gulf that separates potential from actuality as new media forms are born into old systems of power.

Conclusion

IN A LENGTHY VOLUME descriptive of a problematic phenomenon, the tone is expected to turn prescriptive by the final chapter or at the latest within the conclusion. The paradigm shift of chapter 11's analysis of virtual reality (VR) might suggest the approach of just such a change in tone. Certainly, it would not be the first elated celebration of VR's potential. Michael Heim compares this new media form's contribution to human evolution to the invention of fire and writes, "Here, at the end of modern aesthetics, we glimpse a gradual recovery of the world-building function of art. The art of VR reinserts the world function of art. VR is about the synthesis of the senses."[1] The exaltation continues as others chime in with remarks, such as Jaron Lanier's suggestion that virtual reality is "the first new reality since Adam and Eve."[2] If VR does offer some potential for counteracting the effects of the tourist gaze, it is not for the reason that seems most apparent, its incorporation of the body into the simulation. In fact, the body and the notion of corporeal tourism are used similarly, and are similarly misinterpretable, in both chapter 10 and in E. M. Forster's work as described in chapter 7. In neither case is the body being identified as the sole terrain for the experience of authenticity. The critique of touristic vision is not an attempt to banish belief in authenticity only to have it resurface within corporeal experience. In the case of Forster's work, the inscription of his critique of tourism as an authenticity scavenger hunt onto the bruised and battered surface of the body is a literary device rather than an insistence on the resurfacing of authenticity. Within Forster's novels, the exhaustion of the indigenous body during the catalytic conversion of the tourist or the doubling back of violence onto the tourist's body is a suggestion of the epistemic violence of touristic mining for authenticity. It is a suggestion that direct experience through the foreign encounter only exists as a puncturing process, an event marked by displeasure and disorientation.

Within my own analysis, the prominent role of the body is similarly a device to help make tangible a larger process, which may exist on many perceptual and epistemological levels not fully represented within the VR experience. The abstract nature of the VR environment and the disorientation that it may bring provides an exaggerated scenario that nonetheless makes clear the nature of culture shock as a crisis in orientation. Within VR, that crisis may be narrowly understood as a breakdown of spatial orientation and a lack of grounding. Within the actual travel experience, that loss of positionality reverberates on multiple levels including the spatial. VR also provides an interesting scenario in that reaction to one type of strangeness drives the virtual tourist into the arms of another kind of strangeness. The tourist gaze is deployed within the virtual space in order to both understand the illusion of immersion and condense it into flattened spectacle—in other words, to take up a position of distanced immersion. The VR user thus confronts the issue of the ground of a gaze in a body that occupies a position within that space. An acculturation to this strange body is accelerated in order to confirm positionality and to then conquer space through vision. The strangeness of the space is then defused, and one type of culture shock is staved off through the distanced immersion provided through anchored vision. The culture shock that is then experienced is a result of the VR apparatus's shortcomings in the department of interface transparency. The enduring effects are the result of an attempt to assimilate to this inexactly matched bodily overlay.

VR not only isolates effects at the level of the body, where the issue of orientation becomes most literal and most detectable, but provides a paradigm for thinking about the process of acculturation as an adjustment to an overlay. Several fantasies regarding acculturation exist, including perhaps the most fanciful of the bunch, Lawrence Durrell's belief in the "spirit of place" as a knowledge absorbed by the traveler over time, a fantasy reminiscent of the old joke of the student who sleeps with a book under her pillow in order to absorb the knowledge by osmosis.[3] For the anthropologist or the spy such as in the James Bond thriller *You Only Live Twice* (Lewis Gilbert, 1967), acculturation is passed off as a simple matter of the skill of a professional. In each of these cases, acculturation is seen as the equivalent of what I have described as "body hopping," or "culture hopping" in this case. Just as body hopping relies on the fantasy of disembodiment, culture hopping relies on the assumption that the trappings of one's home culture can be shed, making way for direct experience and, eventually, acculturation. Within the travel film, this process is given a metaphoric equivalent that again places the body in a central position. The stripping away of cultural baggage is likened to a liberating denuding of the body to be followed by the immersion of the body in the water or sun of the foreign culture—in other words, the cultural equivalent of skinnydipping or nude sunbathing. While rejecting its premise, this metaphor can be refashioned to bring it into accord with the notion of cultural overlays, the impossibility of direct knowledge, and the displeasurable nature of experiencing the friction or disconnect between two cultures. Just as disembodiment is impossible, one's own cultural filtering of a foreign culture is inescapable. The clothes can be stripped away, but culture is still inscribed on the body by way of bands of pale skin that speak of cultural convention and habit. The inevitable outcome then is a nasty sunburn in those previously unexposed areas. To the extent that those bands of pain are direct-experience merit badges, they reveal only the shapes of the home culture and do not speak authentically about the host culture. The regions requiring salve speak only to the disconnect between cultures, not to the essential nature of the foreign culture. In short, acculturation efforts as the overlaying of one culture on another reveal the points of friction, areas of mismatch between cultures. Culture shock as the experience of this friction is only one half of the equation. It may reveal the ill-fitting nature of the overlay, but it is the phenomenon of reverse culture shock that is the result of one's own culture, or one's own body, becoming strange to oneself. Culture shock alone within VR or another exotic environment may infringe upon pleasure and prompt the reassertion of mastery. Without reverse culture shock as its bookend, culture shock can be recouped as a brief stage within a psychological readjustment that may even involve an outwardly directed anger at the threatening environment. It may be the slight tickling that incites the deployment of attempts at mastery. Reverse culture shock, on the other hand, is a measure of the degree to which the experience of cultural difference has denaturalized the tourist's cultural cocoon. In the same way that VR's overlay of one body on another may produce a temporary shift in body image and increased plasticity of body image, flexibility in cultural standpoint could be a by-product of sustained and repeated reverse culture shock.

While VR's reembodying nature conveniently makes tangible this unique view of the dynamics of culture shock and its reverse counterpart, its true potential lies in the hope that it will operate as a simulation device and an instrument of communication simultaneously. Strangely enough, this notion of multiuser interaction connects with this volume's other brief glimmer of optimism, expressed in chapter 6 within my exploration of the 1960 film *Never on Sunday* as the product of multiproducer interaction. While film charcter Homer Thrace departs by ship, throwing his notes off the bow at the end of the film, director/actor Jules Dassin himself does not leave the shores of Greece. And one might assume that although his character may have abandoned the attempt to reduce a culture to abstractions, Dassin, in his relationship with Melina Mercouri that endured until her death, did not stop in his efforts to understand how culture had inflected one individual. While inequities between actor and director, woman and man, or wife and husband can surely discolor the respectful nature of such cross-cultural interaction, *Never on Sunday*, while in some ways barely more than a simple and light-hearted musical comedy, presents a glimpse of a productive conversation in progress.

Within travel practices, there may indeed be a genuine desire for meaningful cross-cultural interaction. However, the other desires that impel tourism and the various inequities that characterize host/guest relations make it an unlikely terrain for such interactions. And armchair travel delivered through the Western travel broker scarcely leaves a place for a cross-cultural conversation. Even the two-way exchange of films across national borders are subject to the pressures of providing the illusion of spectator mastery through narrative and are susceptible to the objectifying effects of the tourist gaze. Additionally, as confirmed by Rey Chow's analysis of the American reception of Chinese films and by anthropologists' studies of tourism's effects on indigenous cultures, in film and in actual tourist encounters, commercial demands and even economic exigency have encouraged "toured" peoples to portray themselves in ways most salable to American visitors and audiences.[4]

Other zones of cross-cultural contact—Camp David, the international food court, the playground, the overseas conference call—are all marked by the specific demands, inequities, and confounding desires that do not lend themselves to sustained efforts at understanding personal inflections of cultural backgrounds. Such backgrounds, marked by migration, diasporic cultures, mixed heritage, and ethnic subdivisions, demand a recognition of the inutility of cultural essentialism based on location and of other such moves toward abstraction. The use of communication technologies in place of simulation technologies may facilitate dialogue between culturally diverse discussants, and certainly such conversations are already ongoing. However, VR's combination of simulation and communication capabilities can aid in the creation of yet another space for cross-cultural interaction. Interaction within such a space might also circumvent the slip between the ethnographic and the performative, the assumption that visible culture has some truth value while ignoring the performative component of culture, a component that has become more pronounced with tourism's global profusion. The mandatory performance of a VR space in which all participants are marked by expressive—or, conversely, obfuscating—overlays would integrate the potential for politically invested play of the type performed by Guillermo Gómez-Peña and Coco Fusco, to name just two artists working in this vein of antiexotic masquerade. The tournaments hosted by VR entertainment centers such as Virtual World or Cybermind, however, should indicate how far we are from using virtual reality to construct a contact zone marked by a playful equivocation that focuses interaction on the exchange between individuals rather than on cultural abstraction. Tournaments between top scorers in the United States and equally skilled contenders from VR centers in Hong Kong and Japan pit spacecraft against spacecraft in a death race or feature the nearly identical androgynous bodies of Virtuality's 1991 VR game Dactyl Nightmare scurrying after one another with exchange limited to that of gunfire.

NOTES

—— INTRODUCTION   The Filtering Eye of the Tourist

1. My definition of a gaze as mobile and the collapse between the deployment of this gaze in virtual and actual situation borrows much from the work of Anne Friedberg, as will be discussed in chapter I. See Anne Friedberg, *Window Shopping: Cinema and the Postmodern* (Berkeley and Los Angeles: University of California Press, 1993).

2. For another view of how a gaze may characterize entertainment and scientific practice, see Giuliana Bruno, *Streetwalking on a Ruined Map: Cultural Theory and the City Films of Elvira Notari* (Princeton, N.J.: Princeton University Press, 1993).

3. Michelle Kendrick traces the utopic discourses surrounding virtual reality using a similar understanding of the illusion of demediation. See Michelle Kendrick, "Cyberspace and the Technological Real," in *Virtual Reality and Its Discontents*, ed. Robert Markley (Baltimore: John Hopkins University Press, 1995).

4. Dean MacCannell, *The Tourist: A New Theory of the Leisure Class* (1976; reprint New York: Schocken Books, 1989).

5. Ibid., 41.

6. Michael Crichton, *Travels* (New York: Alfred A. Knopf, 1988), x.

7. Robert Eisner, *Travelers to an Antique Land* (Ann Arbor: University of Michigan Press, 1991), 7.

8. Christian Metz, *The Imaginary Signifier*, trans. Celia Britton and Annwyl Williams (Bloomington: Indiana University Press, 1990).

9. Kaja Silverman, *The Acoustic Mirror: The Female Voice in Psychoanalysis and Cinema*. (Bloomington: Indiana University Press, 1988).

10. Steven Connor, *Postmodernist Culture: An Introduction to the Theories of the Contemporary* (Oxford: Blackwell,1989), 56.

11. MacCannell, *The Tourist*, x.

12. Ibid., 3.

13. Ibid., xiv.

14. Georges Van den Abbeele, "Sightseers: The Tourist As Theorist," *Diacritics* 10 (1980): 2–14.

—— CHAPTER ONE   Defining the Tourist Gaze

1. John Urry, *The Tourist Gaze: Leisure and Travel in Contemporary Society* (London: Sage, 1990).

2. Anne Friedberg, *Window Shopping: Cinema and the Postmodern* (Berkeley and Los Angeles: University of California Press, 1993).

3. Giuliana Bruno, *Streetwalking on a Ruined Map: Cultural Theory and the City Films of Elvira Notari* (Princeton, N.J.: Princeton University Press, 1993).

4. Eric J. Leed, *The Mind of the Traveler: From Gilgamesh to Global Tourism* (New York: Basic Books, 1991), 179.

5. David Bordwell, Janet Staiger, and Kristin Thompson, *The Classical Hollywood Cinema: Film Style and Mode of Production to 1960* (New York: Columbia University Press, 1985), 159.

6. Tom Gunning, "The Cinema of Attractions: Early Film, Its Spectator and the Avant Garde," in *Early Cinema: Space—Frame—Narrative,* ed. Thomas Elsaesser with Adam Barker (London: BFI, 1991).

7. Christian Metz, "Identification, Mirror," in *Film Theory and Criticism,* ed. Gerald Mast and Marshall Cohen (1974; reprint New York: Oxford University Press, 1985), 788–90.

8. Jean-Louis Comolli, "Machines of the Visible," in *The Cinematic Apparatus,* ed. Teresa de Lauretis and Stephen Heath (New York: St. Martin's Press, 1980), 122.

9. Gareth Shaw and Allan M. Williams, *Critical Issues in Tourism: A Geographical Perspective* (Oxford: Blackwell, 1994), 176–78.

10. Among these new styles we could include environmental tourism or even the hippie tourism of the 1970s. Of course, travel as a subcultural practice, such as that of gay and lesbian populations or nudists, has a long history that complicates this idea of divergent travel styles emerging only in the last two or three decades.

11. Johannes Fabian, *Time and the Other: How Anthropology Makes Its Object* (New York: Columbia University Press, 1983), 106.

12. Martin Heidegger, "The Age of the World Picture," in *The Question Concerning Technology and other Essays,* trans. William Lovitt (New York: Harper Colophon, 1977), 134.

13. Pierre Bourdieu, *Outline of a Theory of Practice,* trans. Richard Nice (Cambridge: Cambridge University Press, 1977), 96.

14. James Clifford, *The Predicament of Culture: Twentieth-Century Ethnography, Literature, and Art* (Cambridge, Mass.: Harvard University Press, 1988), 212.

15. Dean MacCannell, *The Tourist: A New Theory of the Leisure Class* (1976; reprint New York: Schocken Books, 1989), 78.

16. Lawrence Durrell, *Spirit of Place: Letters and Essays on Travel* (New York: E. P. Dutton, 1969), 156.

17. Ibid., 162.

18. Bill Nichols, *Ideology and the Image: Social Representation in the Cinema and Other Media* (Bloomington: Indiana University Press, 1981), 11, 26.

19. Jonathan Culler, "Semiotics of Tourism," in *Framing the Sign: Criticism and Its Institutions* (Norman: University of Oklahoma Press, 1988).

20. John Frow, "Tourism and the Semiotics of Nostalgia," *October* 57 (1991): 125.

21. Nancy Christine Lutkehaus, "'Excuse Me, Everything Is Not All Right': On Ethnography, Film, and Representation. An Interview with Filmmaker Dennis O'Rourke," *Cultural Anthropology* 4, no. 4 (1989): 422–37.

22. Clifford Geertz, *Works and Lives: The Anthropologist As Author* (Stanford: Stanford University Press, 1988), 77.

23. Bronislav Malinowski, *Argonauts of the Western Pacific* (1922; reprint New York: E. P. Dutton, 1961), 11.

24. Trinh T. Minh-ha, *Woman, Native, Other: Writing Postcoloniality and Feminism* (Bloomington: Indiana University Press), 1989.

25. Claude Lévi-Strauss, *Tristes Tropiques,* trans. John and Dorreen Weightman (1955; reprint New York: Atheneum, 1975), 47–48.

26. John Collier Jr. and Malcolm Collier, *Visual Anthropology As a Research Method* (Albuquerque: University of New Mexico Press), 5–6.

27. Ibid., 19.

28. Fabian, *Time and the Other,* 106.

29. Leed, *The Mind of the Traveler,* 65.

30. James Buzard, *The Beaten Track: European Tourism, Literature, and the Ways to Culture 1800–1918* (Oxford: Clarendon Press, 1993).

31. Wolfgang Schivelbusch, *The Railway Journey: Trains and Travel in the Nineteenth Century,* trans. Anselm Hollo (1977; reprint New York: Urizen Books, 1980), 65.

32. Susan Sontag, *On Photography* (New York: Doubleday, 1990), 9–10.

33. John Berger, *Ways of Seeing* (Harmondsworth, England: Penguin, 1972), 219.

34. Christian Metz, "Identification, Mirror," in *Film Theory and Criticism,* ed. Gerald Mast and Marshall Cohen (1974; reprint New York: Oxford University Press, 1985), 788–90.

—— CHAPTER TWO   Touristic Births

1. Thomas Richards, *The Commodity Culture of Victorian England: Advertising and Spectacle 1851–1914* (Stanford, Calif.: Stanford University Press, 1990), 136, 139.

2. See Brian Street, "British Popular Anthropology: Exhibiting and Photographing the Other," in *Anthropology and Photography 1860–1920,* ed. Elizabeth Edwards (New Haven, Conn.: Yale University Press, 1992).

3. Date and genre label given by G. D. Killam in *African English Fiction 1874–1939,* discussed in Brian V. Street, *The Savage in Literature: Representations of 'Primitive' Society in English Fiction 1858–1929* (London: Routledge: London, 1975), 6.

4. Robert Wiebe, *The Search for Order, 1877–1920* (New York: Hill and Wang, 1967).

5. Robert W. Rydell, *All the World's a Fair: Visions of Empire at American International Expositions, 1876–1916* (Chicago: University of Chicago Press, 1984), 4.

6. Jane Desmond, "Picturing Hawai'i: The 'Ideal' Native and the Origin of Tourism, 1880–1915," *Positions: East Asia Cultures Critique* 7, no. 2 (1999): 462.

7. John Hannavy, *Masters of Victorian Photography* (New York: Holmes and Meier, 1976), 68.

8. Grace Seiberling, *Amateurs, Photography, and the Mid-Victorian Imagination* (Chicago: University of Chicago Press, 1986), 81–82.

9. Richards, *Commodity Culture,* 133.

10. The term *virtual* is used here as it is by Anne Friedberg in her concept of the "mobilized virtual gaze." See Anne Friedberg, *Window Shopping: Cinema and the Postmodern* (Berkeley and Los Angeles: University of California Press, 1993), 204.

11. The use of aerial photography and the elevated perspective for military surveillance and for land surveying related to ownership questions encourages us to consider these traditions of viewing as linked to touristic strategies. It is also worthwhile to point out that the late nineteenth century was also the period in which the science of cartography reached a level of maturity that allowed the consideration of a global map. In 1891, at the fifth International Geographical Congress, a proposal was made to map the world as a totality with the help of a team of cartographers using standardized measurements and a predetermined scale. The project was not completed until 1914, at which time the map could not be released due to the outbreak of World War I. See Lloyd A. Brown, *The Story of Maps* (1949; reprint New York: Dover, 1979).

12. Martin Heidegger, "The Age of the World Picture," in *The Question Concerning Technology and Other Essays,* trans. William Lovitt (New York: Harper Colophon, 1977), 135; Susan Stewart, *On Longing: Narratives of the Miniature, the Gigantic, the Souvenir, the Collection* (1984; reprint Durham, N.C.: Duke University Press, 1993), 162.

13. See Rydell, *All the World's a Fair;* and Annie E. Coombes, *Reinventing Africa: Museums, Material Culture and Popular Imagination in Late Victorian and Edwardian England* (New Haven, Conn.: Yale University Press, 1994).

14. Johannes Fabian, *Time and the Other: How Anthropology Makes Its Object* (New York: Columbia University Press, 1983), 111–12.

15. Rydell provides evidence of this legitimizing of exotic attractions through his comparison of three consecutive American exhibitions. During the 1876 Philadelphia Exposition, many of the freak-show entertainments and honky-tonk amusements were condemned by city officials and burned down. The Chicago fair was marked by public ambivalence over the Midway attractions. By the time of the 1904 St. Louis exhibition, similar attractions were integrated into the main grounds of the fair. Rydell, *All the World's a Fair,* 236.

16. Roslyn Poignant, "Surveying the Field of View: The Making of the RAI Photographic Collection" in Edwards, ed., *Anthropology and Photography,* 55.

17. See Coombes, *Reinventing Africa,* 109–11, on anthropology's bid for acceptance from the state.
18. Poignant, "Surveying the Field of View," 51.
19. Ibid.
20. Ibid.
21. Susan Sontag speaks about the anthropologist as a "necrologist" who explores the world of the lost primitive. Susan Sontag, "The Anthropologist As Hero" in *Against Interpretation and Other Essays* (New York: Octagon Books, 1986), 73. Marianne Torgovnick similarly speaks about the anthropologist's futile quest for the authentic, untouched primitive who is part of a crumbling past. Marianne Torgovnick, *Going Primitive: Savage Intellects, Modern Lives* (Chicago: University of Chicago Press, 1990), 221–23. Tourists also seek an impossible authenticity, an untouched locale, that can only exist before the first tourist's arrival, before the indigene's commodification within the logic of tourism.
22. See Frank Spencer, "Some Notes on the Attempt to Apply Photography to Anthropometry during the Second Half of the Nineteenth Century" in Edwards, ed., *Anthropology and Photography,* 99–107.
23. Exhibit program, cited in Coombes, *Reinventing Africa,* 95.
24. Coombes, *Reinventing Africa,* 96–97.
25. See Sander Gilman, *Difference and Pathology: Stereotypes of Sexuality, Race, and Madness* (Ithaca, N.Y.: Cornell University Press, 1985).
26. Robert Bogdan, *Freak Show: Presenting Human Oddities for Amusement and Profit* (Chicago: University of Chicago Press, 1988), 38.
27. Bernth Lindfors, "African Circus," *Journal of American Culture* 6 (1983): 10.
28. Ibid.; see also Street, "British Popular Anthropology," 129.
29. Street, "British Popular Anthropology," 122.
30. Phineas Taylor Barnum, *Struggles and Triumphs, Or Forty Years' Recollections of P. T. Barnum Written by Himself* (1871; abridged reprint Harmondsworth, England: Penguin, 1981), 103.
31. Poignant, "Surveying the Field of View," 61.
32. Bernard McGrane, *Beyond Anthropology: Society and the Other* (New York: Columbia University Press, 1989), 90.
33. Ibid., 89.
34. Eric J. Leed, *The Mind of the Traveler: From Gilgamesh to Global Tourism* (New York: Basic Books, 1991), 210.
35. Curtis Hinsley, "Ethnographic Charisma and Scientific Routine: Cushing and Fewkes in the American Southwest, 1879–1893," in *Observers Observed: Essays on Ethnographic Fieldwork,* ed. George W. Stocking Jr.; History of Anthropology vol. 1 (Madison: University of Wisconsin Press, 1983), 56.
36. Sontag, "The Anthropologist As Hero," 71.
37. For a reproduction of these two photographs, see Coombes, *Reinventing Africa,* 78–79.
38. See Poignant, "Surveying the Field of View," 54.
39. Street, "British Popular Anthropology, " 127.
40. Alfred Court Haddon, quoted in Street, "British Popular Anthropology," 189.
41. Street, "British Popular Anthropology," 61, 70. It is interesting to note that both Thurn and Haddon were two people who entered anthropology as a former explorer (Thurn), and natural scientist (Haddon), rather than the more typical case of as former armchair anthropologists.
42. George Brown Goode, quoted in Rydell, *All the World's a Fair,* 45.
43. Dean MacCannell, *The Tourist: A New Theory of the Leisure Class,* rev. ed. (New York: Schocken Books, 1989), 101.
44. Norman Bolotin and Christine Laing, *The World's Columbian Exposition: A One-Hundred-Year Retrospective* (Washington, D.C.: Preservation Press, 1992), 77.
45. Coombes, *Reinventing Africa,* 69.
46. Rydell, *All the World's a Fair,* 56.
47. Ibid., 57–58.
48. Ibid., 160.

49. William C. Sturtevant, "Does Anthropology Need Museums?" *Proceedings of the Biological Society of Washington* 182 (1969): 662.

50. Susan Sheets-Pyenson, *Cathedrals of Science: The Development of Colonial Natural History Museums during the Late Nineteenth Century* (Kingston, Ont.: McGill-Queen's University Press, 1988), 9.

51. New York magazine article, quoted in Geoffrey Hellman, *Bankers, Bones, and Beetles: The First Century of the American Museum of Natural History* (Garden City, N.Y.: The Natural History Press, 1969), 100.

52. Nancy Oestreich Lurie, "Museumland Revisted," *Human Organization* 40, no. 2 (1981): 182.

53. See Donna Haraway, "Teddy Bear Patriarchy: Taxidermy in the Garden of Eden, New York City, 1908–1936," in *Primate Visions: Gender, Race, and Nature in the World of Modern Science* (New York: Routledge, 1989).

54. Franz Boas, quoted in Ira Jacknis, "Franz Boas and Exhibits: On the Limitations of the Museum Method of Anthropology," in *Objects and Others: Essays on Museums and Material Culture*, ed. George W. Stocking Jr.; History of Anthropology vol. 3 (Madison: University of Wisconsin Press, 1985), 79.

55. Ibid.

56. Letter written by Franz Boas, quoted in Jacknis, "Franz Boas," 101.

57. Precursors to this kind of immersive museum experience can be found in occasional exhibits by popular museums of the early nineteenth century. For instance, William Bullock's Egyptian Hall housed an 1824 exhibit on ancient and modern Mexico featuring carvings, models of tombs, fish and mineral specimens, and a cast of Montezuma's calendar stone arranged beneath a panoramic view of Mexico City. Two years earlier, the Egyptian Hall in London had been the location of a performance of the Sami and their reindeer against a background of snow-covered mountains. See Richard D. Altick, *Shows of London* (Cambridge, Mass.: Belknap Press of Harvard University Press, 1978), 247–48, 273.

58. Franz Boas, "Some Principles of Museum Administration," *Science* 25 (1907): 922.

59. At the same time, these immersive exhibits' appeal to codes of realism naturalizes the collection and display of other cultures as educational spectacle. James Clifford writes, "The *production* of meaning in museum classificaiton and display is mystified as adequate *representation*. The time and order of the collection overrides and erases the concrete social labor of its making." James Clifford, "Objects and Selves—An Afterword," in Stocking, ed., *Objects and Others*, 239.

——CHAPTER THREE   Technological Identification

1. Sir David Brewster, *The Stereoscope: Its History, Theory, and Construction* (Hastings-on-Hudson, N.Y.: Morgan and Morgan, 1971), 36–37.

2. O. G. Mason, quoted in Edward W. Earle, "The Stereograph in America: Pictorial Antecedents and Cultural Perspectives," in *Points of View: The Stereograph in America—A Cultural History*, ed. Edward W. Earle (Rochester, N.Y.: Visual Studies Workshop Press, 1979), 44.

3. Oliver Wendell Holmes, "The Stereoscope and the Stereograph," *Atlantic Monthly*, June 1859, 744.

4. William C. Darrah, *The World of Stereographs* (Gettysburg, Penn.: W. C. Darrah, 1977), 2.

5. Earle, "The Stereograph in America," 48.

6. Darrah, *The World of Stereographs*, 47.

7. Ibid., 49.

8. Earle, "The Stereograph in America." 78.

9. Holmes, "The Stereoscope and the Stereograph," 742.

10. Another parallel could be drawn between stereograph's planes and visions and those of panoramas with sculpted foregrounds. For instance, in 1881, a London panorama representing the charge of the Light Brigade filled the foreground between the viewing platform and the painted surface of the diorama with bushes, wrecked wagons, cannon balls, and corpses of soldiers and horses made of wax. See Richard D. Altick, *Shows of London* (Cambridge, Mass.: Belknap Press of Harvard University Press, 1978), 506.

11. Timothy Mitchell, *Colonising Egypt* (Cambridge: Cambridge University Press, 1988), 21.

12. The numbers in parentheses refer to the numbers listed on the stereoscopic view cards.

13. James Buzard lists "saturation" as one motif within the trope of the picturesque. James Buzard, *The Beaten Track: European Tourism, Literature, and the Ways to Culture 1800–1918* (Oxford: Clarendon Press, 1993), 188.

14. William R. Scott, *The Americans in Panama* (New York: Statler, 1913), 1.

15. Ibid.

16. Maury Klein refers to the first America as a colony of England, the second as an agrarian economy that continued until the end of the Civil War, and the third as a nation in the midst of an industrial transformation occuring between 1865 and 1920. Maury Klein, *The Flowering of the Third America: The Making of an Organizational Society, 1850–1920* (Chicago: Ivan R. Dee, 1993), 171.

—— CHAPTER FOUR   Moving Postcards

General Note: Director's names are given for the films whenever they are known; however, many films of the late 1800s and early 1900s do not credit directors.

1. Fatimah Tobing Rony, *The Third Eye: Race, Cinema, and Ethnographic Spectacle* (Durham, N.C.: Duke University Press, 1996). Timothy Mitchell, *Colonising Egypt* (Cambridge: Cambridge University Press, 1988).

2. Dana Polan, quoted in Catherine A. Lutz and Jane L. Collins, *Reading National Geographic* (Chicago: University of Chicago Press, 1993), 90.

3. See the *Illustrated and Descriptive Catalogue and Price List of Stereopticons, Lantern Slides, Moving Picture Machines, Accessories for Projection* (Chicago: Stereopticon and Film Exchange, 1903).

4. Joseph North, *The Early Development of the Motion Picture (1887–1909)* (New York: Arno Press, 1973), 71.

5. Irving Wallace, "Everybody's Rover Boy," in *The Man Who Photographed the World: Burton Holmes Travelogues 1886–1938*, ed. Genoa Caldwell (New York: Harry N. Abrams, 1977), 11.

6. Genoa Caldwell, "The Travelogue Man," in Caldwell, ed., *The Man Who Photographed the World*, 25.

7. Leaflet quoted in Wallace, "Everybody's Rover Boy," 16.

8. Wallace, "Everybody's Rover Boy," 16–18.

9. According to the work of Alison Griffiths, ethnographers working for the American Natural History Museum at the turn of the century made differentiations between Native-American dances performed for audiences of tourists and those enacted as a part of traditional tribal ritual. Ethnographers, without always noting how a dance might be altered to accommodate an audience, considered the former to be more degraded and less authentic. However, if the absence of an audience is a necessary precondition for authenticity, then the photographing ethnographer's presence, perhaps not regarded by Native Americans as any different from a tourist's presence, may have created a similar context of staged performance. Alison Griffiths, "Science and Spectacle: Discourses of Authenticity in Early Ethnographic Film," in *Dressing in Feathers: The Construction of the Indian in American Popular Culture*, ed. Elizabeth Bird (Boulder: Westview Press, 1995).

10. For further information on film's introduction into the context of the museum, Griffiths's work again proves valuable. Her dissertation, which was being completed at the time that this chapter was written, documents the conflicted acceptance of film into professional anthropology and the attempt to disassociate the scientific uses of the medium from film's status as an entertainment for urban lower classes.

11. Charles Musser, *Before the Nickelodeon: Edwin S. Porter and the Edison Manufacturing Company* (Berkeley and Los Angeles: University of California Press, 1991), 108.

12. Griffiths's work recounts an anecdote to the contrary. Apparently, some Native-American dances performed at the beginning of the century defied Western conventions of staging, making filming a difficult process. One ethnographer retells his experience of focusing the camera on particular dancers only to have them disappear into the surrounding bushes for long periods of time, yielding a final film product containing

extended shots of the bushes while the dance continued offscreen. Griffiths, "Science and Spectacle," 83.

13. See Caldwell, ed., *The Man Who Photographed the World*. John L. Stoddard, *John L. Stoddard Lectures* (10 vols; Boston: Balch Brothers, 1907).

14. Tom Gunning, "The Cinema of Attractions: Early Film, Its Spectator and the Avant Garde," in *Early Cinema: Space—Frame—Narrative*, ed. Thomas Elsaesser with Adam Barker (London: BFI, 1991), 59.

15. Although a number of valuable articles on cinematic suture have been published, Stephen Heath's discussion of editing, the shifting point of view, and the shot-reverse-shot is most similar to the way I speak about suture within the fictional travel narrative as it develops within silent cinema. However, this kind of suture is preceded by a more simplified form that more closely resembles the spectator's identification with the camera's vision as discussed by Jean-Louis Baudry. Stephen Heath, "Notes on Suture," *Screen* 18, no. 4 (1977–78): 48–76.

16. Tom Gunning, "An Unseen Energy Swallows Space: The Space in Early Film and Its Relation to American Avant Garde," in *Film before Griffith*, ed. John L. Fell (Berkeley and Los Angeles: University of California Press, 1983), 362.

17. Film review quoted in Gunning, "An Unseen Energy," 363.

18. Film review quoted in Charles Musser, "The Travel Genre in 1903–1904: Moving toward Fictional Narrative," *Iris* 2, no. 1 (1982): 53–54.

19. Raymond Fielding, "Hale's Tours: Ultrarealism in the Pre-1910 Motion Picture," in Fell, ed., *Film before Griffith*, 119.

20. Ibid., 118.

21. B. S. Brown , "Hales Tours and Scenes of the World," *Moving Picture World*, July 15, 1916, 373.

22. Fielding, "Hale's Tours," 119.

23. Musser, *Before the Nickelodeon: Edwin S. Porter and the Edison Manufacturing Company* (Berkeley and Los Angeles: University of California Press, 1991), 175.

24. It is worth noting that Dean MacCannell describes tourists' visits to disaster sites as motivated by the same desire that propels touristic adventure in general.

25. Musser, "The Travel Genre," 50–51.

26. Eileen Bowser, *The Transformation of Cinema 1907–1915*, vol. 2 (New York: Maxwell Macmillan, 1990), 154.

—— CHAPTER FIVE   Travel and Adaptation

1. Tom Gunning, "The Cinema of Attractions: Early Film, Its Spectator and the Avant Garde," in *Early Cinema: Space—Frame—Narrative*, ed. Thomas Elsaesser with Adam Barker (London: BFI, 1991), 56.

2. Philip Rosen, "Disjunction and Ideology in a Preclassical Film: *A Policeman's Tour of the World*," *Wide Angle* 12, no. 3 (1990): 20–36.

3. Many critics, with whom I agree, have suggested that Verne was not a science fiction writer but rather a writer of *scientific* fiction.

4. A number of American and French critics have reassessed his work, suggesting that his literary style and innovation has been overlooked by generations of literary critics.

5. Andrew Martin, *The Mask of the Prophet: The Extraordinary Fictions of Jules Verne* (Oxford: Clarendon Press, 1990), 11.

6. Critics such as William Butcher attribute this myth of Verne as an "unnovelist" to poor translations of his work. See Butcher's introduction to Jules Verne's *Around the World in Eighty Days*, trans. William Butcher (1872; reprint Oxford: Oxford University Press, 1995).

7. Martin, *The Mask of the Prophet*, 9.

8. Joe MacDonald, quoted in "CinemaScope: What It Is; How It Works," *American Cinematographer*, March 1953.

9. Lorin Grignon, quoted in "CinemaScope: What It Is; How It Works."

10. However, according to John Belton, Russia claimed they had the invented Cinerama, CinemaScope, and other widescreen systems even before the United States had. John Belton, *Widescreen Cinema* (Cambridge, Mass.: Harvard University Press, 1992), 90.

11. See Belton, *Widescreen Cinema*, 87–88.

12. A publicist for *The Search for Paradise*, quoted in Belton, *Widescreen Cinema*, 95.

13. Belton, *Widescreen Cinema*, 92.

14. Ibid., 176.

15. Martin, *The Mask of the Prophet*, 2.

16. Quoted in Arthur B. Evans, *Jules Verne Rediscovered: Didacticism and the Scientific Novel*, number 27 in *Contributions to the Study of World Literature* (New York: Greenwood Press, 1988), 30.

17. Quoted in Martin, *The Mask of the Prophet*, 2.

18. Evans, *Jules Verne Rediscovered*, 38.

19. Ibid., 2.

20. Martin, *The Mask of the Prophet*, 7.

21. Pierre-Jules Hetzel, quoted in Martin, *The Mask of the Prophet*, 7.

22. In the companion book, Palin often writes about filming inconveniences, such as waking up and then going back to bed so that he can be filmed waking up. Michael Palin, *Around the World in Eighty Days with Michael Palin* (San Francisco: KQED Books, 1995).

23. Evans, *Jules Verne Rediscovered*, 153.

24. Lewis Mumford, *Technics and Civilization* (New York: Harcourt, Brace, and World, 1934), 311.

25. Roland Barthes, *Mythologies*, trans. Annette Lavers (1957; reprint New York: Hill and Wang, 1984), 65.

26. Ibid.

27. Evans, *Jules Verne Rediscovered*, 156–58.

—— CHAPTER SIX   Snapshots of Greece

1. Robert Sullivan, quoted in Shari Roberts, "'The Lady in the Tutti-Frutti Hat': Carmen Miranda, a Spectacle of Ethnicity," *Cinema Journal* 32, no. 3 (1993): 11.

2. Robert Kaplan, *Balkan Ghosts* (New York: Vintage Books, 1993), 247.

3. This article does not represent a search for an effaced modern Greece nor for an authentic Greece hidden beneath foreign paint strokes. In fact, the same critique of cultural authenticity that has been applied to the tourist's search for the "real Italy" or the "true India" can and should be applied to the film critic purporting to identify that which is "uniquely Greek." In this section, I call attention to the obfuscating visions of Greece that have reached American shores and provide some preliminary observations from an outsider's point of view.

4. Benedict Anderson, *Imagined Communities* (London: Verso, 1991), 6.

5. The case of the Greeks' use of cultural heritage or the pedigree argument to argue distinctions between their own people and their conquerors illustrates the concept of national identity as process and construction. Rather than a retained memory of ancient Greek culture providing a preexisting base for the elaboration of a modern Greek identity, many rural Greeks under Ottoman rule had no knowledge of Homer, Pericles, or any other classical Greek character, historical or fictional. A revival of ancient Greek history, literature, language, and mythology accompanied the battle for independence and became integrated into Greek national identity.

6. This historically based means of defining national identity (i.e. as a nation and people historically and culturally distinct from Turkey), has endured hand-in-hand with the stubborn antipathy between Hellenes and their Turkish neighbors. Greeks still entertain, although with less and less seriousness, the *megali idea* (the big idea), the pledge that Constantinople will be, in the words of an oft-quoted Greek folk song, "ours once more."

7. Greeks trace the origins of such "thievery" back to Tito's rewritten historical texts that fallaciously assert Alexander's Slavic ethnicity and the classical legacy carried into modern times by Yugoslavia. Responding to particular wordings within the new "Macedonian" constitution, the Greeks fear that this "thievery" will extend to territories as well.

8. To avoid the confusion between the two regions claiming the name Macedonia, Greeks have suggested that the original claimants use the name Macedonia and that their northern neighbors be called the Skopje Republic or FYROM (an acronym for the name recognized by the United Nations).

9. Lord Elgin removed large numbers of classical artworks from Greece (including the marbles of the Acropolis) in 1805. He justified his role as a British "caretaker" of Greece's past by citing the supposed "uncultivated hands and indifferent minds" of the Greeks, a people unable to appreciate or properly care for the treasures of its past.

10. Lawrence Durrell, *Spirit of Place: Letters and Essays on Travel* (New York: E. P. Dutton, 1969), 156.

11. Greek National Tourist Organization, *Greece '91* (Athens: Char. I. Papadopoulos, 1990), 3.

12. James Buzard, *The Beaten Track: European Tourism, Literature, and the Ways to 'Culture' 1800–1918.* (Oxford: Clarendon Press, 1993), 209–15.

13. Melina Mercouri, *I Was Born Greek* (Garden City, N.Y.: Doubleday, 1971), 138.

14. Kaplan, *Balkan Ghosts*, 252.

15. Mercouri, *I Was Born Greek*, 138. Sound is often used as a signifier of authenticity and in this case is part of an appeal to the power of "being there" to communicate to the foreigner, through some mystical means, the native point of view.

16. Andrew Horton, "Jules Dassin: A Multinational Filmmaker Considered," *Film Criticism* 8, no. 3 (1984): 21–35.

17. Mercouri, *I Was Born Greek*, 12.

18. *Romeic* refers to the Eastern influence of the Turks and other peoples who have lived alongside or ruled over Greeks. Western critics of Greek culture often label the positive aspects of this nation as hellenic and the less progressive aspects as romeic. For instance, Kaplan, in *Balkan Ghosts*, refers to highly educated, liberal leaning Greeks as Hellenes, while describing those with less democratic politics as "romios." This kind of differentiation between the intertwined strands of romeic and hellenic seems oversimplistic and accepting of an ethnocentric devaluation of all that is Eastern in comparison to the West.

19. Emily A. McDermott, *Euripedes' Medea: The Incarnation of Disorder* (University Park: Pennsylvania State University Press, 1989), 43–44.

20. Euripedes, as quoted and translated in McDermott, *Euripedes' Medea*, 46.

21. Kerry Segrave, *The Continental Actress* (Jefferson, N.C.: McFarland, 1990), 105.

22. Mercouri, *I Was Born Greek*, 145.

23. Ibid., 142.

24. Diane Giddis, "The Divided Woman: Bree Daniels in Klute," in *Movies and Methods*, ed. Bill Nichols (Berkeley and Los Angeles: University of California Press, 1976), 194–201.

25. The disorder caused by the prostitutes of *Unforgiven* and *Never* echoes McDermott's thesis about *Medea*. As her title indicates, McDermott considers Euripedes' play a progression toward disorder reaching the climax with Medea's rebellion against the natural order. McDermott, *Euripedes' Medea*.

26. David Morley and Kevin Robins, "Spaces of Identity: Communications Technologies and the Reconfiguration of Europe," *Screen* 30, no. 4 (1989): 10.

—— CHAPTER SEVEN   Corporeal Geographies

1. Lawrence Grossberg, "The In-Difference of Television." *Screen* 28, no. 2 (1987): 28–48.

2. Maria Lugones, "Playfulness, 'World'-Travelling, and Loving Perception," in *Making Face, Making Soul*, ed. Gloria Anzaldúa (New York: Aunt Lute Foundation, 1990), 390.

3. Elspeth Probyn, "Travels in the Postmodern," in *Feminism/Postmodernism*, ed. Linda J. Nicholson (New York: Routledge, 1990), 184.

4. Dean MacCannell, *The Tourist: A New Theory of the Leisure Class* (1976; reprint New York: Schocken Books, 1989), 21.

5. Ibid., 105.

6. John Frow, "Tourism and the Semiotics of Nostalgia," *October* 57 (1991): 128.

7. Davydd J. Greenwood, "Culture by the Pound: Tourism As Cultural Commoditization," in *Hosts and Guests: The Anthropology of Tourism*, ed. Valene L. Smith (Philadelphia: University of Pennsylvania Press, 1977).

8. Frow, "Tourism and the Semiotics of Nostalgia," 128.

9. Jonathan Culler, "Semiotics of Tourism," *American Journal of Semiotics* 1 (1981): 156.

10. E. M. Forster, *Where Angels Fear to Tread* (1905; reprint London: Edward Arnold, 1975), 1; hereafter, page numbers are cited parenthetically in the text.

11. James Buzard, *The Beaten Track: European Tourism, Literature, and the Ways to Culture 1800–1918* (Oxford: Clarendon Press, 1993), 310.

12. Victor Turner and Edith Turner, *Image and Pilgrimage in Christian Culture* (New York: Columbia University Press, 1978), 249.

13. Barbara Rosecrance, *Forster's Narrative Vision* (Ithaca, N.Y.: Cornell University Press, 1982), 92.

14. E. M. Forster, *A Room with a View* (1908; reprint New York: Bantam, 1988), 40.

15. Kaja Silverman, *Male Subjectivity at the Margins* (New York: Routledge, 1992), 210–11.

16. Mary Louise Pratt, *Imperial Eyes: Travel Writing and Transculturation* (London: Routledge, 1992), 204.

17. Buzard, *The Beaten Track,* 188.

18. Andrew Higson, "Re-Presenting the National Past: Nostalgia and Pastiche in the Heritage Film," in *Fires Were Started: British Cinema and Thatcherism,* ed. Lester Friedman (Minneapolis: University of Minnesota Press, 1993), 115.

—— CHAPTER EIGHT   Global Mappings

1. Jorge Luis Borges, "Del rigor en la ciencia," in *El Hacedor,* in *Obras completas* vol. 2 (Buenos Aires: Emecé, 1974), 225.

2. Jean Baudrillard, *Simulations,* trans. Paul Foss, Paul Patton, and Philip Beitchman (New York: Semiotext(e), 1983), 158.

3. Steven Connor, *Postmodernist Culture: An Introduction to Theories of the Contemporary* (Oxford: Blackwell, 1989), 56.

4. Andrew Martin, *The Mask of the Prophet: The Extraordinary Fictions of Jules Verne* (Oxford: Clarendon Press, 1990), 9.

5. Crichton entered the interactive entertainment business early on with Amazon (1982), a game for the Apple II computer that used *Congo*'s story line, but in a different setting. Distributed by Trillium, the game was produced by Crichton's company FilmTrack and reportedly programmed in part by Crichton himself. Based on the film version of the book, the video game Congo: Descent into Zinj was released by Sega in 1995. Signing a ten-year distribution deal with Eidos Interactive in 1999, Crichton and his second (and equally short-lived) video game company, Timeline Computer Entertainment, released a video game version of *Timeline* in 2000.

6. Susan Stewart, *On Longing: Narratives of the Miniature, the Gigantic, the Souvenir, the Collection* (1984; reprint Durham, N.C.: Duke University Press, 1993), 133.

7. Ibid., xi.

8. Michael Crichton, *Congo* (1980; reprint New York: Ballantine Books, 1993), xiii.

9. Lurton Dunham Ingersoll, ed., *Explorations in Africa by Dr. David Livingstone and Others* (San Francisco: Union Publishing Company, 1872), 176.

10. Ibid.

11. Ingersoll, publisher's preface to *Explorations,* n.p.

12. Crichton, *Congo,* 15.

13. Ibid., 19.

14. Ibid.

15. Ibid., 213–14.

16. Ibid., 214.

17. Jody Duncan and Janine Pourroy, *The Making of Congo the Movie* (New York: Ballantine Books, 1995), 21.

18. Michael Crichton, *Timeline* (New York: Alfred A. Knopf, 1999), 401.

19. Ibid.

—— CHAPTER NINE   *Millennium*

1. Marianna Torgovnick, *Gone Primitive: Savage Intellects, Modern Lives* (Chicago: University of Chicago Press, 1990), 222.

2. Jean Baudrillard, *Simulations,* trans. Paul Foss, Paul Patton, and Philip Beitchman (New York: Semiotext(e), 1983), 15.

3. Bronislaw Malinowski, quoted in Trinh T. Minh-ha, "The Language of Nativism: Anthropology As a Scientific Conversation of Man with Man," in *Woman, Native, Other: Writing Postcoloniality and Feminism* (Bloomington: Indiana University Press, 1989), 73.

4. Trinh, "The Language of Nativism," 48.

5. Davydd J. Greenwood, "Culture by the Pound: Tourism As Cultural Commoditization," in *Hosts and Guests: The Anthropology of Tourism*, ed. Valene L. Smith (Philadelphia: University of Pennsylvania Press, 1977).

6. Kenneth Read, *The High Valley* (New York: Columbia University Press, 1965), ix.

7. Clifford Geertz, *Local Knowledge* (New York: Basic Books, 1983), 56.

8. James Clifford, *The Predicament of Culture: Twentieth-Century Ethnography, Literature, and Art* (Cambridge: Harvard University Press, 1988), 95.

9. See George W. Stocking Jr., "The Ethnologer's Magic: Fieldwork in British Anthropology from Taylor to Malinowski," in *Observers Observed: Essays on Ethnographic Fieldwork*, ed. George W. Stocking Jr.; History of Anthropology vol. 1 (Madison: University of Wisconsin Press, 1983).

10. Frank Hamilton Cushing, stranded among the Zuni Indians during an expedition, provides an example of this type of fieldwork, although from an earlier period. Cushing, however, is not given credit for being the forefather of this anthropological methodology since questions surrounding his dedication to scientific exploration persist. See chapter 1 of this volume.

11. Stocking, "The Ethnologer's Magic," 109.

12. Clifford, *The Predicament of Culture*, 22.

13. Stocking, "The Ethnologer's Magic," 107.

14. Bronislaw Malinowski, *Argonauts of the Western Pacific* (1922; reprint New York: E. P. Dutton, 1961), 4.

15. Mary Louise Pratt, "Fieldwork in Common Places," in *Writing Culture: The Poetics and Politics of Ethnography*, ed. James Clifford and George E. Marcus (Berkeley and Los Angeles: University of California Press, 1986).

16. Clifford Geertz, *Works and Lives: The Anthropologist As Author* (Stanford, Calif.: Stanford University Press, 1988), 79.

17. Malinowski, *Argonauts*, 35.

18. In fact, Pratt's article "Fieldwork in Common Places" is based upon the argument that ethnographic writing borrows heavily from travel writing.

19. Geertz, *Works and Lives*, 82.

20. Deborah Gewertz and Frederick Errington, *Twisted Histories, Altered Contexts: Representing the Chambri in a World System* (Cambridge: Cambridge University Press, 1991), 15.

21. For a relatively comprehensive list of sources that compare anthropology and tourism see Deborah Gewertz and Frederick Errington, "Anthropology and Tourism," *Oceania* 60, no. 1 (1989): 37–54.

22. For more information on such programs see the television section of Peter Ian Crawford and David Turton, eds., *Film As Ethnography* (Manchester: Manchester University Press, 1992).

23. Terence Wright, "Television Narrative and Ethnographic Film," in Crawford and Turton, eds., *Film As Ethnography*, 276. It is worth noting that *Millennium* was sponsored by Body Shop and Esprit, two companies that have used the exotic as style in order to sell their products.

24. This phrase is taken from Amy Richlin, "The Ethnographer's Dilemma and the Dream of a Lost Golden Age," in *Feminist Theory and the Classics*, ed. Nancy Sorkin Rabinowitz and Amy Richlin (New York: Routledge, 1993).

25. See Wright, "Television Narrative," 286, concerning televisual ethnography's role in fulfilling audiences' touristic desires.

26. *The Shock of the Other*, episode 1 of *Millennium: Tribal Wisdom and the Modern World*, produced by the Public Broadcasting Company and Channel Four, 1992.

27. Margaret Morse, "An Ontology of Everyday Distraction: The Freeway, the Mall, and Television," in *Logics of Television: Essays in Cultural Criticism*, ed. Patricia Mellencamp (Bloomington: Indiana University Press, 1990), 197.

28. On the subject of the ways in which souvenirs launch narratives, see Susan Stewart, *On Longing: Narratives of the Miniature, the Gigantic, the Souvenir, the Collection* (Durham, N.C.: Duke University Press, 1993), 136.

29. The notion of anticonquest is defined by Mary Louise Pratt in her book *Imperial Eyes: Travel Writing and Transculturation* (London: Routledge 1992).

30. William Crawford, quoted in Melissa Banta and Curtis M. Hinsley, *From Site to Sight: Anthropology, Photography, and the Power of Imagery* (Cambridge, Mass.: Peabody Museum Press, 1986), 121. See also William Crawford, "The Shavanti of Central Brazil," *Polaroid* 14, no. 1(1983): 52-53.

31. David Maybury-Lewis, *Millennium: Tribal Wisdom and the Modern World* (New York: Viking, 1992), 7.

32. Pratt, "Fieldwork in Common Places," 40.

33. Maybury-Lewis, *Millennium*, xxiii.

34. Pratt, "Fieldwork in Common Places," 41.

35. Susan Sontag, "The Anthropologist As Hero," in *Against Interpretation and Other Essays* (New York: Octagon Books, 1986).

36. Claude Lévi-Strauss, *Tristes Tropiques,* trans. John and Doreen Weightman (New York: Atheneum, 1975), 56.

37. This comparison is made more appealing by Malinowski's hopeful claim to being the Conrad of anthropology. See James Clifford, "On Ethnographic Self-Fashioning: Conrad and Malinowki," in *Reconstructing Individualism,* ed. Thomas C. Heller, Morton Sosna, and Davis E, Wellbery (Stanford, Calif.: Stanford University Press, 1986).

38. Gayatri Chakravorty Spivak, "Can the Subaltern Speak? Speculations on Widow-Sacrifice," *Wedge* 7-8 (1985): 120-30.

39. Trinh, "The Language of Nativism," 48.

40. Sontag, "The Anthropologist As Hero," 73.

41. Lévi-Strauss, *Tristes Tropiques,* 37.

42. David Turton argues that this focus on technology is a preoccupation with ourselves. David Turton, "Anthropology on Television: What Next?" in Crawford and Turton, eds., *Film As Ethnography,* 291-93.

43. Lévi-Strauss, *Tristes Tropiques,* 38.

44. On the myth of monoculture, see James Clifford, *The Predicament of Culture: Twentieth-Century Ethnography, Literature, and Art* (Cambridge, Mass.: Harvard University Press, 1988), 16.

45. Maybury-Lewis, *Millennium,* book jacket.

46. Isabel McBryde notes that it was a standard practice among turn-of-the-century anthropologists to recreate the ethnographic past. The Chicago Columbian Exposition of 1893 tried to replicate the living conditions of Native Americans at the time of Columbus's arrival. Similar fictions have been created through photography. For instance, a photograph by ethnographic photographer/hobbyist Thomas Dick, taken in the early twentieth century when it was believed that the Australian aborigines as a race and as a culture would soon die out, re-creates the arrival of Captain James Cook. The negative has been retouched, adding a ship in the distant background as three aborigines watch and wait from the shore. Anthropology becomes romantic fiction making as the camera produces the illusion of capturing a pristine past, of recovering this rare moment of first contact. Isabel McBryde, "Thomas Dick's Photographic Vision," in *Seeing the First Australians,* ed. Ian Donaldson and Tamsin Donaldson (Sydney: George Allen and Unwin), 154.

47. John Frow, "Tourism and the Semiotics of Nostalgia," *October* 57 (1991): 125.

48. Trinh, "The Language of Nativism," 69.

49. Turton, "Anthropology on Television: What Next?" 294.

50. Ibid., 285.

51. Trinh, "The Language of Nativism," 67.

—— CHAPTER TEN   Narrativizing Cybertravel

1. Michel de Certeau, *The Practice of Everyday Life,* trans. Steven Rendell (1984; reprint Berkeley and Los Angeles: University of California Press, 1988), 115.

2. Jurij M. Lotman, "The Origin of Plot in the Light of Typology," trans. Julian Graffy, *Poetics Today* I, nos.I–2 (1979): 167.

3. Ibid.

4. Teresa de Lauretis, *Alice Doesn't: Feminism, Semiotics, Cinema* (Bloomington: Indiana University Press, 1984), 121.

5. Ibid., 119.

6. Eric J. Leed, *The Mind of the Traveler: From Gilgamesh to Global Tourism* (New York: Basic Books, 1991)

7. Ella Shohat, "Gender and Culture of Empire: Toward a Feminist Ethnography of the Cinema," in *Discourse of the Other: Postcoloniality, Positionality, and Subjectivity,* ed. Hamid Naficy and Teshome H. Gabriel. Special issue of *Quarterly Review of Film and Video* 13, nos.I–3 (1991): 45–84.

8. The anthropologist's voyage could be considered oedipal in its search for a mirror image of Western civilization's precivilization savagery and in its contemplation of some essential human nature.

9. Michel de Certeau, *Heterologies: Discourse on the Other,* trans. Brian Massumi; Theory and History of Literature vol. 17 (Minneapolis: University of Minnesota Press, 1986), 69.

10. Susan Stewart, *On Longing: Narratives of the Miniature, the Gigantic, the Souvenir, the Collection.* (1984; reprint Durham, N.C.: Duke University Press, 1993), 148.

11. Mary Fuller and Henry Jenkins, "Nintendo® and New World Travel Writing: A Dialogue," in *CyberSociety: Computer Mediated Communication and Community,* ed. Steven G. Jones (Thousand Oaks, Calif.: Sage, 1995), 58.

—CHAPTER ELEVEN   Virtual Reality and the Challenges of Reembodied Tourism

1. Mark Bolas, quoted in Ken Pimentel and Kevin Teixera, *Virtual Reality: Through the New Looking Glass* (New York: McGraw-Hill, 1993), 152.

2. Kay Keppler, "Art for Art's Sake," *Virtual Reality* I, no. 4 (1994): 5.

3. Dean MacCannell, "Virtual Reality's Place," *Performance Research* 2, no. 2 (1997): 13.

4. Christopher Pinney, "Future Travel," in *Visualizing Theory: Selected Essays from V.A.R. 1990–1994,* ed. Lucien Taylor (New York: Routledge, 1994).

5. Authenticity is referenced in the evaluation of VR training applications, such as for firefighting, surgery, and combat. In these cases, authenticity is a measure of the application's ability to effectively simulate a situation such that mastery of the VR simulated task directly translates into success in the nonsimulated version of the task.

6. Howard Reingold, *Virtual Reality* (New York: Summit Books, 1991).

7. Although several Virtual World locations exist in and outside of the United States, my descriptions are based upon visits to the Virtual World in San Diego.

8. Perhaps this link can be explained in part by the similar epistemologies behind Western tourism and exploration/colonialism.

9. Steve Aukstakalnis and David Blatner, *Silicon Mirage: The Art and Science of Virtual Reality* (Berkeley: Peachpit Press, 1992), 36.

10. Maurice Merleau-Ponty, *The Phenomenology of Perception,* trans. Colin Smith (London: Routledge and Kegan Paul, 1962), 100.

11. Henri Lefebvre, *The Production of Space,* trans. Donald Nicholson-Smith (1974; reprint Oxford: Blackwell, 1992), 182.

12. The phallic implications of the gun are reinforced within VR and CD-ROM games (which use the gun in the foreground to indicate the player's virtual presence), and by the parallel use of the virtual penis or optional dildo placed in the same position, the center foreground, in games such as Virtual Valerie II (Reactor, 1995). Additionally, the invisibility of the rest of the body makes it impossible to ascertain from which point on the body this rigid unit emerges.

13. Jacques Lacan, *Ecrits: A Selection,* trans. Alan Sheridan (London: Tavistock, 1977), 27.

14. Elizabeth Grosz, *Volatile Bodies: Toward a Corporeal Feminism* (Bloomington: Indiana University Press, 1994), 46.

15. Roger Caillois, "Mimicry and Legendary Psychasthenia, " *October* 31 (1984): 28.

16. Ibid., 30.

17. Sigmund Freud, "Civilization and Its Discontents," in *The Standard Edition of the Complete Psychological Works of Sigmund Freud,* ed. James Strachey, vol. 12 (London: Hogarth Press, 1929).
18. Grosz, *Volatile Bodies,* 66.
19. Sigmund Freud, "The Ego and the Id," in Strachey, ed., *The Complete Psychological Works,* vol. 19 (1961).
20. Warren Gorman, *Body Image and the Image of the Brain* (St. Louis: Warren H. Green, 1969), 193.
21. Grosz, *Volatile Bodies,* 80.

—— CONCLUSION

1. Michael Heim, "The Art of Virtual Reality," *Virtual Reality* 1, no. 4 (1994): 21.
2. Jaron Lanier, quoted in Dean MacCannell, "Virtual Reality's Place," *Performance Research* 2, no. 2 (1997): 13.
3. Lawrence Durrell, *Spirit of Place: Letters and Essays on Travel* (New York: E. P. Dutton , 1969), 156.
4. Rey Chow, *Primitive Passions: Visuality, Sexuality, Ethnography, and Contemporary Chinese Cinema* (New York: Columbia University Press, 1995).

BIBLIOGRAPHY

Adler, Judith. "Origins of Sightseeing." *Annals of Tourism Research* 16 (1989): 7–29.
———. "Travel As Performed Art." *American Journal of Sociology* 94, no. 6 (May 1989): 1366–91.
Alloula, Malek. *The Colonial Harem.* Trans. Myrna and Wlad Godzich. Theory and History of Literature, vol. 12. Minneapolis: University of Minnesota Press, 1986.
Altick, Richard D. *Shows of London.* Cambridge, Mass.: Belknap Press of Harvard University Press, 1978.
Ames, Michael M. *Museums, the Public and Anthropology: A Study in the Anthropology of Anthropology.* Vancouver: University of British Columbia Press, 1985.
Anderson, Benedict. *Imagined Communities.* London: Verso, 1991.
Aukstakalnis, Steve and David Blatner. *Silicon Mirage: The Art and Science of Virtual Reality.* Berkeley: Peachpit Press, 1992.
Barthes, Roland. *Mythologies.* 1957. Trans. Annette Lavers. New York: Hill and Wang, 1984.
Baudrillard, Jean. *Simulations.* Trans. Paul Foss, Paul Patton, and Philip Beitchman. New York: Semiotext(e), 1983.
Baudry, Jean Louis. "Ideological Effects of the Basic Cinematographic Apparatus." In *Narrative, Apparatus, Ideology.* Ed. Philip Rosen. New York: Columbia University Press, 1986.
Bazin, André. *What is Cinema?* Trans. Hugh Gray. Berkeley and Los Angeles: University of California Press, 1967.
Belton, John. *Widescreen Cinema.* Cambridge, Mass.: Harvard University Press, 1992.
Benjamin, Walter. "The Work of Art in the Age of Mechanical Reproduction." In *Illuminations.* Trans. Harry Zohn. New York: Schocken Books, 1979.
Berger, John. *Ways of Seeing.* Harmondsworth, England: Penguin Books, 1972.
Bogdan, Robert. *Freak Show: Presenting Human Oddities for Amusement and Profit.* Chicago: University of Chicago Press, 1988.
Bolotin, Norman and Christine Laing. *The World's Columbian Exposition: A One-Hundred-Year Retrospective.* Washington, D.C.: Preservation Press, 1992.
Boorstin, Daniel. *The Image: A Guide to Pseudo-Events in America.* 1961. Reprint, New York: Atheneum, 1985.
Bordwell, David, Janet Staiger, and Kristin Thompson. *The Classical Hollywood Cinema: Film Style and Mode of Production to 1960.* New York: Columbia University Press, 1985.
Bourdieu, Pierre. *Outline of a Theory of Practice.* Trans. Richard Nice. Cambridge: Cambridge University Press, 1977.
Bowser, Eileen. *The Transformation of Cinema 1907–1915.* Vol. 2. New York: Maxwell Macmillan, 1990.

Brewster, Sir David. *The Stereoscope: Its History, Theory, and Construction.* Hastings-on-Hudson, N.Y.: Morgan and Morgan, 1971.

Brigard, Emilie de. "The History of the Ethnographic Film." In *Toward a Science of Man: Essays in the History of Anthropology.* Ed. Timothy H. H. Thoresen. Paris: Mouton, 1975.

Brown, B. S. "Hales Tours and Scenes of the World." *Moving Picture World,* July 15, 1916, 372–73.

Brown, Lloyd A. *The Story of Maps.* 1949. New York: Dover, 1979.

Bruno, Giuliana. *Streetwalking on a Ruined Map: Cultural Theory and the City Films of Elvira Notari.* Princeton, N.J.: Princeton University Press, 1993.

Buzard, James. *The Beaten Track: European Tourism, Literature, and the Ways to Culture 1800–1918.* Oxford: Clarendon Press, 1993.

Caillois, Roger. "Mimicry and Legendary Psychasthenia," *October* 31 (1984): 28.

Cazmanian, Louis and Emile Legouis. *A History of English Literature.* Vol. 2. New York: Macmillan, 1927.

Certeau, Michel de. *Heterologies: Discourse on the Other.* Trans. Brian Massumi. Theory and History of Literature, vol. 17. Minneapolis: University of Minnesota Press, 1986.

———. *The Practice of Everyday Life.* 1984. Trans. Steven Rendell. Berkeley and Los Angeles: University of California Press, 1988.

Chicago Times Portfolio of Midway Types. Chicago: American English Company, 1893.

Chow, Rey. *Primitive Passions: Visuality, Sexuality, Ethnography, and Contemporary Chinese Cinema.* New York: Columbia University Press, 1995.

Clifford, James. "On Ethnographic Self-Fashioning: Conrad and Malinowki." In *Reconstructing Individualism.* Ed. Thomas C. Heller, Morton Sosna, and David E. Wellbery. Stanford, Calif.: Stanford University Press, 1986.

———. *The Predicament of Culture: Twentieth-Century Ethnography, Literature, and Art.* Cambridge, Mass.: Harvard University Press, 1988.

———. *Routes: Travel and Translation in the Late Twentieth Century.* Cambridge, Mass.: Harvard University Press, 1997.

Cohen, Erik. "Authenticity and Commoditization in Tourism." *Annals of Tourism Research* 15, no. 4 (1988): 371–86.

———. "A Phenomenology of Tourist Experiences." *Sociology* 13, no. 2 (1979): 179–201.

———. "Traditions in the Qualitative Sociology of Tourism." *Annals of Tourism Research* 15 (1988): 29–46.

Collier, John Jr. and Malcolm Collier. *Visual Anthropology: Photography As a Research Method.* Albuquerque: University of New Mexico Press, 1986.

Comolli, Jean-Louis. "Machines of the Visible." In *The Cinematic Apparatus.* Ed. Teresa de Lauretis and Stephen Heath. New York: St. Martin's Press, 1980.

———. "Technique and Ideology: Camera, Perspective, Depth of Field." In *Narrative, Apparatus, Ideology.* Ed. Philip Rosen. New York: Columbia University Press, 1986.

Connor, Steven. *Postmodernist Culture: An Introduction to Theories of the Contemporary.* Oxford: Blackwell, 1989.

Coombes, Annie E. *Reinventing Africa: Museums, Material Culture, and Popular Imagination in Late Victorian and Edwardian England.* New Haven, Conn.: Yale University Press, 1994.

Crane, Sylvia. *White Silence: Greenough, Powers, and Crawford: American Sculptors in Nineteenth-Century Italy.* Coral Gables, Fla.: University of Miami Press, 1972.

Crapanzano, Vincent. "Hermes' Dilemma: The Masking of Subversion in Ethnographic Description." In *Writing Culture: The Poetics and Politics of Ethnography.* Ed. James Clifford and James E. Marcus. Berkeley and Los Angeles: University of California Press, 1986.

Crary, Jonathan. *Techniques of the Observer: On Vision and Modernity in the Nineteenth Century.* 1990. Reprint, Cambridge, Mass.: MIT Press, 1996.

Crawford, Peter Ian and David Turton (eds). *Film As Ethnography.* Manchester: Manchester University Press, 1992.

Crawford, William. "The Shavanti of Central Brazil." *Polaroid* 14, no. 1 (1983): 52–53.

Crichton, Michael. *Congo.* 1993. New York: Ballantine Books, 1980.

———. *Timeline.* New York: Alfred A. Knopf, 1999.

———. *Travels.* New York: Alfred A. Knopf, 1988.

Crick, Malcolm. "Representations of International Tourism in the Social Sciences: Sun, Sex, Sights, Savings, and Servility." *Annual Review of Anthropology* 18 (1989): 307–44.

Croutier, Alev Lytle. *Harem: World behind the Veil.* New York: Abbeville Press, 1989.

Culler, Jonathan. "Semiotics of Tourism," *Framing the Sign: Criticism and Its Institutions.* Norman: University of Oklahoma Press, 1988.

Damarin, Suzanne K. "Schooling and Situated Knowledge: Travel or Tourism?" *Educational Technology,* March 1993, 27–32.

Darrah, William C. *Cartes de Visite in Nineteenth Century Photography.* Gettysburg, Penn: W. C. Darrah, 1981.

———. *The World of Stereographs.* Gettysburg, Pennsylvania: W. C. Darrah, 1977.

De Lauretis, Teresa. *Alice Doesn't: Feminism, Semiotics, Cinema.* Bloomington: Indiana University Press, 1984.

Devereaux, Leslie and Roger Hillman, eds. *Fields of Vision: Essays in Film Studies, Visual Anthropology, and Photography.* Berkeley and Los Angeles: University of California Press, 1995.

Dietrick, Ellen Battelle. "The Circassian Slave in Turkish Harems." *Popular Science Monthly* 44 (1894): 481–86.

The Dream City: A Portfolio of Photographic Views of the World's Columbian Exposition. St. Louis: N. D. Thompson, 1893.

Driver, Felix. "Henry Morton Stanley and His Critics: Geography, Exploration and Empire." *Past and Present* 133 (1991): 134–66.

Duncan, Jody and Janine Pourroy. *The Making of Congo the Movie.* New York: Ballantine Books, 1995.

Durrell, Lawrence. "Landscape and Character." In *Spirit of Place: Letters and Essays on Travel.* New York: E. P. Dutton, 1969.

Earle, Edward W., ed. *Points of View: The Stereograph in America—A Cultural History.* Rochester, N.Y.: Visual Studies Workshop Press, 1979.

Eisner, Robert. *Travelers to an Antique Land.* Ann Arbor: University of Michigan Press, 1991.

Ellis, Havelock. *Sexual Selection in Man.* Studies in the Psychology of Sex, vol. 4. Philadelphia: F. A. Davis, 1929.

Evans, Arthur B. *Jules Verne Rediscovered: Didacticism and the Scientific Novel.* Contributions to the Study of World Literature, no. 27. New York: Greenwood Press, 1988.

Fabian, Johannes. *Time and the Other: How Anthropology Makes Its Object.* New York: Columbia University Press, 1983.

Fielding, Raymond. "Hale's Tours: Ultrarealism in the Pre-1910 Motion Picture." In *Film before Griffith.* Ed. John L. Fell. Berkeley and Los Angeles: University of California Press, 1983.

Forster, E. M. *A Room With A View.* 1908. Reprint, New York: Bantam Books, 1988.

———. *Where Angels Fear to Tread.* 1905. Reprint, London: Edward Arnold, 1975.

Freud, Sigmund. "Civilization and Its Discontents." 1929. In *The Standard Edition of the Complete Psychological Works of Sigmund Freud.* Ed. James Strachey. Vol. 12. London: Hogarth Press, 1958.

———. "The Ego and the Id." 1923. In *The Standard Edition of the Complete Psychological Works of Sigmund Freud.* Ed. James Strachey. Vol. 19. London: Hogarth Press, 1961.

Friedberg, Anne. *Window Shopping: Cinema and the Postmodern.* Berkeley and Los Angeles: University of California Press, 1993.

Frow, John. "Tourism and the Semiotics of Nostalgia." *October* 57 (1991): 123–51.

Fuller, Mary and Henry Jenkins. "Nintendo® and New World Travel Writing: A Dialogue." In *CyberSociety: Computer Mediated Communication and Community.* Ed. Steven G. Jones. Thousand Oaks, Calif.: Sage, 1995.

Fussell, Paul, ed. *Abroad: British Literary Traveling between the Wars.* New York: Oxford University Press, 1980.

———. *The Norton Book of Travel.* New York: W. W. Norton, 1987.

Geertz, Clifford. *Local Knowledge: Further Esays in Interpretive Anthropology.* New York: Basic Books, 1983.

———. *Works and Lives: The Anthropologist As Author.* Stanford, Calif.: Stanford University Press, 1988.

Gewertz, Deborah and Frederick Errington. "Tourism and Anthropology in a Postmodern World," *Oceania* 60, no. 1 (1989): 37–54.

——. *Twisted Histories, Altered Contexts: Representing the Chambri in a World System*. Cambridge: Cambridge University Press, 1991.

Gibson, William. *Neuromancer*. New York: Ace Science Fiction, 1984.

Giddis, Diane. "The Divided Woman: Bree Daniels in *Klute*." In *Movies and Methods*. Ed. Bill Nichols. Berkeley and Los Angeles: University of California Press, 1976.

Gilman, Sander. *Difference and Pathology: Stereotypes of Sexuality, Race, and Madness*. Ithaca, N.Y.: Cornell University Press, 1985.

Graham-Brown, Sarah. *Images of Women: The Portrayal of Women in Photography of the Middle East 1860–1950*. New York: Columbia University Press, 1988.

Greek National Tourist Organization. *Greece '91*. Athens: Char. I. Papadopoulos, 1990.

Greenwood, Davydd J. "Culture by the Pound: Tourism As Cultural Commoditization." In *Hosts and Guests: The Anthropology of Tourism*. Ed. Valene L. Smith. Philadelphia: University of Pennsylvania Press, 1977.

Griffiths, Alison. "'Journeys for Those Who Cannot Travel': Promenade Cinema and the Museum Life Group," *Wide Angle* 18, no. 3 (1996): 53–84.

——. "Knowledge and Visuality in Turn of the Century Anthropology: The Early Ethnographic Cinema of Alfred Cort Haddon and Walter Baldwin Spencer." *Visual Anthropology Review* 12, no. 2 (1996–97): 18–43.

——. "Science and Spectacle: Discourses of Authenticity in Early Ethnographic Film." In *Dressing in Feathers: The Construction of the Indian in American Popular Culture*. Ed. Elizabeth Bird. Boulder: Westview Press, 1995. 79–95.

——. "'To Disappoint the Ravages of Time': Precinematic Ethnography at the American Museum of Natural History." In *Le cinéma au tournant du siècle/Cinema at the Turn of the Century*. Ed. André Gaudreault, Claire Dupré la Tour, and Roberta Pearson. Lausanne: Editions Payot/Quebec: Nuit Blanche, 1998. 108–21.

——. "'To the World the World We Show': Early Travelogues As Filmed Ethnography," *Film History* 11, no. 3 (1999): 282–307.

——. "'We Partake as It Were of His Life': The Status of the Visual in Early Ethnographic Film." In *Technologies of Moving Images*. Ed. John Fullerton. Sydney: John Libbey Press, 1999.

——. *Wondrous Difference: Cinema, Anthropology, and Turn-of-the-Century Visual Culture*. New York: Columbia University Press, 2002.

Gronewold, Sylvia. "Did Frank Hamilton Cushing Go Native?" In *Crossing Cultural Boundaries: The Anthropological Experience*. Ed. Solon T. Kimball and James B. Watson. San Francisco: Chandler, 1972.

Grossberg, Lawrence. "The In-Difference of Television." *Screen* 28, no. 2 (1987): 28–48.

Grosz, Elizabeth. *Volatile Bodies: Toward a Corporeal Feminism*. Bloomington: Indiana University Press, 1994.

Gunning, Tom. "The Cinema of Attractions: Early Film, Its Spectator and the Avant Garde." In *Early Cinema: Space—Frame—Narrative*. Ed. Thomas Elsaesser with Adam Barker. London: BFI, 1991.

——. "An Unseen Energy Swallows Space: The Space in Early Film and Its Relation to American Avant Garde." In *Film before Griffith*. Ed. John L. Fell. Berkeley and Los Angeles: University of California Press, 1983.

Gupta, Akhil and James Ferguson, eds. *Anthropological Locations: Boundaries and Grounds of a Field Science*. Berkeley and Los Angeles: University of California Press, 1997.

Hallock, E. S. "The American Circus." *Century*, August 1905, 583.

Hammerton, J. A., ed. *Peoples of All Nations: Their Life Today and the Story of their Past*. 7 vols. London: Amalgamated Press, 1922–24.

Hannavy, John. *Masters of Victorian Photography*. New York: Holmes and Meier, 1976.

——. *Roger Fenton of Crimble Hall*. Boston: David R. Godine, 1975.

Haraway, Donna. "A Manifesto for Cyborgs: Science, Technology, and Socialist Feminism in the 1980s." *Socialist Review* 80 (1985): 64–107.

——. "Teddy Bear Patriarchy: Taxidermy in the Garden of Eden, New York City, 1908–1936."

In *Primate Visions: Gender, Race, and Nature in the World of Modern Science*. New York: Routledge, 1989.

Harris, Marvin. *The Rise of Anthropological Theory: A History of Theories of Culture*. 1968. New York: Thomas Y. Crowell, 1971.

Hayles, N. Katherine. *How We Became Posthuman: Virtual Bodies in Cybernetics, Literature, and Informatics*. Chicago: University of Chicago Press, 1999.

Heidegger, Martin. "The Age of the World Picture." In *The Question Concerning Technology and Other Essays*. Trans. William Lovitt. New York: Harper Colophon, 1977.

Heim, Michael. "The Art of Virtual Reality," *Virtual Reality* 1, no. 4 (1994): 9–22.

Hellman, Geoffrey. *Bankers, Bones, and Beetles: The First Century of the American Museum of Natural History*. Garden City, N.Y.: Natural History Press, 1968, 1969.

Higson, Andrew. "Re-Presenting the National Past: Nostalgia and Pastiche in the Heritage Film." In *Fires Were Started: British Cinema and Thatcherism*. Ed. Lester Friedman. Minneapolis: University of Minnesota Press, 1993.

Hinsley, Curtis. "Ethnographic Charisma and Scientific Routine: Cushing and Fewkes in the American Southwest, 1879–1893." In *Observers Observed: Essays on Ethnographic Fieldwork*. Ed. George W. Stocking Jr. History of Anthropology, vol. 1. Madison: University of Wisconsin Press, 1983.

Holmes, Burton. *The Man Who Photographed the World*. John L. Stoddard, *John L. Stoddard Lectures*. 10 vols. Boston: Balch Brothers, 1907.

Holmes, Oliver Wendell. "The Stereoscope and the Stereograph." *Atlantic Monthly*, June 1859, 744.

hooks, bell. *Black Looks: Race and Representation*. Boston: South End Press, 1992.

Horton, Andrew. "Jules Dassin: A Multinational Filmmaker Considered." *Film Criticism* 8, no. 3 (1984): 21–35.

Illustrated and Descriptive Catalogue and Price List of Stereopticons, Lantern Slides, Moving Picture Machines, Accessories for Projection. Chicago: Stereopticon and Film Exchange, 1903.

Ingersoll, Lurton Dunham, ed. *Explorations in Africa by Dr. David Livingstone and Others*. San Francisco: Union, 1872.

Jay, Martin. "The Scopic Regimes of Modernity." *Vision and Visuality*. Ed. Hal Foster. Seattle: Dia Press, 1988.

Kaplan, Karen. *Questions of Travel: Postmodern Discourses of Displacement*. Durham, N.C.: Duke University Press, 1996.

Kaplan, Robert. *Balkan Ghosts*. New York: Vintage Books, 1993.

Karp, Ivan and Steven D. Lavine, eds. *Exhibiting Culture: The Poetics and Politics of Museum Display*. Washington D. C.: Smithsonian Institution Press, 1991.

Keizer, Gregg. "The Next Generation of Multimedia Software." *Multimedia World* 2, no. 6 (1995): 66–72.

Kendrick, Michelle. "Cyberspace and the Technological Real." In *Virtual Reality and Its Discontents*. Ed. Robert Markley. Baltimore: John Hopkins University Press, 1995.

Klein, Maury. *The Flowering of the Third America: The Making of an Organizational Society, 1850–1920*. Chicago: Ivan R. Dee, 1993.

Kuklick, Henrika. *The Savage Within: The Social History of British Anthropology, 1885–1945*. Cambridge: Cambridge University Press, 1991.

Kuper, Adam. *Anthropology and Anthropologists: The Modern British School*. 1973. London: Routledge, 1983.

Lacan, Jacques. *Ecrits: A Selection*. Trans. Alan Sheridan. London: Tavistock, 1977.

Leaf, Murray J. *Man, Mind, and Science: A History of Anthropology*. New York: Columbia University Press, 1979.

Leed, Eric J. *The Mind of the Traveler: From Gilgamesh to Global Tourism*. New York: Basic Books, 1991.

Lévi-Strauss, Claude. *Tristes Tropiques*. 1955. Trans. John and Dorreen Weightman. New York: Atheneum, 1975.

Lindfors, Bernth. "African Circus." *Journal of American Culture* 6, no. 2 (1983): 9–14.

Loshitzky, Yosefa. "The Tourist/Traveler Gaze: Bertolucci and Bowles's *The Sheltering Sky*." *East-West Film Journal* 7, no. 2 (1993): 110–37.

Lotman, Jurij M. "The Origin of Plot in the Light of Typology," trans. Julian Graffy. *Poetics Today* 1, nos. 1–2 (1979): 167.

Lugones, Maria. "Playfulness, 'World'-Travelling, and Loving Perception." In *Making Face, Making Soul.* Ed. Gloria Anzaldúa. New York: Aunt Lute Foundation, 1990.

Lurie, Nancy Oestreich. "Museumland Revisted." *Human Organization* 40, no. 2 (1981): 180–87.

Lutkehaus, Nancy Christine. "'Excuse Me, Everything Is Not All Right': On Ethnography, Film, and Representation: An Interview with Filmmaker Dennis O'Rourke." *Cultural Anthropology* 4, no. 4 (1989): 422–37.

Lutz, Catherine A. and Jane L. Collins. *Reading National Geographic.* Chicago: University of Chicago Press, 1993.

Lynch, Gertrude. "Racial and Ideal Types of Beauty." *Cosmopolitan* 38 (1901): 223–33.

Maertens, James W. "Between Jules Verne and Walt Disney: Brains, Brawn, and Masculine Desire in *Twenty Thousand Leagues under the Sea.*" *Science-Fiction Studies* 22, no. 2 (1995): 209–25.

MacCannell, Dean. Empty *Meeting Grounds: The Tourist Papers.* London: Routledge, 1992.

———. "Staged Authenticity: Arrangements of Social Space in Tourist Settings." *American Journal of Sociology* 79, no. 3 (1973): 602.

———. *The Tourist: A New Theory of the Leisure Class.* 1976. Reprint, New York: Schocken Books, 1989.

———. "Virtual Reality's Place." *Performance Research* 2, no. 2 (1997): 10–21.

MacDougall, David. *Transcultural Cinema.* Princeton, N.J.: Princeton University Press, 1998.

Malinowski, Bronislaw. *Argonauts of the Western Pacific.* 1922. Reprint, New York: E. P. Dutton, 1961.

Martin, Andrew. *The Mask of the Prophet: The Extraordinary Fictions of Jules Verne.* Oxford: Clarendon Press, 1990.

Maybury-Lewis, David. *Millennium: Tribal Wisdom and the Modern World.* New York: Viking, 1992.

McBryde, Isabel. "Thomas Dick's Photographic Vision." In *Seeing the First Australians.* Ed. Ian Donaldson and Tamsin Donaldson. Sydney: George Allen and Unwin.

McDermott, Emily A. *Euripedes' Medea: The Incarnation of Disorder.* University Park: Pennsylvania State University Press, 1989.

McGrane, Bernard. *Beyond Anthropology: Society and the Other.* New York: Columbia University Press, 1989.

Mercouri, Melina. *I Was Born Greek.* Garden City, N.Y.: Doubleday, 1971.

Merleau-Ponty, Maurice. *The Phenomenology of Perception.* Trans. Colin Smith. London: Routledge and Kegan Paul, 1962.

Metz, Christian. "Identification, Mirror." *Film Theory and Criticism.* Ed. Gerald Mast and Marshall Cohen. 1974. Reprint, New York: Oxford University Press, 1985.

———. *The Imaginary Signifier: Psychoanalysis and the Cinema.* Trans. Celia Britton, Annwyl Williams, Ben Brewster, and Alfred Guzzetti. Bloomington: Indiana University Press) 1982.

Mitchell, Dolores. "Images of Exotic Women in Turn-of-the-Century Tobacco Art." *Feminist Studies* 18, no. 2 (1992): 327–50.

Mitchell, Timothy. *Colonising Egypt.* Cambridge: Cambridge University Press, 1988.

Moore, Alexander. "Walt Disney World: Bounded Ritual Space and the Playful Pilgrimage Center." *Anthropological Quarterly* 53, no. 4 (1980): 207–18.

Morley, David and Kevin Robins. "Spaces of Identity: Communications Technologies and the Reconfiguration of Europe." *Screen* 30, no. 4 (1989): 10.

Morse, Margaret. "An Ontology of Everyday Distraction: The Freeway, the Mall, and Television." In *Logics of Television: Essays in Cultural Criticism.* Ed. Patricia Mellencamp. Bloomington: Indiana University Press, 1990.

Mumford, Lewis. *Technics and Civilization.* New York: Harcourt, Brace, and World, 1934.

Musser, Charles. *Before the Nickelodeon: Edwin S. Porter and the Edison Manufacturing Company.* Berkeley and Los Angeles: University of California Press, 1991.

———. "The Travel Genre in 1903–1904: Moving toward Fictional Narrative." *Iris* 2, no. 1 (1982): 47–60.

Naimark, Michael. "Presence at the Interface; or, Sense of Place/Essence of Place." In *Land-*

scape and Place. Ed. Widdicombe Schmidt and Michael Naimark. Special issue, *Wide Angle* 15, no. 4 (1993): 55.

Nash, Dennison. "Tourism As a Form of Imperialism." In *Hosts and Guests: The Anthropology of Tourism*. Ed. Valene L. Smith. Philadelphia: University of Pennsylvania Press, 1977.

Nichols, Bill. *Ideology and the Image: Social Representation in the Cinema and Other Media*. Bloomington: Indiana University Press, 1981.

———. *Movies and Methods*. Vol 2. Berkeley and Los Angeles: University of California Press, 1985.

North, Joseph. *The Early Development of the Motion Picture (1887–1909)*. New York: Arno Press, 1973.

Palin, Michael. *Around the World in Eighty Days with Michael Palin*. San Francisco: KQED Books, 1995.

Peck, Harry Thurston. "Beauty." *Cosmopolitan*, December 1900, 176–84.

Pedersen, Paul. *The Five Stages of Cultural Shock*. Westport, Conn.: Greenwood Press, 1995.

Pimentel, Ken and Kevin Teixera. *Virtual Reality: Through the New Looking Glass*. New York: McGraw-Hill, 1993.

Pinney, Christopher. "Future Travel." In *Visualizing Theory: Selected Essays from V.A.R. 1990–1994*. Ed. Lucien Taylor. New York: Routledge, 1994.

Pittier, Henry. "Little Known Parts of Panama" *National Geographic* 23, no. 7 (1892): 627–62.

Poignant, Roslyn. "Surveying the Field of View: The Making of the RAI Photographic Collection." In *Anthropology and Photography 1860–1920*. Ed. Elizabeth Edwards. New Haven, Conn.: Yale University Press, 1992.

Pratt, Mary Louise. "Fieldwork in Common Places." In *Writing Culture: The Poetics and Politics of Ethnography*. Ed. James Clifford and George E. Marcus. Berkeley and Los Angeles: University of California Press, 1986.

———. *Imperial Eyes: Travel Writing and Transculturation*. London: Routledge, 1992.

Preston, Douglas J. *Dinosaurs in the Attic: An Excursion into the American Museum of Natural History*. New York: St. Martin's Press, 1986.

Probyn, Elspeth. "Travels in the Postmodern." In *Feminism/Postmodernism*. Ed. Linda J. Nicholson. New York: Routledge, 1990.

Read, Kenneth. *The High Valley*. New York: Columbia University Press, 1965.

Redfoot, Donald L. "Touristic Authenticity, Touristic Angst, and Modern Reality." *Qualitative Sociology* 7, no. 4 (1984): 291–309.

Reingold, Howard. *Virtual Reality*. New York: Summit Books, 1991.

Rice, Anne. *The Tale of the Body Thief*. New York: Ballantine, 1992.

Richards, Thomas. *The Commodity Culture of Victorian England: Advertising and Spectacle 1851–1914*. Stanford, Calif.: Stanford University Press, 1990.

Richlin, Amy. "The Ethnographer's Dilemma." In *Feminist Theory and the Classics*. Ed. Nancy Sorkin Rabinowitz and Amy Richlin. New York: Routledge, 1993.

Riverol, A. R. *Live From Atlantic City: The History of the Miss America Pageant Before, After, and in Spite of Television*. Bowling Green, Ohio: Bowling Green State University Popular Press, 1992.

Roberts, Shari. "'The Lady in the Tutti-Frutti Hat': Carmen Miranda, a Spectacle of Ethnicity." *Cinema Journal* 32, no. 3 (1993): 3–23.

Robertson, George, Melinda Mash, Lisa Tickner, Jon Bird, Barry Curtis, and Tim Putnam, eds. *Travellers' Tales: Narratives of Home and Displacement*. London: Routledge, 1994.

Rony, Fatimah Tobing. *The Third Eye: Race, Cinema, and Ethnographic Spectacle*. Durham, N.C.: Duke University Press, 1996.

Rosecrance, Barbara. *Forster's Narrative Vision*. Ithaca, N.Y.: Cornell University Press, 1982.

Rosen, Philip. "Disjunction and Ideology in a Preclassical Film: *A Policeman's Tour of the World*." *Wide Angle* 12, no. 3 (1990): 20–36.

Rowe, John Howland. "Technical Aids in Anthropology: A Historical Survey." In *Anthropology Today*. Ed. Alfred L. Kroeber. Chicago: University of Chicago Press, 1953.

Russell, Catherine. *Experimental Ethnography: The Work of Film in the Age of Video*. Durham, N.C.: Duke University Press, 1999.

Rydell, Robert W. *All the World's a Fair: Visions of Empire at American International Expositions, 1876–1916*. Chicago: University of Chicago Press, 1984.

Said, Edward W. *Orientalism.* New York: Random House, 1978.

Schivelbusch, Wolfgang. *The Railway Journey: Trains and Travel in the Nineteenth Century.* Trans. Anselm Hollo. 1977. New York: Urizen Books, 1980.

Scott, William R. *The Americans in Panama.* New York: Statler, 1913.

Segrave, Kerry. *The Continental Actress.* Jefferson, N.C.: McFarland, 1990.

Seiberling, Grace. *Amateurs, Photography, and the Mid-Victorian Imagination.* Chicago: University of Chicago Press, 1986.

Shaw, Gareth and Allan M. Williams. *Critical Issues in Tourism: A Geographical Perspective.* Oxford: Blackwell, 1994.

Sheets-Pyenson, Susan. *Cathedrals of Science: The Development of Colonial Natural History Museums during the Late Nineteenth Century.* Kingston, Ont.: McGill-Queen's University Press, 1988.

Shohat, Ella. "Gender and Culture of Empire: Toward a Feminist Ethnography of the Cinema." *Discourse of the Other: Postcoloniality, Positionality, and Subjectivity.* Ed. Hamid Naficy and Teshome H. Gabriel. Special issue, *Quarterly Review of Film and Video* 13, nos. 1–3 (1991): 45–84.

Silverman, Kaja. *Male Subjectivity at the Margins.* New York: Routledge, 1992.

———. *The Subject of Semiotics.* New York: Oxford University Press, 1983.

Sobel, Bernard. "The Historic Hootchy-Kootchy." *Dance* 20 (1946): 13–15.

Sontag, Susan. "The Anthropologist As Hero." In *Against Interpretation and Other Essays.* New York: Octagon Books, 1986.

———. *On Photography.* New York: Doubleday, 1990.

Spencer, Frank. "Some Notes on the Attempt to Apply Photography to Anthropometry during the Second Half of the Nineteenth Century." In *Anthropology and Photography.* Ed. Elizabeth Edwards. New Haven, Conn.: Yale University Press, 1992.

Spigel, Lynn. "Installing the Television Set: Popular Discourses on Television and Domestic Space, 1948–55." *Camera Obscura* 16 (1988): 17.

Spivak, Gayatri Chakravorty. "Can the Subaltern Speak? Speculations on Widow-Sacrifice." *Wedge* 7–8 (1985): 120–30.

Sternberger, Dolf. *Panorama of the Nineteenth Century.* Trans. Joachim Neugroschel. New York: Urizen Books, 1977.

Stewart, Susan. *On Longing: Narratives of the Miniature, the Gigantic, the Souvenir, the Collection.* 1984. Reprint, Durham, N.C.: Duke University Press, 1993.

Stocking, George W. Jr., ed. *Objects and Others: Essays on Museums and Material Culture.* Madison: University of Wisconsin Press, 1985.

———, ed. *Observers Observed: Essays on Ethnographic Fieldwork.* History of Anthropology, vol. 1. Madison: University of Wisconsin Press, 1983.

Street, Brian. "British Popular Anthropology: Exhibiting and Photographing the Other." *Anthropology and Photography 1860–1920.* Ed. Elizabeth Edwards. New Haven: Yale University Press, 1992.

———. *The Savage in Literature: Representations of "Primitive" Society in English Fiction 1858–1920.* London: Routledge and Kegan Paul, 1975.

Sturtevant, William C. "Does Anthropology Need Museums?" *Proceedings of the Biological Society of Washington* 182 (1969): 619–50.

Tomas, David. "Toward an Anthropology of Sight: Ritual Performance and the Photographic Process." *Semiotica* 68, nos. 3–4 (1988): 245–70.

Torgovnick, Marianna. *Gone Primitive: Savage Intellects, Modern Lives.* Chicago: University of Chicago Press, 1990.

Trinh T. Minh-ha. *Woman, Native, Other: Writing Postcoloniality and Feminism.* Bloomington: Indiana University Press, 1989.

———. "All-Owning Spectatorship." *Discourse of the Other: Postcoloniality, Positionality, and Subjectivity.* Ed. Hamid Naficy and Teshome H. Gabriel. Special issue, *Quarterly Review of Film and Video* 13, nos. 1–3 (1991): 189–204.

Turner, Louis and John Ash. *The Golden Hordes: International Tourism and the Pleasure Periphery.* New York: St. Martin's Press, 1976.

Turner, Victor and Edith Turner. *Image and Pilgrimage in Christian Culture: Anthropological Perspectives.* New York: Columbia University Press, 1978.

Turton, David. "Anthropology on Television: What Next?" In *Film As Ethnography.* Ed. Peter Ian Crawford and David Turton. Manchester: Manchester University Press, 1992.

Urry, John. *Consuming Places.* London: Routledge, 1995.

———. *The Tourist Gaze: Leisure and Travel in Contemporary Society.* London: Sage, 1990.

Van den Abbeele, Georges. "Sightseers: The Tourist As Theorist." *Diacritics* 10 (1980): 2–14.

Vermeulen, Han F. "Origins and Institutionalization of Ethnography and Ethnology in Europe and the USA, 1771–1845." In *Fieldwork and Footnotes: Studies in the History of European Anthropology.* Ed. Han F. Vermeulen and Arturo Alverez Roldán. London: Routledge, 1995.

Verne, Jules. *Around the World in Eighty Days.* 1872. Trans. William Butcher. Oxford: Oxford University Press, 1995.

Wexman, Virginia Wright. "The Critic As Consumer: Film Study in the University, *Vertigo* and the Film Canon." *Film Quarterly* 39 (1986): 35.

Wiebe, Robert. *The Search for Order, 1877–1920.* New York: Hill and Wang, 1967.

"Women of All Nations." *National Geographic* 22 (1911): 49–61.

Wrigley, Richard and George Revill, eds. *Pathologies of Travel.* Amsterdam: Rodopi, 2000.

Zurick, David. *Errant Journeys: Adventure Travel in a Modern Age.* Austin: University of Texas Press, 1995.

INDEX

acculturation, 272, 275–276

Adler, Judith, 24

aerial perspective, 32–33, 34, 46, 137–138

aerial photography, 32, 33, 46, 281n11

Africa Trail (computer game), 232

age of the world picture, 25

Akeley, Carl, 70

alienation, 138, 225–226

Amazon (computer game), 288n5

American Museum, 57, 58

American Museum of Natural History (AMNH), 20, 69–70, 72–73, 284n9

American national identity, 158

AMNH. *see* American Museum of Natural History

Ancient Lands (computer game), 244

Anderson, Michael, 124, 128

The Andromeda Strain (Crichton), 196, 200

Angelopoulos, Theodoros, 160

Antarctica: The Last Continent (computer game), 232

Anthropologisch-Ethnologishes (Dammann), 53

anthropologist: armchair, 19, 24, 50; as hero, 24, 215–216; hyphenated, 216, 224–227; as tourist stand-in, 216–217, 221

anthropology: classical, 2, 18, 19, 23, 29–33; critique of ethics in, 214–215, 219–220; dual perspective of, 31–32; ethnographic

film use in, 32–33, 284n10, 284n12–285n12; ethnographic mediation in, 29–31; for popular audience, 49–51, 220–224; professionalization of, 23–24, 59–61; spatialization of time in, 47–49

anthropometry, 54–55, 56, 58, 64

antitourism: collapse of, and Forster, 179–183; in film, 193; mythos of, 4–5; and travel game, 230–231

appropriation, 35, 182

Argonauts of the Western Pacific (Malinowski), 24, 217, 218–219, 223, 224–225

armchair anthropologist, 19, 24, 50

armchair tourist/traveler, 2, 15, 42, 74, 105, 177

Around the Moon (film), 125–126

Around the Moon (Verne), 140

Around the World in Eighty Days (CD-ROM), 144–145, 205, 239

Around the World in Eighty Days (film): affluence in, 132–133; holistic perspective in, 137–138; narrative in, 124, 128, 131, 132, 139, 140; as nostalgic, 138–139; perspective in, 137–138; promotion of, 131, 132; sexualization of female in, 136–137; technology of, 126, 129–131, 135–136, 150; themes in, 128, 137

Around the World in Eighty Days (Verne), 137, 141, 145
Around the World in Eighty Days with Michael Palin (documentary), 140, 142–144, 286n22
assimilation, 192, 206
authenticity: basis of search for, 3–4; as not commodified, 176–177; post-modernism and myth of, 6, 8–10, 178; in simulated travel, 193–194

Baartman, Saartje (Hottentot Venus), 55–56
Balkan Ghosts (Kaplan), 156, 287n18
Barnum, P. T., 57, 64
Barthes, Roland, 146–147
Baudrillard, Jean, 176, 192, 214
Bazin, André, 248
Being John Malkovich (film), 266–267
"being there": as bestowing authority, 31, 61; through film, 20, 287n15; through stereoscopy, 80, 83; in touristic experience, 27, 37; in travel game, 233; at world's fair, 26, 65
Belton, John, 135, 285n10
Beyond Anthropology (McGrane), 219
Bibliothèque d'Education et de Récréation (Hetzel), 145
Bly, Nelly, 132
Boas, Franz, 24, 72–73, 217
body hopping, 266–267, 275–276
body image: comparative analysis of, 48, 49, 50, 53–54; urgency for collecting primitive, 51–53
Bolas, Mark, 250
Bond, James, 275
Boorstin, Daniel, 4, 5
Borges, Jose Luis, 192, 197
Bourdieu, Pierre, 25
Brainstorm (film), 257
Brewster, David, 81
Bruno, Giuliana, 16, 17
Butcher, William, 285n6
Buzard, James, 164, 181, 186

Caesar II (computer game), 230
Canada, 141, 151
cannibalism, 105–106

capitalism, 15, 37, 39, 40, 45; Panama Canal and, 97–101
cartesian space, 35, 255
cartography, 45–46, 192
Catlin, George, 51
The Cell (film), 257
Certeau, Michel de, 241
Chapman, Frank M., 70
Chow, Rey, 277
cinema: history of, 19–21, 24; as tool of muscular perception, 19, 21; panning technology in, 117–119; perspective in early, 18, 33, 117–120; relationship to lantern slide show, 106–107; relationship to visual practices of science, 16; technology of early, 112, 115; wide-screen technology, 129, 131, 133–136, 285n10. *see also* film
cinema of attractions, 19, 115–116
CinemaScope, 126, 129, 140, 150, 285n10
Cinéorama, 117, 129
Cinerama, 129, 130, 133–136, 285n10
Cinerama Holiday (film), 134
Clifford, James, 26, 218, 283n57
Cold Lazurus (film), 257
collection, 35, 46–49
collection vs. context, 80, 83
Collier, John Jr., 33
Collier, Malcolm, 33
colonialism, 1, 39, 41, 42, 63, 97, 249
commodification, 176–177
Congo: Descent into Zinj (video game), 288n5
Congo (Crichton), 196, 198, 200–201, 203–206, 288n5
Congo (film), 209
Connor, Stephen, 8, 9, 193
Conrad, Joseph, 219, 225
consumerism, 15–16, 39, 40, 41, 42
context: recreating within museum, 69–73; vs. collection, 80, 83
Cook, Thomas, 21, 39, 41
Coombes, Annie E., 55, 67
Cooper, Merian C., 133
corporeal overlay, 258, 269, 272–274, 276
cortical homunculus, 271–272
Costa-Gavras, Constantin, 160

Crawford, William, 223
Crichton, Michael: background of, 195–196; on demediating power of travel, 4, 5; influence of Verne on, 196, 197, 198; maps in works of, 195, 197; postmodernism in work of, 9–10; primitivism in works of, 205–206; repeat journey in work of, 140, 195, 198–199, 200–201; success/failure of, 208–210; technology in work of, 203, 204, 207, 209, 210; as writer of scientific fiction, 194, 195, 196, 197
Cronenberg, David, 192
cross-cultural contact, 1, 10, 182, 277–278
Culler, Jonathan, 29, 179
cult of immediate experience, 9, 193
cultural difference, 17–18, 28, 36, 37, 39, 272
culture shock, 18, 28; in virtual reality, 271, 272, 273, 275, 276
Cunningham, R. A., 50–52
curiositas, 16–17
Cushing, Frank H., 59–61, 64, 282n41, 289n10
Cyan, 126, 230
Cybermind VR center, 263, 268, 278
The Cyberstalking (TV movie), 256, 257
Czech film, 150

Dactyl Nightmare (VR game), 262, 268–270, 278
Dammann, Carl, 53
dance, as spectacle, 108–110, 284n9, 284n12–285n12
The Darkest Africa (Stanley), 200
The Dark Labyrinth (Durrell), 180
Dassin, Jules, 165, 166, 171, 277
Davidson, Robyn, 232
de Certeau, Michel, 239
de Laurentis, Teresa, 240
Deleuze, Gilles, 175
demediating mediation, 3, 4, 5, 177, 194–195, 257
demediation, 18, 178
Descarté, Rene, 268
Desmond, Jane, 42
Diary in the Strict Sense of the Term (Malinowski), 217, 219, 225

Dick, Philip K., 193
Dick, Thomas, 290n46
Diggers (computer game), 243
direct experience: anthropology and, 30–31, 215, 217, 218–219, 220, 224–225; film as, 6; travel as, 4–5, 27, 28–29
disembodiment: in virtual reality, 255–256, 266–268; vs. dual embodiment, 266–268
distanced immersion, 27; in cinema, 105–106; in travel game, 233–235; in virtual reality, 275
distantiation, 27–28; in anthropology, 219; of framed mobility, 34–35; and mastery, 25
Doane, Mary Ann, 35
documentary, 142–144
Doyle, Arthur Conan, 39
A Dream of Passion (film), 171
dual embodiment, 258, 266–268
Durrell, Lawrence, 28, 32, 164, 180, 275

East/West dichotomy, 155
Eco East Africa, 246–247
economics of tourism, 11
ego trip, 193–194, 195, 209
Eisner, Robert, 5–6
embodiment: dual, 258, 266–268. see also disembodiment
The Empire State Express (film), 111
environmental bubble, 34–35, 260
epistemology, 2, 3, 11, 24, 25, 137, 182, 219
Errington, Frederick, 213–214, 220
Escher, M. C., 251
essentialism, 32
"Eternal Adam" (Verne), 149–150
ethnographic film, 30, 32–33, 284n10, 284n12–285n12
ethnographic "I", 30, 218, 223
ethnographic novel, 30, 39. see also Malinowski, Bronislaw
ethnography, 24, 30–31. see also fieldwork; fieldworker
Evans, Arthur, 139, 145
exotic body, 49; comparative analysis of, 48, 50, 53–54; exhibition of, 55–59, 109–110, 113

exoticism, 2, 3, 17, 26, 31, 32, 37, 67
exoticization, as fetishization, 18
experiential realism, 249–250
exploration: Lévi-Strauss on, 32; in virtual
    reality, 258–259, 260
Exploration (computer game), 230–231
explorer, 4, 25; fair-goer as, 67–68; traveler
    as, 213. *see also* Livingstone, David;
    Stanley, Henry M.

Fabian, Johannes, 24, 33, 47–48, 219
The Fabulous World of Jules Verne (film), 150
fair, world's. *see* world's fair
Fallmeyayer, Jakob Philip, 169
fetishization, 6, 17, 18, 178, 191–192
Feynman, Richard, 210
fieldwork, 59; birth of prolonged, 24; as
    coming of age experience, 61; confes-
    sional about, 217, 219, 225
fieldworker, 30; and direct experience,
    30–31, 215, 217, 218–219, 220, 224–225;
    early, 49–50
"Fieldwork in Common Places" (Pratt), 223
film: antitourism in, 193; "being there"
    through, 20, 287n15; collective
    consciousness of audience, 256–257;
    early travel, 111–112, 114; experiential
    realism in, 249; labor vs. technology in
    early, 112–113; phantom train, 116, 117;
    silent, 124; as simulated immersion, 177;
    spectacle in, 177–178; spectator position
    in, 5–6, 18, 106, 115–116, 119–120, 184–185,
    255; transportation-focused early,
    113–114; in travel lecture, 108; in
    vaudeville theater, 108–110; virtual
    reality in, 251. *see also* cinema
Five Weeks in a Balloon (Verne), 46, 139–140
Flaubert, Gustave, 85
Fleischer, Richard, 126
Flight Unlimited (computer game), 233
Forster, E. M., 8, 177; and authenticity,
    274–275; and collapse of antitourism,
    179–181; film adaptation of work of,
    183–190; physical violence in work of,
    181; repressed homosexuality in work of,
    182–183; sexual violence in work of,
    181–182; and traveler quest, 178–179

Foucault, Michel, 268
France, and Panama Canal, 93, 95
freak show, 55–57, 281n15
Freak Show (computer game), 244
Freddi Fish (computer game), 239
Freud, Sigmund, 267–268
Friedberg, Anne, 15, 16, 177
From Alice to Ocean: Alone across the
    Outback (computer game), 232, 235, 236
From the Earth to the Moon (film), 125–126
Frow, John, 29, 176, 229
Fuller, Mary, 244
Fusco, Coco, 278
Fussell, Paul, 4

Gadget (computer game), 240, 243
gaze, 24–25. *see also* tourist gaze
Geertz, Clifford, 31, 59, 217
Geisha Girls (film), 110
gender: of character in travel game,
    240–241; and exotic body exhibition,
    55–56, 109–110, 155; film stereotype
    and, 162–163
gendered geography, 155
Gewertz, Deborah, 213–214, 220
Gibson, William, 258, 266, 268
globalization, 1, 2, 98
globe as body, 154–155
Godard, Jean-Luc, 172
"going native", 31, 60, 264
Gómez-Peña, Guillermo, 278
Goode, George Brown, 64
Grand Canyon: The Hidden Secrets (film), 250
The Great Train Robbery (film), 120
Greece: effacement of culture of, 156;
    effacement of history of, 155–156; female
    as metaphor for, 163, 168; gendered
    tourist gaze in, 155; landscape as image
    of, 163–164; national identity in, 158,
    286nn5–6; political crisis in, 158, 159,
    174, 286nn7–8; popular image in West,
    159–162; stereotype of, 169; stereotype of
    female in film about, 163; stereotype of
    male in film about, 162–163; stolen
    heritage of, 158, 287n9
Greece through the Stereoscope (Richardson),
    85–86

Greenwood, Davydd J., 176, 216
Griffiths, Alison, 284nn9–10,
    284n12–285n12
Grignon, Lorin, 129
Grimoin-Sanson, Raoul, 117, 129
Grossberg, Lawrence, 175
Grosz, Elizabeth, 270
Gunning, Tom, 19, 115–116, 124

habitat group, 70, 72–73, 74
Haddon, Alfred C., 64, 217–218, 282n41
Haggard, Rider, 39
Hale, George C., 117, 153, 252
Hale's Tours and Scenes of the World, 117,
    120, 153, 252
Haverstraw Tunnel (film), 116
Hawaii High (computer game), 239
HDTV, 141, 147
Heart of Darkness (Conrad), 219, 225
Heath, Stephen, 285n15
Heidegger, Martin, 25, 45, 47, 137, 138, 203,
    265
Heim, Michael, 274
Henty, G. A., 39
Hetzel, Pierre-Jules, 137, 145
High Season (film), 160, 163
The High Valley (Read), 217
Higson, Andrew, 190
historical recovery, 195
Holmes, Burton, 107–108, 114, 115
Holmes, Oliver W., 80, 81–82, 83–84, 99
Holmes stereoscope, 80, 82, 83–84, 99
Horton, Andrew, 166
host/guest relations, 182
hyphenated anthropologist, 225–227

I Love Lucy (TV), 221
immersion, 28, 34; distanced, 27, 105–106,
    233–235, 275; fair attendance as, 65–69;
    at museum, 69–71, 283nn57&59;
    simulated, 117, 152–153, 177, 249; spatial,
    249; and tourist gaze, 2–6
imperialism, 42, 229
indigenous peoples, 43, 50–51; as dying
    culture, 52–53; photographic repre-
    sentation of, 55–59, 77. see also exotic
    body

interactivity: of computer-based travel
    game, 248–249; of virtual reality, 248, 260
interface: bodily, 192, 254–255, 258, 268–269;
    neurological, 254, 255, 256, 258, 267
Ivory, James, 184, 186

Jameson, Fredric, 247
Jenkins, Henry, 244
A Jewish Dance at Jerusalem (film), 110
The Journey to the Center of the Earth (film),
    140
The Journey to the Center of the Earth (TV),
    140
The Journey to the Center of the Earth
    (Verne), 140, 198
The Jungle Book (Kipling), 39
Jurassic Park (Crichton), 196, 199, 200, 206,
    209–210
Jurassic Park (film), 199, 207, 209–210

kamaki, 163
Kaplan, Robert, 156, 287n18
Keppler, Kay, 250
Keystone View Company, 82, 83, 84, 99
King Solomon's Mines (Haggard), 39, 204, 205
Kipling, Rudyard, 39
Kirby, Lynne, 35
Klein, Maury, 99, 284n16
Klute (film), 172

Lacan, Jacques, 256, 268, 269, 270
Lanier, Jaron, 274
lantern slide show, 106–107
Latuko (film), 20
The Lawnmower Man (film), 251, 254, 256,
    257, 258–259, 261
Lean, David, 178, 184, 186, 187
Leed, Eric J., 34, 240
Lefebvre, Henri, 269
Lévi-Strauss, Claude, 10; on exploration,
    32; as hyphenated anthropologist, 216,
    224, 225, 226; search for natural society,
    214, 227, 228, 229
Le Voyage Dans La Lune. see A Trip to the
    Moon
life group display, 70, 72–73, 76
liminality, 181

live action film, 126
Livingstone, David, 39, 79, 199, 200, 201, 202
local knowledge, 59
Lost World (Crichton), 200, 206–207
Lotman, Jurij, 239
Lugones, Maria, 175
Lukás, George, 225–226
Lumière, Auguste, 116, 128
Lumière, Louis, 116, 128
Lurie, Nancy, 70

MacCannell, Dean: on alienation, 138; on
    authenticity, 3–4; on cultural exoticism,
    67; on tourism, 26–27, 137, 176; on
    tourist as ethnographer, 33; on tourist
    as postmodern figure, 8–9; on touristic
    motivation, 285n24; on virtual reality,
    250
MacDonald, Joe, 129
Macedonian controversy, 158, 159, 174
MacMahon, Thomas, 30
Magic Edge game center, 262, 263
magic-lantern show, 106
Malinowski, Bronislaw, 32; as chameleon
    fieldworker, 215, 217, 218–219, 224–225;
    confessional of, 217, 219, 225; ethno-
    graphic methodology of, 24; on myth of
    direct experience, 31; repeat journey in
    work of, 217–218
map, as extension of self, 192
Marco Polo (computer game), 244
Maréorama, 116
Marked Woman (film), 172
Martin, Andrew, 139
Mashco Piro, 221, 222, 228
Mason, Otis T., 69
mass tourism, 21, 22, 143
mastery, 16–17, 25, 27, 261
Material World (computer game), 232, 235,
    241, 243
The Matrix (film), 8
Maybury-Lewis, David, 10, 215–216, 217,
    220, 221, 222–224; as hyphenated
    anthropologist, 225, 226
McBryde, Isabel, 290n46
McDermott, Emily A., 170, 287n25
McGrane, Bernard, 59, 219

Medea (play), 169–170, 287n25
mediation: demediating, 3, 4, 5, 177,
    194–195, 257; ethnographic, 29–31
medicine, visual practice of, 16
Mediterraneo (film), 155–156, 161, 162, 163,
    169, 173
Méliès, Georges, 124, 125–126, 128, 150
Merchant, Ishmael, 186
Mercouri, Melina, 158, 167–168, 171, 277
Merleau-Ponty, Maurice, 269
Metz, Christian, 5–6, 19, 75, 76–77
*Millennium: Tribal Wisdom and the Modern
    World* (Maybury-Lewis), 215–216
Millennium (documentary), 9; authority in,
    221, 222–223; birth/death/regret in,
    227–229; duality of audience for, 220;
    hyphenated anthropologist in, 225, 226;
    nostalgia in, 227–228; repeat journey in,
    223–224, 228–229; tourist stand-in in,
    221
Miller, Rand, 150
Miller, Robyn, 150
Minh-ha, Trinh, 32, 215, 220, 226, 229
Miranda, Carmen, 155
Mitchell, Timothy, 85, 105
mobility, 2; framed, 34–35; virtual, 35, 231
mobilized virtual gaze, 15
modernism, 3, 6–7, 8, 9, 10
monoculture, 11
To the Moon and Beyond (film), 126
Morley, David, 173
Morse, Margaret, 35, 221
multiculturalism, 175
multiperspectival viewing, 33–34
Mulvey, Laura, 24
Mumford, Lewis, 145
Mundi people, 228, 229
Murrow, Edward R., 124, 128, 131, 132, 139,
    140
muscular perception, cinema as tool of,
    19, 21
museum, 27, 42, 59; exhibiting exotic body
    at, 57; habitat group in, 72, 74; immer-
    sive exhibit at, 69–71, 283nn57&59; life
    group in, 70, 72–73, 74; period room in,
    70, 71, 72; recreating context within,
    69–73

Musser, Charles, 118, 120, 122
Myst (computer game), 126, 148–149, 150, 237, 240
The Mysterious Island (film), 140
The Mysterious Island (TV), 140–141
The Mysterious Island (Verne), 128, 140, 147, 148, 149
myth of direct experience, 177

Nadia: The Secret of Blue Water (film), 140
narrative film, 118, 120–123
national identity, 1; in Greece, 158, 286nn5–6; in United States, 158
nationalism, 133
National Museum of Natural History, 69, 72
National-Physiognomieen (Schadow), 53
natural history museum, 6, 20, 23, 39, 58, 69–71, 72–73, 284n9
Natural History of Man (Prichard), 53
Nautilus (Verne), 141, 146, 147, 150
"The *Nautilus* and the Drunken Boat" (Barthes), 146–146
neurological interface, 254, 255, 256–257, 258, 267
Neuromancer (Gibson), 258, 266
Never on Sunday (film): commercial success of, 165; contradictory image of Greece in, 156; as critique, 159–160; cultural viewpoint of, 166–168; image of prostitution in, 171–173; interpretation of myth in, 169–170, 171; as product of multiproducer interaction, 276–277; stereotype in, 167, 168–169
New Zealand, television in, 141
Nichols, Bill, 29
nomadism, 175
nostalgia: for ancient Greece, 143, 168; documentary as, 143, 227–228; film as, 138–139, 150–151; imperialist, 229
Notes and Queries on Anthropology (Royal Anthropological Institute), 50, 64
Now, Voyager (film), 263

objectification: and mastery, 25; of tourist gaze, 37, 45–46, 105–106, 277; in virtual reality, 272

Oklahoma! (film), 135, 136
"On Exactitude in Science" (Borges), 192
On Longing (Stewart), 198
orientation, 84–85, 86, 239; aerial perspective, 32–33, 34, 46, 137–138; photography and, 35

packaged tourism, 21–23, 41, 263
Pakula, Alan J., 172
Palin, Michael, 140, 142–144, 286n22
Palladium Interactive, 230
Panama Canal. *see* stereograph collection, of Panama Canal
Panorama from the Moving Boardwalk (film), 121
Panorama of the Moving Boardwalk (film), 121
participant observation, 24, 31–32, 61
A Passage to India (film), 178, 180, 182, 183, 185, 186–187, 188–189
A Passage to India (Forster), 178–179, 180
The Passenger (film), 263–264
Pederson, Con, 126
Peploe, Clare, 160
period room, 70, 71, 72
perspective: aerial, 32–33, 34, 46, 137–138; in early film, 18, 33, 117–120; in photography, 35; in stereograph, 74–75, 76
phantom train film, 116, 120
photography: aerial, 32, 33, 46, 281n11; amateur travel, 45; ethnographic, 35, 58, 61–64; as experiential realism, 249; panoramic, 33; roll film technology, 44, 45; surveying human body through, 54. *see also* postcard; stereograph; stereograph collection, of Panama Canal; stereoscopy
physiognomy, 53, 56
picturesqueness, 43, 89, 90–92, 185, 186–188
Pinney, Christopher, 250
Plain Tales from the Hills (Kipling), 39
Polan, Dana, 106
A Policeman's Tour of the World (film), 122, 124–125, 126, 136
popular anthropology, 49–51, 220–224
Porter, Edwin S., 120, 122, 126

postcard, 23, 25, 33–34, 42, 45, 58, 61, 112, 182

postmodernism, 191, 193; and eclipse of authenticity, 6, 8–10, 178; tourist as postmodern figure, 8–9; virtual virtual reality as symbol of, 253–254; in work of Crichton, 9–10

Pote tin Kyriaki. see *Never on Sunday*

Pratt, Mary Louise, 186, 218, 223

Prichard, J. C., 53

primary identification, 19, 21, 75, 77–79, 115, 120

primitives/primitivism, 4, 26, 205–206, 214–215, 228

Prince Henry films, 121–122

Probyn, Elspeth, 175

psychoanalysis, 5–6, 183, 256, 269

Putnam, Frederick W., 64

Pyst (computer game), 230

Qin (computer game), 236–239, 242, 243, 245

Quantum Leap (TV), 266

Read, Kenneth, 216–217

realism: experiential, 249–250; positional, 270–271; representational, 249, 250–251

Red Planet (VR game), 260, 262

reembodiment. *see* virtual reality

repeat journey, 9; in documentary, 223–224, 228–229; in work of Crichton, 140, 195, 198–199, 200–201; in work of Malinowski, 217–218; in work of Verne, 195, 198

representational realism, 249, 250–251

reverse culture shock, 276

Rice, Anne, 266

Richardson, Rufus B., 85–86

Robins, Kevin, 173

Rony, Fatimah Tobing, 105

A Room with a View (film), 184, 185–186, 188, 189

A Room with a View (Forster), 180, 182

Rosaldo, Renato, 229

Rosen, Philip, 120, 122, 124

Rube and Mandy at Coney Island (film), 122

Rusnak, Josef, 8

Rydell, Robert W., 281n15

Said, Edward, 26

Schadow, Gottfried, 53

Schivelbusch, Wolfgang, 35

Schoedsack, Ernest B., 133

science, and tourist, 45–46

scientific fiction, 9, 194–195

Scott, William R., 97

secondary identification, 19, 21, 76–77, 120

The Secret Adventures of Jules Verne (film), 126, 141, 151

The Secret Adventures of Jules Verne (TV), 147

self/other, 26, 47–48, 253

semiotics of tourism, 4, 29

The Seven Wonders of the World (film), 134, 135

sexual difference, 16, 17

Shanghai Street Scene, Scene Two (film), 114

Shirley Valentine (film), 161, 163

"The Shock of the Other" (TV), 221

Shohat, Ella, 240

Shoot the Chute (film), 122

showmen, 50–51

Showscan Entertainment, 152

sightseeing, 25, 33, 86, 184–185, 249

silent film, 111

Silverman, Kaja, 6, 183

simulated immersion: amusement park ride as, 117, 152–153; film as, 177; in virtual reality, 249

simulated travel, 193–194

Smith, Sidney, 124, 128

Smithsonian Institution, 69

Sontag, Susan, 35, 224, 227, 282n21

SouthPeak Interactive, 151, 152

souvenir: as documenting authenticity, 198; filmic image as, 21; function in travel game, 243; photograph as, 35; stereograph as, 77, 78, 82, 91

"space of identity", 173

spatial orientation, 47–49, 239

spectacle, 89, 105, 177–178; dance as, 108–110, 284n12–284n12, 284nn9

spectator position: in film, 5–6, 18, 106, 115–116, 119–120, 184–185, 255; at world's fair, 116–117

Sphere (Crichton), 196, 198, 200
"spirit of place", 28, 164, 275
staged authenticity, 9
Stanley, Henry M., 39, 40, 68, 79, 199, 200–202, 206
Star Trek (TV), 140
Stella (film), 165, 171, 172
stereograph, 42, 45, 63; box set of, 82–84; perspective in, 74–75, 76; planes of vision in, 84, 283n10
stereograph collection, of Panama Canal: as advertisement, 86–91; bridging primary/secondary identification in, 77–79; companion literature for, 85, 86; depiction of capitalism in, 98–101; documentation problems with, 84; as image building, 92–97; indigenous in, 88, 91–92; orientation in, 84–85, 86; picturesqueness in, 89, 90–92
stereoscopy: "being there" through, 80, 83; experiential realism in, 249; history of, 79–82; illusion of reality in, 83–84; primary identification and, 75
Stewart, Susan, 47, 198, 243
Stocking, George W. Jr., 218
Strange Days (film), 254–255, 257
Street, Brian, 63
Streetwalking on a Ruined Map (Bruno), 16
subjectivity, 253, 265, 267, 270
Summer Lovers (film), 161, 162, 163, 169

The Tale of the Body Thief (Rice), 266
Taylor, E. B., 59
technological identification, 76–77
technological spectacle, 177–178
technology: cinema, 112, 115, 117–119, 126, 129, 130, 140, 150; and simulated travel, 202, 203; transportation, 41, 42, 113–114, 132; and travel, 42; travel film, 128–131; wide-screen, 129, 131, 133–136, 285n10; in work of Crichton, 203, 204, 207, 209, 210; in work of Verne, 126, 129–131, 132, 135–136, 148, 149, 150. *see also* photography; stereograph; stereograph collection, of Panama Canal; stereoscopy; virtual reality; virtual virtual reality
technology as fetish, 18, 191–192

Tempest (film), 162–163
theory of evolution, 59
The Thirteenth Floor (film), 8
This is Cinerama (film), 133–134, 136, 153
Thomas Cook travel agency, 133
3-D Atlas (computer game), 234–235, 241, 246
Thurn, Everard im, 64, 282n41
Time and the Other: How Anthropology Makes Its Object (Fabian), 47–48, 219
Timeline (Crichton), 9–10, 208, 210
time travel, 9–10, 89, 141
tobacco product illustration, 38, 41, 43, 45, 80
Todd, Michael, 124, 129, 130–131, 132, 135–136
Todd, Michael Jr., 133
Todd-AO format, 129, 135–136, 150
Torgovnick, Marianna, 26, 214, 282n21
Torrid Zone, 154–155
totalizing vision, 27
Total Recall (film), 193–194, 199, 253
tourism: as beneficial to "peripheral" culture, 7, 11; classical, 19, 23, 24; early study on, 3–4; history of, 19, 21–22; mass, 21, 22, 143; new style of, 21, 23, 280n10
tourist gaze: definition of, 2; gendered, 155; and immersion, 2–6; as mastery, 16–17; and modernism, 3; objectification by, 37, 45–46, 105–106, 277; relationship to mobilized virtual gaze, 15–16; relationship to touristic vision, 18
touristic mastery, 16, 27, 261
touristic pleasures: marketing in precinematic era, 37, 39; in travel game, 236, 249; in works of Forster, 185, 190, 207. *see also* museum; photography; postcard; stereograph; world's fair
touristic vision, 18
Tourists Starting for Canton (film), 114
tourist stand-in, 193–194, 216–217, 221
The Tourist (MacCannell), 3–4, 8–9, 176
tourist/traveler distinction, 4, 5, 36, 179, 193
The Tragedy of the Korosko (Doyle), 39
transportation technology, 41, 42, 113–114, 132
travel agency, 133

travel computer game, CD-ROM: depicting time/space in, 232–233; environments of, 231–232, 237

travel film, 21, 111, 276; authenticity in, 251; narrative, 118, 120–123

travel film, fictional: early, 122, 124–126, 128, 136; gendered narrative in, 240; narrative in, 120–122; use of technology in early, 128–131. see also *Around the World in Eighty Days*; Verne, Jules

travel game, CD-ROM: animation in, 236–239; antitourist in, 244–245; "being there" in, 233; character group in, 239; constructing tale for, 239–244; cultural difference in, 241–242; digitized past in, 244–247; distanced immersion in, 233–235; as form of antitourism, 230–231; gender of character in, 240–241; illusion of reality in, 248–249; interactivity in, 248–249; materialist gaze in, 242–244; photographic representation in, 234–235

travel lecture, 107–108, 114–115

travel literature, 45, 82

travel metaphor, 175–176

travelogue, 108, 114, 133–135, 185

travel photography. *see* postcard; stereograph

A Trip to the Moon (film), 124, 125, 126, 128

Tristes Tropiques (Lévi-Strauss), 214, 216, 224

The Truman Show (film), 8

Turton, David, 229

Twenty Thousand Leagues: The Adventure Continues (computer game), 141, 147–148, 151

Twenty Thousand Leagues under the Sea (film), 126, 140

Twenty Thousand Leagues under the Sea (Verne), 128, 196

Underwood and Underwood, 82, 84, 99

Underwood Traveling System, 82–83

Unforgiven (film), 172, 287n25

Until the End of the World (film), 256

Urry, John, 15

vacation film, 161–162

Van den Abbeele, George, 11

Verhoeven, Paul, 193

Verne, Jules, 9, 10, 46; discovery/rediscovery in work of, 139–140; enclosure metaphor in works of, 147; holistic perspective in work of, 137–138; influence on Crichton, 196, 197, 198; interest in adaptation of themes of, 151–152; maps in works of, 195, 196–197; nonfilmic adaptation of work of, 125, 140–141, 146, 147–149, 151–152; repeat journey in work of, 195, 198; technology in work of, 126, 129–131, 132, 135–136, 148, 149, 150; as writer, 126–128, 147, 149–150, 285n3, 285n6; as writer of scientific fiction, 195, 196

Videodrome (film), 192–193, 199, 253

viewmaster, 150

virtual mobility, 35, 231

virtual reality (VR), 10, 279n3; actual implementation of, 258–259; authenticity in training applications of, 291n5; bodily interface in, 254–255, 258, 268–269; corporeal overlay in, 258, 269, 272–274, 276; cross-cultural interaction and, 277–278; disembodiment in, 255–256, 266–268; early example of, 254; experiential realism in, 250; immersion in, 249; interactivity in, 248, 260; potential of, 274; realism of positionality in, 270–271; theme park chain, 259, 262, 263, 278; touristic pleasures of, 260–261; vs. virtual VR, 252, 253, 258–259, 261. *see also* virtual virtual reality (VR)

virtual reality (VR) game: death/bodily harm denial in, 261–262; experiential realism in, 250; identity/role playing in, 263–265; positional realism in, 268–273; representational realism in, 249, 250–251; spatial immersion in, 249

virtual tourism, 177, 195

virtual virtual reality (VR): as demediating mediation, 257; detrimental effects of, 257; disembodiment in, 255–256; interpersonal exchange in, 257; neurological interface in, 254, 255, 256, 258, 267; sexual encounter in, 254–255;

as symbol of postmodernism, 253–254; vs. actual reality, 252, 253, 261. *see also* virtual reality

Virtual World (VW) theme park, 259, 262, 263, 278

Voyage in Egypt (computer game), 232, 241, 242, 245

Voyages Extraodinaires (Verne), 126–127, 128, 137, 139–140, 147

VR. *see* virtual reality

VR5 (film), 256, 257

Wachowski, Andy, 8

Wachowski, Larry, 8

Weir, Peter, 8

Westworld (film), 207

What Happened in the Tunnel (film), 120

Wheatstone, Charles, 80

Where Angels Fear to Tread (film), 184, 185

Where Angels Fear to Tread (Forster), 179–181

Where in the World is Carmen Sandiego (computer game), 232, 234, 241, 242, 244, 246

White, James H., 111–112, 113–114, 118, 121, 122, 137

wide-screen technology: in amusement park ride, 152; in film, 129, 131, 133–136, 285n10

Wiebe, Robert, 41–42

Wilson, George Washington, 82

world as picture, 25, 45, 137, 203, 265

world's fair, 6, 42, 281n15; "being there" at, 26, 65; cinematic technology at, 133; exhibiting exotic body at, 55, 58, 64–69; life group at, 76; recreating ethnographic past at, 23, 290n46; souvenir of exotica from, 45; spectator position at, 116–117

Wrath of the Gods (computer game), 232, 239, 245

Xavante Indian, 222, 223, 225

You Only Live Twice (film), 275

Z (film), 160

Zorba the Greek (film), 156, 157, 160, 161, 162–163, 165

ABOUT THE AUTHOR

ELLEN STRAIN is an assistant professor of film and multimedia in the School of Literature, Communication, and Culture at the Georgia Institute of Technology in Atlanta. She teaches film history and multimedia design and is a freelance instructional technology designer. She has produced, with coauthor Gregory VanHoosier-Carey, a CD-ROM–based study of the 1915 film *The Birth of a Nation*, entitled *Griffith in Context*. She is also completing the design of a multimedia tool that allows students to use a CD-ROM–based video editing engine to learn about the effects of editing on narrational strategies within the film noir genre.